PORT ROYAL UNDER SIX FLAGS

Books *by* KATHARINE M. JONES:

HEROINES OF DIXIE: *Confederate Women*
Tell Their Story of the War

THE PLANTATION SOUTH

PORT ROYAL
UNDER SIX FLAGS

by

Katharine M. Jones

THE **BOBBS-MERRILL** COMPANY, INC.
A SUBSIDIARY OF HOWARD W. SAMS & CO., INC.
Publishers • INDIANAPOLIS • NEW YORK

To

DAVID LAURANCE CHAMBERS

Table of Contents

7

Illustrations

The following illustrations will be found after page 256:

Proem

A JOURNEY THROUGH HISTORY ALONG THE INNER WATERWAY FROM EDISTO ISLAND TO THE SAVANNAH RIVER[1]

The waterway, at many points within a short ride by rail or air from the metropolises of the eastern seaboard, runs through long stretches inhabited only by the ghosts of legend-haunted cypress swamps where Indian lovers paddle white canoes by night; semitropical jungles in which runaway slaves still lurk, according to local belief; sandy islands where long-dead pirates linger to protect their hidden treasures. . . .

Along the route are facilities for nearly every kind of water sport, and the whole area is rich in game. . . .

For the imaginative the chief interest of the territory lies in its history, for here were enacted many of the most important early scenes in one of the most amazing adventures of all time, that of the expropriation of a continent, so complete that within 300 years after the first settlement the surviving natives had become sideshow curiosities. These are the lands first sighted by many of those hardy scouts of empire of the sixteenth and seventeenth centuries. . . . Visible from the waterway and its tributaries are the very spots on which settled colony after colony of Europeans—missionaries, real-estate promoters, adventurers, religious and political refugees, criminals, and restless freemen and lords—who had dared the long crossing of the Atlantic in foul little ships to find peace or fortune in what to them was a limitless continent filled with savages. Along the waterways are the unmarked graves of the thousands of settlers who died, victims of rival colonizers, of natives fighting desperately for their home lands, of hardship, and disease, before the conquest was complete. . . .

Many acres along the waterway are part of the estates that in less than 150 years so built up the wealth and prosperity of the owners that they dared join in the only entirely successful major challenge of the power of Britain; they are also the acres that gave the power and wealth

[1] Federal Writers' Project of the Works Progress Administration, comp., *The Intracoastal Waterway: Norfolk to Key West* (American Guide Series). Washington, Government Printing Office, 1937, pp. ix-x, 34-40.

13

that 85 years later enabled owners to challenge their own government. Many scars of this conflict are visible. . . .

EDISTO ISLAND, 30.2 miles [south of Charleston] is a beach resort and the site of many summer homes. . . . Prospect Hill, built in 1790, was designed by James Hoban, architect of the White House.

From North Edisto River the waterway passes through North Creek and Watts Cut to SOUTH EDISTO RIVER, 33 miles. SAMSON ISLAND (right) and RACCOON ISLAND (left) are passed; the Dodge Hunting Preserve is on the latter. This region is famous for its bass and trout fishing, as well as for its hunting.

The waterway leads through Ashepoo River and Rock Creek to ST. HELENA SOUND, 44.7 miles, the broadest opening on the Atlantic coast between Chesapeake Bay and the Gulf of Mexico. At places the sound is more than 6 miles wide.

South of St. Helena Sound the waterway leads up to COOSAW RIVER. At 37 miles is COOSAW ISLAND. The name of the island and river comes from the Coosaw tribe of Indians, who once inhabited this section. The island was the home of Captain John Bull. . . . The island, now inhabited solely by Negroes, is unusual in that it has never known an automobile, a telephone, or a bathtub.

Separated from Coosaw Island by a narrow creek is LADY'S ISLAND, named by Spanish explorers in 1526. It is connected with the northern end of ST. HELENA ISLAND by a bridge. Most of the inhabitants of these islands are Negroes who own the land sold for taxes by Federal troops shortly after the Civil War. The islands have been the scene of a number of educational experiments for the Negroes, who were isolated for nearly 70 years before the building of the bridge that connects the islands with the town of Beaufort.

From Coosaw River the route leads through Brickyard Creek to BEAUFORT RIVER. In late afternoon along Beaufort River numerous shrimp and oyster boats, with widespread sails and dripping nets, turn homeword in the sunset.

BEAUFORT, 69.4 miles, is the second oldest town in South Carolina. Laid out in 1710, it was named for the Duke of Beaufort. . . .

Southwest of Beaufort the waterway passes CAT ISLAND (left), the center of much publicity several years ago when it served as the headquarters of a nudist colony.

At 62.5 miles (left) are the ruins of a tabby structure, FORT

FREDERICK, erected in 1731. Only three sides remain, the tides having taken one wall. . . .

At 63.3 miles (left) is BATTERY CREEK, which empties into Beaufort River. One mile north is PORT ROYAL. . . . Although the population has never been more than 800, Port Royal was once a busy shipping point, with boats coming in from all over the world. Railroad coaches were manufactured here in 1870, and the town once boasted the largest cotton compress in the world.

Across Battery Creek is PARRIS ISLAND, on which the United States Marines have headquarters. The barracks and the airport are seen (right). . . .

The southern end of ST. HELENA ISLAND (left) extends for 6 miles. . . . On the island east of the water tower is FORT FREMONT, erected during the Spanish-American War and garrisoned until about 20 years ago, but now privately owned. Southeast of this group of islands is BAY POINT, which was fortified during the attack by Federal forces in 1861.

From Beaufort River the route veers westward through PORT ROYAL SOUND, 69.5 miles. . . .

From Port Royal Sound the waterway leads through SKULL CREEK, 73.7 miles, which flows between HILTON HEAD ISLAND (left) and PINCKNEY ISLAND (right). The name Skull Creek is said to be a corruption of "skulk," which was applied to the creek because Indians used to skulk along the stream in their attacks upon white settlers on the islands. Hilton Head was an island of large plantations before the Civil War. . . . The island's only means of communication with the mainland is the Beaufort-Savannah steamer. Pinckney Island, now occupied by Negroes, was once the site of a palatial home of the Pinckney family. At SEABROOK LANDING, 74.6 miles, is an oyster factory that draws its supplies from the many oyster beds in the vicinity.

South of Skull Creek the waterway runs through CALIBOGUE SOUND. Branching (right) at 80.2 miles is MAY RIVER (navigable only for small boats), on which is BLUFFTON, 6.2 miles, a small village that attracts many fishermen during the summer months.

At 83.3 miles COOPER RIVER (right), one of two streams of that name in the state, enters Calibogue Sound. DAUFUSKIE ISLAND (left) and BULL ISLAND (right) are passed. At HAGUE POINT, locally called Egg Point, on the northern end of Daufuskie Island is an unused lighthouse. On the northeast end of Daufuskie Island is BLOODY POINT. In the early days of the colony frequent Indian attacks occurred, during which Indians from Georgia murdered the settlers and plundered their plantations. On one of their trips, said to have been the last . . . the planters slipped up upon the Indians, cutting them off from their canoes, and murdered all of them except one, who swam across the river to Tybee Island. Since that time, the spot has been called Bloody Point. . . . At RAMS HORN CREEK, 86.5 miles, the tides from Calibogue Sound and Tybee Roads meet and run with considerable strength. . . .

From Cooper River the waterway leads into NEW RIVER, 88 miles. Daufuskie Landing is a regular stopping point of the Beaufort-Savannah steamer.

From New River the waterway leads through WRIGHT RIVER and two cuts to the SAVANNAH RIVER, 93.5 miles, the boundary between South Carolina and Georgia.

PORT ROYAL UNDER SIX FLAGS

PART I

The Spanish Discover the Sea Islands

1520

"Lucas Vásquez de Ayllón was a native of Toledo, judge of the Santo Domingo Court of Appeals, and a very learned and wealthy man. . . . [In 1520 he] joined forces with six of his Santo Domingo neighbors and, signing on Diego Miruello as pilot, they set out for the Lucayan Islands in two vessels. They were looking for Carib Indians (who by them were declared enemies) to work in the mines; but some of the islands were found depopulated and others appeared to be.

"A tempest cast him upon the eastern shore of Florida, where once having made repairs, he began exploration of the land. . . .

"Lucas Vásquez disembarked at various places, of which Chicora, where Santa Elena is located, was the most noteworthy. They named the cape for Santa Elena, having discovered it on that saint's day. The Indians along the coast, watching the ships with awe, were thrown into a panic, for they thought the vessels were new monsters the sea had cast up. On seeing the small boats approach land, they fled in great trepidation. . . .

"In 1521 Lucas Vásquez de Ayllón came to Spain to solicit the right to the conquest and colonization of the province of Chicora and Duharhe. With him he brought an Indian native of Chicora. . . .

He described the lands he had seen to the royal ministers. . . . The King granted . . . the favors he had asked. . . .

"In 1524 he fitted out two ships in Santo Domingo and sent them to Florida . . . to colonize and report what they might discover. When they returned with pearls and some pieces of gold and silver, he resolved to go himself to claim his province of Chicora. He ordered the refitting of two ships but lately arrived, and another that he bought for the pilot Diego Meruelo [Miruello].

". . . He set out, taking this same Meruelo with him as chief pilot. But the pilot could never make a landfall in the province of Chicora which he sought, and consequently became so melancholy that he went insane and died. Lucas Vásquez landed at the place which seemed to him most fertile and suitable for his plans. The Indians made a pretense at peace and received him with soft words and flattery. They betook themselves with such alacrity to serving the Spaniards and handing over all they possessed that Lucas Vásquez thought himself master of the country. . . .

"He therefore dispatched two hundred men to reconnoiter a village which lay a day's march from the coast. In this village the Indians . . . killed all of them at night while they were sleeping. . . . These same Indians, desiring to finish them all, came in a fury to attack the men who stayed with the ships. Sorely pressed, the Spaniards made their way to the boats and set sail. They suffered heavy adversity and sorrow before they reached the island of Hispaniola. The following year certain persons brought an account of the outcome of this misadventure, and said that Lucas Vásquez was among those who died at the hands of the Indians. . . ."

Anthony Kerrigan, trans., *Barcia's Chronological History of the Continent of Florida . . . from the year 1512 . . . until the year 1722*. Gainesville, University of Florida Press, 1951, pp. 145-46.

Barcia's *Ensayo Cronologico* was first published in Madrid in 1723.

PART **II**

The French at Port Royal

1562

"In the year 1562 a cloud of black and deadly portent was thickening over France. Surely and swiftly she glided towards the abyss of the religious wars. None could pierce the future; perhaps none dared to contemplate it: the wild rage of fanaticism and hate, friend grappling with friend, brother with brother, father with son; altars profaned, hearthstones made desolate; the robes of Justice herself bedrenched with murder. In the gloom without lay Spain, imminent and terrible. . . .

"In these days of fear, a Huguenot colony sailed for the New World. The calm, stern man who represented and led the Protestantism of France felt to his inmost heart the peril of the time. He would fain build up a city of refuge for the persecuted sect. Yet Gaspard de Coligny, too high in power and rank to be openly assailed, was forced to act with caution. He must act, too, in the name of the Crown, and in virtue of his office of Admiral of France. A nobleman and a soldier—for the Admiral of France was no seaman—he shared the ideas and habits of his class; nor is there reason to believe him to have been in advance of others of his time in a knowledge of the principles of successful colonization. His scheme promised a military colony, not a free commonwealth. The Huguenot party was already a political, as well as a religious party. At its foundation lay the religious element, represented by Geneva, the martyrs, and the devoted fugitives who sang the psalms of Marot among rocks and caverns. Joined to these were numbers on whom the faith sat lightly, whose hope was in commotion and change. Of these, in great part, was the Huguenot noblesse, from Condé, who aspired to the crown. . . . to the younger son of the impoverished seigneur whose patrimony was his sword. More than this, the restless, the factious, the discontented began to link their fortunes to a party whose triumph would involve confiscation of the bloated wealth of the only rich class in France. An element of the great revolution was already mingling in the strife of religions.

"America was still a land of wonder. The ancient spell still hung unbroken over the wild, vast world of mystery beyond the sea. A land of romance, of adventure, of gold. . . ."[1]

---

[1] Francis Parkman, "The Fleur-de-Lis at Port Royal," in *Atlantic Monthly*, July 1863, pp. 30-32.

René de Laudonnière

"YOU SHALL BE REGISTERED FOR EVER AS THE FIRST THAT INHABITED THIS STRANGE COUNTRY"

To command the expedition to the New World, Admiral Coligny selected Captain Jean Ribaut,[2] a zealous Huguenot and "a man in truth expert in sea causes." On February 18, 1562, one hundred and fifty soldiers, sailors and a few young noblemen sailed from the port of Havre de Grace. After a voyage of more than two months they sighted the coast of Florida, sailed northward, and on May 1 landed near the mouth of the river which is now known as the St. Johns. They called it the River of May. They sailed on north, naming stream after stream for their own French rivers.

On May 24, the Frenchmen came to a "mightie river," and to show their admiration they gave to it the name Port Royal. On a little island, "exceeding faire and pleasant"—known today as Daw Island— they planted a "pillar of hard stone fashioned like a columne, wherein the armes of the King of France were graven."

After exploring "this faire land," they selected a site for a settlement and built a fort which was called Charlesfort in honor of their boy King, Charles IX. The site of the fort is what is now known as Parris Island. Thirty volunteers under the command of Albert de Pierria remained there to hold Port Royal for the King.

On June 11 Captain Ribaut, with his ships and men, departed for France, promising to return within six months with more colonists and provisions. As they sailed away, he commanded his gunners "to shoote off our ordnance to give a farewell to our Frenchmen," who were watching from the shore.

The Frenchmen on that little island, says Parkman, "were alone in those fearful solitudes. From the North Pole to Mexico no Christian denizen but they."

René de Laudonnière, young Huguenot nobleman and Captain Ribaut's lieutenant on the expedition, was the chronicler. His letters, one of which follows, were published in 1586 in the Histoire Notable de la Florida *and later "done into English" and included in Hakluyt's collections.*

---

[2] According to Samuel Gaillard Stoney, Ribault is the original spelling. However, the traditional spelling of Ribaut has been followed in headnotes.

. . . In lesse then the space of threescore leagues wee had found out many singularities along nine rivers. Nevertheless not fully satisfied wee sayled yet further towards the north, following the course that might bring us to the River of Jordan, one of the fairest rivers of the north, and holding our wonted course, great fogges and tempests came upon us, which constrained us to leave the coast to beare toward the maine sea, which was the cause that we lost the sight of our pinnesses a whole day and a night untill the next day in the morning, what time the weather waxing faire and the sea calme, wee discovered a river which wee called Belle à veoir.

After wee had sayled three or foure leagues, wee began to espie our pinnesses which came straight toward us, and at their arrivall they reported to the captaine that while the foule weather and fogges endured, they harboured themselves in a mightie river which in bignesse and beautie exceeded the former. Wherewithall the captaine was exceedingly joyfull, for his chiefe desire was to finde out an haven to harbour his shippes, and there to refresh our selves for a while. Thus making thitherward wee arrived athwart the sayde river, (which because of the fairenesse and largenesse thereof wee named Port Royall). Wee strooke our sailes and cast anker at ten fathom of water, for the depth is such, namely when the sea beginneth to flowe, that the greatest shippes of France, yea, the arguzes of Venice may enter in there.

Having cast anker, the captaine with his souldiers went on shoare, and hee himselfe went first on land, where we found the place as pleasant as was possible, for it was all covered over with mightie high oakes and infinite store of cedars, and with lentiskes growing underneath them, smelling so sweetly that the very fragrant odor only made the place to seeme exceeding pleasant. As we passed thorow these woods we saw nothing but turkeycocks flying in the forrests, partridges gray and red, little different from ours but chiefly in bignesse. Wee heard also within the woods the voyces of stagges, of beares, of lusernes, of leopards, and divers other sortes of beastes unknowen unto us.

Being delighted with this place, we set our selves to fishing with nets, and we caught such a number of fish that it was wonderfull. And amongst other wee tooke a certain kind of fish which we call sallicoques, which were no lesse then crevises, so that two draughts of the net were sufficient to feede all the companie of our two ships for a whole day.

The river at the mouth thereof from cape to cape is no lesse then three French leagues broad. It is divided into two great armes, whereof the one runneth toward the west, the other towards the north; and I beleeve in my judgement that the arme which stretcheth towarde the north runneth up into the countrey as farre as the River Jordan; the other arme runneth into the sea, as it was knowen and understoode by those of our company which were left behind to dwell in this place. These two armes are two great leagues broad; and in the middest of them there is an ile, which is poynted towardes the opening of the great river, in which iland there are infinite numbers of all sortes of strange beasts. There are simples growing there of so rare properties, and in so great quantitie, that it is an excellent thing to behold them. On every side there is nothing to be seene but palmetrees, and other sorts of trees bearing blossoms and fruite of very rare shape and very good smell.

But seeing the evening approach, and that the captaine determined to returne unto the shippes, wee prayed him to suffer us to pass the night in this place. In our absence the pilots and chiefe mariners advertised the captaine that it was needefull to bring the shippes further up within the river, to avoyde the dangers of the windes which might annoy us by reason of our being so neere to the mouth of the river; and for this cause the captaine sent for us. Being come to our shippes, wee sayled three leagues further up within the river, and there we cast anker.

A little while after, John Ribault, accompanied with a good number of souldiers, imbarked himselfe, desirous to sayle further up into the arme that runneth toward the west, and to search the commodities of the place. Having sayled twelve leagues at the least, we perceived a troope of Indians, which, assoone as ever they espied the pinnesses, were so afrayed that they fled into the woods, leaving behind them a yong lucerne which they were a turning upon a spit: for which cause the place was called Cape Lucerne.

Proceeding foorth on our way, we found another arme of the river, which ranne toward the east, up which the captaine determined to sayle and to leave the great current. A little while after they began to espie divers other Indians, both men and women, halfe hidden within the woods; who, knowing not that wee were such as desired their friendship, were dismayed at the first, but soone after were emboldened, for the captaine caused store of marchandise to bee shewed them openly, whereby they knew that we meant nothing but well unto them; and then they made a signe that we should come on lande, which wee would not refuse.

At our comming on shoare divers of them came to salute our generall according to their barbarous fashion. Some of them gave him skins of chamois, others little baskets made of palme leaves, some presented him with pearles, but no great number. Afterwards they went about to make an arbour to defend us in that place from the parching heate of the sunne. But wee would not stay as then. Wherefore the captaine thanked them much for their good will, and gave presents to each of them; wherewith hee pleased them so well before hee went thence that his suddaine departure was nothing pleasant unto them. For knowing him to bee so liberall, they would have wished him to have stayed a little longer, seeking by all meanes to give him occasion to stay, shewing him by signes that he should stay but that day onely, and that they desired to advertise a great Indian lorde which had pearles in great abundance, and silver also, all which things should bee given unto him at the Kings arrivall; saying further that in the meane time while that this great lord came thither, they would lead him to their houses, and shewe him there a thousand pleasures in shooting, and seeing the stagge killed; therefore they prayed him not to denie them their request.

Notwithstanding wee returned to our shippes, where, after wee had bene but one night, the captaine in the morning commanded to put into the pinnesse a pillar of hard stone fashioned like a columne, wherein the armes of the King of France were graven, to plant the same in the fairest place that he could finde.

This done, wee imbarked our selves and sayled three leagues towards the west, where we discovered a little river, up which we sayled so long that in the ende we found it returned into the great current, and in his returne to make a little iland separated from the firme land, where wee went on shore; and by commandement of the captaine, because it was exceeding faire and pleasant, there wee planted the pillar upon a hillock open round about to the view, and invironed with a lake halfe a fathom deepe of very good and sweete water. In which iland wee sawe two stagges of exceeding bignesse in respect of those which we had seene before, which we might easily have killed with our haguebuzes, if the captaine had not forbidden us, mooved with the singular fairenesse and bignesse of them. But before our departure we named the little river which environed this ile the River of Liborne.

Afterward we imbarked our selves to search another ile not farre distant from the former; wherein after wee had gone a land, wee found nothing but tall cedars, the fairest that were scene in this countrey. For this cause wee called it the Ile of Cedars. So wee returned into our pinnesse to go towards our shippes.

A few dayes afterward John Ribault determined to returne once againe toward the Indians which inhabited that arme of the river which runneth toward the west, and to carrie with him good store of souldiers. For his meaning was to take two Indians of this place to bring them into France, as the Queene had commanded him. With this deliberation againe wee tooke our former course so farre foorth that at the last wee came to the selfe same place where at the first we found the Indians, from whence we tooke two Indians by the permission of the King, which, thinking that they were more favoured then the rest, thought themselves very happy to stay with us.

But these two Indians, seeing we made no shew at all that we would goe on land, but rather that wee followed the middest of the current, began to be somewhat offended, and would by force have lept into the water, for they are so good swimmers that immediately they would have gotten into the forrestes. Neverthelesse, being acquainted with their humour, wee watched them narrowly and sought by all meanes to appease them; which we could not by any meanes do for that time, though we offered them things which they much esteemed, which things they disdained to take, and gave backe againe whatsoever was given them, thinking that such giftes should have altogether bound them, and that in restoring them they should be restored unto their libertie.

In fine, perceiving that all that they did avayled them nothing, they prayed us to give them those things which they had restored, which we did incontinent. Then they approached one toward the other and began to sing, agreeing so sweetely together that in hearing their song it seemed that they lamented the absence of their friendes. They continued their songs all night without ceasing; all which time we were constrained to ly at anker by reason of the tyde that was against us, but we hoysed sayle the next day very earely in the morning and returned to our ships.

Assoone as we were come to our ships, every one sought to gratifie these two Indians, and to shew them the best countenance that was

possible. . . . Then we offered them meate to eate, but they refused it,
and made us understand that they were accustomed to wash their
face and to stay untill the sunne were set before they did eate. . . .
Neverthelesse in the end they were constrained to forget their superstitions, and to apply themselves to our nature, which was somewhat
strange unto them at the first. They became therfore more jocunde,
every houre made us a 1000 discourses, being merveilous sory that we
could not understand them.

A few daies after they began to beare so good wil towards mee that,
as I thinke, they would rather have perished with hunger and thirst
then have taken their refection at any mans hand but mine. Seeing
this their good wil, I sought to learne some Indian words, and bagan
to aske them questions, showing them the thing whereof I desired to
know the name, how they called it. They were very glad to tell it me,
and knowing the desire that I had to learne their language, they encouraged me afterward to aske them every thing. So that putting
downe in writing the words and phrases of the Indian speech, I was
able to understand the greatest part of their discourses.

Every day they did nothing but speak unto me of the desire that
they had to use me wel, if we returned unto their houses, and cause
me to receive all the pleasures that they could devise, as well in hunting as in seeing their very strange and superstitious ceremonies at a
certaine feast which they call Toya. Which feast they observe as
straightly as we observe Sunday.

They gave me to understand that they would bring me to see the
greatest lord of this countrey which they called Chiquola, which
exceedeth them in height, as they tolde me, a good foote and a halfe.
They said unto me that he dwelt within the land in a very large place
and inclosed exceeding high, but I could not learne wherewith. And
as farre as I can judge, this place whereof they spake unto me was a
very faire citie. For they said unto me that within the inclosure there
was great store of houses which were built very high, wherein there
was an infinite number of men like unto themselves, which made none
account of gold, of silver, nor of pearles, seeing they had thereof in
abundance. . . .

After they had staied a while in our ships, they began to be sory,
and stil demanded of me when they should returne. I made them
understand that the captaines will was to send them home againe, but
that first he would bestow apparell on them, which fewe dayes after

was delivered unto them. But seeing he would not give them licence to depart, they resolved with themselves to steale away by night, and to get a litle boat which we had, and by the help of the tyde to saile home toward their dwellings, and by this meanes to save themselves. Which thing they failed not to doe, and put their enterprize in execution, yet leaving behinde them the apparel which the captaine had given them, and carrying nothing but that which was their owne, shewing well hereby that they were not void of reason. The captaine cared not greatly for their departure, considering they had not bene used otherwise then well; and that therefore they woulde not estrange themselves from the Frenchmen.

Captaine 'Ribault, therefore, knowing the singular fairenes of this river, desired by all meanes to encourage some of his men to dwell there, well foreseeing that this thing might be of great importance for the Kings service and the reliefe of the Common wealth of France. Therefore proceeding on with his intent, he commanded the ankers to bee weighed and to set things in order to returne unto the opening of the river, to the ende that if the winde came faire he might passe out to accomplish the rest of his meaning. When therefore we were come to the mouth of the river, he made them cast anker, whereupon we stayed without discovering any thing all the rest of the day. The next day he commanded that all the men of his ship should come up upon the decke, saying that he had somewhat to say unto them. They all came up, and immediately the captaine began to speake unto them in this manner:

"I thinke there is none of you that is ignorant of how great consequence this our enterprize is, and also how acceptable it is unto our young King. Therefore, my friendes, (as one desiring your honour and benefite) I would not faile to advertise you all of the exceeding good happe which should fall to them, which, as men of valure and worthy courage, would make tryall in this our first discoverie of the benefits and commodities of this new land—which should be, as I assure my selfe, the greatest occasion that ever could happen unto them, to arise unto the title and degree of honour. And for this cause I was desirous to propose unto you and set downe before your eyes the eternall memories which of right they deserve, which forgetting both their parents and their countrey have had the courage to enterprize a thing of such importance, which even kings themselves, understanding to be men aspiring to so high degree of magnanimitie and increase

of their majesties, doe not disdaine so wel to regard that, afterwards
imploying them in maters of weight and of high enterprize, they
make their names immortall for ever. . . .

"Howe much then ought so many worthy examples to move you to
plant here? Considering also that hereby you shall be registred for ever
as the first that inhabited this strange countrey. I pray you therfore all
to advise your selves thereof, and to declare your mindes freely unto
mee, protesting that I will so well imprint your names in the Kings
eares, and the other princes', that your renowne shall hereafter shine
unquenchable through our realme of France."

He had scarcely ended his oration but the greatest part of our
souldiers replyed: that a greater pleasure could never betide them, perceiving well the acceptable service which by this meanes they shoulde
doe unto their Prince; besides, that this thing should be for the increase
of their honours; therfore they besought the captaine, before he departed out of the place, to begin to build them a fort, which they
hoped afterward to finish, and to leave them munition necessarie for
their defence, showing, as it seemed, that they were displeased that
it was so long in doing.

Whereupon John Ribault, being as glad as might be to see his men
so well willing, determined the next day to search the most fit and
convenient place to be inhabited. Wherefore he embarked himselfe
very earely in the morning and commanded them to followe him that
were desirous to inhabite there, to the intent that they might like the
beter of the place. Having sayled up the great river on the north side,
in coasting an isle which ended with a sharpe point toward the mouth
of the river, haveing sailed a while, he discovered a small river, which
entred into the islande, which hee would not faile to search out.
Which done, and finding the same deep inough to harbour therein
gallies and galliots in good number, proceeding further, he found a
very open place, joyning upon the brinke thereof, where he went on
land, and seeing the place fit to build a fortresse in, and commodious
for them that were willing to plant there, he resolved incontinent to
cause the bignes of the fortification to be measured out. And considering that there stayed but six and twentie there, he caused the
fort to be made in length but sixteene fathome, and thirteene in
breadth, with flankes according to the proportion thereof.

The measure being taken by me and Captain Salles, we sent unto
the shippes for men, and to bring shovels, pickaxes and other instru-

ments necessarie to make the fortification. We travailed so diligently
that in a short space the fort was made in some sort defenciable. In
which meane time John Ribault caused victuals and warrelike munition to be brought for the defence of the place. After he had furnished
them with all such things as they had neede of, he determined to
take his leave of them.

But before his departure he used this speech unto Captaine Albert,
which he left in this place:

"Captaine Albert, I have to request you, in the presence of al these
men, that you would quit your selfe so wisely in your charge, and
governe so modestly your small companie which I leave you, which
with so good cheere remaineth under your obedience, that I never
have occasion but to commend you, and to recount unto the King (as
I am desirous) the faithfull service which before us all you undertake
to doe him in his new France.

"And you companions," quoth he to the souldiers, "I beseech you
also to esteeme of Captaine Albert as if hee were my selfe that stayed
here with you, yeelding him that obedience which a true souldier oweth
unto his generall and captaine, living as brethren one with another,
without all dissention; and in so doing God wil assist you and blesse
your enterprises."

Having ended his exhortation, we tooke our leaves of each of them,
and sayled toward our shippes, calling the forte by the name of
Charlesfort, and the river by the name Chenonceau. The next daye
wee determined to depart from this place, being as well contented as
was possible that we had so happily ended our busines, with good
hope, if occasion would permitte, to discover perfectly the River of
Jordan. For this cause we hoysed our sayles about ten of the clocke
in the morning. After wee were ready to depart Captaine Ribault commanded to shoote off our ordinance to give a farewel unto our Frenchmen, which failed not to doe the like on their part. This being done,
wee sailed toward the north; and then we named this river Porte
Royal because of the largenes and excellent fairenes of the same.

After that we had sailed about fifteen leagues from thence, we espied
a river, whereupon wee sent our pinnesse thither to discover it. At
their return they brought us word that they found not past halfe a
fathom water in the mouth thereof. Which when we understood,
without doing any thing els, we continued our way, and called it the
Base or Shallow River. As we stil went on sounding we found not

past five or sixe fathome water, although we were sixe good leagues from the shoare; at length we found not past three fathomes, which gave us occasion greatly to muse. And without making any farther way we strook our sayles, partly because we wanted water, and partly because the night approached; during which time Captaine John Ribault bethought with himselfe whether it were best for him to passe any farther, because of the eminent dangers which every houre we saw before our eyes, or whither he should content himselfe with that which he had certainely discovered, and also left men to inhabite the countrey. Being not able for that time to resolve with himselfe, he referred it until the next day.

The morning being come he proposed to all the company what was best to be done, to the end that with good advisement every man might deliver his opinion. Some made answere, that according to their judgement he had occasion fully to content himselfe, considering he could doe no more; laying before his eyes that he had discovered more in sixe weekes then the Spaniards had done in two years in the conquest of their New Spaine; and that he should do the King very great service, if he did bring him newes in so short a time of his happy discoverie. Other shewed unto him the losse and spoile of his victuals, and on the other side the inconvenience that might happen by the shallow water that they found continually along the coast. Which things being well and at large debated, we resolved to leave the coast, forsaking the north, to take our way toward the east, which is the right way and course to our France, where we happily arrived the twentieth day of July, the yere 1562.

Jean Ribaut

"NO FAYRER OR FYTTER PLACE THEN PORTE ROYALL"

When Captain Ribaut arrived in France he found the country in the midst of the Protestant and Catholic wars. Reinforcements for the colony at Port Royal were never levied. Ribaut joined Admiral Coligny in the field. After the surrender of Dieppe on October 20, 1562, he fled to England. There, in May 1563, an English translation

of his report to Admiral Coligny on his Port Royal discoveries and the
colony at Charlesfort was published in London.

The following is from Ribaut's account "of that which we had don
and discovered, which is of great consequence. . . ."

Whereas in the yeare 1562 it pleased God to move your grace to chose and appoynt us to discover and vieu a certen long coste of the West Indea from the hed of the lande called la Florida, drawing towardes the northe parte untill the hed of Britons, distant from the said hed of al Florida 900 leages, or therabout, to the ende that we might certifie you and make true reporte of the temperature, fertilitie, portes, havens, rivers, and generally of all the comodities that might be founde and seen in that lande, and also to learn what people were there dwelling, which thing long tyme agon ye have desiered, being stirred thereunto by this zeale, that France might one daye through newe discoveries have knowledg of strange conteries, and also thereof to receave, by meanes of contynewall trafficque, riche and inestimable comodities, as other nations have don, by taking in hand suche farre navegacions, bothe to the honnour and praise of theire Kinges and prynces, and also to thincrease of great proffite and use of their comon wealthes, counteris and domynions.

And which is most of all, withowt comparison, to be considered and estemed, it semeth well that you have byn hereto stirred from God above, and led to yt by the hope and desire you have that a number of brutishe people and ignoraunt of Jesus Christ may by his grace come to some knowledge of his holly lawes and ordynaunces, so as it seemeth that it hathe pleased the lyving God by his godly providence to reserve the care he hathe had of there salvation until this tyme, and will bryng them to our ffaithe, at the tyme by himself alone foreseen and ordeyned.

For if it were nedefull to shewe howe manye from tyme to tyme have gon about to fynd owt this great land, to inhabite there, who never-theles have alwaies failed and byn put by of there intention and pur-pose, some through feare of shipwracke, and some by great wyndes and tempestes that drive them backe, to theire marvelous greif . . . who never could attayne to any habytation or take possesion there of one only fote of grownd, nor yet approche nor enter into those portes and faire rivers, into which God hathe brought us—wherefore, my lorde, it may be well said that the living God hathe reserved this greate lande for the Kinges poore subjectes, as well to the ende they might be made great over this pooer people and rude nation, as also tapprove the former affection which our Kinges have had to this discoverie. . . .

Wherfore, my lorde, trusting that in a thinge so comendable and wortheye to be with good curradge attempted, that God would guyde and kepe us, desiering alwaies to full fill your commaundementes, when we had don our bussines and made our preparations, the 18 daye of February last past, through the favor of God, we departed with our two vesselles owt of the havon of Havor de Grace. . . .

Upon Whitsontide, Sondaye the xvIj [17th] of Maye, [1562], after we had well perceved and considered that there was no remedye but to assaye to fynde the meanes to harborough our shippes, as well for to amend and tryme them as to gett us fresshe water, wood and other necessaries wherof we had nede, being of opynion that there was no fayrer or fytter place for the purpose then Porte Royall. And when we had sounded the entrey and the channell (thanked be God!) we entred salfely therin with our shippes agenst the opynyon of many, finding the same one of the greatest and fayrest havens of the worlde. . . .

In this porte are many armes of the sea depe and lardg, and here and there of all sides many rivers of a meane biggness, where withowt danger all the shippes in the worlde myght be harbored. We founde no Indians inhabyting there abowt the porte and river side nearer then x or xij leages upward into the countryes, although yt be one of the goodlyest, best and frutfullest cunteres that ever was sene, and where nothing lacketh, and also where as good and like[ly] comodities be founde as in the other places therby; for we found there a great numbre of peper trees, the peper upon them yet grene and not redy to be gathered; also the best watter of the worlde, and so many sortes of fishes that ye maye take them withowt nett or angle, as many as you will; also guinea foule and innumerable wildfoule of all sortes, and in a lyttell ilande at the entrye of this haven, on the est notherest side, there is so great numbre of egretes that the bushes be all white and covered with them, so that one may take of the yong ones with his hande as many as he will carry awaye. There be also a numbre of other foule, as herons, bytterns, curleaux, and, to be shorte, so many smale birdes that yt is a straung thing to be sene.

We found the Indians there more doubtfull and fearefull then thothers byfore; yet after we hade byn att there howses, and congratulated with them, and shewed curtysie . . . they were somewhate emboldened; for some of them came to our boate, of the which we carriede two goodly and strong abourd our shippes, clothing and using them as gently and lovingly as yt was possible; but they never ceassed day nor nyght to lament and at lengh they scaped awaye. Wherefore, albeyt I was willing, according to your commaundment and memoriall, to bring away with us some of that people, yet by thadviz of those that were sent with us on the Princes behalf and youres, I forbade to do so for many considerations and reasons that they tould me, and for that also we were in doubte that, leving some of our men to inhabyte there, all the country, man, woman and childre, would not have ceased to have pursued them for to have theires agayn, seing they be not able to consider nor waye to what intent we shuld have carried them awaye. And this may be better don to theire contentation when they have better acquaintance of us, and knowe that there is no suche cruelltye in us as in other people and nations. . . .

This is the River of Jordayne in myne oppynion, whereof so muche hathe byn spoken, which is verry faire, and the cuntrye good and of grete consequence, both for theire easye habitation and also for many other thinges which whuld be to long to wrytt.

The xx of May we planted another colme graven with the Kinges armes, on the south side, in a comodyous pleasant and high place, at the entry of a faire great river, which we have called Lybourne, where there is a faire lake of freshe water verry good, and on the same side, a lyttell lower towardes the entry of the haven, is one of the fairest and best fountaynes that a made [maid] may drynke of. . . .

Ther we saw the fairest and the greatest vynes with grapes according, and yong trees, and smale woodes verry well smelling, that ever were sene, wherby yt aperithe to be the pleasantest and most comodious dwelling of all the worlde.

Wherfore, my lorde, trusting you will not thinke yt amisse, considering the great good and commodyties that may be brought thence into France, if we leve a nombre of men there, that may fortifye and so provide themselves of thinges necessarye, for in all new discovers yt is the chef and best thinge that may be don at the beginning, to fortifye and people the country which is the true and chef possession. I had not so soone sett fourthe this thinge to our company but many

of them offered to tarry there—yea, with suche a good will and jolly
curradg that suche a nombre did thus offre themselves as we had much
ado to staye there importunytie, and namely of our shipmasters and
principall pilottes, and of suche as we could not spare. Howebeyt, we
have leift there but to the numbre of xxx in all, of gentilmen, souldiers
and merryners . . . and have leift unto them for hed and ruler (following therin your goodwill) Capten Alberte della Pirie [Albert de la
Pierria], a souldier of long experyence and the first that from the beginning did offre to tarry; and furthere by there adviz, choice and will,
installed and fortified them in an iland on the northe est side, a place
of strong scytuation and comodyous, upon a river which we have
called Chenonceau and the inhabytacion and fortress Charles forte.

After we had instructed and duclyc admonished them of what they
shuld do as well for there mannour of proceading as for there good and
loving behavior of themselves towardes thes poore and simple Indians
. . . the xi of the mounthe of June last past, we departed from Porte
Royall. . . .

We thought yt mete and necessarye that your grace shuld with
diligence be advertised of that which we had don and discovered,
which is of great consequence. We concluded through the helpe of
God to retourn into France to make relation unto you of the effecte
of our navegation; praying to God that yt may please him to kepe you
in long helthe and prosperytie and give unto you the grace to cause
this faire discoverture of this Newe France to be cuntynewed and
dylligently followed.

René de Laudonnière

THE FATE OF THE CHARLESFORT COLONY

*What happened to these poor Frenchmen abandoned in Charlesfort
on Port Royal? Laudonnière tells the thrilling, terrible, tragic story as
he carefully picked up the details from survivors and put them together.
There were survivors: some were carried to England, and some ultimately reached France. So, after all, the tale has in measure a happy
ending.*

It is believed that the small vessel built by the colonists with the aid of their Indian friends was the first ship contrived by Europeans in the American continent to be used for crossing the Atlantic Ocean.

One Frenchman, seventeen-year-old Guillaume Rufin, had elected to remain at Port Royal with the Indians, and there he married the daughter of King Audusta.

In March 1926 a monument was dedicated on Parris Island by Secretary of the Navy Curtis D. Wilbur in memory of Captain Ribaut and his Frenchmen. The inscription reads:

> Here Stood
> Charlesfort
> Built 1562
> By Jean Ribaut
> For Admiral Coligny
> A Refuge
> For Huguenots
> And to the
> Glory of France

Our men after our departure never rested, but night and day did fortifie themselves, being in good hope that after their fort was finished, they would begin to discover farther up within the river.

It happened one day, as certaine of them were in cutting of rootes in the groves, that they espied on the sudden an Indian that hunted the deere, which, finding himselfe so neere upon them, was much dismayed, but our men began to draw neere unto him and to use him so courteously that he became assured and followed them to Charlesfort, where every man sought to doe him pleasure.

Captaine Albert was very joyfull of his comming, which after he had given him a shirt and some other trifles, he asked him of his dwelling. The Indian answered him that it was farther up within the river, and that he was vassal of King Audusta; he also shewed him with his hand the limits of his habitation. After much other talke the Indian desired leave to depart, because it drew toward night, which Captaine Albert granted him very willingly.

Certaine dayes after, the captaine determined to saile toward Audusta, where being arrived, by reason of the honest entertaynment which he had given to the Indian, he was so courteously received that the King talked with him of nothing else but of the desire which he had to become his friend; giving him besides to understand that, he being his friend and allie, he should have the amitie of foure other Kings, which in might and authoritie were able to do much for his sake. Besides all this, in his necessitie they might be able to succour him with victuals. One of these Kings was called Mayon, another Hoya, the third Touppa, and the fourth Stalame. He told him, moreover, that they would be very glad when they should understand the newes of his comming, and therefore he prayed him to vouchsafe to visit them.

The captaine willingly consented unto him, for the desire that he had to purchase friends in that place. Therefore they departed the next morning very earely, and first arrived at the house of King Touppa, and afterward went into the other Kings' houses, except the house of King Stalame. He received of each of them all the amiable courtesies that might be: they shewed themselves to be as affectioned friends unto him as was possible, and offered unto him a thousand small presents.

After that he had remained by the space of certaine daies with these strange Kings, he determined to take his leave; and being come backe to the house of Audusta, he commanded all his men to goe aboord their pinnesse, for he was minded to goe towardes the countrey of King Stalame, which dwelt toward the north the distance of fifteen great leagues from Charles-fort. Therefore, as they sailed up the river they entered into a great current, which they followed so farre till they came at the last to the house of Stalame, which brought him into his lodging, where he sought to make them the best cheere he could devise. He presented immediately unto Captaine Albert his bow and arrowes, which is a signe and confirmation of alliance betweene them. He presented him with chamoys skinnes. The captaine, seeing the best part of the day was now past, tooke his leave of King Stalame to return to Charles-fort, where hee arrived the day following.

By this time the friendship was growne so great betweene our men and King Audusta that in a manner all things were common betweene him and them: in such sort that this good Indian King did nothing of importance but he called our men thereunto. For when the time drew neere of the celebrating their feasts of Toya, which are ceremonies most strange to recite, he sent ambassadours to our men to request them on his behalfe to be there present. Whereunto they agreed most willingly for the desire that they had to understand what this might be. They imbarked themselves, therefore, and sailed towards the King's house, which was already come forth on the way towards them, to receive them courteously, to bid them welcome and bring them to his house, where he sought to intreat them the best he might. In the meane while the Indians prepared themselves to celebrate the feast the morrow after, and the King brought them to see the place wherein the feast should be kept; where they saw many women round about, which laboured by all meanes to make the place cleane and neat. This place was a great circuit of ground with open prospect and round in figure.

On the morrow therefore early in the morning, all they which were chosen to celebrate the feast, being painted and trimmed with rich feathers of divers colours, put themselves on the way to go from the King's house toward the place of Toya; whereunto when they were come they set themselves in order and followed three Indians, which in painting and in gesture were differing from the rest: each of them bare a tabret in their hand, dancing and singing in a lamentable tune, when they began to enter into the middest of the round circuit, being followed of others which answered them again. After that they had sung, danced and turned three times, they fell on running like unbridled horses, through the middest of the thickest woods. And then the Indian women continued all the rest of the day in teares as sad and woful as was possible, and in such rage they cut the armes of the yong girles, which they lanced so cruelly with sharpe shels of muskles that the blood followed, which they flang into the ayre, crying out three times, "He Toya!"

The King Audusta had gathered all our men into his house while the feast was celebrated, and was exceedingly offended when he saw them laugh. This he did, because the Indians are very angry when they are scene in their ceremonies. Notwithstanding, one of our men made such shift that by subtile meanes he gatte out of the house of Audusta, and secretly went and hid himselfe behinde a very thicke bush, where at his pleasure he might easily discry the ceremonies of the feast.

They three that began the feast are named Jawas; and they are, as it were, three priestes of the Indian law, to whom they give credite and beliefe partly because that by kindred they are ordained to be over their sacrifices, and partly also because they be so subtile magicians that any thing that is lost is straightway recovered by their meanes.

Againe, they are not onely reverenced for these things, but also because they heale diseases by I wotte not what kinde of knowledge and skill they have.

Those that ran so through the woodes returned two dayes after. After their returne they began to dance with a cherfull courage in the middest of the faire place, and to cheere up their good olde Indian fathers, which, either by reason of their too great age or by reason of their naturall indisposition and feeblenesse, were not called to the feast.

When all these dances were ended, they fell on eating with such a greedinesse that they seemed rather to devoure their meate than to eate it, for they had neither eaten nor drunke the day of the feast, nor the two dayes following. Our men were not forgotten at this good cheere, for the Indians sent for them all thither, shewing themselves very glad of their presence. . . .

When the feast therefore was finished, our men returned unto Charles-fort, where, having remained but a while their victualles beganne to waxe short, which forced them to have recourse unto their neighbours, and to pray them to succour them in their necessitie; which gave them part of all the victualles which they had, and kept no more unto themselves than would serve to sow their fieldes. They tolde them farther that for this cause it was needful for them to retire themselves into the woods, to live on mast and rootes untill the time of harvest, being as sory as might be that they were not able any farther to ayde them. They gave them also counsell to goe toward the countreys of King Couexis, a man of might and renowne in this province, which maketh his aboad toward the south, abounding at all seasons and replenished with such quantitie of mill, corne and beanes that by his onely succour they might be able to live a very long time. But before they should come into his territories, they were to repayre unto a King called Ouade, the brother of Couexis, which in mill, beanes and corne was no lesse wealthy, and withall is very liberall, and which would be very joyfull if he might but once see them.

Our men . . . resolved to go thither, for they felt already the necessity which oppressed them. Therfore they made request unto King Maccou that it would please him to give them one of his subjects to guide them the right way thither; whereupon he condescended very willingly. . . . Wherefore after they had given order for all things necessary for the voyage, they put themselves to sea, and sayled so farre that in the end they came into the countrey of Ouade, which they found to be the River Belle. . . . They advertised the King by one of the guides which they brought with them, how they (having heard of his great liberalitie) had put to sea to come to beseech him to succour them with victuals in their great want and necessitie; and that in so doing, he should binde them all hereafter to remaine his faithfull friends and loyall defenders against all his enemies.

This good Indian, as soone ready to doe them pleasure as they were to demand it, commanded his subjects that they should fill our pinnesse with mil and beanes. Afterward he caused them to bring him six pieces of his tapistry made like little coverlets, and gave them to our men. . . . In recompence of all these giftes our men gave him two cutting hookes and certaine other trifles. . . . Wherefore they imbarked themselves and sayled towards Charles-fort, which from this place might be some five and twenty leagues distant.

But as soone as our men thought themselves at their ease, and free from the dangers whereunto they had exposed themselves night and day in gathering together of victuals here and there, lo, even as they were asleepe, the fire caught in their lodgings with such furie, being increased by the winde, that the roome that was built for them before our mens departure was consumed in an instant, without being able to save any thing, saving a little of their victualles.

Whereupon our men, being farre from all succours, found themselves in such extremitie that without the ayd of Almighty God, the onely searcher of the hearts and thoughts of men, which never forsaketh those that seeke him in their afflictions, they had bene quite and cleane out of all hope. For the next day betimes in the morning the King Audusta and King Maccou came thither, accompanied with a very good companie of Indians, which, knowing the misfortune, were very sory for it. And then they uttered unto their subjects the speedy diligence which they were to use in building another house, shewing unto them that the Frenchmen were their loving friends, and that they had made it evident unto them by the gifts and presents which they had received, protesting that whosoever put not his helping hand unto the worke with all his might should be esteemed as unprofitable and as one that had no good part in him, which the savages feare above all things.

This was the occasion that every man began to endeavour himselfe in such sort that in lesse than twelve houres they had begun and finished a house which was very neere as great as the former. Which being ended, they returned home fully contented with a few cutting hookes and hatchets, which they received of our men. . . .

Behold, therefore, how our men behaved themselves very well hitherto, although they had endured many great mishaps. But misfortune—or rather the just judgement of God—would have it that those which could not bee overcome by fire nor water, should be undone by their owne selves. This is the common fashion of men, which cannot continue in one state, and had rather to overthrow themselves than not to attempt some new thing dayly. . . . They entred therefore into partialities and dissentions, which began about a souldier named Guernache, which was a drummer of the French bands; which, as it was told to me, was very cruelly hanged by his owne captaine, and for a smal fault. Which captaine, also using to threaten the rest of his souldiers which staied behind under his obedience, and peradventure (as it is to be presumed) were not so obedient to him as they should have bene, was the cause that they fell into a mutinie, because that many times he put his threatnings in execution. Whereupon they so chased him that at the last they put him to death.

And the principall occasion that moved them thereunto was because he degraded another souldier named La Chere (which he had banished) and because he had not performed his promise—for hee had promised to send him victuals, from eight dayes to eight dayes, which thing he did not, but said, on the contrary, that he would be glad to heare of his death. He said, moreover, that he would chastise others also, and used so evil sounding speeches that honestie forbiddeth me to repeat them. The souldiers, seeing his madnes to increase from day to day, and fearing to fall into the dangers of the other, resolved to kill him. Having executed their purpose, they went to seeke the souldier that was banished, which was in a small island distant from Charles-fort about three leagues, where they found him almost half dead for hunger.

When they were come home againe, they assembled themselves together to choose one to be governour over them, whose name was Nicolas Barre, a man worthy of commendation and one which knewe so well to quite himselfe of his charge that all rancour and dissention ceased among them, and they lived peaceably one with another.

During this time they began to build a smal pinnesse, with hope to return into France, if no succours came unto them as they expected

from day to day. And though there were no man among them that had
any skill, notwithstanding necessitie, which is the maistresse of all
sciences, taught them the way to build it. After that it was finished,
they thought of nothing else saving how to furnish it with all things
necessarie to undertake the voyage. But they wanted those things
that of all other were most needefull, as cordage and sayles, without
which the enterprise coulde not come to effect. Having no meanes to
recover these things, they were in worse case then at the first, and
almost ready to fall into despayre. But that good God, which never
forsaketh the afflicted, did succour them in their necessitie.

As they were in these perplexities King Audusta and Maccou came
to them, accompanied with two hundred Indians at the least, whom
our Frenchmen went forth to meete withal, and shewed the King
in what neede of cordage they stood; who promised them to returne
within two dayes and to bring so much as should suffice to furnish
the pinnesse with tackling. Our men, being pleased with these good
newes and promises, bestowed upon them certaine cutting hookes
and shirtes. After their departure our men sought all means to recover
rosen in the woodes, wherein they cut the pine trees round about,
out of which they drew sufficient reasonable quantitie to bray the
vessell. Also, they gathered a kind of mosse which groweth on the
trees of this countrey, to servie to calke the same withall. There now
wanted nothing but sayles, which they made of their owne shirtes and
of their sheetes. Within few dayes after, the Indian Kings returned to
Charles fort with so good store of cordage that there was found sufficient for tackling of the small pinnesse.

Our men, as glad as might be, used great liberalitie towards them
and, at their leaving of the countrey, left them all the marchandise
that remained, leaving them thereby so fully satisfied that they departed from them with all the contentation of the worlde. They went
forward therefore to finish the brigandine, and used so speedie diligence that within a short time afterward they made it ready furnished
with all things. In the meane season the winde came so fit for their
purpose that it seemed to invite them to put to the sea; which they
did without delay, after they had set all their things in order. But before they departed they embarked their artillerie, their forge and other
munitions of warre which Captaine Ribault had left them, and then
as much mill as they could gather together. But being drunken with
the too excessive joy which they had conceived for their returning into

France, or rather deprived of all foresight and consideration without regarding the inconstance of the winds which change in a moment, they put themselves to sea, and with so slender victuals that the end of their interprise became unlucky and unfortunate.

For after they had sayled the third part of their way, they were surprised with calmes which did so much hinder them that in three weekes they sailed not above five and twentie leagues. During this time their victuals consumed and became so short that every man was constrained to eate not past twelve graines of mill by the day, which may be in value as much as twelve peason. Yea, and this felicitie lasted not long, for their victuals failed them altogether at once, and they had nothing for their more assured refuge but their shooes and leather jerkins which they did eat. Touching their beverage, some of them dranke the sea water, others did drink their owne urine, and they remained in such desperate necessitie a very long space, during the which part of them died for hunger.

Beside this extreme famine, which did so grievously oppresse them, they fell every minute of an houre out of all hope ever to see France againe, insomuch that they were constrained to cast the water continually out, that on al sides entred into their barke. And every day they fared worse and worse; for after they had eaten up their shooes and their leather jerkins, there arose so boystrous a winde and so contrary to their course that in the turning of a hande the waves filled their vessel halfe full of water and brused it upon the one side.

Being now more out of hope then ever to escape out of this extreme peril, they cared not for casting out of the water which now was almost ready to drowne them. And as men resolved to die, every one fell downe backewarde and gave themselves over altogether unto the will of the waves. When as one of them a little having taken heart unto him declared unto them how litle way they had to sayle, assuring them that if the winde held, they should see land within three dayes. This man did so encourage them that after they had throwne the water out of the pinnesse, they remained three dayes without eating or drinking, except it were of the sea water. When the time of his promise was expired, they were more troubled then they were before, seeing they could not descry any land.

Wherefore in this extreme despaire certaine among them made this motion, that it was better that one man should dye than that so many men should perish. They agreed therefore that one should die to sustaine the others. Which thing was executed in the person of La Chere, of whom we have spoken heretofore, whose flesh was divided equally among his fellows: a thing so pitifull to recite that my pen is loth to write it.

After so long time and tedious travels, God of his goodnesse using His accustomed favour, changed their sorrow into joy and shewed unto them the sight of land. Whereof they were so exceedingly glad that the pleasure caused them to remaine a long time as men without sence; whereby they let the pinnesse floate this and that way, without holding any right way or course. But a small English barke boarded the vessel in the which there was a Frenchman who had been in the first voyage into Florida, who easily knew them and spoke unto them, and afterwards gave them meat and drinke. Incontinently they recovered their natural courages and declared unto him at large all their navigation. The Englishmen consulted a long while what was best to be done, and in fine they resolved to put on land those that were most feeble, and to carry the rest unto the Queene of England, which purposed at that time to send into Florida. . . .

PART III

The Spanish at Santa Elena

1564-1587

In June 1564 a Spanish squadron was sent over by Philip II to destroy Charlesfort. The mission performed, they carried off with them to Cuba the pillar set up by Ribaut as a symbol of French dominion, and Guillaume Rufin, the lad who had chosen to stay on the island when his compatriots sailed away. The boy was held prisoner.

Two years later the Spanish returned in full earnest to Santa Elena —the region which they had discovered, claimed and named in 1520— to establish a military post, successive colonies of farmers and a mission of which Jesuit Father Juan Rogel was the first resident priest. For twenty-one years Santa Elena was Philip II's northernmost outpost on the Atlantic coast.

"Unlike the romantic conquistadores who chanced to find the ready-made wealth of the Aztecs and the Incas, the conquerors of La Florida were confronted by the manifold problem of competing with nature, with natives, and with foreign enemies. Life was not easy on the northern frontier. . . . No silver-laden mule-trains made their way southward from the red hills of Chiaha [north Georgia] and Tama [central Georgia] across Guale's pine barrens and dense coastal plains to the sea; nor did dazzling heaps of gold fill the royal coffers at San Augustin and Santa Elena. More often the very storerooms were bare of supplies, while hungry colonists and tall lean Creeks begged for grain."[1]

The Spanish legacy of names survives today: in St. Helena and Lady's islands; in St. Helena Sound; and in old St. Helena's church of Beaufort. From the Spanish we inherited our Carolina plantation system, says Samuel Gaillard Stoney of Charleston. "The nearest thing to an architectural heritage is the system of building in concrete, called tabby. This was made of seashells. . . . Its origin, its name and its tradition are all so distinctively of Spanish derivation."

---

[1] Mary Ross, "French Intrusions and Indian Uprisings in Georgia and South Carolina, 1577-1586," in *Georgia Historical Quarterly*, VII, No. 3 (Sept. 1923), 253.

Gonzalo Solís de Merás

"A FORT WAS BUILT ... AND THE ADELANTADO CALLED IT SAN FELIPE"

When the news reached the Spanish court that the French Hugue-nots had established a second colony in Florida, this time at Fort Caroline on the St. Johns River, some 160 miles south of Port Royal, King Philip II dispatched Pedro Menéndez de Avilés to the scene to drive out the encroachers. On March 20, 1565, he had bestowed on him the title of Adelantado (Governor) of Florida, with a patent for the conquest and settlement of his province.

Menéndez proceeded to carry out the King's orders. He destroyed Fort Caroline and slaughtered the Frenchmen, one of whom was Captain Jean Ribaut. In April 1566 he sailed northward from St. Augustine, where he had established a presidio—his destination, Santa Elena, where the French had built Charlesfort. With him as interpre-ter was the French youth, Guillaume Rufin, whom the Spaniards called Guillermo Rouffi.

Stopping briefly at Guale on what is now the coast of Georgia, Menéndez found the Indians there at war with the Indians at Santa Elena. The Adelantado demanded that they make peace with their enemies, left some of his men as hostages and sailed on toward Santa Elena. There he built a fort which he called San Felipe and established a settlement.

Gonzalo Solís de Merás, who gives the following report, was the brother of Menéndez's wife, Ana María de Solís. He belonged, it is said, to one of the noble families of the Asturias and was a man of letters. He accompanied the Adelantado on this Florida expedition, and he was one of the two men who murdered Ribaut.

Opinions differ as to the site of Fort San Felipe. Dr. David Duncan Wallace, South Carolina historian, says it was Mean's Creek on Parris Island about two miles from the French Charlesfort. A. S. Salley, another authority on South Carolina, holds it could have been on the island today called St. Helena. Major George H. Osterhout, of the U.S. Marines, places it "at the junction of Battery Creek and Beaufort River in the present town of Port Royal." Spanish authorities put it near Charlesfort. N. L. Willett, of Beaufort, says San Felipe was on Parris Island. Woodbury Lowery says, "It appears highly probable

49

*that the Point of Santa Elena was Hilton Head, and that San Felipe
was therefore in the immediate neighborhood of Charlesfort. . . . The
Fort of San Felipe may have been on Parris Island."*

The Adelantado ordered the ship to hoist anchor, and sailed for
Santa Elena with her and the 2 brigantines. . . . They arrived at Santa
Elena the next day in the afternoon, for the 3 Indians they brought
knew the harbor very well. They entered it at the place to which the
Indians guided them, for they were skilful pilots, being accustomed to
going there fishing in their canoes. Having entered the harbor and
gone a league up the river, the Indians ordered that the large vessel
should anchor, as she could not go farther, and they should embark in
the brigantines and go to the village. The Adelantado did this, and
embarked in the brigantines, and took with him Estébano de las Alas
and about one hundred persons.

He arrived at the pueblo of the Indians, which was 2 leagues from
there, and found it burned, and [the inhabitants] beginning to build a
few houses again. A few Indians appeared, much disturbed, with their
bows and arrows and ready for war. The two Indians the Adelantado
had with him told him that those others thought that he and his men
were some of the false Christians who had captured them in the war
while helping Guale; that they would land and tell them we were very
good and enemies of those people, and the reason we came.

The Adelantado let them go, and within half an hour he landed with
all his people, leaving 10 in each brigantine to guard it; and the Indians immediately came to the Adelantado without bows and arrows,
with great humility and making great demonstrations of respect, and
many ran off, some by one trail, others by another. This was to notify
the pueblo, the caciques and captains, that they should come to see
the Adelantado. Then they built a great fire and brought a quantity of
shell-fish, and the Adelantado and his men took supper. Many Indians
came running, all of them to speak and pay their respects to the
Adelantado, for the love and joy these Indians showed him was
something to see.

That night came three caciques, subjects of Orista, and told him
that he should go to a village one league distant from there, as Orista
and others of his captains and caciques would come there to eat. Next
day the Adelantado did this. Orista came and 2 other caciques and

captains. Great was the delight of all on seeing Guillermo, the interpreter, to whom Orista had given a daughter of his for wife at the time he first came there. The Adelantado ordered him to tell Orista to gather his principal Indians, because he wished to speak to them. This was done. The Adelantado commanded Guillermo . . . to tell them (the 3 Indians being present whom the Adelantado had brought with him[2]) all that had passed in Guale concerning the making of peace. Orista said that he would reply presently, and he spoke with his Indians more than half an hour, discussing the subject, without their wanting Guillermo to be there, so that he should not understand what they were treating of. And then they called the interpreter to whom they talked a very long time, and afterward the interpreter told the Adelantado, on behalf of Orista, that it would please him much to make peace, as the Adelantado ordered him to do; and he would be even more pleased to become a true Christian with his people, as those of Guale wanted to be, for those people were not to be better than they; that his Indians, whom the Adelantado had brought from Guale, had told them who God was and how good it was to be Christians; that they wished very much to have the Adelantado live in that land and to take him for an elder brother, in order to do what he should command them; and that they would hold the false Christians as enemies, since they were those of the Adelantado.

He replied to them, showing there was great joy in his heart, that he loved them much, but did not think he could live in that land, because it was bad, and his own was better; and that if Orista's Indians killed his Christians, and if they did any harm, the Adelantado would at once kill him who did it, because the Christians he brought would not hurt the Indians; that he would like to live there solely in order that they might learn to become Christians, so that when they died they might go to heaven. He told them the power and goodness of God, and all that he told the other caciques, that they might become Christians.

They showed great satisfaction at hearing him, and repeated that they wished to become Christians, praying him to leave them someone to teach them. They begged for this with so much earnestness that

---

[2] The three Indians Menéndez had found captives under sentence of death in Guale. He had promised to return them to Guale if his peace negotiations with the Santa Elena Indians failed.

the Adelantado offered to leave a man, but [said] that if Orista or his people killed him, he would return to make war on them and cut off the heads of all of them.

Then came many Indian women, carrying maize, fish boiled and roasted oysters and many acorns; and the Adelantado ordered biscuit, honey and wine to be brought, and divided it among the Indians, who drank the wine well, but ate the biscuit dipped in honey-water, better, because they are very fond of sweets. When the meal was over, during which there was great merriment and rejoicing, they seated the Adelantado in the seat of the cacique, and with various ceremonies Orista came to him and took his hands. Afterward the rest of the caciques and Indians did the same. . . . Then they began to sing and dance, the caciques and several principal Indians remaining with the Adelantado, and the festivities and demonstrations lasted until about midnight, when they withdrew.

The next day, the Indians issued many proclamations in the village, in order that no one should do any harm to the Christians, and the Adelantado said to the cacique that he was going in search of a good site where he could make a settlement for his Spaniards, for it was not right that they should live among the Indians and quarrel afterward. The cacique told him of one, near the place where the vessel was anchored, and he embarked, without any suspicion whatever, with his wife and 12 Indians, in the Adelantado's brigantines; and they all went very gaily together as far as the spot where they were to land. There the Adelantado gave the Indians their midday meal, and the Spaniards landed to go to Orista's village,[3] where they were very well entertained that night. Next morning the cacique took the Adelantado to a very large house and seated him in his seat, going through the same ceremony with him as he had in the previous pueblo, and ordering the same proclamations to be made. They spent the following day in reconnoitring the site to begin the settlement, and it appeared to all of them very good and pleasant; and without losing time, the Adelantado, Estébano de las Alas and other captains marked out the fort, and its erection was committed to the charge of Antonio Gomez, whom he had taken with 50 soldiers and others who were sailors from the ship of the fleet which was in Havanna, so that up to the end of May they could be with him in Florida; and they served him very well.

---

[3] Orista had been Laudonnière's friend. The French called him Audusta. Guale in French was called Ouadé.

A fort was built of stakes, earth and fascines, and the Adelantado called it San Felipe. He named Estébano de las Alas as governor of it and of that land and left him 110 men: then he sent the vessel with 20 on board to Santo Domingo, to be laden with supplies so that the fort might be provisioned, for he had little to leave there. He likewise dispatched a brigantine to St. Augustine and San Mateo, to give news of everything.

He sent some Indians inland to tell the caciques that very good Christians were there; that they did no evil or harm to the natives, but much good, giving them presents; and that Orista and others had taken him for their elder brother, to defend them from their enemies, whereat all the Indians were very much pleased and desired to be Christians; that if those others wished to do the same and to see him, he was waiting for them to give them some of the things he had brought. Within 15 days, the time he tarried there, many caciques came to visit him, and he paid them many attentions, so that they took him for their elder brother, to command them at his will; they told him they wanted to be Christians and he should give them a cross, and some of his men to teach them in their country.

The Adelantado did so, giving to each cacique 1 or 2 Christians, and tools for erecting a cross in each village, admonishing them that every day, morning and evening, they should repeat the Christian doctrine and worship the Holy Cross, in order that the Indians might learn it and imitate them. To all the caciques he gave presents, and a hatchet to each one, with which they were very much delighted, and they gave him well-tanned deerskins and some pearls, of which there are many in that country, although they are of little value because they are burned.

Taking his leave of Cacique Orista, who was very joyful at having Spaniards [left with him], the Adelantado set out for Guale, taking 20 soldiers, 2 of Orista's principal Indians to negotiate the peace, and Guillermo the interpreter. In Santa Elena remained Estébano de las Alas,[4] and the men who were with him, who were pleased because there appeared to be a very good beginning of turning the Indians into Christians, which, next to driving the Lutherans out of the land, was all that they desired; but they had great fear of lack of food, for they had very little remaining; and much work to do in finishing their fort, for each day they expected French Lutherans, who had had tid-

---
[4] First governor of Santa Elena.

ings of the Adelantado's successes against them on sea as well as on
land in destroying them and eradicating them from that country, so
that they should not teach their evil faith to the Indians. . . .

Alonso Martin

"IN THE CITY OF SANTA ELENA"

*By order of the King, Pedro Menéndez de Avilés returned to Spain
in 1571 to build, gather and command a great armada destined for
Flanders and England. On September 17, 1575, shortly before the
armada sailed, he died of a violent fever, defeated in his wish to go
back to Florida and "not to leave it for the rest of my life, . . . for that
is the sum of my longings and happiness."*

*During his absence the Florida settlements were seemingly neg-
lected. At Santa Elena the colonists were unhappy and dissatisfied.
In February 1576 they petitioned to be allowed to return to Spain.
Testimony was taken at the request of Alonso Martin, Procurador
of Santa Elena; the hearings lasted for several weeks.*

In the city of Santa Elena, on the twenty-seventh day of the month
of February in the year [fifteen] seventy-six, the very Illustrious Señor
Hernando de Miranda, Governor and Captain-General of these provinces of Florida for His Majesty, and Adelantado thereof, said—the
other settlers being assembled in the Cabildo of this said city—that
he wished to know which of the colonists wanted to remain to settle
these provinces of Florida: wherefore he ordered us to assemble, and
those who wished to depart from this land of Florida were to say so
and put it in writing, the name of each one being mentioned so that
he could give a report and information thereof to His Majesty, in
order to see how many were those who wished to go, and how many
were those who wished to remain. Wherefore we came together, and
a general *cabildo* took place of the *justicia* and *regimiento*, with all
the other settlers who at present reside in this city. . . .

We, assembled and met together, . . . say that we . . . were enlisted
in Spain . . . captains appointed by the Adelantado, Pedro Menéndez
de Avilés, by virtue of a royal ordinance, wherein many perquisites
were promised to all those who should come to settle these provinces

. . . : giving us all manner of cattle, twelve head with the bull; establishing us on good soil, and giving us allotments of lands for farming and raising cattle. And nothing of all this has been fulfilled to us, unless it be to keep us on an island surrounded by sea water, which is one league long and half a league wide, more or less; the larger part of which island, at every period of spring tides, is over-flowed by the sea; and the land is of the kind aforesaid, and we have no other assistance save our own arms, although by doing some hoeing we have broken up a little land which we sow with maize to sustain our children; because the soil is not of the quality for sowing any other sort. . . .

Besides which, even if the soil were rich and fertile, it has not the [right] climate nor is the earth ever dry, unless it be with the frosts and extreme cold caused therein by the winter, which comes in December and January; for in the months of April and May, when the [grain for] bread ripens in this island, it does nothing but rain all that time, which is when we are sowing and gathering the maize; and so we have suffered and do suffer great hardships, as the harvest is small which we gather therefrom with excessive labor; because the agreement with us has not been carried out, as has been said.

Therefore we have wasted all our means, with which, and with other things, we came well supplied, having been farmers in Spain, where we had all manner of cattle wherewith to work; and so here we feel ourselves lost, and old, and weary, and full of sickness . . . and have been ill-treated and insulted by the governors who have governed, and so we say that we . . . are not for settling. We therefore beg and request Your Honor, one, two and three times, and all the [times] that by law we must, to order permission given to us and a ship to depart from this land, whither His Majesty shall best see opportunity and be most pleased [to send us], outside these provinces. . . .

Don Cristobal de Erraso

"FROM THE SHIPS THEY SAW THE HOUSES BURNING"

Soon after the petition of the Santa Elena settlers was on its way to Spain, the once friendly Indians of the province of Orista became

enraged at the garrison of the fort and massacred two parties of Spanish soldiers. Among the slain was Pedro Menéndez de Avilés the
Younger, twenty-eight-year-old nephew of the great Adelantado. In-
terference in a local quarrel among the Guale Indians by the commander at Santa Elena brought on enmity in that quarter.

Governor Hernando de Miranda, in answer to a call for help, sailed
up from St. Augustine with a small force of fifteen or twenty young
soldiers. He ordered San Felipe dismantled. Apparently he planned
to leave Santa Elena without the "weeping and wailing" widows who
begged him to take them away; for when he refused, "they seized him,
took him by force, and put him on board."

The following is from the report which the "Very Illustrious Señor,
Don Cristobal de Erraso, Knight of the Order of Santiago, Captain-
General for his Majesty of the royal armada for the protection of the
Indies, caused to be made concerning the uprising of the Indians of
the province of Florida, and the capture [abandonment seems a bet-
ter word] of the fort of Santa Elena. . . ."

[La Yaguana, Hispaniola, January 19, 1577]
. . . His lordship caused to appear before him . . . Domingo Martin,
a sailor of the boat called Nuestra Señora de la Luz; and he said that
he is a native of the town of Avero, in Portugal. . . . And being ques-
tioned . . . he said that he has knowledge of the province of Florida
and the forts of Santa Elena and St. Augustine, which are therein,
because he has seen them and been there; and that what he knows,
and what is occurring, is that this witness, having gone in a boat from
Havana to the said Florida with meat and other supplies from His
Majesty for the people of the said forts, . . . arrived . . . at the said
fort of Santa Elena and anchored there, as it seems to him, in the
month of July or August.

When this witness arrived, he found the men of the said fort and
the women all gathered therein and in arms, because the Indians one
month previous had slain Ensign Moyano and twenty soldiers with
him; and that the occasion of their killing them, as those of the said
fort declared, was that the said ensign with the others had gone to
a pueblo they call Oristan, where they had found Cacique Oristan
and other caciques who were holding a certain feast, whom they
asked to give them something to eat. That the said caciques or Indians
had answered, [inquiring] how it was that they came in that manner,

with their fuses lighted; they must extinguish them if they wished to be given what they asked; that the said ensign had told the said soldiers to do this; that he alone was sufficient for those Indians; and that as soon as they had extinguished them, the Indians had sprung upon them and killed them all, except one sailor who had escaped through the forest and come to the fort to give notice thereof. That within a month of the arrival of this witness at the said fort of Santa Elena, there came news of how the Indians had slain Pedro Menéndez [the Younger] . . . likewise His Majesty's factor and treasurer, who were on their way from the fort of St. Augustine to pay the men who were in the said fort of Santa Elena.

And it was said that the manner in which they killed them was that the aforesaid were coming in a shallop by the inland waterway, with five or six other persons, nine altogether, . . . to the fort of Santa Elena, for the aforesaid purpose, bringing the King's money on board a vessel; that on arriving at a village they call Guale, they had stopped to speak with the Indians, and a cacique had told them they should land and eat and rest themselves; and that when they landed, the Indians killed all nine of them, not one remaining.

At the same time that this happened, this witness being at the fort of Santa Elena, the son of a resident of the fort they called Rodrigo Menca was missing, for his father had sent him to look after some hogs, and he never returned. The General of the said Florida, whom they called Hernando de Miranda, ordered a captain they called Diego de Solis to set out with nine soldiers to learn about the said youth and ascertain if there were Indians on the island. He went forth in the morning, before sunrise, and within two or three hours the men at the fort heard shots, and they at once said and suspected that the said captain and those who went with him had been slain by Indians, and the said suspicion was confirmed, because it afterward appeared that they had all been killed, not one being left alive.

Then the next day, this witness being in the said fort, a great number of Indians came upon it and began to shoot many arrows at those within, to which they replied with the artillery and arquebuses. This may have lasted about two hours or more, and because the Indians' arrows gave out, they fled. Two or three days after this happened, the women at the said fort pestered the said General with great weeping and wailing, telling him that they were left alone, that their husbands had been killed, that he must take them away from there; and as the said General would not do so, they seized him, took him by force and put him on board [one of] two boats and one vessel which were there. When the said General saw this, and that in the said fort there were no more than fifteen or twenty soldiers, all young boys, he commanded that they should embark with their belongings in the said ship and two boats, and so they all did; and while they awaited good weather, having crossed the bar, they saw how a great number of Indians attacked the fort and set fire thereto, and from the ships they saw the houses burning. . . .

Bartolomé Martinez

"GIVE ME SOME GRANT OF LAND THERE, WHERE I MIGHT LIVE FOR ALWAYS"

Bartolomé Martinez had served as Keeper of Supplies at Santa Elena and later as Accountant. He was there during the Indian uprising in the summer of 1576.

The following request is from a letter he wrote to Philip II from Havana. No record shows that the King granted his wishes, for apparently Martinez was never again to see the land "so marvelously good" where, like Pedro Menéndez de Avilés before him, he longed to spend the rest of his life. Some months later he killed an ensign in the Florida forces and was condemned to slavery in the galleys.

[Havana, February 17, 1577]

. . . I have served Your Majesty enough . . . years in these provinces of Florida, for the Adelantado brought me hither as a soldier, and during that period I have suffered much misery, and many torments from hunger and nakedness, not because the country is as bad as they think it is, but because of the bad system its governors have had, and because its funds are small for conquering so many people and such an extensive territory.

I have travelled over the the larger part of the coast of these provinces, and thirty leagues round about Santa Elena; and what may be said to Your Majesty of this country, whereof every one speaks ill, is that it is marvellously good, for where I have gone there are the richest lands for cultivation and cattle-raising; mighty, fresh-water rivers, great plains and mountain ridges inland, very great indication of there being therein very fine pearls and mines of silver.

And what may be truthfully told to Your Majesty is that in Santa Elena I planted with my own hands grape-vines, pomegranate trees, orange and fig trees; wheat, barley, onions and garlic. All the vegetables which grow in Spain were raised in that fort; and although I know that there are persons in those kingdoms who have a contrary opinion, I offer to prove what I say with reliable witnesses, and I wish I had the opportunity to beseech Your Majesty to give me some grant of land there, where I might live for always, for it is the healthiest country, with most abundant shooting and fishing, and very good for cultivation, which is all that can be desired.

If Your Majesty should be pleased that I remain in office, I know that *Visitador* Baltasar del Castillo will give Your Majesty a report on my capacity. And either way, or whatever Your Majesty may will, I entreat Your Majesty to have compassion on me, for I am very poor, and I am married to a niece of the wife of the Adelantado, Pedro Menéndez, . . . and I have not enough clothes in which to fall dead, on account of the loss of the city of Santa Elena, of which I was a resident. . . .

May Our Lord preserve the Very Royal Catholic person of Your Majesty for long years, with an increase of kingdoms and dominions! . . .

Your Majesty's humble servant
and vassal, who kisses your royal feet,
BARTOLOMÉ MARTINEZ

Pedro Menéndez Marqués

SANTA ELENA REBUILT

When King Philip II learned that Santa Elena had been abandoned and Fort San Felipe destroyed by the Indians, he commanded Pedro Menéndez de Marqués, nephew and successor to the late Adelantado, to go back there and rebuild the fortification, "because it so befits Your Majesty's service and the safety of the rest of the Indies."

In June 1577 Marqués, aboard the Espiritu Santo, a well-armed vessel carrying forty men under the command of Captain Vincente Gonzales, sailed away to Santa Elena. Near the ruins of San Felipe a new fort was built which was called San Marcos, and "floating high above the gleaming cannon . . . the proud banner of old Castile was once more triumphant, all crimson and gold in the Carolina breeze."⁵

Unbeknown to the Spanish, French corsairs led by Nicolao Strozzi and Gilberto Gil had entrenched themselves in a fortification on "the point of Santa Elena." They allied themselves with the natives and planned to destroy the Spanish strongholds at San Augustin and Santa Elena. "Only the bravery of the Spanish forces at Santa Elena in the presidio of San Marcos and the clear-headed generalship and watchfulness of the Spaniard, the renowned Pedro Menéndez de Marqués, saved the day for Spain and defeated the design for a French occupation of the coast."⁶

Marqués, who continued to serve as Governor of Florida until 1589, regularly informed the King of affairs at Santa Elena. "This is well," wrote the King upon hearing of the building of the village at Santa Elena.

Late in 1587 or very early in 1588 the fort of Santa Elena was finally abandoned and the garrison withdrawn.⁷

The following excerpts are from the letters of Governor Pedro Menéndez de Marqués to King Philip II of Spain.

[Santa Elena, October 21, 1577]
. . . I came to this fort with seventy-nine men, and fourteen soldiers the patache brought . . . ; and on the way I ran into a storm, so that one of the ships was forced to throw much of the lumber overboard. At last, in spite of all these troubles, I arrived here with all the men well; where, on the same day, I started to build the fort, one hundred and fifty paces away from the nearest woods, because [against] Indians there is no greater protection than the open country. When the In-

---

⁵ Mary Ross, "French Intrusions and Indian Uprisings in Georgia and South Carolina, 1577-1580," in Georgia Historical Quarterly, Vol. VII, No. 3 (Sept. 1923), 251-281. Mary Ross was a pupil of Professor Herbert E. Bolton at the University of California. Her study of affairs at Santa Elena is based on manuscript material in the Archives General de Indies of Seville.

⁶ Ibid., p. 251.

⁷ John R. Swanton, Early History of the Creek Indians and Their Neighbors. Washington, D.C.: Bureau of American Ethnology Bulletin 73, 1922, p. 59.

dians saw us coming, they surrounded us from all the forests, as was apparent from the smoke they made, in order to see where we would go to cut timber for the fort; but they were deceived, for within six days of my arrival here I had all the curtains done. When the enemy saw this, and a blockhouse at a distance, and in such a short time, they tried through spies to learn how many people there were; and so I know not whether they were Frenchmen or Indians who came during three nights to reconnoitre us; but up to now they have never been able to ascertain or find out the number I had, for I have seven outposts beyond the fort, every twenty-five or fifty paces, which prevent them from knowing anything. May it please God that they learn nothing henceforth! I hold it as my opinion that, with the aid of the French, they will not fail to come here or to St. Augustine, to see if they can get in, although we are so much on the lookout that we shall not give them that opportunity. . . .

It appears to me that Your Majesty has need of sending some succor to these provinces, and within a short time. . . . It may be that [against] Indians only, one hundred and fifty [men] are sufficient, although it is to be said to Your Majesty that if the one hundred and fifty shall happen to lack supplies they will die, for there are not people [enough] to remain in the forts, and to go and seek food; and let not Your Majesty count on the farmers, for at two hundred paces they dare not do any ploughing, and all they cultivate is but a little air in comparison with what they eat and what they exact. The laborers here are all youths, who are soldiers married to daughters of the older farmers; they serve in soldiers' *plazas* because there are no other [men], and they have forty-four women, sixty-two children and eleven pregnant women, about to be confined; which makes, in all, one hundred and six persons who perforce must eat, and each day they beg me to give them level land where they can do their sowing, or to turn them out of the country.

Let Your Majesty consider what I shall do with one hundred and six persons who beg me to feed them, and I with no order therefor from Your Majesty. I brought to this fort five women only, only with their husbands; they are married to five sawyers. [I brought them] because of the need there was of them, although against their will, as they did not wish to come, saying that there was nothing to eat. So I have given and now give them rations as I do their husbands; and to the others I give nothing until I hear what Your Majesty com-

mands. God knows what this costs me from my poverty! I beseech
Your Majesty to order that there be speedy provisions made in this. . . .

It will likewise be needful that Your Majesty command that there
be provided fifty quintals of lead. . . . It will also be necessary to send
thirty quintals of wicks, for it is an extraordinary thing how much is
used thereof; since I have been here there has not been a night that we
have not consumed about twenty pounds [of candles], because we
dare not extinguish them until we are well fortified. . . .

Let Your Majesty be pleased to command that there be decreed
therein what best befits Your Majesty's service, and within a short
time. May Our Lord preserve your R.C.P.,[8] and prosper you for many
and happy years, with an increase of larger kingdoms, as Christendom
has need thereof, and we, Your Majesty's servants, desire it! . . .

Your R.C. Majesty's humble servant,
who kisses your royal hands,
P° MENÉNDEZ MARQUÉS

[St. Augustine, June 15, 1578]

. . . I heard in Santa Helena that Frenchmen were alive among the
Indians, and I knew it likewise by some arquebus shots which I heard
one night. . . . I remained there a few days, for, as it was already summer, [when] they are in the habit of coming forth to lie in ambush, they
came many times to the island; but, although I set some ambushes . . . ,
never did they dare show themselves. At last a few showed themselves.
When I went after them, however, they took to the woods, for they
are like deer. While I was there, one evening a ship arrived off the
harbor, and as it was night it cast anchor; and that night God was
pleased to send such a storm that it disappeared the next day, and I
have seen it no more up to now. I suspect that it was French, and had
news of the people who were lost at Santa Helena. . . .

I did my utmost to learn where the French had fortified themselves
after they were shipwrecked, and at last I found it, in a wood near a
river. According to the plan thereof, there were more people than I
thought, because it was shaped in a triangle, with three cavaliers, all
made of sod and fagots, with its curtain largely of wood, and it had
from cavalier to cavalier sixty-six paces. I found five houses within, one
piece of bronze artillery of about twelve quintals, one man who was

---

[8] Royal Catholic Person.

hanged, and many bones of dead people. I burned and destroyed the whole fort. I learned afterward that the man who was hanged was a Spaniard. . . .

There is much need that your Majesty command that one hundred and fifty suits of Mexican armor [*escopiles*] be provided. . . . And if any greater number of men should come, let Your Majesty order that one suit of armor be brought for each of them. . . .

PEDRO MENÉNDEZ MARQUÉS

[St. Augustine, January 3, 1580]
. . . I went to Santa Helena to distribute the pay to the soldiers who live there, and, as the Indians would not come to talk with me, I sent a boat with twelve men to seek information from them. The men spoke to them from the boat, and the Indians answered that they did not desire friendship, and began to shoot arrows at them. The boat returned, and when I heard this, I sent a boat a second time, with twenty men, notifying them to make peace; and they were so rebellious that the soldiers grew angry and wounded five men. When I heard this, I went there with sixty men, and landed; and they waited with great courage, so much so that I marveled, and they wounded fourteen of my men, but no one was killed. I worked a trick on them as well as I knew how, in such wise that many Indians were slain, and they all fled and quit the country.

I returned to the fort, which was fifteen leagues from there, and before they could spread the news to other villages, I went back and attacked a large village called Cocapey, which was very well fortified and in the midst of a swamp. I fell upon it at midnight and did much damage, and I captured a son of the cacique, his wife, a sister and his mother. More than forty Indians were burned to death, and I seized two Frenchmen, and thereupon I returned to the fort. I learned from the Frenchmen that there were twelve other Frenchmen in that village. Among them was the pilot who, on another occasion, about seven years ago, escaped from here.

I sent word to the Indians to give me the Frenchmen and I would give them the women, and they did so although they took their time. I kept the cacique's son as a hostage. They are in such a mood that I have little hope concerning them. I went to the province of Guale and they behaved well, for they delivered to me at once the captain who called himself Nicolao Estroci, and the others they had, except two

boys and one soldier who were far away; and all the caciques came to
see me, and renewed their allegiance to Your Majesty. To all appearances they are friendly, although one cannot much rely on them. . . .
I did not at once work justice upon the Frenchmen; not until now.
I sent a boat to Santa Helena for some of them, and then justice was
worked upon the rest there. I added those who were brought to those
who were here, so that those on whom I worked justice, here and at
Santa Helena, numbered twenty-three altogether. There remain three
boys, one barber and one gunner, who are needed in these provinces
as interpreters. From what has been heard, only two men and one boy
are now left among the Indians. They have agreed to surrender them.
. . . The captain was rich, because he offered me three thousand ducats
as ransom, if I would grant him his life. It did not appear to me expedient for Your Majesty's service that a man like him should get back
to France. He was of the Florentine nation, and of good lineage. . . .[9]

P° MENÉNDEZ MARQUÉS

[Santa Elena, March 25, 1580]

After I had given Your Majesty an account, in the month of January last past, of what news there was, and how I had worked justice
on the French, I came later to this province, as I heard that there remained alive among the Indians a captain and other Frenchmen; and
here I learned from the Indians that there were more Frenchmen, and
so I tried by all the ways possible to me to get them into my power.
The Indians, because of the fear they have, offered to deliver them
to me, and so they went to seek them, and brought me the captain . . .
with three other Frenchmen, young boys. The captain was a young
man of twenty-eight years, but in my opinion very warlike and of very
fine appearance. He was a native of Rouen and was called Captain
Roque. I worked justice upon him, and the three I left for the last. I
have news that there remain three others, whom the Indians say they
will deliver to me within a very brief space. I suspect that there must
be more. I shall do my utmost so that none shall remain.[10]

All the Indians are peaceful, those of this province as well as those

---

[9] Nicolao Strozzi (written Astroco, Astroci, Estroci or Estrozi by the Spaniards) was a cousin of Catherine de Medici.

[10] "This is well," written in the margin of this paragraph, was evidently the
King's comment.

of the others, as far as St. Augustine. I hope in our Lord that satisfactory results will be obtained among them.

This village is being very well built, and because of the method which is being followed any of the houses appear fortified to Indians, for they are all constructed of wood and mud, covered with lime inside and out, and with their flat roofs of lime. And as we have begun to make lime from oyster-shells, we are building the houses in such manner that the Indians have lost their mettle.

There are more than sixty houses here, whereof thirty are of the sort I am telling Your Majesty. As this letter is going on the chance of its overtaking some dispatch boat in Havanna, I do not give Your Majesty a longer account of other things. . . .

P° MENÉNDEZ MARQUÉS

PART IV

The English

1629-1670

Despite the fact that Philip's ambassador warned a company of Englishmen that, if they settled in Florida, Spain would cut off their heads as she had done with Ribaut and his men, Charles I granted to Sir Robert Heath, his attorney-general, all "of a territory in America betwixt 31 & 36 degrees of North Latitude, not inhabited by the subjects of any Christian King, but partly inhabited by barbarous men who have not any knowledge of the Devine Deity." This territory was to be known as "Carolana, or Province of Carolana." The charter was dated October 30, 1629.

Sir Robert Heath did little or nothing toward settling his province and eventually his grant elapsed.

On March 24, 1663, Charles II granted to eight of his "right trusty and right-beloved cousins and counselers" the territory lying between the 31st and 36th parallels of north latitude and extending from the Atlantic Ocean to the South Seas, "described in the parts of America not yet cultivated or planted, and only inhabited by some barbarous people who have no knowledge of Almighty God. . . ." This province was to be called henceforth "the Province of Carolina."

The eight Lords Proprietors were the Earl of Clarendon, the Duke of Albemarle, Lord Craven, Lord Berkeley, Lord Ashley, Sir George Carteret, Sir William Berkeley, and Sir John Colleton.

The prospect on the mainland gained the interest and attention of English settlers in Barbados who were looking for "new areas of expansion."

William Hilton

"ALL THEY THAT WANT A HAPPY SETTLEMENT
OF OUR ENGLISH NATION"

The ship Adventure, *under the command of Captain William Hilton, reached the Carolina coast in August 1663 on a voyage of exploration sponsored by "Several Gentlemen and Merchants of the Island of Barbadoes." The expedition entered St. Helena Sound which, according to Hilton's report, "was but four leagues or thereabouts N.E. from Port Royal, which by the Spaniards is called St. Ellens." On what is now known as Parris Island they found the Spanish Captain Alonso Arguiles and a company of soldiers from St. Augustine. Letters—the English were unable to read the Spanish ones—and gifts were exchanged.*

Captain Hilton rescued a party of shipwrecked Englishmen and then sailed away, while from the shore of St. Ellens an Indian "shot an arrow at us."

Upon his return to Barbados, Captain Hilton wrote a highly favorable account of his discoveries, including "Proposals made by the Commissioners of the Lords Proprietors, to all such persons as shall become the first settlers on the rivers, harbors and creeks there."

Captain Hilton's name survives today in Hilton Head Island which the Spanish called Isla de los Osos, *the "Island of Bears," and the French called* Ile de la Rivière Grande. *From the ship* Adventure *waved the first English flag to enter Port Royal.*

After sixteen days of fair weather and prosperous winds, Wednesday the 26 instant [August 1663], four of the clock in the afternoon, God be thanked, we espied land on the coast of Florida, in the lat. of 32 deg. 30m., being four leagues or thereabouts to the northwards of St. Ellens, having run five hundred and fifty leagues: and to the westward of the Meridian of Barbadoes, three hundred and thirty and one leagues. This evening and night following we lay off and on.

Thursday the 27th instant in the morning, we stood in with the land and coasted the shoar to the southward, ankering at nights, and sending our boat out a mornings, till we came into the lat. of 31 deg., but found no good harbour that way.

On Sunday the 30th instant, we tacked and stood northward; and on

Wednesday the second of September, we came to an anchor in five fathoms at the mouth of a very large opening of three leagues wide, or thereabouts, in the lat. of 32 deg: 30 min: and sent our boat to sound the channel.

On Thursday the third we entered the harbour, and found that it was the River Jordan,[1] and was but four leagues or thereabouts N.E. from Port Royal, which by the Spaniards is called St. Ellens: within land, both rivers meet in one. We spent some time to sound the channels both without and within, and to search the rivers in several branches, and to view the land.

On Saturday the fifth of September, two Indians came on board us, and said they were of St. Ellens; being very bold and familiar; speaking many Spanish words, as *cappitan*, *commarado* and *adeus*. They know the use of guns and are as little startled at the fireing of a piece of ordnance as he that hath been used to them many years. They told us the nearest Spaniards were at St. Augustins, and several of them had been there, which as they said was but ten days journey, and that the Spaniards used to come to them at St. Ellens sometimes in conoas within land; at other times in small vessels by sea, which the Indians describe to have but two masts. They invited us to come to St. Ellens with our ship, which they told us we might do within land.

Monday the 14 September, our long-boat went with twelve hands within land to St. Ellens.

On Wednesday the 16th came five Indians on board us. One of them, pointing to another, said he was the Grandy Captain of Edistow; whereupon we took especial notice of him, and entertained him accordingly, giving him several beads and other trade that pleased him well. He invited us to bring up our ship into a branch on the N.E. side, and told us of one Captain Francisco, and four more English that were in his custody on shoar; whereupon we showed him store of all trade, as beads, hoes, hatchets and bills, etc., and said he should have all those things if he would bring the English on board us; which we promised should be done the next day. Hereupon we wrote a few lines to the said English, fearing it to be a Spanish delusion to entrap us.

In the dark of the same evening came a canoa with nine or ten Indians in her with their bowes and arrowes, and were close on board

---

[1] The harbor was St. Helena Sound, and the "River Jordan" was the Combahee.

before we did discern them. We haled them, but they made us no answer, which increased our jealousie. So we commanded them on board, and disarmed them, detaining two of them prisoners, and sending away the rest to fetch the English; which if they brought, they should have theirs again. At length they delivered us a note written with a coal, which seemed the more to continue our jealousie, because in all this time we had no news of our long boat from St. Ellens, which we feared was surprised by the Indians and Spaniards. But to satisfie us that there were English on shoar, they sent us one man on board about twelve of the clock in the night who related to us the truth of the matter, and told us they were cast away some four or five leagues to the northward[2] of the place we then rode, on the 24th of July past, being thirteen persons that come on shoar, whereof three of them were kill'd by the Indians.

On Thursday the 17th of September the long-boat returned from St. Ellens, which presently we sent on shoar to fetch the other English, the Indians delivering us three more; and coming aboard themselves, we delivered them their two men. Then we demanded of the chief commander where the rest of our English were. He answered, "Five were carried to St. Ellens, three were killed by the Stonohs,[3] and the other man we should have within two days."

We replyed to him again, that we would keep him and two more of his chief men till we had our English that were yet living; and promised them their liberty, with satisfaction for bringing us the English.[4]

Now to return to the business of our design—the entertainment we had at S. Ellens put us in great fear of the Indians treachery; for we observed their continual gathering together, and at last began with stern-look'd countenances to speak roughly to us, and came to search our mens bandileers and pockets, yet inviting us to stay that night with them. But we made a sudden retreat to our boat, which caused the Indian King to be in a great rage, speaking loud and angry to his men, the drift of which discourse we understood not. That which we noted there was a fair house builded in the shape of a dove-house, round, two

---

[2] They were cast away at North Edisto, or between there and Stono River which separates James Island and Johns Island.

[3] The Stono Indians.

[4] Shadoo and Alush went with Hilton to Barbados; the third Indian escaped. The first two returned to their homes and were there to receive Sandford on his arrival in 1666.

hundred foot at least, compleatly covered with palmeta-leaves, the
wal-plate being twelve foot high, or thereabouts, and within lodging
rooms and forms; two pillars at the entrance of a high seat above all
the rest; also another house like a sentinel-house, floored ten foot high
with planks, fastened with spikes and nayls, standing upon substantial
posts, with several other small houses round about. Also we saw many
planks, to the quantity of three thousand foot or thereabouts, with
other timber squared, and a cross before the great house. Likewise we
saw the ruines of an old fort, compassing more than half an acre of
land within the trenches, which we supposed to be Charles Fort,[5] built,
and so called by the French in 1562. . . .

On Monday September 21, one English youth was brought from St.
Ellens aboard us by an Indian, who informed us that there were four
more of their company at St. Ellens, but he could not tell whether the
Indians would let them come to us—for, saith he, our men told me
that they had lately seen a frier and two Spaniards more at St. Ellens,
who told them they would send soldiers suddenly to fetch them away.
This day we sayled up the river with our ship to go through to St.
Ellens.

On Tuesday the 22 instant, three Indians came on board: one of
them we sent with a letter to the English prisoners there.

On Wednesday the 23d, we sent our boat and men to sound the
channel and finde out the most likely way to St. Ellens with our ship
by Combeheh. In the mean time came many canoas about us with
corn, pompions and venison, deer-skins, and a sort of sweet-wood. One
of the men, looking into an Indian basket, found a piece of Spanish
rusk: it being new, we demanded of the Indian where he had it—who
said, of the Spaniards. In the interim, while we were talking, came a
canoa with four Indians from St. Ellens, one standing up and holding a
paper in a cleft stick. They told us they had brought it from the Spanish captain at St. Ellens. We demanded how many Spaniards were
come thither—who said seven, and one Englishman. We received their
letter writ in Spanish, but none of us could read it. We detained two
of the chiefest Indians, one of them being the Kings son of St. Ellens[6]
and that kept one of the English prisoners; the other two we sent
away with a letter to the Spaniard, wherin we gave him to understand

---

[5] This was not Charlesfort but the Spanish fort San Marcos.
[6] Wommony. He also was taken to Barbados where he remained for a time
before returning to his home.

that we understood not his letter; and told the Indians when they brought the English, they should have their men again, with satisfaction for their pains.

On Thursday, 24 instant, we sayling further up the river to go through, at last came to a place of fresh water, and anchored there, sending our boat ashoar with a guard to get water. Towards night came the first Indian that we sent to St. Ellens with a letter to the English, who brought us another letter from the Spaniards, and an answer of ours from the English, writ in the Spaniards letter. The Spaniard sent us a quarter of venison, and a quarter of pork, with a complement, that he was sorry he had no more for us at that time. We returned him thanks, and sent him a jug of brandy, and withal that we were sorry we understood not his letter. This night about twelve of the clock we had a most violent gust of winde, but of no long continuance.

On Friday 25 September we weighed and returned down the river six leagues or thereabouts, because we perceived the Indians had gathered themselves in a body from all parts thereabouts and moved as the ship did; and being informed by an Indian that the Spaniards would be there the next day, we took in fire-wood, and continued there that night, at which time one of our Indian prisoners made his escape by leaping over board in the dark.

On Saturday the 26, we weighed, and stood down to the harbour's mouth, and stayed there till Monday the 28. In all which time came no one to us, though we stayed in expectation of their coming continually; therefore put out to sea, concluding their intentions not to be good. Being out of the River Jordan, we directed our course S.W. four leagues of thereabouts for Port Royal, to sound the chanel without from the poynts of the harbour outwards; for we had sounded the harbour within from the points inward when our boat was at St. Ellens. . . .

Now our understanding of the land of Port Royal, River Jordan, River Grandie or Edistow is as followeth: the lands are laden with large tall oaks, walnut and bayes, except, facing on the sea, it is most pines tall and good. The land generally, except where the pines grow, is a good soyl, covered with black mold, in some places a foot, in some places half a foot, and in other places lesse, with clay underneath mixed with sand; and we think may produce any thing as well as most part of the Indies that we have seen. The Indians plant in the worst land because they cannot cut down the timber in the best, and yet have plenty of corn, pompions, water-mellons, musk-mellons. Although the land be over grown with weeds through their lasinesse, yet they have two or three crops of corn a year, as the Indians themselves inform us. The countrey abounds with grapes, large figs and peaches; the woods with deer, conies, turkeys, quails, curlues, plovers, teile, herons; and as the Indians say, in winter with swans, geese, cranes, duck and mallard and innumerable of other water-fowls whose names we know not, which lie in the rivers, marshes, and on the sands; oysters in abundance, with great store of muscles; a sort of fair crabs, and a round shelfish called horse-feet. The rivers [are] stored plentifully with fish that we saw play and leap.

There are great marshes, but most as far as we saw little worth, except for a root that grows in them the Indians make good bread of.

The land, we suppose, is healthful; for the English that were cast away on that coast in July last were there most part of that time of year that is sickly in Virginia; and notwithstanding hard usage, and lying on the ground naked, yet had their perfect healths all the time. The natives are very healthful; we saw many very aged amongst them. The ayr is clear and sweet, the countrey very pleasant and delightful. And we could wish that all they that want a happy settlement, of our English nation, were well transported thither. . . .

Robert Sandford

"THAT NEVER-ENOUGH-TO-BE-VALUED COUNTRY"

Lieutenant Colonel Robert Sandford, "Secretary and Chiefe Register for the Lords Proprietors of their County of Clarendon"—a small Cape Fear River settlement which was abandoned after two years— sailed from there to explore the Carolina coast in the Port Royal region in the summer of 1666.

His discovery over, Sandford sailed away to Barbados to write his Relation of a Voyage on the Coast of the Province of Carolina.

Young Woodward, the surgeon he had left behind and the first English settler in South Carolina, learned the language of the Indians and gained their favor. "He remained some considerable time amongst the natives of these parts, being treated with the greatest love and courtesye

. . . until the Spanish, having notice of his abode at St. Helena, carried him thence to St. Augustine, where necessarily he must have remained a prisoner if Serle [Captain Robert Searle, the buccaneer] surprising the town had not transported him to the Leeward Islands, where, shipping chyrurgeon of a privateer, . . . [he] unfortunately, the 17th of Aug. 1669, was cast away in a hurricane at Meavis [Nevis]."[7] *He managed to return to Carolina, and because of his service as an interpreter and discoverer, the Lords Proprietors for "his industry and hazard" granted him 2000 acres and commissions as Deputy and Indian Agent of the colony. Among his distinguished descendants were Paul Hamilton Hayne, General John Barnwell of the Revolutionary War, General Stephen Elliott of the Confederate War, Senator Robert Y. Hayne and Robert Barnwell Rhett.*[8]

About midnight the third of July [1666] I came to an anchor within the river[9] in seaven fathum water, the least depth I could finde, a little above the entrance into Brayne Sound[10] or the passage which goes through to Yeamans Harbour. . . .

The next morning I removed opposite to the principall Indian Towne and there anchored before itt, where I had not ridd long ere the cassique himselfe came aboard mee with a canoa full of Indians, presenting mee with skinns and bidding mee welcome after their manner. I went a shoare with him to see their towne which stood in sight of our vessel. Found as to the forme of building in every respect like that of Eddistowe, with a plaine place before the great round house for their bowling recreation, att the end of which stood a faire woodden crosse of the Spaniards ereccon. But I could not observe that the Indians performed any adoracon before itt.

All round the towne for a great space are severall feilds of maiz of a very large growth. The soyle nothing inferior to the best wee had seene att Eddistowe, apparently more loose and light, and the trees in the woods much larger and rangd att a greater distance; all the ground under them burthened exceedingly and amongst it a great variety of

---

[7] Letter from "Council at Ashley River" to the Lords Proprietors, Sept. 11, 1670. *South Carolina Historical and Genealogical Magazine*, VIII (Jan. 1907).

[8] Joseph W. Barnwell, "Dr. Henry Woodward, the first English settler in South Carolina, and some of his descendants." *South Carolina Historical and Genealogical Magazine*, VIII (Jan. 1907).

[9] Broad River above the entrance of Port Royal River.

[10] Brayne Sound was Port Royal River.

choice pasturage. I saw here, besides the great number of peaches
which the more northerly places doe alsoe abound in, some store of
figge trees very large and faire, both fruite and plants and diverse grape
vines which, though growing without culture in the very throng of
weedes and bushes, were yett filled with bunches of grapes to admira-
con. . . . The towne is scited on an island[11] made by a branch which
cometh out of Brayne Sound and falleth into Port Royall about a mile
above where wee landed, a cituacon not extraordinary here. Rather the
whole country is nothing else but severall islands made by the various
intervenings of rivers and creekes, yett are they firme good lands (excepting what is marsh) nor of soe smale a seize but to continne many
of them thowsands of acres habitable wood land, whose very bankes
are washed by river or creeke, which, besides the fertility, adde such a
comodiousnesse for portage as fewe countryes are equally happy in.

After a fewe houres stay to view the land about the towne I returned
to my vessell and there found Ensign Brayne with his shallope come
that morning through Brayne Sound from Yeamans Harbour att the
mouth of which wee had seene him two days before. Hee told mee
that the same morning that I made Harvey Haven, hee came in with
the shoare more to the eastward and sayled along it till towards evening when hee entred Yeamans Harbour, supposing it Port Royall,
and not findeing mee there nor any knowledge of mee, and guessing
that I might be more southerly, hee came through to Port Royall and
acquainted himselfe with Wommony, the cassiques sonne (who had
alsoe beene att Barbados), whome hee easily prevailed with to beare
him company from place to place into severall creekes and branches
betweene this and Yeamans Harbour, soe becomeing both his guide
and proteccon that hee had by this meanes a large leasure and opor-
tunity of viewing all that part of the country which hee did soe loudly
applaud for land and rivers. . . .

The 7th of July I tooke in some fresh water, purposing that night to
leave Port Royall and retorne homeward, haveing, in the discovery
already made, exceeded all our owne and therefor confident to answere
all other expectacons. Besides, each mans proper occasions hastened
him, and the consideration of the charge of the vessell hired att five
and twenty pounds sterling per month made us earnest not to detaine
her a minute of time unnecessarily. . . . But a little before night the

---

[11] The Indian town was on what is now known as Parris Island.

Cassique of Port Royall came aboard and brought with him a propper younge fellowe whome hee made mee understand to bee his sister's sonne. Hee demanded of mee when I would retorne thither, and, shewing mee the moone, asked whether within three times of her compleating her orbe. I told him noe, but in tenn monthes I would. Hee seemed troubled att the length of time and, as it were, begged mee to come in five. But I continued my first given number.

Att length hee gave mee this young fellowe, told mee hee should goe and retorne with mee and that I must clothe him, and then hee asked mee when I would sayle. I told him presently that night, but hee very much importuned mee to stay until the next day that hee might prepare mee some venison, and made signes as wee parted that, if in the morning hee should not see mee, hee should crye, and soe hee left mee and the Indian with mee.

I was somewhat pleased with the adventure, haveing, before I came on the discovery, wished that if I liked the country I might prevaile with the Indians to lett one of their nacon goe with mee, I leaving an Englishman in their roome for the mutual learning their language, and to that purpose one of my company, Mr. Henry Woodward, a chirurgeon, had before I sett out assured mee his resolucon to stay with the Indians if I should thinke convenient; wherefore I resolved to stay till the morning to see if the Indians would remaine constant in this intencon, according to which I purposed to treate further with them on the morrowe. Therefore I went a shoare to their towne, took Woodward and the Indian with me, and in presence of all the inhabitants of the place and of the fellows relacons, asked if they approved of his goeing along with mee. They all with one voyce consented.

After some pause I called the cassique and another old man (his second in authority) and their wives, and in sight and heareing of the whole towne delivered Woodward into their charge, telling them that when I retorned I would require him att their hands. They received him with such high testimonyes of joy and thankfullness as hughely confirmed to mee their great desire of our friendshipp and society. The cassique placed Woodward by him uppon the throne and after lead him forth and shewed him a large field of maiz which hee told him should bee his. Then hee brought him the sister of the Indian that I had with mee, telling him that shee should tend him and dresse his victualls and be careful of him, that soe her brother might be the better used amongst us. I stayed a while being wounderous civilly treated after this manner and, giveing Woodward formall possession of the whole country to hold as tennant att will of the Right Honorable the Lords Proprietors, I retorned aboard and imediately weighed and fell downe.

An Indian that came with mee from Eddistowe with intencon to goe noe further than Port Royall, seing this kindness and mutuall obligation betweene us and the people of this place that his nacon or tribe might bee within the league, voluntarily offerred himselfe to stay with mee alsoe and would not bee denyed. And thinking that soe hee should be the more acceptable, hee caused himselfe to be shoaren on the crowne after the manner of the Port Royal Indians, a fashion which I guesse they have taken from the Spanish fryers, thereby to ingratiate themselves with that nation, and indeed all along I observed a kinde of emulacon amongst the three principall Indians of this country (vizt., those of Kywaha, Eddistowe and Port Royall) concerning us and our friendshipp, each contending to assure it to themselves and jealous of the other though all be allyed. . . .

The 12th of July about noone I entered Charles River and before darke night landed att Charles Towne in the country of Clarendon to the great rejoicing of our ffreinds, who yett received not our persons more gratefully then they did the sound comendacons which they heard from every one of us, without one dissonant note of that never-enough-to-be-valued country which we had seene and searcht, in which may be found ample seats for many thowsands of our nation in a sociable and comfortable vicinity, secured from any possible generall and from all probable particle massacres, with such other accomoacons to boote as scarce any place cann parralell, in a clime perfectly temperate to make the habitacon pleasant, and where such a fertile soyle cannot faile to yeild soe great a variety of produccons as will not onely give an absolute selfe subsistance to the place without all manner of necessary forraigne dependence, but alsoe reach a trade to the Kingdome of England as great as that shee has with all her neighbours, and render our Soveraigne Lord the King, within his owne dominions and the land possessed by his naturall English subjects, universall monarch of the traffique and comodity of the whole world.

ROBT:SANDFORD

For a further confirmacon hereof take this testimoniall given of this country by the principall gentlemen with mee in this discovery, who have attested under their hands as much as I have sayd and yett noe more than what thowsands, had they beene there, would alsoe have affirmed. . . .

Wee whose names are hereunto subscribed, haveing accompanied Lt. Colonell Robert Sandford in a voyage of discovery on the coast and rivers of this province to the southward and westward of Cape St. Romane as farre as the River Port Royall, and being all of us persons well experienced in the nature and quallity of the severall soyles in theise regions, and some of us by means of our travels throughly acquainted with most part of America, Northerne and Southerne Continent and islands, does hereby declare and testefie to the whole world that the country which wee did search and see, from the River Grandy, nowe Harvey Haven, to Port Royall inclusive, doth for richness and fertillity of soyle, for excellency of rivers, havens, creekes and sounds, for aboundance of good timber of diverse sorts and many other requisites both to land and sea, building and for sundry rare accomodacons both for navigation and plantacon, exceed all places that wee knowe in posescon of our nacon in the West Indies. And wee doe assure our selves that a colony of English here planted, with a moderate support in their infant tendencey, would in a very short time improve themselves to a perfect comon wealth, injoying a selfe sufficiency of all the principall necessaryes to life and abounding with a great variety of superfluity for the invitacon of foraigne comerce and trade, and which for its scite and produccons would be of more advantage to our native country, the Kingdome of England, and to the grandeur of Our Soveraigne Lord the King, his crowne and dignity, than any (wee may say all) his other dominions in America. And wee doe further a vouch that this country may bee more securely setted and cheaply defended from any attempts of its native inhabitants than any of those other places which our countrymen have refined from the drosse of Indian barbarisme.

In witness whereof wee have hereunto sett our hands this 14th of July, 1666.

Henry Brayne
Richard Abrahall
Thomas Giles
George Cary
Samuel Harvey
Joseph Woory

Nicholas Carteret

"THE LAND WAS GOOD LAND"

Robert Sandford's enthusiastic report on Port Royal induced the Lords Proprietors to settle a colony there. Joseph West commanded the fleet of three ships, the Carolina, the Port Royal and the Albemarle, which arrived at Barbados in October. There a storm wrecked the Albemarle. Several weeks later they sailed on for Port Royal, stopping briefly at Nevis where they were joined by Dr. Henry Woodward whom we left at Port Royal. The Port Royal was wrecked in the Bahamas. At Bermuda, according to instructions, Colonel William Sayle assumed command as governor of the colonists.

Only the Carolina reached its destination. Those aboard sighted the Carolina coast on March 15, 1670, at Bull's Bay. On March 21 they reached Port Royal, where the "freemen" elected five men "to be of the council," a first election in South Carolina.

Nicholas Carteret, who gives the following account, was one of the passengers that sailed from England with their servants. The colonists did not settle at Port Royal, but sailed to Kiawah on the bank of the river which Sandford had named the Ashley. They called their town Albemarle Point; later the Lords Proprietors changed the name to Charles Towne.

Barmuda, Febry 26th [1670]. Sayling from thence we came up with the lande between Cape Romana and Port Royall, and in 17 days, the weather being faire and the winde not friendly, the longe boate went ashoare the better to informe as to the certainty of the place where we supposed we were. Upon its approach to the land few were the natives who upon the strand made fires and came towards us, whooping in their own tone and manner, making signes also where we should best land, and when we came a shoare they stroaked us on the shoulders with their hands, saying *Bony Conraro Angles*, knowing us to be English by our collours (as wee supposed). We then gave them brass rings and tobacco at which they seemed well pleased, and into the boate after halfe an howre spent with the Indians we betooke our selves. They liked our company soe well that they would have come a board with us.

We found a pretty handsome channell about 3 fathoms and a halfe from the place we landed to the shippe, through which the next day we brought the shipp to anchor, feareing a contrary winde and to gett in for some fresh watter. A day or two after the Governor, whom we tooke in at Barmuda with severall others, went a shoare to view the land here, some 3 leagues distant from the shipp, carrying along with us one of the eldest Indians who accosted us the other day, and as we drew to the shore, a good number of Indians appeared clad with deare skins, haveing with them their bows and arrows, but our Indian calling out "*Appada*," they withdrew and ledged theire bows, and returning ran up to the middle in mire and watter to carry us a shoare, where when we came they gave us the stroaking compliment of the country and brought deare skins, some raw, some drest, to trade with us, for which we gave them knives, beads and tobacco, and glad they were of the market.

By and by came theire women clad in their mosse roabs, bringing their potts to boyle a kinde of thickening which they pound and make food of, and as they order it, being dryed, makes a pretty sort of bread. They brought also plenty of hickery nutts, a wall nut in shape, and taste onely differing in the thickness of the shell and smallness of the kernell. The Governor and severall others, walking a little distance from the water side, came to the hutt pallace of His Majesty of the place, who, meeteing us, tooke the Governor on his shoulders and carryed him into the house in token of his chearful entertainment.

Here we had nutts and root cakes such as their women useily make, as before, and watter to drink, for they use no other lickquor as I can learne in this countrey. While we were here, His Majestyes three daughters entered the pallace, all in new roabs of new mosse which they are never beholding to the taylor to trim up, with plenty of beads of divers collours about their necks. I could not imagine that the savages would so well deport themselves, who coming in according to their age and all to sallute the strangers, stroaking of them.

These Indians, understanding our business to St. Hellena, told us that the Westoes, a rangeing sort of people reputed to be the man eaters, had ruinated that place, killed sev'all of those Indians, destroyed and burnt their habitations, and that they had come as far as Kayawah doeing the like there, the casseke of which place was within one sleep

of us (which is 24 hours, for they reckon after that rate) with most of
his people whome in two days after came aboard of us.

Leaveing that place which is called Sowee, carrying the Casseeka
of Kayawah with us, a very ingenious Indian and a great linguist in
this maine, the winde being very lofty soe that we could not deale with
the shoare, we drove to the southward of Port Royall, where we made a
faire opening and, findeing by observation and otherwayes the contrary,
we stood five minutes to the northward and soe gott the shipp into
Port Royall River . . . against which shoales ley of about five leagues
to sea, W.N.W., Hilton head boare from us when we steared in, and
in stearing in, W.N.W. and N.W. by W., we had 2½ fathoms at low
water with breakers on both sides, but when you are within you have
5, 6, 7, 8 and 9 fathoms water and a cleare river. I cannot say much
of the channell, being but a land man, but this Governor, Captain
Brayne and myself took the longe boate to goe upon discovery and
stood off to sea about 5 or 6 miles close aboard the northwardmost
breakers. We had no lesse than 5 fathoms at low water. The tyde being
spent and the winde proving calme, we were forst to make in for the
shoare with the tyde of flood. . . .

A small kinde of whale, white about the head and joule, is very plenty
in this river. In two howres time I beheld about 10 or 11 of the kinde,
and some pretend and undertake to say to be of the sparma kinde that
were worth the experiment to finde out the truth of it.

We were two dayes at anchor ere we could speake with an Indian.
When we did they confirmed what [we] heard at Sowee. We weighed
from Port Royall River and ran in between St. Hellena and Combohe
where we lay at anchor. All the time we staide neare the place where
the distressed Indians sojourned, who were glad and crying "*Hiddy
doddy Comorado Angles Westoe Skorrye*" (which is as much as to
say, "English very good friends, Westoes are nought"). They hoped by
our arrivall to be protected from the Westoes, often making signes they
would ingage them with their bowes and arrows, and wee should with
our guns. They often brought us veneson and some deare skins which
wee bought of them for beads. Many of us went ashoare at St. Hellena
and brought back word that the land was good land, supplyed with
many peach trees and a competence of timber, a few figg trees and
some cedar here and theire, and that there was a mile and a halfe of
cleare land fitt and ready to plante. Oysters in great plenty, all the
islands being rounded with bankes of the kinde, in shape longer and

scarcely see any one round, yet good fish though not altogether of soe pleasant taste as your wall fleet oysters. Here is also wilde turke which the Indian brought but is not soe pleasant to eate of as the tame, but very fleshy and farr bigger.

The sloupe which wee have with us, bought at Barmuda, was dispatcht to Kayawah to veiwe that land soe much comended by the casseeka, [and] brings back a report that the lande was more fit to plant in than St. Hellena, which begott a question whether to remove from St. Hellena theither, or stay. Some were of opinion it were more prudent forthwith to plant provisions where they were than betake themselves to a second voyage, though small, it would not prove a better change, the enterance into that harbour being as difficult as the other. The Governor adheraing for Kayawah, and most of us, being of a temper to follow though wee knew noe reason for it, imitating the rule of the inconsiderate multitude, cryed out for Kayawah, yet some dissented from it, yet being sure to take a new voyage but difident of a better convenience. Those that inclyned for Port Royall were looked upon straingely. Soe thus wee came to Kayawah....

PART V

The Scotch at Port Royal

1684-1686

"There being severall Scotch going from Glasgow to Carolina," the Lords Proprietors informed Governor Joseph Morton on March 4, 1683/4, "you are to permitt them to settle at Port Royal if they desire it and direct their lands to bee run out to them according to our agreement with Sir John Cochran and Sir George Campbell."

As early as 1682 a group of Scotch Covenanters, weary of persecution in their own country, planned a settlement in Carolina. Henry Erskine, third Lord Cardross, thirty-three-year-old leader of the Covenanters, had suffered imprisonment and had been outlawed, his estate wasted by the King's army, his dwelling and gardens destroyed. He was commissioned Governor of the proposed colony at Port Royal with "authority independent of the Governor at Charles Town."

On July 21, 1684, the ship *Carolina Merchant* sailed from Gourock Bay on the Clyde, carrying one hundred and forty-eight Covenanters. The ship was commanded by Captain James Gibson and flew the white cross of St. Andrew.

Lord Cardross

"IT SHALL BE A PORT TOUN FOR EVER"

On November 2, 1684, Lord Cardross and his colonists arrived at Port Royal Island. Here they built Stuart Town, sometimes spelled Stewart Town, on "a verie convenient place" midway between the present towns of Beaufort and Port Royal. Its name honored Lady Cardross, who was Catherine Stuart, daughter of Sir James Stuart.

Many months after arriving at Port Royal, Lord Cardross and his associate, the Reverend William Dunlop, sent a belated report of affairs at Stuart Town to the Lords Proprietors in London.

Lord Cardross had his own peculiar ideas of spelling, syntax and logic. He had so much to say that it was hard for him to pause and catch his breath.

Stewartstown on Port Royall
March 27 day 1685

To Sir Peter Colleton

Honored Sirs,

If occasion had offered since our arraival at this place, we had befor this givine you the trouble of a lyne which now by this we give. Sir, we safelie arrived at Charlestoun on Ashley River on the 2nd of October last, having beine ten weeks at sea. There wer in our veshell 148 persons, whereof none dide at sea except one after our arrivell, at which tyme we delyvered the Lords Proprietors' letters to Collnell West who, upon Sir Richard Kerle's death, was made Governour. We found the place so extrordinerie sicklie that sickness quickley seased many of our number and took away [a] great many of our number and discoraged others, insomuch that they desarted us when we wer come to this place and sold of[f] ther servants, and besides ther were some upon the place who wold be esteemed grate men there, who not only did what they could to discoradge us to setle here, but also used us uncivilie and dealt with severall of our number to deserte us, which some did; but we love not to complaine, yet we cannot but in justice acknowledge we wer civilie receaved, treated, and encouraged by the Governour Colnell West, Landgrive Mortoun, Mr. Percevall, Mr. Grimball, and some others.

The great report of the Spaniards invading the province wanted not

its own discoragement and not without ground, seeing he had lately
ruined Providence and threatened to do so to Carolina;[1] the loss likewayes of a ship which came from Belfast filled with our countriemen
who desyned to setell with [us, and] the number of those who fixedly
resolved to adhere to us being redused almost to these of our own families and being not bot 51, did so much discouradge others of our
countriemen who desyned to settle with us that arrived in one other
veshell from Scotland, that none of them would setell with us, many
of them going off againe. Others, being persuaded by thos about
Charilstoun who had litle kyndnes to us, did setle therabouts. And
altho' the sicknes had seased both of us, the one by a fever and the
other by an ague, so that one of us was caried abord the veshell that
brought us hither, yet we, being the onlie two persons who had from
the beginning of our treaties with the Lords Proprietors been under-
takers for the plantations who were personally upon the place and
fixedlie resolved to doe our outermost indeavors to performe our part
of the contract and treatis past betwixt the Lords Proprietors and our
Commissioners, as we are verie confident you and the other Lords
Proprietors will be ready to perform your parts, thought we could do
nothing less than make a trayell of setling heire.

We came here the beginning of November. Sicklie as we were, we
most confess the countrie is verie pleasant and desirable and promiseth
weell enough, better by far than any other place in Carolina that we
had occasione to see. We setled ourselves altogether in a verie convenient place for a toun, being about twentie miles from the mouth
of the River Port Royall where its all along navigabell by [vessels of]
200 or 300 tuns, free of swamps and marishes, a high bloffe land ex-
cellently weell watered, of such wholesome air as many of us quickly
recovered, and none have contracted sicknes since we came, tho many
died of the sicknes they contracted at Charelstoun at our first arravell.

We have determined that this place shall be a toun and, ac [cording]
to the Lords Proprietors' condescensions to us, have ordered that it
shall be a port toun for ever and the seat of justice for severall yeirs;
we have so framed the modell of the toun that everie toun lot hath
a garden adjasent to it, and two ackers of toun land lying near the
toun. We have devyded it into two hundreth and twentie lotts; the
toun itselfe, the streets and ackers of toun land, will in all consist of

---

[1] Providence, the capital of the Bahamas, was taken by a force of 250 Spaniards
on January 19, 1684.

six hundreth ackers of land, Inglish measure; there are already fourty one toun lots takin up by ourselves and severall Inglish who have resolved to setle with us and are transporting ther families hither, to whom we give such incoragement so that we demanded not so much as a proporteine of the expenses we have beine at in the affair. Ther are severall families coming to us from Antego and other plantations; one planter cam already in persone from Antego to us to see the place, and is so confident that it will produce not onley indigoe but good sugar that he and five or six other families who had sent him to see the countrie are expected heire in August nixt, and we have oblidged ourselves to give him one thousand five hundredth ackers of land, having a familie of twentie persones. All who take lotts in our toun are oblidged to build houses theron within two yeirs; we have already built severall as fair houses as is in all Charlestoun, and more are in building.

Sir, we have inclosed here some articles which we desyre ye wold in our name present to the rest of the Lords Proprietors; we hope bothe you and they will find what we demand is necessarie, and what we offer is fair on our pairt; and we most say we ['d] rather have made the offer of ensureing the quit-rent to manifest the sinceritie we resolve to daill with the Lords Proprietors than expecting any grait gain therby, it being otherwayes out of the road to us as to our way of living, and we shall wish that uthers in Carolina may be found also ready to buy or pay ther quit-rent as we shall.

Albeit we be heir upon the place, yet our wifes and childrine are not; and we declare that nothing les than what we have demanded will confirme our stay here; bot if the Lords Proprietors will give us incouradgement to fixe our setilment here we will trewlie performe what we promise, and effectuallie lay out ourselves and intrissis in Scotland to make this a noble plantatione; and if the Lords Proprietors will trust us they shall find this place (by God's assistance and without any expense to the Lords Proprietors) shall flourish at ane other rait than Charlestoun, and that we shall be more for the Lords Proprietors' trew intrest than any in Carolina, and shall study that this setelment be filled with persones who will be willing to performe what they ingadge to us.

We find it will be necessarie that . . . the Lords Proprietors send a commissarie for deputations to persons receiding amongst us, and who shall have plantations here, that thereby the Proprietors be represented

as weell as at Charlestoun and Roanock (untill the countrie be so
planted that the constitutions take effect). And if the Lords Proprietors shall be pleased to send the deputations blank to us as to the persones named who are to be deputies—at least so many of them as you
know not what names to insert in them—we shall take care that they
bee persons who may answer the trust put upon them by you and the
recommendations givine them by us.

We have all beine to view this cuntrie but cannot find any oar
within the cuntrie, except that of iron which is frequent here. We
discovered likewayes the mouth of the West River, and went up the
same a good way, and went near to Saint Catharina, which we hear
the Spainards have desarted on the report of our setling here, and we
desyre this summer to vew it and tak possessione of it in His Majesties
name for the behove of the Lords Proprietors; for it hath beine still
formerlie in the Spanish dominions you may advyse with the other
Lords Proprietors whether it will be necessarie for you to obtaine from
His Majestie a patent for it, and if you find it nidfull we hope ye will
not be forgetfull of us, and we will not be unmindfull of the Lords
Proprietors concernes therin with our owne. We thought fit lykewayes
to acquaint you that ther may be pasage opened from this place to
New Mexico, which with all the mines there about the Indians of that
countrie have takin from the Spainard, and that they are desyrous of
trade and comerice with His Majestie's subjects here, which if effec-
tuated wold be a matter of vast importance both to you and us.

We are in order to this plan laying down a method for correspondence and treade with Cuita and Cussita [Cussatoe], nations of Indians,
who leive upon the passages betwixt us and New Mexico, and who have
for severall yeirs left off any comercie with the Spanirds; but, Sir, these
our endeevors do already provock the inevey of severall particular persones, who, meinding their own privat intrist mor than that of the
Lords Proprietors or good of the province, doe so grudge both at the
situation of this place doth give us advantage for trade more than
these and that they find us ready to improve that advantage, that they
doe opres our designe and endevour to render us contemptible in the
eyes of the Indians about us; yet our cariage towards all our nightbour
Indians heath beine sutch as we have a firme peace and comerce with
them; particularlie we have obliged the Jamessie [Yamasee] nation
which is the most considerable of them all, and which wer laitlie under
the Spainzard at St. Augustine and admited to setle heire within our

bounds by the Government of Charlestoun the last year since our contract with you; and we have consented to them that they remaine here during their good behaviour, and the truth is they are so considerable and warlike that we would not doe utherwayes. The wholl nation is not yet come which we cannot weell opposse, nor is it atte your or our intrist; that nation they appear verie effectionit to us are inveterat enemies to the Spainzard, and continues still in ware with the most considerable Spanish Indians.

The trade, Sir, we expect by these discoveries may verie probablie be considerable and advantageous; if you plees to put in with us for a share, it will be verie acceptable and we shall be as careful of your share (since we are here upon the place) as of our own and indevoure to imploy fit persones in it. Sir, we expect ye will procure a speedy answer from the Lords Proprietors to our demands which we desyre they may signey and seall as we have done.

<table>
<tr><td></td><td>Sirs</td></tr>
<tr><td>Direct your letters to</td><td>Your most humble servants</td></tr>
<tr><td>the Lord Cardross or</td><td>CARDROSS</td></tr>
<tr><td>William Dunlope or both</td><td>Willm. Dunlope</td></tr>
<tr><td>of us at Stuartstoun one</td><td></td></tr>
<tr><td>Port Royall River Carolina.</td><td></td></tr>
</table>

Sir William Craven

"STEWARTS TOWN AT PORT ROYAL IS THE FRONTIER OF THE WHOLE SETTLEMENT"

"Wee desire you cause deliver to the bearer those six guns the Lords Proprietors appoynted for us," wrote Lord Cardross on March 25, 1685, to Governor Robert Quary and the Grand Council at Charles Town. *"We have ground to apprehend the invasion of a Forraigner."*

More than six months passed before Sir William Craven, writing from Whitehall in London, directed Governor Joseph Morton of Carolina to deliver the cannon.

The "Forraigner" who threatened Stuart Town was Spain. In the treaty of 1670 Spain and England acknowledged the rights of each other to their settlements, and Spain conceded Charles Town but not

Port Royal. *"I charge and order you,"* wrote Governor Cabrera of St. Augustine, *"to continue the operations . . . until you succeed in dislodging the enemies, Scotch, English and Yamassees, who were settled on the said islands of Santa Elena and Santa Catharine. . . ."*[2]

Whitehall, Novemb. 18th, 1685

Wee being well informed that Alexander Dunlope, Esq., is a man of good understanding, loyalty, prudence and justice, and well qualified to be sherriffe of Port Royall County, doe hereby require that you commissionate him to be sheriffe of that county. And also that you commissionate four such others to be Justices with him, as shall be recommended to you by the Rt Honoble the Lord Cardrosse, the said Alexander Dunlope and Mr. Wm. Dunlope as men fitting for their loyalty, prudence, and intergrity to administer justice in the county court of that county.

And whereas we are told that there are divers pieces of our cannon that lye unmounted and useless at Old Charles Town, and having taken into our consideration that Stewarts Town at Port Royall is the frontier of the whole settlement towards the Spaniard and most lyable to be hurt by them whenever they shall be disposed to disturb us,

We doe therefore order that you deliver five of the aforesaid peeces of cannon to the said Lord Cardross and the said Alexander Dunlope or either of them or their order, they giveing you security for the transporting the said five peeces of cannon to Stewarts Town . . . and there to mount the same for the safety thereof. . . .

William Dunlop and others

"THE SPANIARDS BURNT THE TOWNE DOWNE TO THE GROUND"

On August 17, 1686, a hundred Spaniards, under Thomás de León, and a force of Indians destroyed Stuart Town and ravaged the surrounding islands. On Edisto Island they burned the home of Paul Grimball, Secretary of the Province.

---

[2] Herbert E. Bolton, ed., *Arredondo's Proof of Spain's Title to Georgia.* University of California Press, 1925, p. 345.

Lord Cardross returned to Europe, "*attached himself to the friends of liberty in Holland*" *and went with William of Orange to Scotland in December 1688. The next year Parliament restored to him his rights, privileges and estates. He died in Edinburgh in 1693 at the age of forty-four.*

William Dunlop served the province in many official positions until 1690. Then William III appointed him Principal of the University of Glasgow.

When Lord Cardross went back to Scotland, he took with him the governmental seal of Stuart Town. A hundred years after his death, his great-grandson, David Stuart Erskine, presented it to Major General Thomas Pinckney, United States Minister at the Court of St. James's. Today the seal of Stuart Town reposes in the museum of the Charleston, S.C., Library.

The following report of the destruction of Stuart Town was sent to the Lords Proprietors by William Dunlop and other leaders of the Carolina province.

September, 1686

May it please Your Lordships

Our present afflictions and misfortunes are soe many and great that it would bee as tedious for Your Lordships to heare them as its impossible for us by words to express them. To tell Your Lordships that your whole country, with the lives and estates of all the inhabitants are now, without some speedy and effectuall remedy, exposed to utter loss and irreparable ruin, will not sufficiently demonstrate our deplorable condition. Wee will therefore presume on Your Lordships patience and for your greater satisfaction decend to these following particulars.

On the 17th Augt last about noone came up Port Royall River 3 Spanish perreaugoes or halfe galleys, but they were no sooner discovered than they landed their men a little belowe Stuart's Towne, being guided thither by some Indians and English runagados who exactly knew the place. The few inhabitants of that towne having scarcely given the alarum to their neighbors by fyring great guns, when the Spanish came running thro' the woods, enter'd the plancons [plantations] and approached in two bodyes, ere the small number of people then there could gett together, soe that being unable to oppose soe great a force as the enemie apprared to bee, they betook themselves to woods. The Spaniards immediately possessed themselves of the towne, where they continued 3 days, and haveing plundr'ed the houses, destroyed the plancons, killed a great quantity of hoggs and cattle, they burnt the towne downe to the ground and took away two men and a boy prisoners.

On the 20th Augt following, my Lord Cardross with much difficultie came to the Governor's house[3] and informed him that the Spaniards had invaded Port Royall with three vessells and that they had landed (as his Lordship thought) near 200 men; whereupon the Governor issued out an order to alarum the country and for his Councell to meet him at Chastowne Monday the 23d Augt following: whereupon the Councell being mett accordingly, the Governor orderred the regiment of Berkley County to remaine at Charles Towne (except Capt Godfrey's[4] company which was to bee on James's Island) and the millitia of Colleton County to bee drawne together to the borders of that county. The 24do the Governor, with the advice of the Councell, ordered Major Boon[5] to march with Capt Godfrey's company (which still guarded the ffrontiers on the north side of Stonoh) and joyn'd with those of Colleton County for the defence and security of the same. Major Boon no sooner arrived to Capt. Godfrey but hee received and sent us intelligence that the enemies were 500 men and 2 or 3 great ships without the barr and were come to Mr. Grimballs[6] house on Edeston [Edisto] Island and had destroyed it. Whereupon the Governor with all diligence sent Capt. Daniell the next morneing, being the 25do, with about nynety men taken out of the severall companys of the regiment to reinforce those under Major Boon and to recall him as a person more usefull in gathering our neighbors, the northern Indians, to our assistance. The same day the Governor, takeing all further care for the better management of affairs in this extremity, in the evening received newes that the Spaniards had been att his house, plundered it and taken two white people prisoners. As the night came, exceeding blacke and manaceing clouds began to shew themselves and were the next morning (being the 26do) succeeded by a hurricane wonderfully horrid and distructive. . . .

---

[3] Landgrave Joseph Morton, governor from May 1682 to April 1684 and again from September 1685 to 1686. His house was on Edisto Island.

[4] Captain John Godfrey, later Lieutenant Colonel Godfrey.

[5] Major John Boone, Council member in 1683 and later, had large land holdings. His plantation in Christ Church Parish is still known as Boone Hall.

[6] Paul Grimball, Secretary of the Province. His home was on Edisto Island.

In the meantime Capt Daniell,[7] haveing information that the enemie was att Capt Blacke's,[8] went up to the head of Stonoh River to oppose them, but they were not there according to intelligence. And Capt. Daniell, haveing received much damage in his boates by the hurricane, sent to the Governor for more men and boates. But the Governor, in the interim positively informed by two fugitives from the Spaniards . . . that the enemye was on Edeston Island att Mr. Grimballs, ordered Major Stephen Bull[9] with another party of 100 men, and boates convenient, to goe by water directly to the enemye and to call to his assistance p[ar]ties under the command of Capt. Daniell. About which tyme the Governor received further intelligence that the Spaniards had been att his new plantacon near London[10] and carried away 13 Negroes and two white men prisoners. Major Bull therefore on the 29do hastened away from Charles Towne, but the enemye was departed from Mr. Grimballs ere hee came thither, haveing left severall markes of his malice, especially the half burnt body of one of our people whom hee had taken prisoner. Notwithstanding Major [Bull] instantly pursued them down to Port Royall where hee received intelligence that they were gone a day or two before in great hast, heareing of his persueing them, haveing likewise lost one of their galleys and their comander in chiefe, Senior Alexandro, in the storme. Whereupon the Major gave over the present pursuit and returned.

Whilst these things were transacting, the expedition of the severall parties was much impeded by frequent contrary and false intelligence together with continuall wett and windy weather which day by day succeeded the hurricane, the violent extremity whereof continued not above 4 or 5 houres, yet was attended with such dismall, dreadfull and fatall consequences that the hand of Almighty God seemes to concur with the malice of our enemies to hasten our ruin and desolation.

Your Lordships cannot imagine the distracting horror that these united evills plunged us into. All the ships and vessells in the road and harbours were drivin up on the land, and whether any of them can bee fitted out againe may bee yett a question. The whole countrey seemes to bee one entire map of devastation, the greatest part of our houses

---

[7] Colonel Robert Daniel (1646-1718) came to South Carolina from Barbados in 1679; Landgrave 1691; Governor from April 25, 1716, to April 30, 1717.
[8] Probably Captain Benjamin Blake who had a plantation on the Stono River.
[9] Stephen Bull was Lord Ashley's deputy; settled Ashley Hall plantation.
[10] New London or Willtown on the South Edisto River, settled about 1683.

are blowne downe and still lye in their ruine, many of us not haveing the least cottage to secure us from the rigour of the weather. The long incessant raines have destroyed almost all our goods which lye intombed in the ruines of our houses. Our corne is all beaten downe and by meanes of continued wett weather lyes rotting on the ground. Our fences are laid flatt soe that the little corne that escaped the storme is devoured or destroyed by our hoggs and cattle. Aboundance alsoe of them were killed in the tempest, by the falls of trees which in infinite numbers are blowne and lye in confused heapes all over the countrey, soe that most of our cattle are in great danger of runing wild, there being scarce any probabillity of finding them out or possibillity of driveing them home when they are found.

In some places ffor 3 or 4 miles together there is scarce one great tree standing, all pathes being soe impassable that there is no travelling on horseback and scarce any on ffoot, whereby all society and communication with our neighbours, one of the greatest comforts of our lives, is for many yeares render'd extraordinary difficult with the ffalls of the trees. The ffoods of our hoggs is likewise distroyed, which will cause them all to run wild or, which is as bad, they will all be starved from these and the like calamityes which now attend us. Wee have too great reason to ffeare the neare approach of famin to compleat all our miseryes, which we pray to God in His mercy to direct from us. . . .

Ribaut and His Followers (from a drawing by G. Bourgain)

Map of Port Royal,

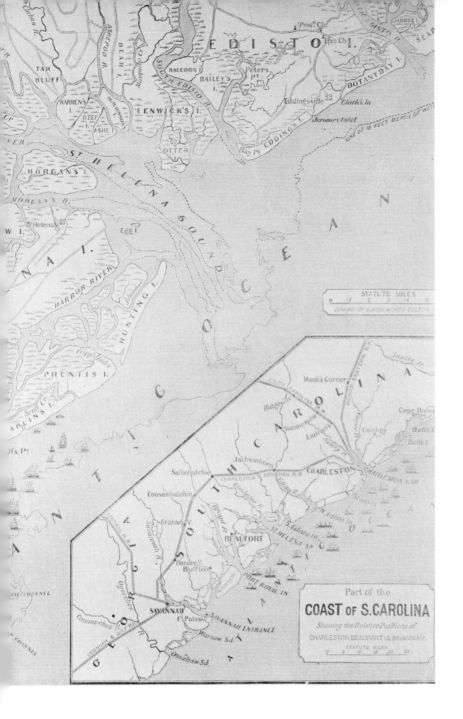

Beaufort and Vicinity

Pedro Menéndez de Avilés (from an old Spanish engraving)

HS

HERE STOOD
CHARLESFORT
BUILT 1562
BY JEAN RIBAUT
FOR ADMIRAL COLIGNY
A REFUGE
FOR HUGUENOTS
AND TO THE
GLORY OF FRANCE

Official Marine Corps Photograph

Monument to Ribaut

Above: Pre-Revolutionary Cemetery

Below: Calibogue Cat

Above: The Beaufort Arsenal, Headquarters of the Beaufort
Volunteer Artillery, organized in 1776

Below: Another View of the Beaufort Arsenal

Above: A Majestic Live Oak Tree, Parris Island, S.C.

Below: View of Sea Pines Beach and Golf Course

PART VI

An English Frontier Colony
1699-1745

"Old Beaufort was a block-house, surrounded with a few scattered dwellings, in the days of the Yamassee wars, and it needed strong arms and stout hearts to win acre after acre of the rich hunting lands which spread round it. Surely and slowly the men stretched out their hands and grasped all that beautiful and bountiful country that lay between the Combahee and the Pocotaligo and along the great water of Broad River. Upon the lands which they took from the savage whom they could not tame, they placed the savage whom they could tame. . . . And . . . they worked together to send cargo after cargo of rice and indigo to the mother country."

William Henry Trescot, September 8, 1866

"THE YAMMOSEES . . . FELL UPON PORT-ROYAL"

*The Lords Proprietors in 1699 began bestowing grants to tracts of
"land commonly called Port Royall." On December 20, 1710, they
agreed that a seaport town—to be called Beaufort Town in compliment
to the Duke of Beaufort—should be built at Port Royal in Granville
County.*

*On Easter Sunday, April 15, 1715, the Yamasee Indians, from their
town of Pocotaligo, suddenly opened war on the colonists at Port Royal.*

*The two accounts of the Yamasee War that follow tell what hap-
pened: the first, anonymous; the second, from the Governor of South
Carolina to the Governor of Massachusetts, published in the Boston
News of June 13, 1715.*

In the year 1715, the Indians adjoining to this colony, all round
from the borders of Fort St. Augustino to Cape Fear, had formed a
conspiracy to extirpate the white people. This war broke out the week
before Easter. The parish of St. Helen's had some apprehensions of a
rising among the adjoining Indians, called the Yammosees.

On Wednesday before Easter, Captain Nairn, agent among the Indians, went, with some others, to them, desiring to know the reason
of their uneasiness, that if any injury had been done them, they might
have satisfaction made them. The Indians pretended to be well content, and not to have any designs against the English. Mr. Nairn therefore and the other traders continued in the Pocotaligat-Town, one of
the chief of the Yammosee nations. At night they went to sleep in the
round-house, with the King and chief War-Captains, in seeming perfect friendship; but next morning, at break of day, they were all killed
with a volley of shot, excepting one man and a boy, who providentially
escaped (the man much wounded) to Port-Royal, and gave notice of
the rising of the Indians to the inhabitants of St. Helen's. Upon this
short warning, a ship happening to be in the river, a great number
of the inhabitants, about 300 souls, made their escape on board her
to Charles-Town . . . having abandoned all their effects to the savages;
some few families fell into their hands, who were barbarously tortured
and murdered.

The Indians had divided themselves into two parties; one fell upon
Port-Royal, the other upon St. Bartholomew's parish; about 100 Christians fell into their hands, the rest fled. . . . The women and children,

with some of the best of their effects, were conveyed to Charles-Town; most of the houses and heavy goods in the parish were burnt or spoiled. The Yammosees gave the first stroke in this war, but were presently joined by the Appellachee Indians. On the north side of the province, the English had, at first, some hopes in the faithfulness of the Calabaws and Creek Indians, but they soon after declared for the Yammosees.

Upon news of this rising, the Governor (the Honourable Charles Craven, Esq.) with all expedition raised the forces in Colleton County, and, with what assistance more could be got presently, put himself at their head, and marched directly to the Indians, and the week after Easter came up with them and attacked them at the head of the River Combahee; and after a sharp engagement put them to flight, and stopped all farther incursions on that side. . . .

The inhabitants of the Parish of St. Helen's in Port-Royal Island, before mentioned, had been all drove from their settlements by the Yammosees; but upon the suppressing of the Indian ravages, the people returned to their plantations. They were encouraged to do so the sooner because Port-Royal Island had a very capacious and safe harbour, and was likely to become a place of great trade, as being a commodious station for shipping, and the country around affording plenty of all provisions. Here are now computed to be above 70 families. . . .

Boston *News*, June 13, 1715

On Tuesday last arrived here His Majesty's ship *Success*, Captain Meade, Commander, about 12 days' passage from South Carolina, by whom His Excellency, our Governor, had a letter from the Honourable Governor Craven, of South Carolina, acquainting him that all their Indians, made up of many various nations, consisting of between 1000 to 1200 men (lately paid obedience to that Government), had shaken off their fidelity, treacherously murdering many of His Majesty's subjects.

Governor Craven, hearing of this rupture, immediately despatched Captain Nairn and Mr. John Cockran, gentlemen well acquainted with the Indians, to know the cause of their discontent, who accordingly, on the 15th of April, met the principal part of them at the

Yamassee Town, about 130 miles from Charlestown, and after several debates, pro and con, the Indians seemed very ready to come to a good agreement and reconciliation, and, having prepared a good supper for our messengers, all went quietly to rest; but early next morning their lodging was beset with a great number of Indians, who barbarously murdered Captain Nairn and Messieurs John Wright and Thomas Ruffly. Mr. Cockran and his wife they kept prisoners, whom they afterwards slew. One Seaman Burroughs, a strong robust man, seeing the Indians' cruel barbarity on the other gentlemen, made his way good through the middle of the enemy, they pursuing and firing many shot at him. One took him through the cheek (which is since cured) and coming to a river, he swam through, and alarmed the plantations; so that by his escape, and a merchantman that lay in Port Royal River [that] fired some great guns on the enemy, several hundreds of English lives were saved.

At the same time that Governor Craven despatched Captain Nairn and Mr. Cockran to make enquiry of the rupture between us and the Indians, he got himself a party of horse, and being accompanied with several gentlemen volunteers, intended for the Yamassee Town, in order to have an impartial account of their complaints and grievances, to redress the same, and to rectify any misunderstanding or disorders that might have happened. And on his journey meeting with certain information of the above murder, and the rebellion of the enemy, he got as many men ready as could be got, to the number of two hundred and forty, designing to march to the enemies' head quarters and engage them.

At the same time the Governour despatched a courier to Colonel Mackay, with orders forthward to raise what forces he could, to go by water and meet him at Yamassee Town. The Governour marched within sixteen miles of said town, and encamped at night in a large savanna or plain, by a wood-side, and was early next morning by break of day saluted with a volley of shot from about five hundred of the enemy that lay ambuscaded in the woods, who, notwithstanding of the surprise, soon put his men in order and engaged them so gallantly three quarters of an hour that he soon routed the enemy; killed and wounded several of them, among whom some of their chief commanders fell, with the loss on our side of several men wounded, and only John Snow, sentinel, killed. The Governour, seeing the great numbers of the enemy, and wanting pilots to guide him over the river, and then having vast woods and swamps to pass through, thought best to return back.

Captain Mackay, in pursuit of his orders, gathered what force he could, and embarked by water, and landing marched to the Indian Yamassee town; and though he was disappointed in meeting the Governour there, yet he surprised and attacked the enemy, and routed them out of their town, where he got vast quantities of provision that they stored up, and what plunder they had taken from the English. Colonel Mackay kept possession of the town; and soon after hearing that the enemy had got into another fort, where were upwards of 200 men, he detached out of his camp about 140 men, to attack it and engaged them. At which time a young strippling named Palmer, with about sixteen men, who had been out upon a scout, came to Colonel Mackay's assistance, who, at once, with his men, scaled their walls and attacked them in their trenches, killed several, but meeting with so warm a reception from the enemy that he was necessitated to make his retreat; yet on a second re-entry with men, he so manfully engaged the enemy as to make them fly their fort. Colonel Mackay, being without, engaged them on their flight, where he slew many of them. He has since had many skirmishes with them.

The Governour has placed garrisons in all convenient places that may be, in order to defend the country from depredations and incursions of the enemy, till better [provision] can be made. We had about a hundred traders among the Indians, whereof we apprehend they have murdered and destroyed about ninety men, and about forty more men we have lost in several skirmishes. . . .

Episcopal Churchmen of St. Helena Parish

"WE BEING A FRONTIER PARISH"

St. Helena's Episcopal Church was established in 1712 and erected, as we see from the following letter, in 1724. Since then it has been twice enlarged.

In answer to the request[1] of the Vestry and Churchwardens of the Parish of St. Helena, "The Society for the Propagation of the Gospel in Foreign Parts" sent the Reverend Lewis Jones from London. He arrived the next year, 1725, and remained until his death in 1746.

To the Reverend Father in God
    Lord Bishop of London
The humble Address of the Vestry and Church
Wardens of the Parish of St. Helena in Granville County (South Carolina).

We, Your Lordships most dutifull and affectionate people of said parish, beg leave to represent to Your Lordship that we have been an erected parish for above ten years, but through the misfortune of an Indian warr have been without the blessing of haveing either church or minister. Now it has pleased God to restore us to the blessing of peace, by the bounty of the General Assembly and subscriptions of His Excellency and several other persons have a handsome brick church, a building which will be finisht in three months. Our humble petition to Your Lordship is that Your Lordship would be pleased to send us a sober and learned person to be our minister. We being a frontier parish and most of our people inclineable to the church, but for want of injoying the blessing of the gospel and publick worship as by law established, they are daily tempted and led away to a dis-senting meeting that has for some years settled among us. A person as above mentioned will prevent that growing mischief and be a means of settling the place which is now a great objection against it. There is allowed fifty acres of good land joyning to the town and a house to be erected for the use of the minister, as also one hundred pounds proclamation money per annum, allowed the minister by act of As-sembly.

We hope Your Lordship will use your interest with the Society for their bounty as usually allowed ministers in these parts. We can't doubt but Your Lordship will think our case is very hard and that all due incouragement ought to be given us as being a frontier people and haveing the best harbour in the province and a place well situated

---

[1] The original letter is in Lambeth Palace Library, London. Copy through the courtesy of Miss Ellen Perry, Greenville, South Carolina, in St. Helena's Epis-copal Church of Beaufort.

for trade, and are daily in hopes of it being made a port of entry, which will be a great incouragement to severall persons who are desirous of settling here and a great strengthening to the whole province.

We hope Your Lordship will take us under your serious consideration and beg leave to subscribe our selves—

Your Lordship's most obedient and most humble servants,

JOHN WOODWARD }
JOHN DE LE BEZEL } Church Wardens

JOHN HORTON   ROWLAND EVARES
AQUA [illegible]   WILLIAM HAZZARD
                                     JAMES HATCHER
                                     THOMAS STONE
                                                      Vestrymen

Beaufort, July 22, 1724

South Carolina Gazette

THE SWISS SETTLE PURRYSBURG

John Pierre Purry, of Neufchatel, Switzerland, was granted a charter by the British Crown and the Carolina Assembly to establish a colony of Swiss settlers in Granville County. The site which he selected in the "Carolina paradise" was twenty-two miles from the mouth of the Savannah River. The first colonists arrived in 1732; and by 1735 more than seven hundred were settled in the town which they called Purrysburg.

During the American Revolution, Purrysburg was headquarters of the American army under General Benjamin Lincoln in 1779, and later of General William Moultrie. The British General Prevost fortified it as a base and left some of his cannon there.

Today Purrysburg is only a name on a granite cross which bears the inscription: "The Site of Purrysburg—the Settlement of Swiss and Huguenots established here in 1732."

The South Carolina Gazette reported the arrival of the Swiss settlers.

October 28 to November 4, 1732

On Wednesday last, a ship arrived here in about 12 weeks from London, having about sixty Switzers on board, the Master of whom reports that we may expect Col. Purry with more every day.

Wednesday, December 20, 1732

On Wednesday last Col. John Peter Purry set out in three pettiaugus, with eighty-seven Switzers, in order to settle a colony on Savannah River in Granville County and was saluted with seven guns from the bastion at their passing by. His Excellency our Governor has been pleased to appoint Mr. Joseph Edward Flowers to be captain; and Mr. John Savy to be lieutenant under the said Col. Purry.

November 9 to November 16, 1734

Col. Purry is lately arrived from England at Purysburg in the ship *Simmon*, Capt. Cornish, with 260 Switzers, Protestants, and their minister Mr. Chiefelle; one hundred and odd more are expected there every day, who were ready to embark at the beginning of October last, among those are 40 persons of the persecuted Protestants in Piedmont and a collect has been made for them in England. Where we hear that James Oglethorpe Esqr has subscribed 40 £ Sterling, the Duc de Montague and several other persons of distinction have likewise handsomely subscribed. 'Tis hoped the province will be kind enough to afford them the necessary provisions, tools, cattle, etc., in order to help foreward an infant colony which is now almost two years old.

November 16 to 23, 1734

We hear that on Saturday last the petition of Coll. Purry was read and examined by the Hon. the Commons House of Assembly wherein he demanded (1) that the 200 £ Sterling, due to him for having carried over to South Carolina even a greater number of people than he had engaged for, might be paid to him, 100 £ Sterling now and the other 100 in the month of March next. (2) That the necessary provisions be given to the 260 persons he brought over with him last, the same as it was given to them that came over before. (3) And lastly

that the debts made at Georgia by the passengers that landed there
fore Purrysburg, for victuals and other necessaries, likewise for periaw-
gus to carry them to the said place might be paid. Both the Hon.
Houses, finding his demands very reasonable, readily granted them.

To the petition of the minister at Purrysburg, Mr. Cheffelle, it was
answered that the pension of a minister could not yet be allowed to
him till the town of Purrysburg should be erected into a parish; in
the meantime one hundred pounds should be paid to him for defray-
ing the charges of his voyage, and further care be taken to satisfy him.

April 19 to 26, 1735

By a letter from Purrysburg of April 10 we are informed that of the
200 Protestant Swiss who were to embark in London for that place,
110 having been put a shore in Georgia by Capt. Thompson were arrived there, that the King has given them out of his own money 1200 £
Sterling to pay their passages on condition that they should settle in
Purrysburg and no where else; that upon this fund notes were made
amounting to the said sum, payable in five years with interest according to the usage of Carolina to reckon from the day of their arrival,
the money accruing by the reimbursement of these notes to be employed for the use of that town to fortifie it, and to render it more
commodious to its inhabitants.

April 26 to May 3, 1735

On Monday arrived here the Scooner *Dolphin*, James Lusk, in 7
weeks from London with about 30 Swiss for Purrysburg.

John Wesley

VISITS TO PORT ROYAL

*John and Charles Wesley, the founders of Methodism, came to
Georgia in 1735 and served as rectors of Christ Church at Frederica
on Saint Simons Island. Charles served also as secretary to General
Oglethorpe and as Secretary for Indian Affairs.*

Charles resigned in the summer of 1736 and John accompanied him as far as Charleston where the brothers made arrangements for the publication of their Collection of Psalms and Hymns.

John remained in Georgia until December 1737. His Journal describes, in the following entries, his experiences in the Port Royal region on two occasions: in July 1736, in company with Charles; and in December 1737, as he journeyed toward Charleston to take his leave of America—"though if it please God, not forever." On this last trip through Port Royal, Wesley was the guest of the Reverend Lewis Jones, rector of St. Helena's Church in Beaufort.

Mon. 26 [July, 1736]. My brother and I set out for Charlestown, in order to his embarking for England; but the wind being contrary, we did not reach Port-Royal, forty miles from Savannah, till Wednesday evening. The next morning we left it. But the wind was so high in the afternoon, as we were crossing the neck of St. Helena's Sound, that our oldest sailor cried out, "Now every one must take care for himself." I told him, "God would take care for us all." Almost as soon as the words were spoken, the mast fell. I kept on the edge of the boat, to be clear of her when she sunk (which we expected every moment), though with little prospect of swimming ashore, against such a wind and sea. But "how is it that thou hadst no faith?" The moment the mast fell, two men caught it, and pulled it into the boat; the other three rowed with all their might, and "God gave command to the wind and seas"; so that in an hour we were safe on land.

Mon. Aug. 2. I set out for the Lieutenant-Governor's seat, about thirty miles from Charlestown to deliver Mr. Oglethorpe's letters. It stands very pleasantly, on a little hill, with a vale on either side, in one of which is a thick wood; the other is planted with rice and Indian corn. I designed to have gone back by Mr. Skeen's, who has about fifty Christian Negroes. But my horse tiring, I was obliged to return the straight way to Charlestown.

I had sent the boat we came in back to Savannah, expecting a passage thither myself in Colonel Bull's. His not going so soon, I went to Ashley-Ferry on Thursday, intending to walk to Port-Royal. But Mr. Belinger not only provided me a horse, but rode with me himself ten miles, and sent his son with me to Cumbee-Ferry, twenty miles farther; whence, having hired horses and a guide, I came to Beaufort (or Port Royal) the next evening. We took boat in the morning; but, the wind being contrary, and very high, did not reach Savannah till Sunday, in the afternoon. . . .

Sat. 3 [December 1737]. We came to Purrysburg early in the morning, and endeavoured to procure a guide to Port-Royal. But none being to be had, we set out without one, an hour before sunrise. After walking two or three hours, we met with an old man, who led us into a small path, near which was a line of blazed trees (that is, marked by cutting off part of the bark), by following which, he said, we might easily come to Port-Royal in five or six hours.

We were four in all; one of whom intended to go to England with me; the other two to settle in Carolina. About eleven we came into a large swamp, where we wandered about till near two. We then found another blaze, and pursued it, till it divided into two: one of these we followed through an almost impassable thicket, a mile beyond which it ended. We made through the thicket again, and traced the other blaze till that ended too. It now grew toward sunset; so we sat down, faint and weary, having had no food all day, except a ginger-bread cake, which I had taken in my pocket. A third of this we had divided among us at noon; another third we took now; the rest we reserved for the morning; but we had met with no water all the day. Thrusting a stick into the ground, and finding the end of it moist, two of our company fell a digging with their hands, and, at about three feet depth, found water. We thanked God, drank, and were refreshed. The night was sharp: however, there was no complaining among us; but after having commended ourselves to God, we lay down close together, and (I at least) slept till near six in the morning.

Sun. 4. God renewing our strength, we arose neither faint nor weary, and resolved to make one trial more, to find our path to Port-Royal. We steered due east; but finding neither path nor blaze, and the woods growing thicker and thicker, we judged it would be our best course to return, if we could, by the way we came. The day before, in the thickest part of the woods, I had broke many young trees, I knew not why, as we walked along: these we found a great help in several places, where no path was to be seen; and between one and two, God brought us safe to Benjamin Arieu's house, the old man we left the day before.

In the evening I read French prayers to a numerous family, a mile from Arieu's; one of whom undertook to guide us to Port-Royal. In the morning we set out. About sunset, we asked our guide if he knew where he was; who frankly answered, "No." However, we pushed on till, about seven, we came to a plantation; and the next evening, after many difficulties and delays, we landed on Port-Royal island.

Wed. 7. We walked to Beaufort, where Mr. Jones,[2] the minister of Beaufort with whom I lodged during my short stay here, gave me a lively idea of the old English hospitality. On Thursday Mr. Delamotte[3] came; with whom, on Friday the 9th, I took boat for Charles-Town. After a slow passage by reason of contrary winds, and some conflict (over provisions falling short) with hunger as well as cold, we came thither early in the morning, on Tuesday the 13th.

Thurs. 22. I took my leave of America (though if it please God, not for ever), going on board the *Samuel*, Captain Percy, with a young gentleman who had been a few months in Carolina, one of my parishioners of Savannah, and a Frenchman, late of Purrysburg, who was escaped thence with the skin of his teeth.

Journal of the Commons House of Assembly

FORT FREDERICK

Port Royal, the Lords Proprietors' "Southern Frontier," was defended by Fort Frederick, built between the years 1731 and 1734. The following items from the Journal of the Commons House of Assembly are concerned with affairs there.

In 1758 it was noted in the Journal that "Fort Frederick is gone in decay and a new fort has been lately constructed near Beaufort which is known by the name of Fort Lyttelton."

A visitor to Beaufort in 1763 wrote: "The harbour is defended by a small fort, lately built of tabby, a cement composed of oister shells

---

[2] Lewis Jones, rector of St. Helena Church in Beaufort.
[3] Charles Delamotte, son of a sugar merchant in London.

beat small, with a mixture of lime and water, and is very durable. . . .
The barracks are very good, and will lodge one hundred men, with
their officers."

Thursday the 3d of March, 1736/37

. . . On motion ordered, that the Commissary do provide three hogs-
heads of rum and a barrel of sugar for the use of the men in garrison
at Fort Frederick, Port Royal, and a suite of colours. . . .

Friday the 4th day of March, 1737

On motion, ordered that a magazine for powder be built of brick
within Fort Frederick.

Thursday the 6th day of December, 1739

. . . Mr. Cramahé, the Master in Chancery, brought down a message
from the Honourable the Lieutenant Governour together with an account of what powder had been expended at Fort Frederick on Port
Royal and also a message from the Honourable the Upper House of
Assembly. The message from His Honour the Lieutenant Governour
is in the following words (that is to say):

I have received a letter from General Oglethorpe who writes to the
following effect, that Capt. Norbury having acquainted him that there
is great want of powder in the garrison at Port Royal, and this being
a dangerous time, he desires that I would order them to be supplied.
And that Capt. Norbury acquaints him further that the flag is worn
out, that the barracks want repair, and that they have great occasion
for a boat. The General recommends this matter to me and hopes
the Province of Carolina will take such measures as His Majesty's
troops may have what is necessary for the service.

Before I received this letter I had taken care to send a supply of 300
pounds weight of gun powder to Fort Frederick; and desired Col.
Prioleau, who went up with it, to acquaint Capt. Norbury that powder
was scarce with us, and that therefore it should not be used but in
the defence of the province. Notwithstanding that caution, the powder had been all expended in little more than a month's time, without
firing one alarm, or one gun for the defence of this province; as appears by an account sent me signed Edward Davis, who calls himself

Gunner, a copy of which I herewith send you, and recommend these affairs to your consideration. . . .

The 8th day of December, 1739

By Order of the House
Charles Pinckney Speaker

Andrew Rutledge, Esq., from the Committee appointed to take under consideration the message from His Honour the Lieutenant Governour of the 4th Day of this instant relating to General Oglethorpe's application for powder, etc., being supplied to Captain Norbury's company garrisoned at Fort Frederick on Port Royal Island made a report. . . .

1. That upon examining the account of Edward Davis, who calls himself Gunner at Fort Frederick, it appears to your Committee that the firing of morning and evening guns at the said fort would occasion an expence of powder almost equal to the whole quantity of powder arising from the powder duty accruing to the public of this province, which your Committee think an unnecessary and unreasonable expence; and that no allowance should be made for the firing of morning and evening guns.

2. But your Committee recommend that the quantity of 100 pounds weight of powder should be supplied at the said fort, for firing salutes on His Majesty's birth and coronation days.

3. And that a further quantity of 300 pounds weight of powder, with 15 fathom of match, and 60 sheets of cartridge paper, should be put under the care of some person in the said fort.

4. Your Committee also recommend that a flag of 30 pounds value be provided for the use of the said fort.

5. And also a boat of 100 pounds value. . . .

A survey of Fort Frederick was made at the request of William Bull, Lieutenant Governor, by Colonel Nathaniel Barnwell, Richard Woodward, Ephraim Mickell, Thomas Wigg and Richard Wigg. The report was read in the Commons House of Assembly in Charleston.

Friday the 8th day of February, 1739/40

May it please Your Honour
We did in company with Col. Barnwell go down to view Fort

Frederick; and shall give Your Honour a faithful account of the state of the same.

That garrison at this time is in a most miserable and forlorn condition, being entirely out of order.

The new work (which is esteemed the best battery and of the most defence) is almost gone to river, and all down on the land side. The repair of which is certainly necessary as the chiefest part of the cannon are mounted therein.

The fort in general is so very low all round that there is no cover or shelter for the men in time of action, who would be too much exposed to the fire of an enemy if it should be ever attacked; and must be raised if intended for service at least 3 feet on the land side, and four feet fronting the river; and ought to be done after the same manner as Broughton's Battery is, with plank framed in, and filled up with mud or dirt, which would be the cheapest and best way, and will make it a good place of defense against any assault.

The barracks would be more durable were they rough plaistered, and are daily decaying for want of it, the weather boards being leaky and very uncomfortable in driving rains, and inconvenient for the sick and ailing soldiers.

The magazine also is very leaky, and so very close it is not fit (on any account) to put ammunition in. It gives very much (having no air holes) that powder will dammage in a very short time, as has been found by experience. They are obliged to keep it at present in the upper part of one of the barracks, which is dangerous on account of fire, and other accidents.

The officers of the garrison there complain (very justly) for want of a convenient place to keep the King's stores in, which might be built out of the fort, and would be of great use and service to the same.

We understand there is an £100 appropriated for purchasing a boat for the use of the garrison. It is true such a sum will purchase one fit for the private use of the fort, but considering we are on the frontier (and especially now in a state of war) Your Honour will certainly be of opinion that it is proper they should have a good substantial one, fit on all occasions to send a party of men in. And had there been such a boat at that fort when the Negroes (who belonged to Capt. Davis and other persons) run away, we should undoubtedly have taken them; having had notice a few hours after their departure; and the officers were ready and willing to have assisted in the pursuit of those fugitives; but had not nor could not get a boat fit for the purpose in due time.

There is not at this time ½ a pound of musket shot in the garrison; scarcely sufficient to mount the guard with.

As to the expence that will attend the necessary repairs of this fort, so as to put it in order of defence, it is impossible for us to judge of it. But in case the government shall think proper to put it in a condition of security, we believe the best way will be to hire Negroes at so much a day, who will both saw the stuff and do the other work, and some careful man who will act with justice, both for the service of his country and his own preservation; especially such an one living this way, who being nearly concerned to have a good place of defence in time of need, will perhaps apply himself more closely to the dispatch of the same; which will both hasten the work and lessen the charge of the expence.

However, this we submit to Your Honour's judgment, and take leave to subscribe ourselves,

Your Honour's most obedient and most humble Servants,

NATHANIEL BARNWELL
RICHARD WOODWARD
EPHRAIM MICKELL
THOMAS WIGG
RICHARD WIGG

Tuesday the 3rd day of July, 1744

. . . The Upper House of Assembly have read a petition of several of the inhabitants of Granville County,[4] in behalf of themselves and others, and recommend the same to the consideration of this House.

And the said petition was read to the House, setting forth that, as Granville County is the southern frontier, it was thereby the most exposed to the attempts of our enemies, either by sea or land. That, as a war is declared with France, the Petitioners apprehend their dangers are greatly encreased; and therefore beg leave to represent the defenceless condition of that part of the province, for want of proper forts, garrisons, rangers and such other assistance as might enable them

---

[4] Granville County became Beaufort District under the Court Act of 1769. This district included four parishes, St. Luke's, St. Peter's, Prince William's and St. Helena's.

to repel the attempts which may be daily expected will be made. That there was a party of Indians (about 15 in number) who had made their camp between Salkatchee and Pocatalaga Rivers, and had been very impertinent and troublesome to several of the inhabitants. And therefore humbly praying that His Excellency and Their Honours would be pleased to take the premisses into consideration, and to grant such relief therein, as they, in their great wisdom, should think proper. . . .

Post Meridiem

. . . Mr. Stephen Bull reported, from the Committee to whom the petition of several of the inhabitants of Granville County in behalf of themselves and others was referred, that the Committee had examined the matter of the said petition. . . .

That they have, in pursuance of the order of the House, taken under consideration the petition of the inhabitants of Granville County, and in order to obtain the best information concerning the allegation therein set forth, they waited upon His Honour the Lieutenant Governour (who lately came from those parts) who acquainted your Committee with several instances of the disorderly behavior of the Indians mentioned in the petition, which occasions great uneasiness to the inhabitants of those parts.

The Committee therefore are of opinion, in order to restrain the insolence and disorders which, by impunity, these Indians may be guilty of, and to prevent or intercept the escape of runaway Negroes, as well as to quiet the minds of the inhabitants of Granville County, many of whom 'tis feared would otherwise leave their settlements, that a troop of Rangers, consisting of 25 men, officers included, be established to scout and range between Savanna and Salkatchee Rivers.

As this House, out of its great care and concern for the protection of those frontier parts, hath already resolved that one fort should be built at Beaufort to receive and shelter the inhabitants of Port Royal Island upon any sudden invasion, and that a fort should be built at Cochran's Point to secure the passage over the ferry from Port Royal Island over to the main, and one other fort on the main at Bryan's Ferry, sufficient to contain a considerable body of men, women and children.

The Committee proceeded to take into consideration the state and condition of Fort Frederick, and, as the same is in a ruinous and defenceless state, and in a very improper situation, as it is commanded on a rising ground on the back of it, your Committee therefore apprehend it unnecessary to repair the same, and are of opinion it should be built on the rising ground before mentioned; but, as the expence of such a fort as might be tenable against an invasion of His Majesty's enemies would be greater than the circumstances of the province would well bear, your Committee are therefore further of opinion that an humble representation thereof be made to His Majesty, and his royal assistance prayed for, to fortify an harbor which is most commodious for the reception of His Majesty's ships from Virginia to Cape Florida, and is so much desired by the Spaniards as to have occasioned their forming formidable armaments to take the same. . . .

PART VII

War for Independence

1775-1783

The sea islands suffered invasion, occupation and ravages of war during the Revolutionary War. Battles or skirmishes occurred on Port Royal Island February 12, 1779; at Coosawhatchie May 3, 1779; at Fort Balfour, Pocotaligo, April 18, 1781; at Savannah River February 24, 1782; and at Beaufort on March 17, 1782.

"In Beaufort," wrote Dr. John Archibald Johnson, "the dwelling . . . at the corner of Carteret and Port Republic was used as the headquarters of the British officer Prevost, during the occupancy . . . by the Royalists. It is due to the memory of this officer to state that he kept his men, quartered here, under the strictest discipline, having promptly 'put in irons' a party of them who were reported to him for attempted theft of silver plate from Mrs. R. Johnson. I have heard this incident from the lips of that venerable lady. . . .

"The only remaining memorials of that war within our present view are the two redoubts in our northwestern suburbs, thrown up to command the approaches of the town by the public highway, now known as the shell road; and the building at the corner of New and Port Republic streets, through which a cannon shot passed, just over the head of its occupant, Mrs. R. Johnson, killing a horse near the site of the present Baptist Church. It was discharged from a British gunboat lying in the stream. . . ."[1]

---

[1] Dr. John Archibald Johnson, *Beaufort and the Sea Islands;* typed copy in Beaufort Township Library from articles which appeared originally in *The Beaufort Republican*, January 16-July 3, 1873.

When the South Carolina Convention that ratified the Constitution of the United States met in Charleston, May 23, 1788, the following delegates represented St. Helena Parish: John Barnwell, John Joyner, William K. Wigg, Robert Barnwell, William Elliott and James Stewart.

Edward Blake

"PROCEED WITH THE SLOOP BEAUFORT"

South Carolina's little navy was used to good advantage in the protection of inland navigation. Her vessels on the high seas succeeded in capturing several prizes while others sailed to the Dutch and French West Indies Islands with cargoes of goods.

Captain John Mercier of the sloop Beaufort *received many assignments—one of particular importance. He was ordered to pick up a cargo of "good new rice at Beaufort" and proceed to "one of the French Islands" and there dispose of it "at the highest price you can obtain."*

Instructions to Captain John Mercier of the Navy of South Carolina
Capt. John Mercier
    Sir.

    The Commissioners of the Navy desire that you will with all possible dispatch have the Sloop *Beaufort* got ready to proceed to sea. They are hopefull you will have her ballasted and ready by tomorrow night.

EDWARD BLAKE
first Commiss^r

Sunday 23d Febry. 1777

Navy Board [Charleston]
28th February 1777

Capt. John Mercier
    Sir.

    The Commissioners of the Navy direct that you do proceed with all possible dispatch to Beaufort, Broad River, or Savannah River, whichever the commanding officer of the troops (now going to Georgia) may direct, and you are, during the time you have the troops or stores on board, to follow the directions of the Commanding Officer in respect to landing of them, and by all means endeavor to cultivate harmony between the troops and your own people. Should you be obliged to go of the outside keep as close along the shore as you can with safety, and you are particularly recommended to keep company with the other vessels, and give them every assistance in your power

during the passage and by no means to remain at sea all night with
the troops on board, if you can possibly get into any one of the inlets.
As soon as the troops and stores are landed, you are to proceed to
Beaufort, and there employ Mr. Black to make such alterations as is
necessary to compleat her for the purpose she is intended. As soon as
that is done and the vessel cleared you are to proceed with the sloop
to Charles Town, with all possible dispatch. You are to advise the
Commissioners by every opertunity of every transaction relating to the
vessel worth communicating to them.

EDWARD BLAKE
first Commiss^r

23d July 1777

Captⁿ. John Mercier
   Sir.

    With the sloop *Beaufort* under your command, you are to pro-
ceed with all possible dispatch to Beaufort, and there deliver to
Captⁿ. James Dohartie of the Beaufort Galley, all the cordage, sails,
and other stores, you have on board for the use of the said galley.
You'll also please to have the sloop *Beaufort* immediately fitted with
all necessary bolts, blocks, and other stores to compleat her for an
armed vessell, to mount six carriage guns and ten swevels. As soon as
the sloop is compleat you'll please return with her to Charles Town
with all possible dispatch, but by no means venture out to sea either
going or coming unless you are well advised that the coast is clear of
men of war and cruizers.

    I am, Sir, Your Most Hbl^e Servt

EDWARD BLAKE
first Commiss^r

[July 31, 1777]

Captⁿ. John Mercier.
   Sir.

    The Commissioners of the Navy having received directions from
his Excellency the President[2] to send the sloop *Beaufort* with a load

---

    [2] John Rutledge was chosen president of a South Carolina government in
March 1776. In January 1776 a provincial congress had met at Charles Town, a
secret committee had been appointed, paper currency issued for military defense
and officers elected.

of rice to one of the French islands, they desire to know if it will be agreeable to you to go in her as captain and transact the business, for which the usual commission will be allowed. If you accept of the offer, you'll please purchase a load of good new rice at Beaufort, and draw on the Commissioners of the Navy for amount . . . and as your vessel is loaded and fit for sea, you are to proceed with all possible dispatch to Cape Francois, or some harbour in Hispaniola, there dispose of the cargo of rice at the highest price you can obtain, and purchase as much rum as you can conveniently store. If any money remains after paying for the rum and the necessary charges of the vessell, you are to invest it in good osnaburgs or sail duck, and proceed with all possible dispatch to Charles Town, or the first convenient inlet in the State of South Carolina. If any provissions or other stores are wanted that cannot be got in Beaufort, advise the Commissioners as early as possible that they may be sent from Charles Town, or if it should not suit you to proceed on this voyage, pray make all possible haste in getting the sloop fitted and loaded for the sea, and proceed with her to Charles Town.

I am, Sir, Your Most Hble Servt.

EDWARD BLAKE
first Commissr Navy Board

Thomas Pinckney

"MY DEAR HARRIOTT"

Thomas Pinckney, son of Chief Justice Charles and Eliza Lucas Pinckney, was twenty-five years old when he camped with General Benjamin's army at Purrysburg in the early months of 1779. His only brother was Charles Cotesworth Pinckney. Thomas was educated in England and had lived there from the age of three until he was twenty-four, when he returned to Charles Town to practice law. The next year he joined the First South Carolina Regiment and was ordered to help recruit soldiers for the Continental cause. He received the rank of Captain.

The following letters,[3] written from camp at Purrysburg, are to his

[3] The original letters are in the Pinckney collection in the Library of Congress.

sister Harriott, wife of Daniel Huger Horry, of Hampton Plantation on the Santee.

Thomas married Elizabeth Motte of Fairfield on South Santee, July 22, 1779. In later years he served as minister to both England and Spain; in the War of 1812 he received the rank of Major General. He served his state as Governor, 1787-1789.

Camp at Purysburg
Mond:Night Janry 18th, 1779

I have wrote so frequently to all my friends and among the rest to my dearest Harriott without rec[eivin]g any answer that as this is a place barren of events, my materials are all exhausted, but as Colo. Tennant, the Inspector Genl who takes the trouble of this, purposes riding very fast and staying but six hours in Charles Town, the hope of so speedy a return makes me again trouble you with a letter containing nothing. . . .

We fare very well here with respect to the ammunition de bouche, being in the neighborhood of many of our friends plantations who are very bountiful to us. Captn Cattell has again joined us here. J. Kinloch is also with us, both of them are in Genl Moultries' family. Major Butler and Mr. Pendleton are now on a visit to us, we have also been favor'd with the company of the two T. Middletons, Mr. Wright, Mr. N. Hall, Genl Bell and his brother William and several other gentlemen of fortune in this part of the country. By these means and the more favorable season, this campaign is render'd infinitely more agreeable in itself than the last, but peculiarly situated as I am, and at all times of a most domestic disposition, which I believe you can testify, you may imagine that the hours do not "dance or down away." The constant correspondence of my dear sister and my friends in Charles Town would make them pass more lightly; of this I suppose I have hitherto been deprived by your being at Santee, but if you had thought of getting Mr. J. L. Dart to forward your letters, I might have still enjoyed that satisfaction tho' you were absent from town. Pray tell Mr. Daniel Horry Junr that I shall at all times be proud of his correspondence; give your little Harriott a kiss for me, and write me all her improvements and alterations. Present my duty to my mother and love to the family and believe me to be my dear girl's

Sincerely Affectionate Brother,
THOMAS PINCKNEY

Camp at Purysburg, Janry 28th, 1779

Your favor of the 14th, my dear Harriott, has remained unanswered hitherto pursuant of some intelligence which I was hopeful might have been conveyed to you, but the same scarcity of events has continued ever since I recd it. Captn Cattell, however, setting off for town tomorrow, I was unwilling to let so good an opportunity pass without informing you of our being all well at this post. I can not say I understand your manouvres at Santee, I fancy you must have been out general'd this time or you would undoubtedly be now attending your duty in the Senate, but you may possibly chuse to make a winters campaign *as we do*; and determine not to go into winter quarters at all. For my part I must own I had rather be campaigning on the banks of Santee than on those of Savannah; which service might be most dangerous, you perhaps may be able to tell better than I can. . . .

We have hitherto fared exceedingly well and provided Genl Prevost continues on the south side of Savannah, we shall, I believe, continue to do so, as we seem to be in no situation for paying him a visit. . . .

Ladson is now moving in the tent beside me and I think it high time for me to join the concert. Wishing you all therefore the best of good nights, I remain my dearest Harriott's

Sincerely Affectionate Brother,

THOMAS PINCKNEY

For charity's sake write often, if it is only to add a little variety to the dull record of camp duty. . . .

Camp at Purysburg, Febry 22d, 1779

My Dear Harriott

. . . Your husband joined us here with 130 horse on Thursday morning and left us again on Saturday. Genl. Lincoln took his corps and Genl. Rutherford's Brigade of North Carolina Militia towards Augusta with himself. We have recd no intelligence from the westward since they left us but are in daily expectation of hearing that something has been done that way. If our forces get together in the west, they will form a body I imagine of 3,000 men, and we are stationed here with about 1500, so that unless the enemy are speedily reinforced, I am still hopeful that we may soon be on the south side of Savannah.

You have undoubtedly heard that our movement some time ago scared Campbell from Augusta, where he left a number of flat bottom'd boats nearly finished. Ashe and Williamson had orders immediately to cross the river after him and we are told that Col. Hammond by forc'd marches got into his rear and destroyed the bridge at Briar Creek (a deep water course he has to pass). It is imagined that in consequence of this a very considerable reinforcement has been sent up the country to Campbell and that some skirmishing may ensue that way. For our parts the General is so exceedingly careful of us that I am inclined to believe we shall not have our coats tarnished with smoak this campaign but shall continue what we have hitherto been, mere parade soldiers.

The extraordinary bounty given by our State for the recruiting service, will, I am hopeful, greatly replenish our regiments. We have enlisted 10 men here and are informed that our officers had got 33 in Charles Town more than a week ago.

The weather has been so unseasonably warm here that the fruit trees are in full blossom, the forest trees begun to be cloathed with leaves and the yellow jessamins hang in abundance on every bush.

Febry 23d. Your husband is just returned with General Lincoln. They went two days journey up the river but finding that the enemy had crossed Briar Creek and burnt the bridge after them (which we were informed our people had previously destroyed but it proved to be a bridge over Briar River), they returned in order to oppose their main body which must now be opposite to us. General Ashe with his whole force is by this time at Briar Creek about 30 miles above this, and we now, I imagine, wait only for him for reinforcements in order to strike a blow. . . .

If we had you on this campaign, you would improve wonderfully in one respect, as you would be obliged to rise before the dawn of day; which I apprehend would be 4 hours in a day clear gain to you. . . .

. . . With my duty, love and compliments where due, conclude my dearest Harriott's

Most Truly Affectionate Brother,
THOMAS PINCKNEY

My brother and Genl Moultrie are not yet returned from town.

Camp at Purysburg Mar 1st, 1779

The first of March is arrived, my dear Harriott, and we are as far advanced in repelling the enemy as we were the 1st of January; I wish the 1st of next month may not make April Fools of such as expect to be much forwarder at that time. . . .

We rise here a little before day break, the men turning out with their haversacks and blankets on their backs. They immediately are sent to their tents to wait 'till the sun rises to dispel the fog. We then turn out to exercise again for two hours, next eat our breakfast of coffee and johney cake, with plenty of milk, as we got a cow from Harry's Tom Middleton. We then lounge about, read a little, write a little, or ride a little, till two, when we eat our rations of pork or beef and whatever addition we can pick up, with strong grog and glass of brandy. At 4 o'clock exercise again 'till six, at seven drink tea and eat johney cake again, at 8 turn out in battalion, post the officer's and men so that they may run to their places at a moments warning; at 9 pull off our coats, caps and boots, wrap ourselves up in our blanket, lay down upon our bear skins, and sleep 'till day break again, when guilty conscience does not keep us awake. The sameness of this round is somewhat diversified by our going on duty once in 6 or 7 days, when we have the satisfaction of sitting up all night, riding the out posts of the army, and ruminating on past pleasures and joys to come. Adieu, my dear girl. I am now infringing one of our rules by sitting up at past 9 o'clock. Give my love to my mother, my love to Daniel, and believe me

Your Most Sincerely Affectionate Brother,
THOMAS PINCKNEY

General William Moultrie

BATTLE FOR BEAUFORT

"Port Royal is looked on as conquered already, by the report of several people from the southward road yesterday. . . . General Bull . . . is much alarmed and thinks Granville County is gone." So wrote Colonel Charles Pinckney to General William Moultrie on January 29, 1779.

The British were already on Port Royal Island. On the second day of February General Moultrie with General Stephen Bull and some three hundred militia crossed Port Royal Ferry, attacked the enemy and drove them from the island.

General Bull had both a patriotic and personal interest in the battle. Near by was his family home, Sheldon Hall, which was burned later by the British as was the old Sheldon Church.

In the following letter General Moultrie reports to General Benjamin Lincoln, commander of the American army in the Southern Department.

Beaufort, February 4th, 1779

Dear Sir,

I wrote you a few days ago from Gen. Bull's when I was there; the militia requested me to cross the river with them; which I readily consented to. The next morning, after leaving a proper guard to our camp, we began to cross the ferry, and got near three hundred over by sun set; we immediately marched off, and continued till we got within one mile of Beaufort. Here I rested the troops a few hours, and then proceeded to the town which we entered at sun rise next morning.

Having ordered the troops into quarters, and reposed myself a little, I rode down to view the fort with Gen. Bull and two or three other gentlemen. We had scarce been a moment there when an express arrived informing that the enemy were in full march for Beaufort, and not more than five miles off. Upon this I requested Gen. Bull to ride on to town, and have the men turned out. I followed immediately and found them all paraded, and had another account that the enemy were coming very fast. I then moved off the troops in order to meet them, and having marched two miles, was again informed they were within four miles of us. I then proceeded very slowly, looking for a proper piece of ground to form upon; having soon found a very advantageous spot, I continued there, waiting an hour for the enemy, and was then informed that they had, after halting awhile, altered their march, and were going towards our ferry.

I followed them and had gone about three miles, when I learnt that they were upon their return from the ferry, in full march towards us, and not more than one mile distant. Having sent my aid, Mr. Kinlock, to reconnoitre and bring me a particular account, he soon returned and informed me they were just at hand. I hastened our march to gain a swamp, which was near; but finding the enemy had already got possession of the ground I intended to occupy, I halted at about two hundred yards distance from the enemy, and drew up the troops to the right and left of the road, with two field-pieces (6 pounders) in the centre, and one small piece (2 pounder) on the right in the wood. On the enemy's near approach, I ordered Capt. Thomas Heyward to begin with the two field-pieces, and advanced my right and left wings nearer the swamp, and then the firing became pretty general. This action was reversed from the usual way of fighting between the British and Americans—they taking to the bushes and we remaining upon the open ground. After some little time finding our men too much exposed to the enemy's fire, I ordered them to take trees.

About three quarters of an hour after the action began, I heard a general cry through the line, of "no more cartridges," and was also informed by Captains Heyward and Rutledge[4] that the ammunition for the field-pieces was almost expended, after firing about forty rounds from each piece. Upon this I ordered the field-pieces to be drawn off very slowly; and their right and left wings to keep pace with the artillery to cover their flanks, which was done in tolerable order for undisciplined troops. The enemy had beat their retreat before we began to move, but we had little or no ammunition, and could not of consequence pursue. They retreated so hastily as to leave an officer, one sergeant and three privates wounded in a house near the action, and their dead lying on the field. It is impossible as yet to be particular with respect to the latter. Two officers we have found and seven men. They fought from behind the bushes.

Capt. John Barnwell,[5] with a few light horse, was of infinite service in giving us frequent intelligence of the enemy's motions, and attacking their rear. He had at one time Capt. Brewer, who is much wounded, two sergeants and twelve privates, prisoners; but a party of the enemy, having rallied in their retreat, retook the captain, one sergeant and six men; the remainder, however, he brought off with twelve stand of arms. Barnwell had about fifteen men.

It makes me happy to assure you that our militia have that spirit which they have always been allowed to possess; nothing but discipline is wanting to make them good troops. The Charlestown artillery behaved gallantly; they stood to their pieces like veterans, and served them well, until I was constrained to order them to retire, in consequence of their ammunition being nearly expended. I had in action only nine Continental troops; Capt. DeTreville,[6] two officers, and six

---

[4] Captain Heyward, Jr., and Captain Edward Rutledge, signers of the Declaration of Independence.

[5] Captain John Barnwell was later wounded at John's Island, and after the capture of Charles Town he was confined on a British prison ship. The first John Barnwell settled near Beaufort in 1701; both he and his Revolutionary namesake are buried at St. Helena churchyard in Beaufort.

[6] Captain John Labouladrie DeTreville, member of an Acadian family sent to Beaufort County in 1755.

privates, with one brass two-pounder, and only fifteen rounds. I must, in justice to them, say that they behaved well. It seems absolutely necessary for me to remain here a few days longer, in order to have the wounded properly taken care of, and other matters put in a right channel.

This moment died a valuable officer and good citizen, of the wound he received yesterday, Lieut. Benjamin Wilkins, of the Charlestown artillery. We have three other officers wounded: Capt. Heyward in the arm, Lieut. Sawyer and Brown, both of the light infantry, with six or seven privates killed in the field, and fifteen wounded. I cannot be very particular; as yet have had no regular return made me. The enemy's brigade consisted of two companies of the 60th and one of the 16th regiment, all picked light infantry.

We had five deserters from them immediately after action, who informed us of several particulars already mentioned: also, that our second shot from the field piece had disabled a Howitz, which they had fired but once.

I am, etc.,
WILLIAM MOULTRIE

P.S. The Chehaw company was sent back before the action, about 125 men, on a report that the enemy had landed there.

Orders by Gen. Moultrie.

Beaufort, February 4th, 1779

Gen. Moultrie takes the early opportunity of returning his thanks to the troops for their gallant and spirited behavior on the field in the action of yesterday, and doubts not but they will always acquit themselves in the like spirited manner, especially when fighting in the glorious cause of liberty.

A return to be made immediately, of the killed and wounded, in the action of yesterday.

Second Company,

S. Wilkins, John Fraser, mortally wounded.
John Anthony, John Calvert, Anthony Watts, John Green,
  John Laurence, wounded.

Third Company,

John Collins, John Righton, John D. Miller, wounded.

Mary Lucia Bull

"I EXPECTED NOTHING BUT DEATH"

Mary Lucia Bull, who writes the ensuing letter to her friend Susanna Stoll, was the great-granddaughter of Stephen Bull, the emigrant "Caseeka of the Itawanas," and the grand-niece of William Bull, first Lieutenant Governor of the Province.

At this time General Augustine Prevost was occupying St. Andrew's Parish on his expedition against Charleston. Mary Lucia Bull, a refugee from her home in Beaufort District, describes her frightening experience with the British soldiers and their Indian allies. In the following year she married Jacob Guerord. Their home was in Prince William's Parish in Beaufort District.

[May 1779]

Many thanks, my dear Sukey, for your kind inquiry's about me and still more thanks for acquainting me of your situation. We left Prince Williams the day after you parted with us. My brother attempted bringing his Negroes with him, but we were obliged to leave them in Pon Pon River, from whence they returned home; thear was a few put on board Mr. River's schooner—which arrived safe in Charles-Town; Nancy and self have six among them, they went about the town for their victuals. We have our two maids with us; Mariah is with the rest of our Negroes at Oakatees (I believe) under the care of Mr. Flower and Mr. M. Garvey.

It is impossible for me to describe to you what I felt while the British army was on this side Ashley-Ferry. We never went in to our beds at night, had candles constantly burning and were alarmed at every noise that we heard. Mrs. Bull was plundered of some of her clothes, my Aunt Bellinger's chamber door was burst open and a great many of her things taken; in short everybody in the house lost something except Nancy and myself. As soon as we saw them taking things about the house we went into our chamber, had the window shut and stood against the door (for it could not lock). One man came and turned the brass but did not push against it hard enough to find out it was not lock'd. But, good Heavens, my Sukey, think what we must have suffered when a parcel of Indians came bolting into the house! As for my part I expected nothing but death, and indeed, at that moment, it was indifferent to me whether I lived or died, yet I could not bear the thought of being murder'd by the savages. One of the British colonels came to the house. We told him we were very uneasy about the Indians and common soldiers. He was sorry they disturbed us, he said, but he had better fee him to stay with us, for he had good spirits, cou'd sing a good song and had a deal of chitty-chatty. Whether he said that to divert us (for we were very dull) or whether he felt as little for our distress as he appeared to do, I will not undertake to say.

You ask me what we intend doing—that is a question that I know not how to answer. I am as yet quite undetermined what to do. I wait for my brother's advice, who is at the Indian-Land.[7] Mrs. Kelsall, my brother informed me, has invited us to go to Georgia, but I see no possibility of our accepting her invitation. I am very glad to hear your mamma has been so lucky; please remember us all kindly to her, if you have any opportunity of writing to her. I wish, my Sukey, I knew how to go and see you before you go to River-May. I would not mind your being at a strangers; I believe I would jump up behind Isaac now, if Nancy would let me, but she wants to see you as much as I do, and she is so selfish she won't let me have the pleasure of seeing you alone.

And now, my Sukey, I must beg that you will not be uneasy about me, I am as happy as your absence and the times will permit me to be. Mrs. Bull, Nancy and Miss Polly Cameron desire to be remembered to you. I remain your unchangeable friend,

MARY LUCIA BULL

P.S.—Mrs. Garvey and Miss Cameron stay'd at Prince William's.

General William Moultrie

"THE ENEMY HAVE LANDED AT BEAUFORT"

After their defeat on June 19, 1779, the British, under General Prevost, evacuated their post at Stono, and after retiring along the sea

---

[7] Indian Land was in Beaufort District.

islands they reached Port Royal Island. At Beaufort, Prevost estab-
lished a strong post of strategic importance, for now by means of inland
navigation the British could easily penetrate into all parts of the sur-
rounding rich plantation country.

Placing the garrison at Beaufort under the command of Lieutenant
John Maitland, Prevost, with the rest of his army, moved on to Georgia.

These letters from General Moultrie to General Lincoln give an
account of the situation at Beaufort.

Stono, Sommer's, July 3d, 1779

Dear Sir,

. . . By a letter from Colonel [Daniel] Horry, which is dated Port-
royal-ferry, July 1st, I am informed that the enemy's army are not yet
got to Beaufort, that only a party of marines were on that island, and
stationed opposite his post, but upon his appearance they were called
in, and went on board the *Vigilant* and two transports which lay there,
that they had no more than 200 men altogether at that place, including
the *Vigilant's* crew. By three deserters from the enemy's gallies yesterday, I am informed that they are still on Edisto-Island, but they agree
that their intention is to go for Beaufort. I think it not adviseable to
move from hence, while they remain where they are. . . .

I am, etc.

Wm. Moultrie

Stono, July 5th, 1779

Dear Sir,

I have just received information from different quarters, that the
enemy are now upon Port-royal-Island. In consequence, I have ordered
Colonel Pinckney's and the Georgia brigade to be ready to march to-
morrow morning early, and shall order General Sumner's to follow the
next day; I shall march them in divisions, because it would be inconvenient to have them all together when they came to cross the rivers. I
propose forming my camp near Colonel [Benjamin] Garden's, and keep
my picquets on the river side; I shall order two field-pieces with each
division, the remainder of the artillery I think may be as well sent to
town; but for this I shall wait your orders. . . .

I am, etc.

Wm. Moultrie

Stono, July 10th, 1779

Dear Sir,

. . . I have just now received a letter from Col. Horry, informing me that the enemy have landed at Beaufort, and mean to maintain the island: they still talk of taking post on the Main. This last I give but little credit to. A party of our troops went on the island and brought off a young man, a prisoner, whom I have sent to town; he says they have landed their sick and wounded, and placed them in the court-house and gaol, which they have converted into hospitals: this looks as if they intended staying there. Is it not scandalous to America that a handful of men, with two small men-of-war, should ride-triumphant and distress these southern states, when perhaps our continental vessels are cruizing for the emolument of their commanders? . . . Should not this be represented to Congress? At all events I shall set off Monday for camp at Port-royal-ferry. I fear we are beginning a new campaign.

I am, etc.

WM. MOULTRIE

Sheldon, July 17th, 1779

Dear Sir,

. . . The last information I received from the enemy, and from good authority, is, that they have sent some of their troops to Savannah, and have kept the 71st, the light-infantry and some Hessians posted in the following manner: the 71st at Beaufort, and the Hessians at Mile-End, throwing up some works. This place is a narrow neck of land, about a mile from the town, not more than 300 yards across; on each side is a navigable river, which makes it a very strong post indeed. The light-infantry (between 3 and 400) are opposite Port-royal-ferry, in sight of one of our guards at the redoubt. The whole of their number does not exceed 1,000 men. It appears to me as if they would leave the place before long. I imagine they have not shipping enough to take them off at one trip, and are therefore obliged to wait the return of the vessels which carried the first division.

. . . The business here, in my opinion, will be only to wait on the motions of the enemy, which I think will be passive enough; they only mean to keep possession of the Island in peace while they stay. . . . I have been employed, these two days, in reconnoitering the country in this neighborhood. Col. Garden, with about 100 men, has taken post at

Gordon's plantation on Scotch-neck, and detached about 20 men to Page's-point, where the battery is built. Col. Hammond is here with about 40 men. These are all the militia of this state that are now in the field near this place. I have changed my opinion relative to commencing a new campaign. I rather think the enemy are lingering out the old one. . . .

I am, etc.

WM. MOULTRIE

Paul Hamilton

"I HAD SOME HAIR BREADTH ESCAPES"

Paul Hamilton, son of Archibald and Rebecca (Brandford) Hamilton, joined the militia company called Wiltown Hunters at the age of sixteen soon after the British invaded South Carolina. He was at the siege of Savannah. After the surrender of Charles Town he went with the army to North Carolina and Virginia. Along the way he and his friend James Moore concocted a scheme to purchase homemade brandy and retail it to the army, from "which we expected to derive a great profit." Young Hamilton joined the army under Baron de Kalb at Hillsborough, N. C., and remained until after its defeat, August 16, 1779, under General Gates. He then joined General Francis Marion on the Santee. The following diary account begins at this point.

Paul Hamilton married Mary Wilkinson, October 10, 1782, and for some years engaged in the planting of indigo and later rice. He held many state offices including that of Controller of Finance; and from 1804 to 1809 he was Governor of South Carolina. In 1809 President Madison appointed him Secretary of the Navy. Upon his resignation in 1812 Madison wrote of his "faithful zeal, uniform exertions and unimpeachable integrity." He died in Beaufort in 1816.

Having remained sometime with Marion, I availed myself of an opportunity that offered of returning homeward with Col. Harden, who had fled from the Parish of Prince William to Marion's Camp and, assembling about 70 followers, determined to return southward, and by stirring up his friends who had submitted to the enemy to cover that part of our country. Him I joined as a volunteer, having previously received, while with Marion, a letter from my good mother, with a supply of money and clothes, most wonderfully conveyed to me through the country then overrun by the enemy.

With Harden I approached Jacksonboro, and hearing that my mother was then at the plantation of my deceased Grand-father Branford, two miles off, I, with leave, quitted the party, galloped off to the plantation opposite (then Dupont's, now Jacob Walter's) where, finding a small canoe which I ordered a Negro man to enter, I threw thereon my arms, and on my horse swam the river. Arriving near the house I was informed that my grand-father's widow was then in a most dreadful state with small pox, which I had not had, and that my mother had that morning gone to her house at Wiltown. An express was sent for her and in a very short time she was at Mrs. Slann's, whose husband I had left northwardly, arrived.

To avoid the infection of small pox I had remained at the fence of the plantation near the swamp, where I met the best of mothers. What our meeting was I cannot describe. Neither had for minutes the power of utterance; at length a flood of tears on her part enabled her to break silence, when such affectionate expressions were poured out as I can never forget, nor the warmth of that maternal embrace, in which I was clasped to her aching bosom, after an absence of 12 months lacking 6 days, during which she had received but one letter from me and had often heard of my having been killed. I remained with her for two hours. I then left her with her blessing on my head, and an assurance that I would shortly again see her. She presented me with some clothing which she had prepared for me; these she had tied up hastily in a pillow case, and I tucked them behind my saddle, a circumstance which had well nigh cost me my life that very night.

On regaining my party we proceeded southwardly, and at midnight encountered a body of British cavalry near Saltketcher Bridge. The onset was in our favor, but Harden being but an indifferent commander we were defeated and in the rout I suffered a hard pursuit, in which my pursuers were guided by the whiteness of the pillow case that contained the clothes behind me. A good horse and some presence of mind at last secured me from pursuit. Our whole party was dispersed, and about 15 severely wounded with the sabre. In two days we were again collected and retorted this defeat by surprising and making prisoners of part of this cavalry at Pocotaligo, among them their Colonel Fenwicke, and other officers. This success led to the surrender of the British Fort Balfour, at the above place, under the ramparts almost of which this surprise was made.[8]

I must, as I am writing of myself, be allowed to be somewhat particular as to this little but handsome military exploit. Colonel Harden, knowing that we had some staunch friends who had been compelled to enter and garrison the fort, thought that if he could destroy the cavalry, he might induce a surrender of the remainder of the garrison, which were Militia and perhaps one half of them friendly to the American cause—some of whom were men of considerable influence and weight. He therefore drew near the fort and with the effective force he had remaining formed an ambuscade.

Twelve well mounted young men, of whom I was one, named as Light Horsemen, were selected and ordered to decoy the cavalry out. With this view we moved on briskly and openly toward Von Bitters Tavern, which stood almost a quarter of a mile from the fort and in full view. While approaching we discovered that some of the enemy were at the tavern, on which we darted forward and captured as follows: Col. Fenwicke, Lieut. Bond, a sergeant and 15 privates of the cavalry with Lieut. Col. Lechmere of the British Militia. Lechmere was taken as he ran within 100 yards of the fort, and brought off by one of our young men named Green. Our prisoners had come out on foot to the tavern to regale themselves; having only their swords, [they] made no attempt to resist. They were hurried off to the ambuscade and delivered. After which, reinforced by eight more swordsmen, we returned, 20 in number, to the tavern, drew up in the adjoining pasture, offered battle to the British cavalry whose number we had reduced now to about our standard, a part of their force having been previously detached to Charleston immediately after we had been defeated by them at Saltketchie. The cavalry made a show of advancing to the charge but finding us firm they turned about and were insulted by us as they retired to the fort.

Col. Harden now came up with the remainder of his force, leaving the servants and baggage just partly in view to keep up the appearance

---

[8] Fort Balfour at Pocotaligo. Colonel William Harden, the American commander, defeated the British on April 18, 1781. He was a native of Beaufort District and a valued member of Marion's band of soldiers.

of a reserve. Major Harden, the brother of the colonel, was now sent to summon the fort to surrender with threats of an assault if refused. I accompanied the major. We were met by Major DeVeaux (after, Col. DeVeaux who took the Bahamas from Spain) at so short a distance from the fort that we could recognize countenances and exchanged an occasional nod with some of the garrison.

At first the answer through Major DeVeaux was a refusal from Col. Kitsall, who commanded the fort, to surrender, on which I was desired by Major Harden to communicate to his brother this answer. The Col. inquired of me if we could distinguish any of our friends in the fort. I replied that Major Harden had recognized Cols. Stafford and Davis, and Mr. Thos. Hutson, with none of whom I had any acquaintance, but that I thought that I discovered some confusion and clamour in the fort. On which the Col., his countenance brightening, formed his men in column and ordered them to prepare for immediate action. This done he turned to me and said, "Go to Major Harden and say to him that I allowed 10 minutes to Col. Kitsall to consider of a surrender, after which if he refuses you are both to return immediately to me and by God I will be in the fort!" The Major communicated this to Major DeVeaux with whom he had been chatting with great familiarity, being acquaintances and closely related by blood. The latter went in and delivered this last message to Col. Kitsall, who, having discovered a division among his Militia, agreed to lay down arms. Thus was Fort Balfour, which had for some months completely bridled that part of the country, surrendered without a shot. The garrison consisted of 92 Militia, about 25 Regulars, cavalry well mounted and equipped, and uniformed as Light Dragoons. In the fort we found an abundance of provisions, some muskets and a six-pound cannon, with a good supply of ammunition for it.

We had just completed this and paroled our prisoners when a body of British composed of artillery, cavalry and infantry appeared within a mile of us, far too strong for us. We therefore drew off, leaving them Fort Balfour in ruins. From this time war was carried on by Harden (whose force was much augmented by the coming in of our Militia friends) with several successive British detachments, in this desultory warfare. Ambuscades, skirmishes and surprises were frequent, but not important, through the Parishes of St. Bartholomew's and St. Paul's. I was mostly with Harden, but frequently at Wiltouns with my friends when I had some hair-breadth escapes from the enemy's irregular and other cavalry, and visiting Mary until the arrival of Gen. Greene in the latter end of 1781 in the Low Country confined the enemy in the walls of Charleston. . . .

The arrival of Gen. Greene . . . left us free to resume our homes and a safety to which we long had been strangers. I now devoted myself to the company of my friends and the sports of the chase of which I was immoderately fond. My chief delight was to converse with Mary whom I now considered as entirely mine, as soon as prudence would admit of our being united. . . . Every day appeared an age till the 10th of October, 1782, united me to Mary, she then turned 18 and I short by 6 days of being 20 yrs of age. . . .

In a few days after our marriage, I carried my wife home to the house of my venerated mother, who insisted that we should make that our residence until we could settle ourselves in our minds. . . .

Reverend Archibald Simpson

"RAVAGES OF WAR"

The Reverend Archibald Simpson, a native of Glasgow, came to South Carolina in 1752. After serving some years in Charleston, he was appointed to the Stoney Creek Independent Presbyterian Church in Prince William's Parish, established in 1740 in what was then called the "Indian Land."

Mr. Simpson returned to Scotland in 1772 and remained there during the war. In the fall of 1783 he was again in South Carolina to see his old plantation and church. This is the sad visit described in his diary.

When he went back to Scotland, he was appointed to the church in the town of Renfrew. There he died. His grandson, Archibald Simpson Johnson, came to South Carolina and lived in Beaufort County until his death in 1819.

On the 3d of November, 1783, . . . got to Mr. Hatcher's Landing, up St. Helena Sound; met Mrs. Hatcher, her nephew, James Ferguson, &c.; was much affected to hear of the dreadful, horrid ravages of war in this parish and neighborhood. . . . The British and American armies have carried off all fine breed of horses and several hundred head of cattle. . . .

Wednesday, Nov. 5th. I rode around by my old parsonage which is still standing; stopped on the road and viewed it for some time, with a heart ready to burst at the remembrance of the past. There my dear children were born; there they and their ever dear mother died; there I had many a sweet, pleasant and comfortable—many a sick, melancholy and sorrowful hour. Proceeded all alone to my old meeting-house at Stoney Creek, which, to the surprise of many, is left standing, while they burned the grand Episcopal church at Sheldon, the most elegant country church in the state. Lighted from my horse; viewed the tomb where the bodies of my dear Jeany Muir, Sacheverel, Archibald, and Jeany Simpson, the mother and the children, lie interred; was greatly affected, yet could not drop a tear, but heaved many a deep-fetched sigh from a troubled heart; went into my old study; sat some time in mournful silence; knelt down and offered up fervent prayers and praises to God—praised the Lord for his sparing mercy to me and mine, and for bringing me back again to this land; prayed for grace, mercy, and counsel for myself while in this country, and that I may again be made useful in it; prayed for the present minister, Mr. James Gourlay, whose circumstances in Scotland being somewhat peculiar, I prevailed with him to come to America; proceeded with a heart full of the most tender feelings past the Stoney Creek store.

All was desolation, and indeed all the way there was a gloomy solitariness. Every field, every plantation, showed marks of ruin and devastation. Not a person was to be met with in the roads. All was gloomy. . . . It is impossible to describe in words how altered these once beautiful fields are; no garden, no enclosure, no mulberry, no fruit trees, nothing but wild fennel, bushes, underwood, briars, to be seen—and a very ruinous habitation.

Some of my Negroes were at work in the woods. They saw me and ran with transports of joy, holding me by the knees as I sat on horseback, and directly ran off to the plantation to give notice to Mr. Lambert.[9] They asked me if I was going to leave them when they had stayed on the plantation when the British wanted them to go away;

---

[9] Mr. John Lambert was the manager of Mr. Simpson's plantation.

abused the two who had left me and gone with Col. Moncrieff.[10] . . .
They indeed live easy and comfortable to what many of their color do,
and much more comfortably not only than many of the peasants in
Britain, but much more than thousands of the farmers or country
people of Scotland. Happy, very happy, should I be if I could be useful
to their souls. . . .

Rev. Mr. Gourlay is much altered and old like, but is very brisk and
lively to what he used to be when I saw him in Scotland. He lives at
Mr. Main's plantation and has acted as teacher to a few boys as well
as minister at Stoney Creek. He, like all other Presbyterian ministers,
was prevented from preaching while the British army was in these
parts. . . .

I have not a horse to ride out anywhere. Every person, every family
in both parishes, and through all this district of country, appears to
be in the same situation. No one comes to see me, for none have horses.
All society seems to be at an end. Every person keeps close on his own
plantation. Robberies and murders are often committed on the public
roads. The people that remain have been peeled, pillaged, and plundered. Poverty, want, and hardship appear in almost every countenance. A dark melancholy gloom appears everywhere, and the morals
of the people are almost entirely extirpated. A general discontent, dis-
satisfaction, and distrust of their present rulers and of one another
prevails throughout the country. In Charleston they appear to be more
happy.

I am greatly disappointed since I came to the country, and could not
have believed that these distresses had been so great had I not seen. It
is evident that the British army came here to plunder, and not to fight
or conquer the people, far less to conciliate them to submit to the
British government. The appearance of the whole country shows it
here, and the vast fortunes that the officers of the British army have
carried home with them and realized in Britain, shows it there. It is
with great difficulty people can get to public worship. Hardly such a
thing as a chair or one-horse chaise is to be seen, and these are so plain
and coarse, and without paint, and made by Negro carpenters, much
like the covered carts we formerly used for carrying our children to
school. . . .

---

[10] Colonel Moncrieff was the British engineer who constructed the defenses of
Savannah.

November 25th. . . . Attend vendue at Godfrey's. . . . The vendue was of the clothes, books, medicines and a horse, belonging to a Dr. Brown, who lodged at Mr. Dunnom's, the son of a Presbyterian minister in Virginia, who had given offense to a company of villains who prowl around the state by his endeavoring to discover the murderers of another young man, Dr. Orr, murdered about four months ago; both shot, scalped, and otherwise most barbarously used, while riding in the public road in the way of his practice, by persons who lay in the woods waiting for him. Both these murders were committed within six miles of the house where I now live. Of the people a few were the children of my former friends, who knew me, and whom I could remember, and were the only persons who made a decent appearance. The two principal murderers, —— and ——, were said to be present. One of them was pointed out to me. . . .

Saturday, March 13th [1784]. Put my things aboard Capt. Rankin's vessel; am to pay ten guineas. Capt. Rankin goes first to Savannah. . . .

PART VIII

Periclean Age of the Sea Islands

1783-1861

"If I see no carriages under the visitors' shed when I return from my fields to dinner, I say to myself, my friends have not treated me well to-day."

Anonymous planter

George Washington

PRESIDENT WASHINGTON PASSED THIS WAY

On his Southern tour in 1791 President George Washington traveled from Charleston to Savannah in early May. Along the way he spent a night with his kinsman, Colonel William Washington, who had married Jane Elliott of Sandy Hill during the Revolution.

Accompanied by his old friends General William Moultrie and Major Pierce Butler, he arrived at Pocotaligo in Prince William's Parish on May 11. Here, reported the City Gazette of Charleston, a crowd awaited him, and a handsome dinner was served at which fourteen toasts were drunk. The President gave a toast to "The Parish of Prince William's."

That night he slept at White Hall, home of Judge Thomas Heyward.

At Purrysburg, site of the Swiss colony and General Lincoln's old headquarters, he was provided with "a handsome eight-oared barge," and the party proceeded down the Savannah River.

According to Beaufort legend, President Washington visited his friend Chancellor Henry William de Saussure, director of the United States mint when the first gold eagles were coined. His house in Beaufort, known today as the Gold Eagle Tavern, may well have provided one of the many beds in which the President slept.

Monday, 9th [1791]. At six o'clock I recommenced my journey for Savanna; attended by a Corps of the Cincinnatti and most of the principal Gentlemen of the City as far as the bridge over Ashley River, where we breakfasted, and proceeded to Colo. W. Washington's at Sandy-hill with a select party of particular friends—distant from Charleston 28 miles.

Tuesday, 10th. Took leave of all my friends and attendants at this place (except General Moultrie and Majr. Butler the last of whom intended to accompany me to Savanna, and the other to Purisburg, at which I was to be met by Boats) and breakfasting at Judge Bee's 12 miles from Sandy hill, lodged at Mr. Obrian Smith's 18 or 20 further on.

Wednesday, 11th. After an early breakfast at Mr. Smith's we road 20 miles to a place called Pokitellieo [Pocotaligo] where a dinner was provided by the Parishoners of Prince William for my reception, and an address from them was presented and answered. After dinner we proceeded 16 miles farther to Judge [Thomas] Hayward's where we lodged, and, as also at Mr. Smith's were kindly and hospitably entertained. My going to Colo. Washington's is to be ascribed to motives of friendship and relationship; but to Mr. Smith's and Judge Haywards to those of necessity; their being no public houses on the Road and my distance to get to these private ones increased at least 10 or 12 miles between Charleston and Savanna.

Thursday, 12th. By five o'clock we set out from Judge Hayward's, and road to Purisburg 22 miles to breakfast.

At that place I was met by Messrs. Jones, Colo. Habersham, Mr. Jno. Houston, Genl. McIntosh and Mr. Clay, a Com[mitt]ee from the City of Savanna to conduct me thither. Boats also were ordered there by them for my accomodation; among which a handsome 8 oared barge rowed by 8 American Captns. attended. In my way down the River I called upon Mrs. [Nathanael] Green the Widow of the deceased Genl. Green, (at a place called Mulberry Grove) and asked her how she did. At this place (2 miles from Purisburg) my horses and Carriages were landed, and had 12 miles farther by Land to Savanna. . . .

William John Grayson

RECOLLECTIONS OF AN ISLAND BOYHOOD

William John Grayson, who tells about his island boyhood, was educated in the North and at the South Carolina University. After serving in the South Carolina state legislature he was sent to Congress from 1833 to 1837. He was the author of a number of books and poems and a frequent contributor to local magazines and newspapers. His most popular work is a once-famous pro-slavery poem, "The Hireling and the Slave," published in 1854. He died a refugee from his island home on October 4, 1863.

Mason Locke Weems, who appears in Grayson's recollections, is remembered now chiefly because he was responsible for the story about George Washington and the cherry tree. But in his time he was a famous and unique figure.

He was born in Anne Arundel County, Maryland, in 1759. His Life of Washington *appeared in 1800, and his* Life of General Francis Marion *in 1809. He was employed by Matthew Carey, pioneer publisher of New York, to sell books for him. Around the South the "Parson" went, engaged not only in peddling his books and pamphlets, but in fiddling freely and "preaching when invited."*

"Parson" Weems died and was buried in Beaufort in 1825. Later his body was removed to Virginia.

According to the Duellist's Looking Glass, *Grayson's father killed the Frenchman.*

I was born in November 1788, in the town of Beaufort, So. Ca. The town is situated in the southern corner of the state, on Port Royal, in a parish of the island.... During the Revolution of 1776, British troops occupied the luckless place....

The little town has not encreased as American towns are accustomed to do. It is remarkable for the conservative property of standing still. Its population is no greater than it was fifty years ago and its condition as to all material advantages is very much the same. It has always been on good terms with itself nevertheless and for better reasons than usually accompany self complacency. It is quiet, healthy, religious, dresses well, is of good manners and morals and not a little addicted to mental cultivation....

My father, John Grayson, was an officer of artillery in the continental army during the Revolutionary War. My father's father was an Englishman, a native of Yorkshire. He had carried on commercial business in the West Indies and afterwards in Carolina and Georgia.... He married the daughter of Col. Thomas Wigg whose father had been among the earliest emigrants from England to Port Royal. Col. Wigg left five children, three daughters ... and two sons.... The name, so common at one time as to comprise a majority of the vestry in St. Helena Parish, is now confined to Mr. William Wigg and his family, lately residents of St. Luke's Parish.

My father entered the army at the age of seventeen as a lieutenant of artillery in Roberts' regiment. He was one of the garrison in Charles-

ton when it was surrendered by Lincoln after a brave defense to the
British forces, in May 1780. After the surrender the officers, prisoners
of war, were placed in cantonments, at Haddrel's Point, over against
the city, where Mount Pleasant village now stands. While there the
young lieutenant was forced into a quarrel with a brother officer, a
Frenchman and professed duellist. Although no longer able to fight
the enemy, the prisoners, it seems, were at liberty to fight each other.
It relieved the tediousness of captivity in a way conformable to the
Soldier's pursuits.

The cause was trivial enough, but not smaller than is common in
"affairs of honour." It was as weighty, perhaps, as many that have produced long conflicts among states and nations. To help out their
scanty rations while prisoners one of the combatants raised chickens,
the other cultivated a garden. The chicken of the poultry breeder
made marauding expeditions on the cabbages of the gardener. It was
a very natural proceeding and in the spirit of the times. But the chicken
raid gave occasion to high words, and high words led to a challenge
and duel.

The Reverend M. L. Weems, formerly pastor of a church in Alex-
andria and "chaplain," as he called himself, of General Washington,
made the affair a subject of one of the curious pamphlets of which he
was the author and vender. He called them by quaint names: the
Gambler's Looking Glass, the *Drunkard's Looking Glass*, the *Duellist's Looking Glass*. These pamphlets with histories of bloody murders, psalm books, testaments, his life of Marion and of Washington,
he carried through the country in a light waggon, for sale, fiddling as
he went and preaching when invited. His favourite text was "God is
love" and his favourite topics for illustrating God's goodness to mankind were George Washington and Langdon Cheves. His fiddle, like
Goldsmith's flute when the poet travelled on foot through Europe,
made the eccentric traveller welcome wherever he went.

[Mr. Weems's] custom was to give his old horse the reins and as the
horse walked the road slowly the master amused himself and cheered
the way with the sounds of his violin. Whenever night overtook them,
he was sure of a welcome at farmhouse or cabin and of hospitable entertainment for man and horse.

The old traveler was returning from one of these periodical circuits
when he was seized with a painful disease and was landed from a
passing steam boat on the wharf at Beaufort, in a destitute and de-

plorable condition. There was no hotel. . . . A good Samaritan, the Reverend Benjamin S. Scriven, took him to his house. Mr. Scriven's excellent wife tenderly nursed the poor old itinerant book-seller and chaplain of Washington thus picked up by the way side, and at his death they buried him in the graveyard of the Episcopal Church. His grave is unmarked by any memorial. Mr. Weems is entitled to a place among the earliest cultivators of literature in the Southern States. His "looking glasses" were tracts for the times—moral lessons in the shape of stories founded on facts. They were popular, widely circulated in the country, and useful in their day. His Life of Marion and of Washington were narratives of a higher order. . . .

My father died when I was about ten years old. I remember very little of him. He was reserved in disposition, I think, and I was shy and sensitive. . . .

The chief pleasures I remember of my early boyhood are those I enjoyed in the house of my father's mother. I spent my holidays of Easter and Christmas at her plantation on Parris Island. I was a favourite child, the son of a favourite son, and was petted accordingly. How well I remember the eagerness with which I looked forward to the months of April and December; how I regretted the rapidity with which the days passed by; how much I enjoyed them; how reluctantly, at their close, I returned home to school and its troubles! My grandmother was an admirable specimen of loveable old age. I still see the dear old lady, at seventy, actively ordering her household. The white muslin cap with the broad black ribbon round it, the ample folds of the same material covering her neck and bosom, the clear eye undimmed by age, the grave and gentle expression of countenance, the fair and delicate features, all rise up before me as of yesterday. I never had from her a harsh word or angry look at my boyish mischief. All my memories respecting her are of unmixed reverence and love.

She had a neighbour, Mrs. Ann Rippon, of her own age whose plantation lay on the opposite side of the Island, on the Broad River shore, about three miles off. . . . I was a frequent and willing guest at Mrs. Rippon's. Never was the hostess more devoted to the comfort and enjoyment of her friends or better pleased at having a house full. She was wonderfully active, bustling, hospitable and addicted to scolding. The finest hams of her own curing, the fattest turkeys of her own raising, the choicest fish and oysters and puddings and pies and dainties without number were marshalled on her dinner table in suitable order.

How she insisted on your eating! There was no escaping. No knife and fork were ever active enough or sufficiently persevering at her table. If you eat never so much, she earnestly pressed you to eat more, not for form sake or imaginary politeness, but with an air of absolute distress to see you, as she would say, so delicate in your appetite or so little satisfied with her fare. Should there be twenty guests at her table her eye appeared to be on every one. If she saw the smallest falling off in the enjoyment of her dishes, she became at once restless, fidgety and unhappy at having nothing that could please you. Her plantation abounded in all good things. Her garden was excellent, producing every fruit and vegetable. Oranges were plentiful, figs without number, peaches and pomegranates in profusion.

At that time and before people lived on their plantations and all useful and pleasant things flourished accordingly. Now plantations are cotton fields rearing a crop for foreign markets and little more. . . . The planter's whole attention now is absorbed by his cotton crop. . . .

During the holiday times that I spent in the country I learned the arts of fishing and shooting at an early age, as all boys do in Carolina. At first my fishing was confined to minnows and a pack thread line with pin hooks. Attended by a retinue of little Negroes, I caught, in the shallow creeks of the marshes, mud fish and sometimes an eel, which we ran away from, thinking it a snake. Next I attempted yellow-tail and whiting. In due time I became initiated in the noble sport of drum fishing. Port Royal, or Broad River as it is locally called, is the favourite haunt of the drum. It is a large heavy fish, weighing fifty or sixty pounds and sometimes more. It makes a singular noise in spring of the year like the tap of a drum, which explains its name. The sound is heard distinctly from the bottom of the river at a depth of five or six fathoms. The fish afford excellent sport to the fisherman and no bad dish for the table. Among sea or river delicacies the roe of the drum in an unsurpassed dainty. They bite only in the spring of the year but seem never to leave the rivers in the vicinity of Port Royal. . . . The largest number ever caught, as far as I have heard, was caught a half century ago.

In this great success it was my fortune to have a share. With ten lines, from half ebb to low water, we took ninety six great fish and when the sport was at an end the fish were biting as rapidly as before. Our bait gave out and we rowed away from the ground, in our loaded boat, unsated with the day's sport and eager to continue it. It was a beautiful day, a bright sky, a gentle south wind just sufficient to ripple the green sea-water of the bay and moderate the warmth of an April sun, and the landscape around us with Hilton Head and Parris Island and Saint Helena and the single palm tree on Dawes Island[1] looked out through the pure atmosphere, in all its beauty, clearly and distinctly defined.

In the eagerness of competition through the day we lost a great number of fish after hooking them. The hook tore out, or the line broke, or the hook or strap gave way, and the mortified and impatient fisherman was obliged to stop and repair his tackle while his companions were catching more fish by his side.

Since the great achievement of ninety six, I have never known more than forty drum caught in a day's fishing and that but seldom. It has become common to toil a whole tide and take only two or three. . . .

During my boyhood many men of the Revolution were still alive. They were a jovial and somewhat rough race, liberal, social, warm-hearted, hospitable, addicted to deep drinking, hard-swearing, and practical-joking and not a little given to loose language and indelicate allusions. . . . They were fond of dinners, barbacues and hunting clubs. The abundance of deer in the country led to associations for sport in every neighbourhood. They met monthly or oftener to hunt and dine. Afterwards when deer became less numerous, the club assembled to eat, drink and talk of politics and planting.

At these festivals no man was permitted to go home sober. It was contrary to good manners and good manners were observed so rigidly that force was used if necessary to secure a just attention to them. Drink round and off with your heel-taps were fundamental rules. No man was permitted to disregard them.

I have been told of one exception only. In my younger days I heard an old friend, himself one of the set, relate that it was customary with a member of the Beaufort Hunting-club, a distinguished man in social and political life, to throw himself on the generosity of his companions. He would appeal to them by saying, "Gentlemen, if I drink when you drink and as you drink I shall be disabled before the day is half over. I shall lose a great part of the conversation and enjoyment. Al-

---

[1] Daw's Island, where Ribaut planted his column in 1562.

low me to drink as I please. I pledge my honour that I will be as drunk as any of you at the close of the meeting, but let it be in my own time and way." The privilege claimed was yielded accordingly and was never abused. The pledge was always redeemed. . . .

On one occasion at the club it was proposed to sit in a circle on the ground, to sing a song and, with the chorus at the end of every stanza, to beat the ground with their hats. It was put to vote. The majority ruled. The song was sung and the hats battered. The joke of this boisterous merriment was in the fact that one of the party, a raw member or guest, wore a new beaver of which he seemed proud while the rest of the company brandished their old hats that were none the worse for the sand or the beating.

At another time a foreigner, very timid about insurrections, made one of the meeting. It was the period when the horrors of St. Domingo were in every mouth. An alarm was given, every one pretended to be frightened, the stranger took to the woods; guns were fired and yells and other noises kept up during the night. The next morning, the victim was found in a tree half-dead with fear and shivering with cold. He was consoled by being told that the attempt had failed and that they had escaped the threatened danger. Many more similar tales of the old campaigners in the seven years war I have heard related by one who had taken no inactive part in the sport.

At this period it was customary to lock the door at dinner parties in the city. No man was permitted to leave the room. The close of the feast found the weaker vessels under the table. The stronger heads staggered, or were assisted, home. It was to escape from one of these potations that Marion, it is said, leapt from a window during the siege of Charleston and broke his leg. The accident compelled him to leave the city and was the means of giving his partizan services to the State. We may infer from the incident that there happened occasionally other revolts besides the great Revolution against legitimate authority.

During the prevalence of these customs of the good old times I can remember seeing the veterans of the day, after dining with one of the party, going the rounds to each other's houses, as long as they could walk, drinking and breaking the wine glasses and tumblers. In addition to the drinking and swearing there was much laxity of morals in various ways. Religion was very little regarded. Church going was for the most confined to the women. They are always better behaved

than their lords. Sunday was a day of boat-racing, foot-racing, drinking and fighting. The Negroes from the country assembled in town
and broils were common among them. . . . Quarter-races and cock-
fighting were popular amusements. . . . Seven years of war and licence
had not strengthened self-denial or led to the control of appetites and
passions, whatever effect they may have had in promoting the exercise
of other virtues.

There was one evil custom which the war had served specially to
promote and which time and increasing civilization have greatly
modified and lessened. Duelling was common. For many years after
the close of the Revolution, the professed duellist was a popular member of society however mischievous his influence. He was the incarna-
tion of cool, systematic, deliberate homicide. Expert at the pistol, he
kept his hand in by assiduous practice. He was usually detested by
the better part of the community but was every where tolerated. . . .

The comparative rudeness of manners in the time of the Revolution and immediately after may be illustrated from another point of
view—from an incident exhibiting the barbarity of judicial proceedings
in the good old times. In the early part of the century I happened to
be near the scene of a Negro conspiracy. It was not far from the plantation of Major Hazzard on the Euhaw. Major Hazzard was the first
cousin of my father, their mothers being sisters, and he had taken me,
a boy of sixteen, on a visit to Hazzard Hall. While there I saw a neighbour of the Major's ride up to the house, late in the day, and hold a
whispered conference with my host. The visitor went away in a few
minutes and that night the guns were taken at bed time from the
parlour to the chambers. It was not a common proceeding. I heard
the reason for it the next day. There was a rumor afloat of a threatened
insurrection among the slaves. But like almost every other plot of the
kind, the scheme failed. Information was given by one of the Negroes,
wiser or more timid than the rest. The ringleaders were seized a few
hours before the time appointed for the outbreak. They were tried
without delay, and ten or a dozen condemned to be hanged. Their
heads were cut off, stuck on poles and set up along the highway leading
from Purrysburg, the place of trial, to Coosawhatchie, the judicial capital of the District. The sight was so disgusting that some of the
younger people refused to bear it. They so far disregarded the majesty
of the law as to take down the hideous butcher's work and bury it
where it stood. . . .

Charles Cotesworth Pinckney

"SENT THE BOAT A DRUM FISHING"

Pinckney Island, lying between Hilton Head Island and the main-land, came into the possession of the Pinckney family in 1734. Earlier it was known as Mackey's Island.

Charles Cotesworth Pinckney inherited the island from his father, Charles Pinckney, in 1758. Sea-island cotton was the staple crop of the three plantations, called Old Place, Cresent and The Point.

The drum fish referred to in the extracts from his diary were said to range in weight from thirty to eighty-five pounds. "The smaller fish were highly esteemed for both the meat and the roe; the larger ones, when properly cured, were not unlike the cod in flavor," writes the editor of the diary.

General Pinckney was seventy-two years of age when he visited his island in 1818. He was then a Charleston attorney. He had served his state and country in many distinguished positions: as commander of Fort Moultrie during the siege of Charles Town; as a member of the Constitutional Convention of 1787; as Minister to France in 1796. He declined President Washington's appointment to the Supreme Court, and later appointments as Secretary of War and Secretary of State. He was the Federalist candidate for President in 1804 and again in 1808.

The original diary is the property of the College of Charleston. It was edited by Dr. J. H. Easterby, director of the South Carolina Archives.

[Pinckney Island,] April 7th [1818]. Arrived at the island about nine o'clock this morning. Sent the boat a drum fishing and caught 7 drum. Gave a drum to each of the overseers and one among the fishermen.

April 8th. Sent the small yawl a fishing with George, Handy and Little Abram from the Old Place and York and Dago from the Cresent; they caught four dozen shrimps for bait last night and 14 drum fish today. Gave two to the fishermen.

April 9th. The fishermen caught 3 dozen shrimps as bait last night. Captain Bythewood landed the articles from Charleston this morning. Took out of the storeroom over the kitchen 8 hams, 4 shoulders and 8 sides and out of a box in the smoke house 1 ham and 2 shoulders and hung them up to smoke. Mr. Cannon sent to-day the meat of three hogs (with the hog's lard well-cured). Mr. Johnston sent to-day the meat of three hogs (with the hog's lard) well-cured. Put the whole in boxes in the store room over the kitchen. Mr. Johnston sent yesterday one dozen fowls, four dozen eggs and one half bushel of corn for the pigeons. Mr. Cannon sent yesterday 2 fowls and one dozen and one eggs. Sent Captain Rogers of the steamboat a cauliflower, three white brocoli and a drum fish. . . . Gave three to the fishermen and one to each of the overseers. Twenty-three were in the whole caught.

April 10th. The fishermen caught fourteen drum. Gave two to the fishermen.

April 11th. Gave to the Negroes of each plantation 14 heads, 19 backbones and 37 sides of drum fish. . . . The fishermen caught 15 drum. Gave the fishermen two drums.

April 12th. Gave to the Negroes of both plantations and at the Point, pipes, tobacco and salt.

April 13th. The fishermen caught 10 drum fish. Gave one to each of the overseers. . . .

April 15th. Cupid's Abram and Ned from the Old Place and Kitt and Dick from the Cresent commenced today fishing for drum. The fishermen caught five drum fish. Gave one between them.

April 16th. . . . The fishermen did not catch a single fish to-day. . . .

April 17th. . . . The fishermen caught five drum to-day. Gave one between them, and one to each of the overseers.

April 18th. The two cows fed at the pen gave five quarts of milk this morning. The three cows out gave four quarts. There was a great deal of thunder, lightning and hail last night. The fishermen caught six drum to-day. Gave one among them.

April 19th. Gave to the Negroes of each plantation 12 sides, 8 backs and 2 heads. . . .

April 24th. The fishermen caught no drum, but one turtle. . . .

April 25th. The fishermen changed their situation to-day to the northward of the Devil's Elbow, but still caught no drum. . . .

Carolina Gazette

PRESIDENT MONROE VISITS BEAUFORT

Beaufort was the third South Carolina city to welcome James Monroe when he toured the South in 1819. After leaving Washington on March 30, the President had stopped at Norfolk, Wilmington, Charleston and Georgetown. Before he got back to the White House in August, he would be feted in Savannah, Augusta, Tennessee via the Cherokee Nation, Louisville and Lexington.

In his official party were his private secretary, Samuel L. Gouvernour, and the distinguished Secretary of War, John C. Calhoun, and family.

Dr. R. B. Screvin was chairman of the Beaufort occasion. The Carolina Gazette story was printed on Saturday May 15.

On Tuesday the 3d inst. information having been received that the President of the United States would honor the town of Beaufort with a visit, a deputation of citizens were requested by the Town Council and a committee of citizens to meet him on his route, to inquire when it would suit His Excellency to reach Port Republic Ferry. At Mrs. Radcliffe's, a distance of about 31 miles, the committe met him at 8 o'clock at night, and were instructed by his private secretary that he would be with us in the afternoon of the succeeding day.

This information being received, the citizens generally, at a very short notice, assembled on horseback, and at 6 miles from the town had the grateful satisfaction to behold the Chief Magistrate of the

Union. On his approach, the chairman of the committee advanced and welcomed him in behalf of the inhabitants of Port Royal Island. On entering the town he was handsomely saluted by a company of artillery, commanded by Capt. Burke, and received the salutations of the Intendant, by deputation, who regretted that indisposition prevented his waiting on him. The President was then conducted, through the greetings of all classes of citizens, to a comfortable dwelling provided by the city.

After receiving some refreshments, the City Council and committee of arrangement waited on him, and, through their chairman, Dr. Screvin, delivered the following Address:—

MR. PRESIDENT,

In behalf of the Town Council and Citizens of Beaufort, permit me to welcome the Chief Magistrate of the Union. In a visit to a place of minor importance, in a commercial point of view, we recognize a patriarchal regard to the whole American family. The town of Beaufort, from the general salubrity of its climate, and convenience of the bar and harbor, presents great inducements to a maritime foe to make it a place of rendezvous.

In a country where a people are the legitimate dispensers of rewards due to merit, your great patriotism and unwearied exertions are duly appreciated. Your fellow citizens have witnessed your various gradations, through an useful life, with the highest applause. In war, Sir, you were the associate of the great Washington, in praise of whom eulogy is dumb. In your diplomatic character you well sustained the interest and honor of your country. On your return home your illustrious predecessor at a crisis peculiarly interesting, called you to fill one of the most important departments of government. The duties of a second you did not shrink from. The last reward which a free people have to give, you now hold.

Nations seem at length inclined to regard our just rights and moderate claims. The Floridas, heretofore the fruitful source of annoyance and suspicion, particularly to the Southern States, will hereafter have rank in the American family. The unhappy of Europe, attracted by our political rights and the fruitfulness of our soil, are hastening to our shores, adding thereby strength to the nation. Every where the unprofitable forests are fast yielding to the luxuriant cultivation.

When increasing years shall admonish you to relinquish the cares of government, may you long live in peaceful retirement with Adams, Jefferson and Madison, to witness the growing prosperity of your country! On the remaining part of your tour—our hearts go with you. May a kind Providence guard you from evil and, after a grateful and happy interview with your fellow citizens, conduct you safely into your native state!

To which the President was pleased to reply:

To R. B. Screvin, chairman of the committee in behalf of the town council and citizens of Beaufort:

On the same principles and for similar purposes that I have taken a view of the ports of our maritime frontier north of this, have I visited Beaufort and shall examine its harbor and approaches from the ocean. Every part of the coast had a strong claim to attention, and it has been my object, so far as it has been practicable, to meet that claim. For your kind reception and attention, accept my grateful acknowledgment.

The spectacle of prosperity which is now exhibited to the admiring world by the United States cannot fail to be highly gratifying to the philanthropist of every country: a people in the full enjoyment of every right, and strangers to every kind of oppression; increasing harmony at home and increasing respect abroad; agriculture and commerce flourishing; our population expanding on principles which increase, rather than diminish, our national strength. These are blessings for which we ought to be profoundly grateful to the Supreme Author of all good. To what causes they are justly imputable, there is no diversity of sentiment among us. All unite in ascribing them to the excellence of the free government under which we live. Let us then unite in cherishing the principles of that government. Let us unite in promoting intelligence and virtue among the people, as the present foundation and best means of supporting it.

From the acquisition of Florida, I anticipate, with you, the most favorable consequences, among which may be considered the security in which it places our peaceful relations with Spain. It must afford to us all a peculiar satisfaction that it has been obtained by amicable arrangement, and on conditions honourable to both nations.

To have been placed by my fellow citizens in the highest trust in their power to confer, is the best proof which they could give of their approbation of my public conduct. To merit the continuance of their favorable opinion will be the object of my unwearied labors, looking always in my future retirement for the consolation so eminently enjoyed by my illustrious predecessors as the best reward for toils and cares—an approving conscience and an approving country.

JAMES MONROE

Beaufort, S. C., May 7, 1819

The succeeding day, the President, in a carriage provided for him, attended by his suite and Colonels Condy and Ford and a number of citizens, made a visit to Fort Marion. On his return to town the citizens generally were presented to him—all received his hand with the most gratifying emotions, because all love him. A 5 o'clock he partook of a dinner provided by the citizens of the College, at which a number of patriotic toasts were drank.

About 8 o'clock His Excellency retired to his drawing room, where he received an elegant assemblage of ladies in a most affable manner. This morning at an early hour, himself and suite, General Gaines and his suite, and the Governor's aids, some strangers, and a few elderly citizens, partook of a breakfast with Doctor Screvin. At about 9 o'clock, he bid adieu to us in an elegant 10-oared canoe provided for the occasion by the city—the Charleston city barge in which General Gaines and family had arrived and General Pinckney's barge in company, on their way to Savannah. After a review of the harbour and inlet, the President, we understand, will pass this night with the venerable General Pinckney on Pinckney's Island; and tomorrw resume his route by way of Colleton Neck.

Carolina Gazette

BEAUFORT CELEBRATES THE ANNIVERSARY OF AMERICAN INDEPENDENCE

A truly great and bibulous celebration! All present must have joined enthusiastically in the gracious toast volunteered by a Mr. Ludlow of New York: "The inhabitants of Beaufort, characterized for

*hospitality and social virtues—may the smiles of Hebe and Ceres ever
greet them."*

*That glorious sportsman, Mr. William Elliott, whom we shall hap-
pily meet again, presided over the festivities, including the thirty-one
toasts which were punctiliously recorded by the* Carolina Gazette *of*
Charleston *on Saturday July 17, 1819.*

BEAUFORT, S. C., July 6, 1819

The following toasts were drank on the 5th inst. at the celebration
of the anniversary of American Independence by a number of citizens
of Beaufort:—

1. The Fourth of July—The Day that Liberty consecrates to herself: let tyrants tremble at the thought.

2. Independence—Our sacred heritage, 'twas achieved by the blood
of our fathers—by our own shall it be defended.

3. The memory of Washington—The records of departed worth
furnish not his parallel, and time as it increases the number of contrasts
adds lustre to his character.

4. The Constitution of the United States—Embodying the accu-
mulated wisdom of ages, may it become the political creed of every
American.

5. The Federal Union—May it receive daily strength by an increasing unanimity of sentiment and feeling.

6. James Monroe—The President in whom rival parties have become amalgamated.

7. The American Navy—In whose stripes we behold the rainbow,
which betokens freedom on the ocean.

8. The Officers and Soldiers of the late war—Who in acquiring
"deathless fame" for themselves exalted the character of their country.

9. Our Naval Warriors—The glory which encircles them flashes a
new light upon the world: it enables our own government to discern
the natural defences of a commercial nation, and it beams a portentous
ray upon our future enemies.

10. The Governor of the State of S. Carolina.

11. The Hon. Wm. Lowndes—The enlightened statesman and
firm patriot. His country wishes him a safe return.

12. The Hon. Langdon Cheves, President of the Bank of the United

States—His powerful genius has restored order to an institution which was fast resolving into chaos.

13. Internal Improvement—May the shores of Port Royal soon be washed by the waters of the Savannah.

14. The Literary Institutions of the United States—May they ever be distinguished for virtue and sound learning.

15. The East India trade—The vampyre that feeds upon the blood of our republic.

16. Patriots of South America—May success crown your exertions! In your struggles for freedom you have the sympathy of freemen.

17. Gen. C. C. Pinckney—The veteran soldier, the patriotic statesman, the virtuous sage.

18. The memory of the gallant Lieut. Archibald Hamilton, who fell in defence of the "Star Spangled Banner"—*"Dulce et decorum est pro patria mori."*

19. The Heroes of the Lake—Their fame, like the voice of Niagara's cataract, shall speak to the latest posterity.

20. The present genial season—The sure harbinger of health and plenty.

21. The fair sex—
"Without our hopes, without our fears,
Without the home that blighted love endears,
Without the smile from partial beauty won,
Oh what were man? a world without a Sun."

The following, among others, were drank as volunteer toasts:—

By William Elliott, Esq., President of the day—May the virtue with which our government is administered be equal to the wisdom with which it has been framed.

By Stobo R. Perry, Esq., Vice-President—Our fellow citizens throughout the Union now engaged in celebrating this glorious day— May the Fourth of July be the National Jubilee of America, till time shall be no more.

By Mr. Ludlow, from New-York—The inhabitants of Beaufort, characterized for hospitality and social virtue—may the smiles of Hebe and Ceres ever greet them.

By B. G. Allston, Esq.—Woman—"The Divinity that shapes our ends rough-hew them how we will."

By Dr. J. D. Guerard—The Union of the States, the Gordian knot of our Independence—May there never arise an Alexander to cut it asunder.

By Mr. E. Barnwell—The memory of Gen. Alexander Hamilton, truly the favorite of both Minervas.

By Dr. A. S. Moore—Maj. Gen. Gaines—The waters of Erie may run dry, but the gallant victory obtained on its banks can never be forgotten.

By Dr. Stewart—Our Country—May neither the fame nor the services of the violators of its Constitution protect them from punishment.

By Mr. W. Barnwell—Gen. Huger—The firm and bold asserter of the interests of his country.

By Dr. Fuller—The Hon. John C. Calhoun.

LAFAYETTE COMES TO THE SEA ISLANDS

General Lafayette's Southern tour in 1825 led him along the inland water route from Charleston to Savannah. Accompanying him were his son, George Washington Lafayette, and his secretary, Auguste Levasseur.

On Edisto Island he was the guest of Mr. William Seabrook, whose baby daughter was christened Carolina Lafayette during the festivities.

At Beaufort Lafayette was entertained by John Mark Verdier. The Verdier house was built on the "bay," where within a stone's throw the owner could look out on his own ships moored to his own wharf on Beaufort River (called also Port Royal River). Ever since then it has been known as the "Lafayette House."

Levasseur tells about Lafayette's visit to Edisto, and the Southern Patriot and Commercial Advertiser, *of Charleston, about the one to Beaufort.*

Auguste Levasseur

[March 1825]

Before we lost sight of Charleston, we directed our course towards the fort on Sullivan's Island, which saluted General Lafayette with all its guns. . . .

We then proceeded on our course, involving ourselves between the

Above: The Ruins of Sheldon Church. The church was twice burned, first by the British during the Revolution and then by Sherman's army in 1865.

Below: Another View of the Ruins of Sheldon Church

THE SITE OF
PURRYSBURGH
THE SETTLEMENT OF
SWISS AND HUGUENOTS
ESTABLISHED HERE IN 1733

Purrysburg Monument

St. Helena Episcopal Church, Beaufort

Courtesy of Frank H. Ramsey

Above: A Rural Businessman's Non-sport Coupe, Lady's Island, S.C.

Below: Approach to the Golden Eagle

Courtesy of James W. Busch

Courtesy of James W. Busch

Lafayette House, Beaufort. The home of John Mark Verdier when Lafayette
was entertained there in 1825. Since that time it has
been known as the Lafayette House.

Courtesy of James W. Busch

Above: Shrimp Boats, Beaufort Dock

Below: The Beaufort Water Front

Courtesy of James W. Busch

Above: The Great Expedition on the Way to Port Royal Inlet, October 1861

Above: The Bombardment of Forts Walker and Beauregard, November 1861
Below: The Landing of United States Troops at Fort Walker
After the Bombardment

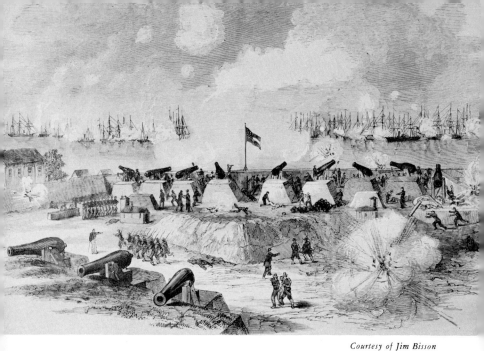

Above: Fort Walker under Bombardment. View of the Interior

Above: Interior of the United States Hospital at Hilton Head, S.C.
Below: Government Buildings Erected on Hilton Head by the
Federal Forces under General Sherman

continent and the islands with which it is lined, all the way to Savannah. We landed on one of these, called Edisto, where General Lafayette was expected. As it was impossible for him to remain there more than two or three hours, the inhabitants, who were collected at one of the principal proprietors', decided to offer him at once all the festivals they had prepared for several days. We had, at the same time, the harangue, the public dinner, the ball and even the baptism of a charming little infant, to which the name of "Lafayette" was given. We then rapidly traversed the island in carriages to join our steamboat, which awaited us on the side next to the ocean.

What we saw of the island in this short ride appeared to us enchanting. The vegetation was particularly striking because of its variety. Odoriferous shrubs of the most elegant forms were agreeably interspersed among large forest trees, and on the downs which border the seashore we saw some beautiful palm trees, which gave to the small dwellings they shaded an aspect altogether picturesque. This island, which lies at the mouth of the Edisto River, forty miles southwest of Charleston, is twelve miles in length and five broad. . . .

During the remainder of our voyage to Savannah, we passed the islands of Hunting, Beaufort, Port Republican, Hilton Head, etc., and often through channels so narrow that the sides of our vessels almost touched the land on each side—and it had rather the appearance of rolling over the prairies that surrounded it than of gliding upon the water that disappeared beneath. It was almost midnight when we passed near Beaufort, and every one on board was asleep, but we were soon awakened by the cries of the citizens, who still awaited us on the shore; and General Lafayette, having risen, acceded to the wish they expressed to him, of landing for a short time. . . .

Southern Patriot and Commercial Advertiser, March 23, 1825

The General was expected to arrive at Beaufort on the morning of the 18th, but did not reach there until half past 10 o'clock on the night of that day. He was received by a committee of the citizens, consisting of Dr. James Stuart and Messrs. John A. Stuart, Richard DeTreville, and by the Beaufort Artillery and Volunteer Guards. As the steam boat came in front of the town, a salute of 13 guns was fired; and the committee was introduced to the General by the Hon. James Hamilton.[2] He was then conducted to the reception room—the military and the carriages (in which were the General and his family and the military gentlemen that accompanied him from this place) forming a procession, preceded by music. The carriages were flanked on the right and left by the Beaufort Volunteer Artillery in single file. A detachment of the St. Luke's Troop of Cavalry and the officers of the battalion mounted, under the command of Maj. Jacobs, flanked the whole procession.

The General passed through a Triumphal Arch, illuminated for the occasion. On his reaching the reception room, he was welcomed by an Address from Wm. Elliott, Esq., Intendant, to which the General replied. He was then led to the Ball Room, where several ladies and gentlemen were assembled to receive him; and, after remaining about three hours, he was reconducted to the landing, in the same order of procession, and left the town of Beaufort, accompanied by the regrets of the inhabitants that his engagements permitted so short a stay among them.

PLANTATION MISSIONS

In 1712 the Parish of St. Helena received the first of a number of missionaries from "The Society for the Propagation of the Gospel in Foreign Parts." This Society, under the Church of England, was incorporated during the reign of William III.

After the Revolutionary War, the evangelization of the slaves on the cotton and rice plantations continued, the first contributions coming from the slaveholders themselves. "The enterprise gained momentum with such rapidity that at the time of the Civil War it was easily the most significant missionary effort in the world. All of the churches were interested and all contributed to the movement, but the

---

[2] James Hamilton, Jr., was born in Charleston, 1786; served in the War of 1812 as major; elected to Congress, 1822-1829; Governor, 1830-1832. He came down from Washington to be with Lafayette. The Charleston *City Gazette*, March 3, 1825, had quoted him: "From Charleston, on his way to Savannah, the General has promised me that he will touch at Edisto Island, to receive the salutations of my constituents. . . ."

Methodist . . . made what appears to be the most significant contribution. . . ."[3]

Reverend George W. Moore

The Pon Pon Mission, when I took charge of it, embraced Col. Morris's place on the Bluff, with several places on the other side of the river belonging to the estate, and Gov. Aiken's[4] place on Jehossee Island. I generally preached in an old cooper shop opposite the Bluff place, where the Negroes from all the other plantations attended. Here we usually held a sunrise prayer meeting and catechised the children from the estate place. . . . The Negroes from the Bluff and the estate all worshipped in the cooper shop, and O how often has my heart rejoiced in their joy at the knowledge of the gospel of Christ Jesus.

Col. Morris and others would attend sometimes with their families and with the overseers and their families, and often around the same altar you could see several of those white persons mingling their cries for mercy with those of the blacks, and many together found the pearl of great price. . . .

We generally preached at the estate place in the morning, and in the afternoon at Jehossee. Here we preached in a room next to the hospital, so that the sick might hear as well as those who were not sick. Gov. Aiken was exceeding kind to us; so was his overseer, Mr. Bagwell. The first letter I received from Gov. Aiken, inclosing his donation of $100, impressed me sensibly.

The overseers would generally send up to the estate place for us a large boat rowed by six or eight hands. I remember a conversation that took place between Dr. Capers[5] and one of the hands on the boat. The Doctor asked him, among other things, how he liked the overseer, which is the test question among the Negroes. In reply he

---

[3] Mason Crum, *Gullah: Negro Life in the Carolina Sea Islands*. Durham, North Carolina: Duke University Press, 1940, p. 198.

[4] William Aiken, Governor of South Carolina, 1844-1846; U.S. Congress, 1851-1857.

[5] Dr. William Capers, the first superintendent and chief exponent of plantation missions, and later Bishop of the Methodist Church.

said: "Massa he good man; he nebber promise nuffin he no gib you.
If he promise you whippin', you's as sho' to git 'em as if you had 'em on
you' back."

I soon found the secret of the good government on this place; it
was decision of character. I visited it at all times during the year, and
I never, to my recollection, heard the overseer swear, get in passion,
or whip a Negro during all that period, and it was all because the
Negroes understood that he meant what he said, and a promise was
as good as performed.

In preaching at Mr. Charles Baring's we occupied a room near to
his dwelling. Adjoining this was another of smaller dimensions, where
the white persons who attended sat, among whom could generally be
seen Mr. and Mrs. Baring, who took a deep interest in the welfare of
their people. I have often seen Mrs. Baring, when the Negroes were
singing, catch the motion of their bodies and do just as they did. On
one occasion, when I was taking my seat at the dinner table, Mr.
Baring took my hand and, . . . said, with emphasis: "Sir, this must do
good, it will do good, it *shall* do good." And he pressed my hand very
warmly in his.

At another time, when about leaving for their summer residence,
they asked me to retire with them to a private room and there engage
in prayer for the salvation of their people.

On one occasion I preached to a British admiral, who was an
American-born citizen on a visit to the family. He sat in the rear of
the Negroes and was quite attentive during the service.

Mr. Baring was most generous in the support of the mission, and I
believe at one time carried it entirely. His good wife was not one whit
behind him in zeal.

The Beaufort Mission was attached to the Combahee and Pon Pon
in 1832, and John R. Coburn sent with me to serve the work. The
Beaufort Mission had its origin through a religious revival that took
place among the Baptists and Episcopalians in Beaufort and vicinity,
instigated by Rev. Mr. Daniel Baker, a Presbyterian minister. The
stores were closed and business in the town suspended for several
days, so great was the interest taken. This revival caused the planters,
several of whom made Beaufort their summer residence, to turn their
attention to the condition of their slaves. Not being able to get the
services of an Episcopal or Baptist minister, they, through the influence
of Mr. Pinckney, who at the time had the services of a Methodist

minister on his plantation on the Santee, applied to our Conference for help, and Beaufort Island was taken in along with Combahee, Pon Pon and Wappahoola, the mission having that name at the time.

One pleasing part of the Beaufort work was that the young ladies took quite an active part in the instruction of the colored children, both in Beaufort and on the plantations of their fathers. Frequently I found them under the shade of the spreading oak, with a group of little Negroes around them, instructing them in the catechism. The planters too were active in the work. Some of the wealthiest and most distinguished gentlemen would spend every Sabbath afternoon in imparting religious instruction to the Negroes, young and old.

I commenced my labors in Beaufort by preaching to the Negroes in the old Tabernacle Church, which belonged to the Baptists, and holding prayer meetings, with the assistance of a few Christian gentlemen, in the Episcopal lecture room. We soon enjoyed as great a revival among the colored people as there had been among the whites. I extended my labors to Paris, Cat, St. Helena, Dathan, Coosa, Lady's, Beaufort, and Big islands, and on the mainland, where we soon enjoyed much prosperity. I left the converts free to join the church of their choice. At one time, with my full consent, over two hundred of them were added to the Baptist church.

The mission was similar to a circuit; I went regularly round, week day and Sunday. We preached on Paris Island on Sunday, the Negroes from all the plantations attending. We had no church building at that time, but occupied a house on the plantation of our patron, Mr. Robert Means. We would also preach at some of the other places at night. I recollect on one occasion preaching with a Negro holding a lightwood torch at my back to throw light on my Bible and hymn-book. At first we preached at two or three places on the island on Sunday, as we confined our labors a good deal to plantation preaching. We catechised during the week, and also preached at several places on week days. Robert Means, Esq., Dr. Thomas Fuller, Rev. S. Elliott, Mrs. Habersham and William Eddings owned the entire island, and we had access to all the plantations.

From Paris Island we went to Cat Island, owned by Rev. R[ichard] Fuller. Here we preached on week nights, the Negroes assembling in a vacant house on the place. On one occasion when Brother Coburn preached, the Negroes were so much pleased . . . that they begged him to remain for the next day and preach again. This he consented to, and

at an early hour the place was filled. One fact I have often noticed is
that not only on the cotton but also on the rice plantations those
Negroes who are industrious can accomplish their task during the
hoeing season by the middle of the day, and thus have the afternoon
to themselves.

Our next appointment was on St. Helena Island at Rev. Mr. Field's,
Col. Stapleton's, and Dr. Scott's. From there we went to Dathan,
owned by Dr. B. Sams and Mr. L. Sams, his brother. At the different
places on Dathan we preached at night and catechised the children
during the day. At Dr. Sams's, however, we preached on a week day,
the Negroes coming out of the fields to assemble at the appointed time
in a large cotton house. At the close of the services the smaller Negroes
would remain to be catechised. At Mr. L. Sams's we preached at night
and had some most attentive hearers. Here there was soon erected a
very comfortable house of worship.

From Dathan we crossed to Mr. Barnwell's place on Coosa Island
and preached at night, and then crossed over to Lady's Island in a
canoe, swimming our horses alongside the boat. Here we also preached
at another of Mr. Sams's places.

On Beaufort Island, where my family lived, we preached at Mr.
Josiah Smith's plantation, at the Misses Elliott's, and the place now
owned by Mr. L. Sams. All these appointments were on Sunday. We
also preached at Rev. Mr. Barnwell's on Laurel Bay, Broad River.
Rev. Mr. Barnwell commenced his ministerial career by preaching to
his own blacks and holding prayer meetings with them every morning
before sunrise. We also had an appointment at a place called Myrtle
Bush in an old brick dwelling. Here we had some refreshing times.

While preaching at this place once, in reference to besetting sins,
I touched upon a sin then prevalent among them, that of taking cotton out of the house and carrying it to the field and bringing it back
at night, saying that they had picked it. While speaking a woman fell
upon her knees and looked very earnestly at me, as if to question:
"How did you find that out?"

One of the most flourishing places on the mission was Big Island,
owned by Mr. Thomas Cuthbert, who was greatly interested for his
people, and among the most liberal patrons of the work. He very soon
built a comfortable church, and allowed his people to attend week
days as well as Sundays. On preaching days he would not permit any
of his people to do anything to interfere with the hour of service.

Every time we visited his place he gave up the labor of sixty hands for half the day. On this place I baptized thirty at one time, twenty-nine by immersion and one, the driver, by pouring. Mr. Cuthbert and his little daughter, he being a widower, were generally present at the church. He would always commune with his people.

In going to and fro on my work on the mission, I have ridden horse-back, in a gig, and often on a Negroe's back. Sometimes it would be in a boat pushed through the mud. Often I have had to be pushed some distance through the mud to get to water to baptize the Negroes.

Our great enemy was superstition, which prevailed to an alarming extent. Idolatry too entered greatly into Negro worship. . . .

Reverend Charles Wilson

I spent four years on the Pon Pon Mission. At the end of that time, my health being sadly impaired through repeated attacks of fever, I was given an assistant, Brother Nathan Bird. Having now more leisure, I was again pressed with the old desire to add new fields to my work. Through the invitation of Col. Morris, who had his summer home at Edingsville, I now began preaching on Edisto Island. I found the fields white to the harvest, and the planters almost unanimous in their de-sire to have the work of evangelization pushed among their people. One of them, Mr. J. J. Mikell, had already gone so far as to erect a comfortable chapel on one of his plantations, not knowing whom he might get to serve his people.

My first preaching appointment on this island, the second Sunday in October, 1840, was a memorable one to me. Mrs. Townsend, a zealous and pious member of the Baptist Church, and its most active member on the island, invited me, there being no pastor in charge, to preach at her church. At the hour appointed I reached the building in company with Col. Morris, at whose home I was staying, and found a large collection of blacks and a considerable number of the planters. I next had an invitation from Mr. Lee, the Presbyterian minister, to preach in his church. I again had a crowded house and spoke with much freedom. The day following I returned home with the deep conviction that here was a promising door for mission work waiting to be opened. The mission was subsequently established, and I have been sent to serve it. Six hundred dollars a year for the support of the missionary was readily subscribed by Messrs. J. J. Mikell, William Seabrook, Maj. Murray, and the Messrs. M. A. and S. Seabrook.

I had on the Edisto Mission, to begin with, six preaching places and eleven plantations to serve. One of these was Gov. Aiken's place on Jehossee Island, which for convenience sake was taken from the Pon Pon Mission and attached to the Edisto. Unlike Edisto, which is a cotton-growing island, Jehossee is most a rice plantation and owned entirely by Gov. Aiken. It is naturally a part of Edisto, but has been made into a separate island by the opening of a creek by a canal connecting the two rivers.

The mission on Jehossee had from the first been one of the most promising in the bounds of the Conference. I became acquainted with it in 1834, my first year in the mission fields; and from then to the present time, a period of twenty-two years, I have preached regularly on the place, with the exception of 1837 and '38, when it was in charge of Dr. Boyd.

There is quite a commodious chapel on this island, which has been erected by Gov. Aiken as a place of worship for his blacks. At first it stood in a grove of live oaks on the lawn in front of his dwelling; but his plantation enlarging, it was subsequently removed to a more central spot. Here an addition of twenty feet was made to the building, which had become too small to accommodate the crowds. A portico has also been attached to the front. This chapel has a bell, and a regular sexton in attendance. The occasion is rare when it is not filled to the door with the blacks, with the exception of a small space reserved for the whites. In this church alone sixty-two couples of blacks have been united by the sacred ties of Christian marriage. I recollect to have married here at one time five couples....

One of my most important fields on the Edisto Island Mission was the plantation of Mr. J. J. Mikell. He had a new and commodious chapel which was largely attended. Though a firm and decided Presbyterian, Mr. Mikell nevertheless gave his hearty and unswerving support to the Methodist mission. Always, when at home, he and his family attended the preaching at the Negro chapel. He was an exceedingly liberal man. Unaided he built a mission house at a cost of $300 in the village, besides providing a winter residence for me nearly all the time of my stay.

In the plantation of Mr. Edward Whaley we had another interesting class. He too was a most liberal patron of the mission.

My labors for the first two years on the Edisto Mission were hard, preaching once a fortnight at all my appointments, and catechising the children and visiting the sick and aged during the week. I have on some occasions preached five sermons and ridden on horseback forty-five miles all in a day, leaving home at 4 o'clock in the morning and returning at 8 in the evening, sometimes much later. But the Lord mercifully supported me through it all. . . .

Reverend A. M. Chreitzberg

In the year 1843, which was the fifth of my itinerancy, I was sent to preach the gospel to the slaves on the Beaufort Mission. I was only the junior on the work, that noble old veteran in the cause, Rev. Thomas E. Ledbetter, being the senior.

Both Brother Ledbetter and myself had our families with us, he in his own house at Beaufort and I in a hired one at the same place.

Our work lay in and around Beaufort, principally around it, among the plantations situated upon Lady's Island, Paris Island, Dawfuskie, and others not necessary to mention. These were reached from the mainland by boats which the planters kindly placed at our service. We could cross and recross at any time we pleased.

The plantations served belonged to some of the most prominent families in the state: the Smiths, Barnwells, Cuthberts, Elliotts, etc. With but one or two exceptions the planters were all sincerely in sympathy with the work of evangelization among their slaves. They threw no hindrance in our way, but put forth every effort to interest the Negroes in the religious services. In many instances they and their families were members of other Churches, yet frequently attended our appointments.

During the week myself and colleague visited the different plantations, catechising the children. In some instances there were as many as two or three hundred of these children, all kept together under the care of an elderly female, and orders were given to have them all assembled whenever the preacher came on his catechising rounds. In no instance that I can recall were these children kept away at work or for other purposes during the occasions of the missionary's visit; but, on the other hand, were always assembled, generally smiling and clean for their instruction.

On Sundays we would preach twice, thrice, and even four times a day, to old and young alike. It was no holiday time, this work of a plantation missionary, but one that required the utmost concentration of effort, the most unflagging spirit of zeal, and, in some instances, a self-sacrifice that was heroic. Especially was this true of those whose labors lay among the slaves of the rice plantations. Here their lives were constantly in jeopardy from the deadly miasmatic exhalations of the rice fields; but thanks to the watchful care of a beneficent Providence, and to the retreats afforded by the pine lands, but few of them died. As to the slaves themselves they seemed to thrive better in these localities, owing to their similarity in temperature and topographical features to their own country.

But despite these drawbacks and the many hardships and discouragements with which I had often to meet, my year on the mission was pleasant and of much satisfaction to me. There were many charming families. In the home of one of these especially were many happy hours passed. This was the family of Capt. John Joiner Smith, himself one of nature's truest noblemen. His plantation was known as "Old Fort," and was situated on a bend of the river about five miles distant from Beaufort, and in plain view of the city. The place was so called from the remains of a structure, composed of shells and lime, supposed to have been built by the Spaniards.

Capt. Smith and his wife were Episcopalians, but were both earnestly devoted to the Methodist mission, giving liberally of their substance to its support. They took a personal interest in each slave's spiritual condition, constantly inquiring thereinto with the devotedness of the missionary himself.

At this plantation there was a most comfortable church, which its black members took great delight and pride in adorning for their missionary's coming, with such simple material as the forest gave them. Around the upright posts of the neat pine pulpit their zealous hands would twine the beautiful drapery of the long gray moss, while graceful festoons of the same moss would hang in front with cords and tassels attached, the latter formed by the bur of the pine. In the rear swept the waters of the river, while in a grove that surrounded the building was the burial ground of the Negroes, kept ever clean and neat. Here year after year, ever since the coming of that noble old pioneer, George W. Moore, the founder of the mission in 1833, the slave had been taught of Jesus and the resurrection; had been pointed to the Lamb of God who taketh away the sins of the world. . . .

Another duty of the missionary, in addition to catechising the children and preaching to the adults, was to visit the sick and aged at their cabins. . . . It was on one of these visits that I first became acquainted with old Friday. He was a genuine African, not so long from his native wilds and greegree worship that the shadows of them did not still hover about him. . . .

Friday was fully eighty years old at the time I met him, but his mind was still vivid with memories of his native land. In the clear, peaceful light of the gospel that had come upon him, he was a living illustration of the power of the word of Jesus Christ to tame and make as new creatures of his savage race. All Friday's remembrances of having had any form of religion in his native land was that of prostrating himself when the sun or moon rose, and in crying: "Allah! Allah!" . . .

I asked him if they knew anything about God in his country.

"Dey no t'ink 'pon um; dey t'ink dey mek demself."

Friday rarely attended preaching, his age and infirmities confining him closely to the house. When he did, it was an occasion that made its impression upon all. . . . I could not refrain from asking him if he was sorry he had been brought to this country.

You should have seen his countenance as he replied: "Ough, mausa, buckra country too much better dan Negro country! Too much better! too much better! Negro country you can't go from here to nex' place by yerse'f; Negro meet you in de path; he got knife, he kill you. All you got do in dis country is worrack [work]. Friday got good mausa, good missus; he ole. Friday do not'ing, mausa tek care o' him; anyt'ing Friday want he get um. Berry well den, I jis de wait till de good Massa way up top senna for me."

It was not uncommon often to be sent for to go to see dying Negroes. I thank my Master that I never once turned a deaf ear to any of these calls. Once I performed the burial rite over one of these humble slaves at night. The memory lingers vividly to this day.

I left home about sunset, on a calm and pleasant evening, and took my way along the high bluff of the river. The distance was four or five miles, so that it was dark ere I arrived at the plantation. Just before the dead man's door was the corpse, already in its narrow house. Beside it sat the widow, and to her I addressed myself, bidding her trust in

God. His fellow-servants were seated around, the deep-drawn sigh showing their sorrow for the departed, their sympathy with the bereaved. I addressed them on the uncertainty of life, the necessity of making preparation for death . . . and by the glimmering of the lightwood fire was the burial service read, and the body committed to the dust.

It was after 9 o'clock as I took my way homeward, and passed through the dark avenue of oaks, trusting to the instinct of my horse to find the way, illumined momentarily by the fitful flash of the firefly. It was a time for serious thought, for a communion with the heart and with God. I asked myself if I had tried in every way to fulfill my duty since I had come to these perishing souls to teach them the way, the truth, and the life. Sweet indeed was the whisper that came in answer to that question. Forgotten now were all the pains and toils of the way. . . . I felt that God had indeed been with me; that he had blessed my labors. . . .

William Elliott

DEVIL FISHING AT HILTON HEAD

William Elliott was born at Beaufort in 1788 and died there in 1863. He was an accomplished planter, a successful writer and a famous fisherman. Mr. Elliott's classic on Carolina Sports by Land and Water, *published first in 1859, was widely read and enjoyed by sportsmen from far and near.*

We have met Mr. Elliott before, in the celebration of the Fourth of July at Beaufort, and as a host to General Lafayette.

Bay Point, June 20th, 1844

Came down this afternoon (Thursday), after a rough passage, having been detained at Beaufort until the tide was two-thirds spent, by a very heavy rain.

Friday, 21st.—Went across to Hilton Head to look for devil-fish. Thunder clouds formed while crossing the river at high water; wind southwardly; had just time to land and reach the house, when it poured. At an hour's ebb, partially cleared off; on reaching the landing, saw numbers of devil-fish close into the shore. Put off, but found them shy, showing themselves but a few seconds at a time above water, then disappearing. Could not get a chance to strike, and, after half an hour's trial, put ashore to avoid another thundercloud, which was following exactly in the track of the former. It rained in torrents. After it ceased, returned to Bay Point without seeing any more fish, though I traversed the ground on which they were usually found. It seems to me that I have this day seen twenty different fish; but their stay at the surface is very short—shorter, I think, than when observed later in the season.

Saturday, 22d June.—Reached Hilton Head beach at high water. Two devil-fish were playing off the landing, not thirty yards from shore. Put off after them; the noise of the oars (the water being shallow) seemed to alarm them, and they disappeared. In a short time, some others made their appearance, coming down with the tide from Skull Creek. Did not succeed in calculating their visits to the surface so accurately as to get a throw of the harpoon. After seven or eight fish had passed down with the first ebb, none others appearing, concluded to anticipate them by rowing up to the flats under Pinckney Island. Did not find them there—returned to the beach in front of the avenue at Hilton Head—remained there beyond the time of tide at which they rose the day before—they did not appear. Coasted down to Pope's, and seeing nothing, returned to Bay Point at half ebb, sorely disappointed in my cruise.

Doubtless it is the state of the weather which has produced so great a change in the run of the fish, in so small an interval of time. It was raining on the first day—the wind was off shore; and from both wind and rain, the shrimps and small fish, which are the food of the devil-fish, would congregate near the shore, and hence their appearance in such numbers. On the night of this day, it blew violently from the west, in such a way as to sweep the shores which had been protected the day before; hence, the small fish were driven off, and the devil-fish were not there, because their food was not there. To find subsistence easily and abundantly, is an impulse that pervades all animal life. It is the great law which governs the inferior animals, as well as man. Hunters and fishermen must not lose sight of this rule, but seek their game by seeking their feeding-places.

Some years back, the devil-fish were sought for only in August. Last year, for the first time, in July, and now, it appears, they may be taken in June. I am now convinced, from what I have myself observed, that they visit our inlets not occasionally only, and in limited numbers, but annually and in considerable shoals; and it indicates a very extraordinary want of observation or enterprise in our predecessors that they have not noticed these fish and converted them into objects of sport or profit. There is danger enough in the pastime to give it the highest relish (it is, in fact, whale-fishing in miniature); nor is it objectionable on the score of cruelty: it is not killing in mere wantonness, for the liver yields an oil useful for many agricultural purposes, and the body cut into portions convenient for transportation, and carted out upon the fields, proves an excellent fertilizer of the soil. . . .

Monday, 24th June.—Wind very fresh at northeast. Mr. W. Cuthbert came on board, and we sailed for Hilton Head, and reached the avenue an hour before high water. Saw a devil-fish at the landing and gave chase, but to no purpose—he was apparently feeding, and would show his wings only at long intervals, and for a few seconds at a time; so that before the boat could reach the spot he was gone. He sometimes came very close to the beach (I should say in five feet water), but would sheer off at the approach of the boat. After a fruitless pursuit of an hour, we gave him up, and cruised up to the mouth of Skull Creek. Saw nothing—returned to the landing, and visited the cotton-field. It was now four o'clock, P.M., and full quarter ebb. In a last hope to see them, loitered a while on the beach, when, just as we were making ready to get on board, a shoal of devil-fish came sweeping along the beach, travelling rapidly downward with the tide, and showing themselves more freely than any I had seen this year. I pushed at one that showed his back fairly above water, as he swam; and he sank just before I reached him, and I drove the harpoon at a venture. He had a narrow escape, for the staff struck him.

At this moment, three showed themselves below and one above. I pushed for the latter, and when I approached the spot, I saw the water boiling up like a caldron—from which sign I knew that the fish was throwing his somersets below the surface (in the way which is so very peculiar to them). Making the oarsmen check the headway with their oars, I looked anxiously for a view, when, unexpectedly, I saw the white of his belly far beneath the water, and quite toward the stern. He was thus behind me, but wheeling suddenly to the right, I pitched the harpoon at him, across the oars, and felt a sensation of surprise, as well as pleasure, in finding that I had struck him.

The fish dashed out violently for the channel, and we payed him out thirty fathoms of rope, until, headway being given to the boat, we brought him to a dead pull: and now his motions were very erratic; unlike some I had before struck, he did not take a direct course for the sea, but sometimes drew the boat against the tide—then suddenly turned and ran directly toward us, so as to give slack line. I inferred from these signs, that he was mortally hurt. As often as he approached the Middle Bank and shoaled the water, he drew off in alarm, and would not cross it until he had got to its tail; his course was then for Paris Bank, which suiting well with our intention to land him, if we could, at Bay Point, we did not interrupt.

About this time he came to the surface without being pulled, and showed great distress—and we resolved, then, to draw upon him and get a second harpoon planted. It was after various fruitless efforts, and by shortening the rope as far as we prudently could, that we at length drew him so far up that the dark shadow of his body was indistinctly seen beneath. The second harpoon was now driven, and the gush of blood to the surface showed that it had done its work. We now drew mainly on this second, leaving only a moderate strain upon the first— and after a few convulsive runs, brought him up helplessly to the surface, and with a spear dispatched him outright.

With a hatchet we now cut a hole in one of his feelers, and inserting a rope, passed it to the stern, drawing solely on this, so that the resistance of the fish through the water should be as small as practicable. The wind was now due east, and moderately fresh; we raised both sails, and, helped at the same time by the oars, made some way in our tedious progress of towing our prize to land.

At this time, espied a boat beating down from Beaufort, and on signalizing her, she proved to be that of Col. DeTreville, then on his way to Bay Point. His offer of assistance was accepted, and a tow line being passed to his boat, we landed our fish at the Point exactly at sunset.

This fish measured sixteen feet across, which I suppose to be the medium size of those that visit our waters. . . .

On the first of July, 1846, I launched my boat at Bay Point, and

crossed over to the Hilton Head shore in search of devil-fish. I was
accompanied by Henry M. Stuart, Esq.

It was high water about four o'clock, P.M., and on reaching the landing at Mrs. Elliott's, just as the tide was turning, we saw three or more.
They did not show themselves somersetting for some time, but after a
while began to sport and throw somersets under the water, but so near
to the surface as to show their bellies in the evolution. We saw, I do
not doubt, as many as twenty fish. We counted eleven that leaped entirely out of the water. They were in the channel, and were further
from shore than where we had usually met with them; and, on approaching near to them in our boat, we remarked that those which
leaped entirely out of the water did not again show themselves on the
surface, until they had silently gone a mile or so toward the sea, when
they reappeared, gambolled awhile, threw new somersets, and again
disappeared for a new seaward movement. The fish which were behind came along sporting, until they had reached the spot where the
first had thrown their somersets. They, too, then threw their somersets
and disappeared like the first. Usually they leaped twice—leaping from
their backs, and falling likewise on their backs; leaping, I should say,
at least ten feet above the water.

After some delay (for early in the season they do not stand the
point), I struck a fish, which resisted very moderately for a good half
hour, when it made some furious runs, giving me to think that the
sharks had gotten the scent of his blood and were in fierce pursuit.
The winds had been hard from the south for several days, and the
weather was now so squally and threatening that I became anxious to
complete the capture of the fish before night; so I planted a second
harpoon, and then, as occasion offered, gave him the spear. When
drawn up alongside, he began to make short, circular runs, and twisted
the two ropes together, so that they could not be separated. The
thunder muttered, and the dark cloud still approached us from the
southwest, spreading its wings beyond us on every side, so as to leave
no chance of escape; so we had to force him on the lines, and draw
the fish close up to the boat. When the lurching from the high sea
snapped off, first one, and then the other of the stout ropes, leaving
both harpoons fixed in the fish, which was thus uselessly killed. Soon
as we were released, we pushed for the shore at Bay Point, which we
scarcely reached before the storm was down upon us.

Thursday, 2d July.—Set out on another cruise to-day. The weather threatening; wind blowing fresh from the south. . . . Saw but few leap to-day; did not find them so numerous under the Hilton Head shore. Struck at one while somersetting below the surface; the harpoon bounded off without entering; probably it encountered the fore part of the head, in which point they are invulnerable. Soon after, found myself in a group where four were sporting. Pushed at one on the right; he disappeared, when a very large fish unexpectedly rose to my left, and showed himself so fairly that I unadvisedly pitched the harpoon into him.

The first draw of the rope—*was across my neck!* Not so pleasant that. Spinning myself out of the coil, I leaped clear of it, and he ran out the whole line before we checked him with the weight of the boat. Like the fish struck the day before, he made some violent runs, and left us this time no doubt as to the cause; for, when drawn up, he thrust out one of his fins, still bleeding, from which the tip had been just cut by a shark; his enemy, in all likelihood, being yet in pursuit. I plunged the spear so deeply into his body that it passed through him, and the cord attached to it was drawn through my hand as he ran and carried it off along with the spear. When next drawn up, I gave him a desperate wound on the back with my remaining spear. He was now much exhausted, and we brought him up to the stern with a short rope, and attempted to draw him to the land.

The wind was very high from south, and the fish had taken us down the centre channel, abreast of Joyner's Bank, and, by setting the foresail, and bearing him down toward the Bay Point shore, I was getting the leeway for my reckoning when the rising of the squall obliged me again to look for safety.

The clouds seemed highly charged with electricity and came sweeping onward with fearful rapidity. While there was any chance of killing the fish in time for reaching the shore in advance of the storm, I held on to my play, which would eventually have succeeded, but night and the tempest were both upon me, and I drew him closer to the stern, that I might kill him at once, or, if that were impracticable, might, at least, disengage my harpoon.

At this moment, the rope parted. But what was my surprise at beholding the fish, though now released, still keeping company with us, swimming close to the boat and following us with his horns projected on each side of the stern, moving exactly with our speed, and in our direction! I caught at my spear; but one glance at the lowering sky served to show the futility of making further onslaught on him. To reach the shore before the storm should burst on us was the imperious demand now made on us by controlling circumstances, and we spread our main-sail, and flew away from the gale and from the devil-fish. . . .

The squall struck us before we gained the shore, and the rain fell upon us with a stunning and bewildering effect; but all was unheeded in the satisfaction of finding ourselves once more on firm land, safe from the tempest and the startling and unwelcome pursuit to which we have just referred!

Sir Charles Lyell

"WE PASSED BETWEEN LOW SANDY ISLANDS"

Sir Charles Lyell, President of the Geological Society of London, made his second visit to North America in 1845. "I had been warned," he wrote in 1841, before beginning his first tour of the South, "by my scientific friends in the North, that the hospitality of the planters might greatly interfere with my schemes of geologizing in the Southern States. In the letters, therefore, of introduction furnished to me at Washington, it was particularly requested that information respecting my objects, and facilities of moving speedily from place to place, should be given me, instead of dinners and society. These injunctions were every where kindly and politely complied with. . . ."[6]

Sir Charles spent nine months in the United States, traveling from Boston to the Georgia coast; from Savannah to Alabama, Louisiana, Mississippi, Kentucky, Ohio and Pennsylvania. The end-of-the-year entry in his diary describes his journey from Charleston to Savannah by the inland water route.

The "racoon oysters" he mentions were called "coon oysters" by Jefferson Davis. During his imprisonment at Fort Monroe Mr. Davis spoke to Dr. John J. Craven, the prison physician, about "the coon

---

[6] Charles Lyell, *Travels in North America, in the years 1841-2* . . . New York: 1845, Vol. I, p. 123.

oysters of the Southern coast—the long, razor-shaped oysters, growing on high ledges, and referred to the Negro version of how the coons obtained their flesh. Their story is, that the coon takes in his mouth a blade of bluebent, or meadow grass, and when the oyster opens his shell, drives the stiletto point of the grass into his flesh, killing him instantly, so that he has no power to close his defences. This, though ingenious, is not true. The coon bites off the thin edges of the shell at one point, and then sucks out all the softer parts of the body...."[7]

Dec. 28, 1845.—A fine steam-ship, the *General Clinch*, conveyed us to Savannah. I was surprised when sailing out of the beautiful harbor of Charleston, on a bright scorching day, to see a cloud of smoke hanging over the town, and learned that they burn here not a little of what is called Liverpool coal. Among others on board, was a female passenger from one of the Western states, who, having heard me make inquiries for my wife, went up to her in the ladies' cabin and said, "Your old man is mighty eager to see you"; "Old man," as we afterwards found, being synonymous with husband in the West.

We were to go by inland navigation, or between the islands and the coast. After passing Edisto Point, we ran aground at the entrance of St. Helena's Sound, in mid-passage, and were detained some hours till the tide floated us off to the westward, through the winding mazes of a most intricate channel, called the Beaufort River. We passed between low sandy islands, and an equally low mainland, covered with evergreen oaks, and long-leaved pines and palmettos, six or seven feet high. Sometimes we sailed by a low bluff or cliff of white sand, two or three feet in height, then by a cotton plantation, then by large salt marshes covered with reeds, on which the cattle are supported when fodder is scarce in winter. The salt water in this narrow channel was as calm as a lake, and perfectly clear. Numerous wild ducks were diving as our steamboat approached, and beds of oysters were uncovered between high and low water mark. It was a novel and curious scene, especially when we approached Beaufort, a picturesque town composed of an assemblage of villas, the summer residences of numerous planters, who retire here during the hot season, when the interior of South Carolina is unhealthy for the whites. Each villa is shaded by a verandah, sur-

[7] John J. Craven, *Prison Life of Jefferson Davis* ... New York: Carleton, 1866, p. 93.

rounded by beautiful live oaks and orange trees laden with fruit, though with leaves slightly tinged by the late severe frost. The Pride-of-India tree, with its berries now ripe, is an exotic much in favor here. A crowd of Negroes, in their gay Sunday clothes, came down to look at our steamboat, grinning and chattering, and looking, as usual, perfectly free from care. . . .

Had it not been for the dense beds of oysters between high and low water mark, hundreds of which adhere to the timbers of the pier at Beaufort, as barnacles do in our English ports, I might have supposed the channel to be really what it is called, a river.

An old Spanish fort, south of Beaufort, reminded me that this region had once belonged to the Spaniards, who built St. Augustine, still farther to the south, the oldest city in the United States, and I began to muse on the wonderful history of the Anglo-Saxon race in settling these Southern states. To have overcome and driven out in so short a time Indians, Spaniards, and French, and yet, after all, to be doomed to share the territory with three millions of Negroes!

Of this latter race, we had not a few passengers on board. Going into the steerage to converse with some of them, my curiosity was particularly attracted to a group of three, who were standing by themselves. The two younger, a girl and a lad, were very frank, and willing to talk with me, but I was immediately joined by a young white man, not ill-looking, but who struck me as having a very determined countenance for his age.

"These colored people," he said, "whom you have been speaking to, belong to me, and they have probably told you that I have brought them by railway from Augusta to Charleston. I hope to dispose of them at Savannah, but if not, I shall take them to Texas, where I may sell them, or perhaps keep them as laborers and settle there myself."

He then told me he had fought in the wars for the independence of Texas, which I afterward found was quite true, and, after telling me some of his adventures, he said, "I will take 450 dollars for the girl, and 600 for the boy; they are both of pure blood, would stand a hot climate well; they can not read, but can count up to a thousand."

By all these qualities, negative and positive, he evidently expected to enhance in my eyes the value of the article which he meant me to buy; and no sooner did he suspect, by one of my questions, that I was a foreigner traveling for my amusement, than he was off the subject, and I attempted in vain to bring him back to it and to learn why the power of counting was so useful, while that of reading was undesirable.

About three weeks after this incident, when we were at Macon in Georgia, there was a hue and cry after a thief who had stolen five Negroes near Augusta, and had taken them to Savannah in the *General Clinch*, where he had sold one of them, a girl, for 450 dollars. From Savannah he had been traced with the remaining four, by railway, to Macon, whence it was supposed he had gone south. The description of the delinquent left me no doubt that he was my former fellow-traveler, and I now learnt that he was of a respectable family in Georgia, the spoiled child of a widowed mother, self-willed and un-manageable from his boyhood, and who had gone off against the wishes of his relations to Texas. I recollected that when we were at Beaufort, none of his Negroes had gone ashore, and that he had kept his eye always anxiously on them during our stay there. I also re-marked that the planters on board, who, for the most part, were gentlemanlike in their manners, shunned all intercourse with this dealer, as if they regarded his business as scarcely respectable.

A vast majority of the slave-owners acquiesced originally in the pro-priety of abolishing the external slavetrade; but the internal one can not, they say, be done away with, without interfering with the free cir-culation of labor from an overpeopled district to another where hands are scarce. To check this, they maintain, would injure the Negroes as much as their masters. When they are forced to part with slaves, they usually sell one to another, and are unwilling to dispose of them to a stranger. It is reckoned, indeed, quite a disgrace to a Negro to be so discarded. When the former master bids for one of his "own people," at a sale of property forced on by debt, the public are unwilling to bid against him. It is clear, therefore, that a dealer must traffic in the lowest and most good-for-nothing class of laborers, many of whom, in Europe, would be in the hands of policemen, or in convict ships on their way to a penal settlement. . . .

The species of oyster which is so abundant here (*ostrea virginica*) resembles our European *ostrea edulis* in shape, when it lives isolated and grows freely under water; but those individuals which live gre-gariously, or on banks between high and low water, lose their round form and are greatly lengthened. They are called racoon oysters, be-cause they are the only ones which the racoons can get at when they come down to feed at low tide. Captain Alexander, of the U.S. Artil-lery, told me that, in the summer of 1844, he saw a large bald-headed eagle, *Aquila leucocephala*, which might measure six feet from tip to tip of its extended wings, caught near the bar of the Savannah river by one of those racoon oysters. The eagle had perched upon the shell-fish to prey upon it, when the mollusk suddenly closed its valves and shut in the bird's claw, and would have detained its enemy till the rising tide had come up and drowned it, had not the captain in his boat secured it with a noose, and disengaged it from the oyster. He flapped his wings violently as they approached, but could not escape. . . .

PART IX

The Confederate Flag Waves
over Port Royal

"There are many Who acknowledge the right of a State to secede."

—John C. Calhoun

Twelve delegates were elected by the Beaufort District to represent her at the South Carolina Secession Convention; and on December 20, 1860, the delegates signed the Ordinance of Secession by which South Carolina declared herself once more a free and independent state. The Beaufort delegates were as follows:

From *Prince William Parish*: John E. Frampton, forty-nine-year-old planter who owned 131 slaves; W. F. Hutson, forty-five-year-old lawyer who owned four slaves.

From *St. Helena Parish*: R. W. Barnwell, fifty-nine-year-old planter who owned 158 slaves; Joseph D. Pope, thirty-year-old lawyer who owned fourteen slaves.

From *St. Luke's Parish*: R. J. Devant, fifty-five-year-old lawyer who owned 36 slaves; E. M. Seabrook, fifty-seven-year-old planter who owned 40 slaves.

From *St. Peter's Parish*: Langdon Cheves, planter who owned 289 slaves; George Rhodes, fifty-eight-year-old planter who owned 63 slaves.[1]

---

[1] *South Carolina Historical Magazine*, Vol. 55 (1954), p. 185.

On January 1, 1861, Governor Francis W. Pickens was authorized "to receive into the service of the State for a period not exceeding 6 months, such volunteer companies as may tender their services."

On the recommendation of General Beauregard, two forts were built to defend Port Royal Harbor: Fort Walker on Hilton Head Island and Fort Beauregard at Bay Point, which is usually located in Port Royal Harbor, adjacent to Phillips Island.

Brigadier General Thomas Fenwick Drayton commanded the defenses. In June the Beaufort Artillery, under command of Captain Stephen Elliott, was ordered from Fort Lyttelton near Beaufort to the uncompleted fort at Bay Point.

On November 1, 1861, J. P. Benjamin, Acting Secretary of War, notified officials in South Carolina "that the enemy's expedition [then outfitting at Hampton Roads] is intended for Port Royal."[2]

On November 5 Special Orders No. 206, from Richmond, stated: "The coasts of South Carolina, Georgia, and East Florida are constituted a military department, and General R. E. Lee, C.S. Army, is assigned to its command."[3]

---

[2] Q. R., Vol. 6, p. 306.
[3] Ibid., p. 309.

A. W. Dimock

"PLEDGING ALLEGIANCE TO THE CONFEDERATE STATES OF AMERICA"

Shortly after the Governor's call for volunteers, the young men of St. Helena Island offered their services. First Lieutenant T. G. White gave to A. W. Dimock the data about the organization of the St. Helena Mounted Volunteer Riflemen.

. . . The entire fighting population of St. Helena Island, numbering thirty-two, met in the hall of their Agricultural Society on the occasion of one of their periodical dinners. There were guests and speakers from Beaufort and elsewhere, and with unanimity and great enthusiasm resolutions presented by Dr. T. G. White were passed, severing themselves forever from the Union called the United States, and pledging allegiance to the Confederate States of America. A company was organized entitled the St. Helena Mounted Volunteer Riflemen, W. O. P. Fripp elected captain, and T. G. White, first lieutenant. A richly embroidered silken flag, inscribed on one side "St. Helena Mounted Volunteer Riflemen, organized Jan. 20, 1861," and bearing on the other a palmetto and the motto *Ubi Libertas Ibi Patria*, was made by the ladies of St. Helena Island, and presented to the company with due formality and all the pomp and pageantry of a real tournament.

In serious provision for an anticipated campaign, it was required of each warrior that he provide himself with a horse, saber, pair of Colt's revolvers, Maynard rifle, trappings, and uniform. He was to be allowed as much baggage as he could carry in his own wagon, and it was understood that he would keep ready packed for immediate service a small tent, mattress, blankets, and bedding sufficient and suitable for a campaign. The company was divided into messes, between which much rivalry developed in the provision of superior cooking outfits. The number of servants was not limited, but it was expected that only one servant would accompany a member of the company in time of action, to carry extra weapons and reload them when discharged, but under no circumstances was a Negro to fire a shot. Obnoxious as the Yankees were, they were to be fought as gentlemen by gentlemen.

The company was mustered into the Confederate srevice at White

Hall Ferry by General Drayton, Captain Young, adjutant and inspector-general of the defenses of Beaufort, Hilton Head and St. Helena Island, and others. . . . The company drilled with some regularity, practiced tilting at rings, and gaily prepared for the coming conflict, to which they looked eagerly forward as did knights of old to the tournaments where they were to win their spurs.

William Howard Russell

ASPECTS OF A SEA ISLAND PLANTATION

In the spring of 1861 William Howard Russell was sent by the London Times to report on affairs between the North and the South. After witnessing the fall of Fort Sumter the famous correspondent left Charleston to visit Mr. William Henry Trescot's cotton plantation on Barnwell Island.

Mr. Trescot was born in Charleston on November 10, 1822. He was a graduate of the College of Charleston and had studied law. Russell tells something of his diplomatic career and writing. Subsequently he was to serve in the state legislature, hold a staff position, and on behalf of the Confederate Government conduct some negotiations with agents of Great Britain and France.

April 26th, 1861.—Bade good-by to Charleston at 9.45 A.M. this day, and proceeded by railway, in company with Mr. Ward, to visit Mr. Trescot's Sea Island plantation. Crossed the river to the terminus in a ferry steamer. No blockading vessels in sight yet. The water alive with small silvery fish, like mullet, which sprang up and leaped along the surface incessantly. . . .

On the move again. Took our places in the Charleston and Savannah Railway for Pocotaligo, which is the station for Barnwell Island. Our fellow-passengers were all full of politics—the pretty women being the fiercest of all. . . .

The country is a dead flat, perforated by rivers and watercourses, over which the rail is carried on long and lofty tressle-work. But for the fine trees, the magnolias and live oak, the landscape would be unbearably hideous, for there are none of the quaint, cleanly, delightful villages of Holland to relieve the monotonous level of rice swamps and wastes of land and water and mud. At the humble little stations there were invariably groups of horsemen waiting under the trees, and ladies with their black nurses and servants who had driven over in the odd-looking old-fashioned vehicles which were drawn up in the shade. Those who were going on a long journey, aware of the utter barrenness of the land, took with them a viaticum and bottles of milk. The nurses and slaves squatted down by their side in the train, on perfectly well-understood terms. No one objected to their presence—on the contrary, the passengers treated them with a certain sort of special consideration, and they were on the happiest terms with their charges, some of which were in the absorbent condition of life, and dived their little little white faces against the tawny bosom of their nurses with anything but reluctance.

The train stopped, at 12.20, at Pocotaligo; and there we found Mr. Trescot and a couple of neighbouring planters, famous as fishers for "drum," of which more by-and-bye. I had met old Mr. Elliot[4] in Charleston, and his account of this sport, and of the pursuit of an enormous sea monster called the devil-fish, which he was one of the first to kill in these waters, excited my curiosity very much. Mr. Elliot has written a most agreeable account of the sports of South Carolina, and I had hoped he would have been well enough to have been my guide, philosopher and friend in drum fishing in Port Royal; but he sent over his son to say that he was too unwell to come, and had therefore dispatched most excellent representatives in two members of his family. It was arranged that they should row down from their place and meet us to-morrow morning at Trescot's Island, which lies above Beaufort, in Port Royal sound and river.

Got into Trescot's gig, and plunged into a shady lane with wood on each side, through which we drove for some distance. The country, on each side and beyond, perfectly flat—all rice lands—few houses visible —scarcely a human being on the road—drove six or seven miles without meeting a soul. After a couple of hours or so, I should think, the gig turned up by an open gateway on a path or road made through a waste of rich black mud, "glorious for rice," and landed us at the door of a planter, Mr. Heyward, who came out and gave us a most

---

[4] This is the William Elliott of the section "Devil Fishing at Hilton Head" in Part VII.

hearty welcome, in the true Southern style. His house is charming, surrounded with trees, and covered with roses and creepers, through which birds and butterflies are flying. Mr. Heyward took it as a matter of course that we stopped to dinner, which we were by no means disinclined to do, as the day was hot, the road was dusty, and his reception frank and kindly. A fine specimen of the planter man; and, minus his broad-brimmed straw hat and loose clothing, not a bad representative of an English squire at home.

Whilst we were sitting in the porch, a strange sort of booming noise attracted my attention in one of the trees. "It is a rain-crow," said Mr. Heyward; "a bird which we believe to foretell rain. I'll shoot it for you." And, going into the hall, he took down a double-barreled fowling-piece, walked out, and fired into the tree; whence the rain-crow, poor creature, fell fluttering to the ground and died. It seemed to me a kind of cuckoo—the same size, but of darker plumage. I could gather no facts to account for the impression that it's call is a token of rain.

My attention was also called to a curious kind of snake-killing hawk, or falcon, which makes an extraordinary noise by putting its wings point upwards, close together, above its back, so as to offer no resistance to the air, and then, beginning to descend from a great height, with fast-increasing rapidity, makes, by its rushing through the air, a strange loud hum, till it is near the ground, when the bird stops its downward swoop and flies in a curve over the meadow. This I saw two of these birds doing repeatedly to-night.

After dinner, at which Mr. Heyward expressed some alarm lest Secession would deprive the Southern States of "ice," we continued our journey towards the river. There is still a remarkable absence of population or life along the road, and even the houses are either hidden or lie too far off to be seen. The trees are much admired by the people, though they would not be thought much of in England.

At length, towards sundown, having taken to a track by a forest, part of which was burning, we came to a broad muddy river, with steep clay banks. A canoe was lying in a little harbour formed by a slope in the bank, and four stout Negroes, who were seated round a burning log, engaged in smoking and eating oysters, rose as we approached, and helped the party into the "dug-out," or canoe, a narrow, long, and heavy boat, with wall sides and a flat floor. A row of one hour, the latter part of it in darkness, took us to the verge of Mr. Trescot's estate, Barnwell Island; and the oarsmen, as they bent to their task, beguiled the way by singing in unison a real Negro melody, which was as unlike the works of the Ethiopian Serenaders as anything in song could be unlike another. It was a barbaric sort of madrigal, in which one singer beginning was followed by the others in unison, repeating the refrain in chorus, and full of quaint expression and melancholy:

> "Oh, your soul! oh, my soul! I'm going to the church-yard
>   to lay this body down;
>   Oh, my soul! oh, your soul! we're going to the church-yard
>   to lay this body down."

And then some appeal to the difficulty of passing "the Jawdan" constituted the whole of the song, which continued with unabated energy during the whole of the little voyage. To me it was a strange scene. The stream, dark as Lethe, flowing between the silent, houseless, rugged banks, lighted up near the landing by the fire in the woods, which reddened the sky—the wild strain, and the unearthly adjurations to the singers' souls, as though they were palpable, put me in mind of the fancied voyage across the Styx.

"Here we are at last." All I could see was a dark shadow of trees and the tops of rushes by the river side. "Mind where you step, and follow me close." And so, groping along through a thick shrubbery for a short space, I came out on a garden and enclosure, in the midst of which the white outlines of a house were visible. Lights in the drawing-room—a lady to receive and welcome us—a snug library—tea, and to bed: but not without more talk about the Southern Confederacy, in which Mrs. Trescot explained how easily she could feed an army, from her experience in feeding her Negroes.

April 27th.—Mrs. Trescot, it seems, spent part of her night in attendance on a young gentleman of colour, who was introduced into the world in a state of servitude by his poor chattel of a mother. Such kindly acts as these are more common than we may suppose; and it would be unfair to put a strict or unfair construction on the motives of slave owners in paying such attention to their property. Indeed, as Mrs. Trescot says, "When people talk of my having so many slaves, I always tell them it is the slaves who own me. Morning, noon and night, I'm obliged to look after them, to doctor them, and attend to them in every way." Property has its duties, you see, madam, as well as its rights.

The planter's house is quite new, and was built by himself; the principal material being wood, and most of the work being done by his own Negroes. Such work as window-sashes and panelings, however, was executed in Charleston. A pretty garden runs at the back, and from the windows there are wide stretches of cotton-fields visible, and glimpses of the river to be seen.

After breakfast our little party repaired to the river-side, and sat under the shade of some noble trees waiting for the boat which was to bear us to the fishing-grounds. The wind blew up stream, running with the tide, and we strained our eyes in vain for the boat. The river is here nearly a mile across—a noble estuary rather—with low banks lined with forests, into which the axe has made deep forays and clearings for cotton-fields.

It would have astonished a stray English traveller, if, penetrating the shade, he heard in such an out-of-the-way place familiar names and things spoken of by the three lazy persons who were stretched out— cigar in mouth—on the ant-haunted trunks which lay prostrate by the seashore. Mr. Trescot spent some time in London as *attaché* to the United States Legation, was a club man, and had a large circle of acquaintance among the young men about town, of whom he remembered many anecdotes and peculiarities, and little adventures. Since that time he was Under-Secretary of State in Mr. Buchanan's administration, and went out with Secession. He is the author of a very agreeable book on a dry subject, *The History of American Diplomacy*, which is curious enough as an unconscious exposition of the anti-British jealousies, and even antipathies, which have animated American statesmen since they were created. In fact, much of American diplomacy means hostility to England, and the skilful employment of the anti-British sentiment at their disposal in their own country and elsewhere. Now he was talking pleasantly of people he had met—many of them mutual friends.

"Here is the boat at last!" I had been sweeping the broad river with my glass occasionally, and at length detected a speck on its broad surface moving down towards us, with a white dot marking the foam at its bows. Spite of wind and tideway, it came rapidly, and soon approached us, pulled by six powerful Negroes, attired in red flannel jackets and white straw hats with broad ribands. The craft itself—a kind of monster canoe, some forty-five feet long, narrow, wall-sided, with high bow and raised stern—lay deep in the water, for there were extra Negroes for the fishing, servants, baskets of provisions, water buckets, stone jars of less innocent drinking, and abaft there was a knot of great strong planters—Elliots all—cousins, uncles, and brothers. A friendly hail as they swept up alongside—an exchange of salutations.

"Well, Trescot, have you got plenty of crabs?"

A groan burst forth at his *insouciant* reply. He had been charged to find bait, and he had told the Negroes to do so, and the Negroes had not done so. The fishermen looked grievously at each other, and fiercely at Trescot, who assumed an air of recklessness, and threw doubts on the existence of fish in the river, and resorted to similar miserable subterfuges; indeed, it was subsequently discovered that he was an utter infidel in regard to the delights of piscicapture.

"Now, all aboard! Over, you fellows, and take these gentlemen in!" The Negroes were over in a moment, waist deep, and, each taking one on his back, deposited us dry in the boat. . . .

The vessel was soon moving again, against a ripple, caused by the wind, which blew dead against us; and notwithstanding the praises bestowed on the boat, it was easy to perceive that the labour of pulling such a dead-log-like thing through the water told severely on the rowers, who had already come some twelve miles, I think. Nevertheless, they were told to sing, and they began accordingly one of those wild Baptist chants about the Jordan in which they delight—not destitute of music, but utterly unlike what is called an Ethiopian melody.

The banks of the river on both sides are low; on the left covered with wood, through which, here and there, at intervals, one could see a planter's or overseer's cottage. The course of this great combination of salt and fresh water sometimes changes, so that houses are swept away and plantations submerged; but the land is much valued nevertheless, on account of the fineness of the cotton grown among the islands. "Cotton at 12 cents a pound, and we don't fear the world!"

As the boat was going to the fishing-ground, which lay towards the mouth of the river at Hilton Head, our friends talked politics and sporting combined—the first of the usual character, the second quite new.

I heard much of the mighty devil-fish which frequents these waters. One of our party, Mr. Elliot, sen., a tall, knotty, gnarled sort of man, with a mellow eye and a hearty voice, was a famous hand at the sport, and had had some hair-breadth escapes in pursuit of it.

The fish is described as of enormous size and strength, a monster ray, which possesses formidable antennae-like horns, and a pair of huge fins, or flappers, one of which rises above the water as the creature moves below the surface. The hunters, as they may be called, go out in parties—three or four boats or more—with good store of sharp harpoons and tow-lines, and lances. When they perceive the creature, one boat takes the lead, and moves down towards it, the others following, each with a harpooner standing in the bow. The devil-fish sometimes is wary, and dives, when it sees a boat, taking such a long spell below that it is never seen again. At other times, however, it backs, and lets the boat come so near as to allow of the harpooner striking it, or it dives for a short way and comes up near the boats again.

The moment the harpoon is fixed, the line is paid out by the rush of the creature, which is made with tremendous force, and all the boats at once hurry up, so that one after another they are made fast to that in which the lucky sportsman is seated. At length, when the line is run out, checked from time to time as much as can be done with safety, the crew take their oars and follow the course of the ray, which swims so fast, however, that it keeps the line taut, and drags the whole flotilla seawards. It depends on its size and strength to determine how soon it rises to the surface; by degrees the line is warped in and hove short till the boats are brought near, and when the ray comes up it is attacked with a shower of lances and harpoons, and dragged off into shoal water to die.

On one occasion, our Nimrod told us, he was standing in the bows of the boat, harpoon in hand, when a devil-fish came up close to him; he threw the harpoon, struck it, but at the same time the boat ran against the creature with a shock which threw him right forward on its back, and in an instant it caught him in its horrid arms and plunged down with him to the depths. Imagine the horror of the moment! Imagine the joy of the terrified drowning, dying man, when, for some inscrutable reason, the devil-fish relaxed its grip, and enabled him to strike for the surface, where he was dragged into the boat more dead than alive by his terror-smitten companions—the only man who ever got out of the embraces of the thing alive. "Tom is so tough that even the devil-fish could make nothing out of him."

At last we came to our fishing-ground. There was a substitute for the favourite crab, and it was fondly hoped our toils might be rewarded with success. And these were toils, for the water is deep and the lines heavy. But to alleviate them, some hampers were produced from the stern, and wonderful pies from Mrs. Trescot's hands, and from those of fair ladies up the river whom we shall never see, were spread out, and bottles which represented distant cellars in friendly nooks far away. "No drum here! Up anchor, and pull away a few miles lower down." Trescot shook his head, and again asserted his disbelief in fishing, or rather in catching, and indeed made a sort of pretence at arguing that it was wiser to remain quiet and talk philosophical politics; but, as judge of appeal, I gave it against him, and the Negroes bent to their oars, and we went thumping through the spray till, rounding a point of land, we saw pitched on the sandy shore ahead of us, on the right bank, a tent, and close by two boats. "There is a party at it!" A fire was burning on the beach, and as we came near, Tom and Jack and Harry were successively identified. "There's no take on, or they would not be on shore. This is very unfortunate."

All the regret of my friends was on my account, so to ease their minds I assured them I did not mind the disappointment much.

"Hallo, Dick! Caught any drum?"

"A few this morning; bad sport now, and will be till tide turns again."

I was introduced to all the party from a distance, and presently I saw one of them raising from a boat something in look and shape and colour like a sack of flour, which he gave to a Negro, who proceeded to carry it towards us in a little skiff. "Thank you, Charley. I just want to let Mr. Russell see a drum-fish." And a very odd fish it was—a thick lumpish form, about 4½ feet long, with enormous head and scales, and teeth like the grinders of a ruminant animal, acting on a great pad of bone in the roof of the mouth—a very unlovely thing, swollen with roe, which is the great delicacy.

"No chance till the tide turned"—but that would be too late for our return, and so unwillingly we were compelled to steer towards home, hearing now and then the singular noise like the tap on a large unbraced drum, from which the fish takes its name. At first, when I heard it, I was inclined to think it was made by some one in the boat, so near and close did it sound; but soon it came from all sides of us, and evidently from the depths of the water beneath us—not a sharp rat-tat-tap, but a full muffled blow with a heavy thud on the sheepskin. Mr. Trescot told me that on a still evening by the river-side the effect sometimes is most curious—the rolling and pattering is audible

at a great distance. Our friends were in excellent humour with everything and everybody, except the Yankees, though they had caught no
fish, and kept the Negroes at singing and rowing till at nightfall we
landed at the island, and so to bed after supper and a little conversation, in which Mrs. Trescot again explained how easily she could
maintain a battalion on the island by her simple commissariat . . .
and that it would therefore be very easy for the South to feed an army
if the people were friendly.

April 28th—The church is a long way off, only available by a boat
and then a drive in a carriage. In the morning a child brings in my
water and boots—an intelligent, curly-headed creature, dressed in a
sort of sack, without any particular waist, barefooted. I imagined it
was a boy till it told me it was a girl. I asked if she was going to church,
which seemed to puzzle her exceedingly; but she told me finally she
would hear prayers from "uncle" in one of the cottages. The use of the
words "uncle" and "aunt" for old people is very general. . . . In the
course of the day, the child, who was fourteen or fifteen years of age,
asked me "whether I would not buy her. She could wash and sew very
well, and she thought missus wouldn't want much for her." The object
she had in view leaked out at last. It was a desire to see the glories of
Beaufort, of which she had heard from the fishermen; and she seemed
quite wonder-struck when she was informed I did not live there, and
had never seen it. She had never been outside the plantation in her
life.
After breakfast we loitered about the grounds, strolling through the
cotton-fields, which had as yet put forth no bloom or flower, and
coming down others to the thick fringes of wood and sedge bordering
the marshy banks of the island. The silence was profound, broken
only by the husky mid-day crowing of the cocks in the Negro quarters.
In the afternoon I took a short drive "to see a tree" . . . and looked
in at the Negro quarters and the cotton mill. The old Negroes were
mostly indoors, and came shambling out to the doors of their wooden
cottages, making clumsy bows at our approach, but not expressing any
interest or pleasure at the sight of their master and the strangers. . . .
The huts stand in a row, like a street, each detached, with a poultry-
house of rude planks behind it. The mutilations which the poultry
undergo for the sake of distinction are striking. Some are deprived of
a claw, others have the wattles cut, and tails and wings suffer in all

ways. . . . Heaps of oyster-shells, broken crockery, old shoes, rags, and feathers were found near each hut. . . . I observed that many of the doors were fastened by a padlock and chain outside.

"Why is that?"

"The owners have gone out, and honesty is not a virtue they have towards each other. They would find their things stolen if they did not lock their doors."

Mrs. Trescot, however, insisted on it that nothing could exceed the probity of the slaves in the house, except in regard to sweet things, sugar and the like; but money and jewels were quite safe. . . .

On our return to the house, I found that Mr. Edmund Rhett, one of the active and influential political family of that name, had called— a very intelligent and agreeable gentleman, but one of the most ultra and violent speakers against the Yankees I have yet heard. He declared there were few persons in South Carolina who would not sooner ask Great Britain to take back the State than submit to the triumph of the Yankees.

"We are an agricultural people," he said, "pursuing our own system, and working out our own destiny, breeding up women and men with some other purpose than to make them vulgar, fanatical, cheating Yankees—hypocritical, if as women they pretend to real virtue; and lying, if as men they pretend to be honest. We have gentlemen and gentlewomen in your sense of it. We have a system which enables us to reap the fruits of the earth by a race which we save from barbarism in restoring them to their real place in the world as laborers, whilst we are enabled to cultivate the arts, the graces, and accomplishments of life, to develop science, to apply ourselves to the duties of government, and to understand the affairs of the country."

This is a very common line of remark here. The Southerners also take pride to themselves, and not unjustly, for their wisdom in keeping in Congress those men who have proved themselves useful and capable. "We do not," they say, "cast able men aside at the caprices of a mob, or in obedience to some low party intrigue, and hence we are sure of the best men, and are served by gentlemen conversant with public affairs, far superior in every way to the ignorant clowns who are sent to Congress by the North.". . .

Mr. Rhett is also persuaded that the Lord Chancellor sits on a cotton-bale. "You must recognize us, sir, before the end of October."

In the evening a distant thunder-storm attracted me to the garden, and I remained out watching the broad flashes and sheets of fire worthy of the tropics till it was bed-time.

April 20th—This morning up at 6 A.M., bade farewell to our hostess and Barnwell Island, and proceeded with Trescot back to the Pocotaligo station, which we reached at 12:20. On our way Mr. Heyward and his son rode out of a field, looking very like a couple of English country squires in all but hats and saddles. The young gentleman was good enough to bring over a snake hawk he had shot for me. At the station, to which the Heywards accompanied me, were the Elliots and others, who had come over with invitations and adieux; and I beguiled the time to Savannah reading the very interesting book by Mr. Elliot, senior, on the Wild Sports of Carolina. . . .[5]

Eugenia Ellis

"OUR COAST WILL BE ATTACKED"

Eugenia Ellis wrote this letter[6] to her fifteen-year-old brother De-Treville, who was away at school. They were children of Edmund S. Ellis of Cedar Point Plantation near Grahamville, a favorite resort of the planters.

The family become refugees in Lawtonville, and the grandmother, who had found it hard to take "a rational view of the war," died there, with no stone to mark her grave. When the war was over the others returned to their "desolate home" at Cedar Point, where Eugenia herself was soon to die, at the age of twenty-eight.

Before the war Admiral Samuel F. DuPont had spent many summers at Grahamville. After his death his son came down to see the place his father had loved, and was drowned on the return voyage.

Sept. 16th [1861], Cedar Point Plantation

Dear Bubs

I suppose you have been expecting a letter from me and perhaps you

---

[5] William Elliott's *Carolina Sports by Land and Water*.

[6] Manuscript letter by permission of Mrs. Nellie Fripp, Beaufort, South Carolina.

have been not a little disappointed at not getting one before. But as
you know . . . it is near a month since we have had a line from you,
dear Bubs. . . .

I got a letter from Grandma a few evenings ago. She sent her love
to you and wanted to know why you had not written to her. She told
me that there has been such a crowd at the Ellis' all summer that Henry
has had to sleep in the drawing room and Rose in a passage way.

Of course we have not moved, but I don't mind it much for it is not
near as lonely here as it used to be and there is no amusement anywhere
in these times, except sewing for the soldiers. . . .

How unfortunate that Cape Hatteras affair[7] was and they are making so much of it. Well, it is the only conquest the poor things have
had to brag about so far, but I am afraid they will have something
else to boast of before long, for now it is certain that our coast will be
attacked, and do you know that it is very far from being ready for such
an attack? Of course they are doing everything which they can for its
defense but it is now September and things are not near complete.
People are already leaving Beaufort; indeed they were completely
panic-stricken a few weeks ago. One night a bright light was seen out
on the Atlantic, and they took it for granted that the town was about
to be attacked by a fleet and of course this created quite a sensation.

Mr. John Scriven's Company of Guerrillas, numbering over a hundred men with another regiment of one thousand, are stationed in
Beaufort. A regiment—I have forgotten the name—has been ordered
to take the place of the Guerillas in Grahamville.

On the first approach of danger we will move to Grahamville,
though I hope there will be no necessity for it.

Grandmother has begun at last to take a rational view of the war
and quickly gave Tommy up to his duties. Tommy and Uncle Stephen
[Ellis] and Wilson Hall are at Bay Point where they will probably
remain until next April. Father spent two days with them on his way
to Beaufort last week. One of the officers remarked to him that he
would not be at all surprised if they should all be taken prisoners any
night and carried off.

I . . . have read a great many books this summer. Mr. William
Heyward sent us a large lot of them, and Mr. Jn. Fripp sent me some
pretty ones a few days ago. Only wish, dear Bubs, that you were here

---

[7] Union troops successfully landed on Cape Hatteras on August 28.

to enjoy them with us. . . . Mamma and all the children unite with
me in love.

Goodbye

Your affectionate sister

I. Jenkins Mikell

THE LAST TRIP FROM EDISTO

*Among those who greeted General Lafayette at Edisto Island there
were, of course, members of the Mikell family of Point Pierre (or
Peter's Point) Plantation. The Mikells had been identified with Edisto
since before 1686.*

*Isaac Jenkins Mikell, Senior, had been born there in 1808 and after
his graduation from Princeton had become one of the leading cotton
planters of the South. He was married four times and was the father
of sixteen children.*

*When the sea islands, early in the conflict, were ordered abandoned,
the younger members of the family were moved to the up-country.
Three older sons wore the Confederate gray.*

*The junior I. Jenkins Mikell who tells of the last trip was born on
the island in 1851, was graduated from the University of Georgia in
1871, and became a civil engineer and the author of a number of books
and articles.*

*When in due time the Mikells moved back to Edisto, they found
their houses—the family dwelling and the Negro cottages—had all
escaped the ravages of war. "But," Mr. Mikell wrote, "they were all
in the possession of former slaves, and it required the authority of the
United States officer in command of the troops stationed here to
dispossess them."*

Charleston harbor was fortified and all the rivers leading to her rear
harbor were supposed to be guarded at their respective mouths. The
Edisto River, some forty miles south of Charleston, was not over-
looked. The Artillery Company of Edisto Island—strictly of an am-
ateur nature—composed of wealthy planters and their sons, each of

whom was a law unto himself, and organized as a pastime—was ordered to the duty of "repelling the invaders." With its thirty-odd men
and two shining, brass-muzzled loading cannon—or was it only one?—
six-pounders, they left their gun shed and marched the five miles to
their post. I do not know but what most, if not all, of them rode in
their buggies! At any rate, they finally arrived, prepared to shed their
blood for their country.

They made camp, or at least their body-servants did, each soldier
being provided with one, and then sat down to a two-hour dinner. It
was really too bad, but, as it was so late in the afternoon, it was
scarcely worth while to begin soldiering until next day. The day began
with a dispute with the officer of the day as to who should or should
not "walk sentry" during meal hours. This was compromised finally
by no one doing sentry duty during meals. All congratulated each
other on the happy settlement of that dilemma. Orders from Head
Quarters were then read. In brief: "Sink every ship attempting to cross
the bar. Spare none. Show no mercy." The men then gave three cheers
—and took a drink.

Time passed and no ship appeared, so none were sunk. The monot-
ony of camp life was soon broken by the announcement that General
Beauregard would visit the camp on the following day, on a tour of
inspection. Then there was bustle and confusion. The cannon was
polished until it was dazzling, shoes were cleaned, hair cut, faces
shaved, everything was put in order. The General arrived and was ac-
corded military honors. His first act was the inspection of the artillery
commanding the river. Going up to the shot piled in pyramidal form,
he gazed in silent awe at the sanguinary preparation for the defense of
Charleston's back door. Saying nothing, he took a six-pound shot
in each hand and tossed them to and fro, from one hand to the other,
back and forth, gently laid them down in place, gave the salute that
signified inspection was over, then retired—to dinner.

There has ever been some discussion as to the significance of the
General's tossing the cannon-balls to and fro. Some ill-natured and
critical persons construed it as poorly veiled contempt of the whole
"lay out.". . . Soon after, the encampment was broken up, and the men
ordered to a less exposed position.

Finding that the Sea Islands had little or no strategic value and
could not be held without too great a sacrifice of men (and six-pounders!) they were ordered abandoned [early in November 1861]. Each

family postponed leaving until the last moment, consequently means of leaving were wanting and confusion ensued. . . .

The limit of time allowed by the Confederate Government for leaving had expired when my father had finished getting ready his cotton for market, and no extension of time was granted. Our slaves were hurried across the river to the mainland and were finally settled in the middle of the state, away from the coast. Our work animals and implements we likewise got off. All our cattle, sheep and the bulk of our provisions were left behind. All the luxuries of our own production attending a well-appointed plantation in a semi-tropical climate shared the same fate. The household effects of "master and man" we could not remove—some old pieces of mahogany, old family relics and priceless—were left behind. . . .

Our crop of Sea-Island cotton from all of my father's plantations that he bent all his energies to get out for market, alas, never reached its destination! There were no means of transportation. It was a problem that sorely puzzled him, but only for a while. He was a man quick to act, and he acted. With a torch in his hand he went to his storehouse, applied it, and standing there saw going up in flames the labor of himself and slaves for one year. . . . "To leave it was to enrich the enemy" was his plea. . . .

The last trip our family made from Edisto Island to Charleston was in our twelve-oared boat. . . . One side of her was hewn out of an immense cypress log, likewise her other side, and a third log furnished the bottom and keel—the three pieces most deftly and artistically joined and fashioned by experts trained for that purpose. In the stern was a collapsible cabin of wood with seats and berth room for a large family. The middle portion—"amidships"—contained seats for twelve oarsmen. In the prow, or "forward," was stored the luggage. The Negroes called her *Nellie Fier*. Since that time I have learned to know that it was *Nullifier*, from the spirit of those days, when the talk was all of nullification. Our home was on the South Edisto River, some eighty miles, by water, from Charleston. By crossing the Island by carriage and embarking from North Edisto River, some seven miles from home, however, we saved a water trip of forty miles, leaving only forty miles to go. So we sent the boat ahead the day before and met her the next day at the point of embarkation.

We had twelve colored oarsmen aboard, with "Old Andrew" as stroke oar. He was a fine specimen of manhood, six feet, two inches tall, with size of body in proportion, with a length of "reach" of arm that Ben-Hur would have been proud of. He had trained his crew of eleven men, and he was a martinet. Any oar that failed to "bite" the water at the same time as his own had to explain why this was so. He set the pace for the others, whether fast or slow, and by some nautical intuition never failed to "get" him. With such a boat and such a crew, we raced against time—and tide also, as it happened—to reach Charleston harbor before the sunset gun should be fired.

We reached "Church Flats," the head-waters of the Stono River, the usual place to dine and rest up, about one P.M., a little behind schedule time, which necessitated curtailing the period of rest for the men, for which we paid later, for we had to reach the harbor by sunset. It is necessary to explain that the only gateway by which the enemy could attack Charleston in the rear was by Wappo Cut, a narrow and crooked stream about three miles long, connecting the upper harbor with all the rivers to the south, with the enemy ships anchored off their respective mouths. The Confederate Government was not slow in estimating the importance of this small stream and fortified it against any attempt of small boats to pass through—it was not navigable for large craft—with the strictest orders that no boat of any kind or description be allowed to pass after the sunset gun had been fired, permitting of no exceptions. Any boat attempting to pass the "dead line" must be sunk without being challenged.

It was to reach this dead line in time that we were racing, with twenty miles still to go and three hours to make it in. The responsibility and nerve-racking strain on my old father was terrible; with no one to help him bear it, with an invalid wife, young daughters and small children under his protection, the burden was crushing. At four o'clock of a winter's afternoon, with the sun an hour high, we were still seven miles or more from the line. Fortunately the tide had begun to favor us, which helped somewhat.

My father would call out to his stroke oar, "A little more speed, Andrew, more speed!"

"Yes, sir, Maussa!" he replied.

Then the call for the reserve power in his men was made. Raising his mighty voice, Andrew began to sing the great boat song "Roll, Jordan, Roll," which, when sung by twelve oarsmen, keeping time with their oars, was inspiring. One could feel the great canoe quiver and spring forward under the spiritual exaltation of the men. Then, as the tune died away into a distant echo, the boat would slide back into its old stride. But time was too precious for this.

A short period to allow of their catching their breath, and again the old command from the anxious helmsman: "More speed, Andrew, faster!"

"Yes, sir, Maussa!" was again the reply and again his rough but earnest voice would sing out their old camp-meeting song, "The Jews cast Daniel in the lion's den," to be taken up in short order by his willing crew, when the boat would again quiver and respond to the increased power. But, alas, she was "under forced draught and the crown sheets were warping!" The pace was gruelling and killing. The spurt soon slackened and down her speed came to normal.

Realizing that his boys were doing all that mortal man could do, the master waited a while, then spoke again. This time there was more of pathos and entreaty in his voice than of command, and he spoke now to the crew, to all: "One more mighty effort, boys, for your mistress! We all depend on you!"

And that mighty effort was made. Old Andrew began that old, old song of their revivals, which would nerve them if any song would: "Where, oh, where are the Hebrew children?" and the crew would respond: "Away over in the Promised Land."

The boat seemed to take in the situation and sped forward. They had not strength to sing more, and the effort to sing was always the last effort they had in reserve. From this on it was a dogged, spiritless pull, silent and hopeless.

I had been sitting at my father's side at the stern of the boat, and to pass away the time had launched over the side a little toy boat of my own and was towing it along. As I could gather more string, my tow line became longer and dragged in the water for quite a length behind, impeding our progress to some little extent.

Old Andrew looked up and saw me and called out: "Maussa, look what 'Junior' am doing!"

My father looked, took in the situation and loss of power I was causing and gave me a slap that sent me howling into the cabin. . . . Young as I was, I took in its meaning. . . . We had to make the dead line, and I was keeping the boat back. We had reached that state of high tension when something was liable to give way. This side of the line meant cold, discomfort, a sleepless vigil on the boat and a possible capture; beyond the line, home and all the blessings the word expresses.

The men were expending their last ounce of reserve power, their faces were ashen, eyes protruding, breath coming through their open mouths like steam escaping, and yet they kept on, their loyalty to the family goading them to action. The sun had dropped below the tops of the trees. Before us was the last straight stretch of water. Near half a mile ahead we saw the guard preparing to fire the evening gun. My father, standing bare-headed, with his white locks lifted by the evening breeze, with eyes closed, was praying that we might be seen before it was too late.

And we were seen. Sensing something out of the ordinary, the soldiers soon took in the situation and gave us three cheers, which acted like wine on our exhausted crew. We were just in time. As the prow of the good old boat crossed the imaginary line there was a flash, a roar. The sunset gun had been fired. We were safe. The men rested on their oars, the boat slowed down. Some of the oarsmen fell from their seats, others were unable to stand. My sisters wept hysterically, the children cried in sympathy, and my invalid mother swooned. . . .

We hobbled across the Ashley River with our exhausted crew and landed at one of the rice mills, where our carriage awaited us. Then— home. And night with all its tragedies settled down over land and sea. The good boat *Nullifier* passed out of my life. I never saw her again. She was taken over by the military and used in its service in the harbor. . . .

A. W. Dimock

"THE FLEET IS UPON US"

Lieutenant White and Mr. Dimock collaborated to give us the first glimpse of the St. Helena Mounted Volunteer Riflemen, the former with information and the latter with his pen. Now they combine again to give us the last look.
The attack of the Yankee fleet will be recounted in Part X.

On Sunday, November 4, the inhabitants of St. Helena Island assembled at the old church where for generations their people had worshiped. It was a lovely day, and although it was remembered afterward that upon that afternoon a crimson sun sank in a sea of blood, no one at the time attached sinister significance to the warlike portent. The quiet of the service was disturbed by the fast galloping of a horse, and a man strode up the aisle bearing a despatch for Captain Fripp, which was handed to the pastor and read from the pulpit. It announced that the Yankee fleet had passed Charleston and was probably bound for Port Royal. The news was received without apprehension or any real appreciation of its significance. . . .

No valuables were removed or concealed, and not a step taken in contemplation of any possibility of being compelled to abandon the island. A special order was served upon the members of the company of Riflemen:

Headquarters St. Helena Mounted Volunteer Riflemen

Order No. 1. The United States fleet, which for the past few months has been fitting out at Fort Monroe, is upon us and premeditates probably an incursion on our shores. The St. Helena Mounted Riflemen are hereby requested to appear properly armed and accoutered at Dr. Jenkins' house at Seaside, prepared to meet the dastardly foe.

2d—Private William Jenkins is hereby ordered to have a good and substantial dinner provided for the Company at three o'clock.

3d—Lieutenants White, Fripp, and Capers, who live at conveniently different sections of the island, are hereby requested to impress all boats, flats, and means of transportation and congregate them at Dr. Jenkins' place on Station Creek, dividing St. Helena Island from Bay Point, in readiness, in case it may become expedient, to conduct a retreat from the latter place.

W. O. P. FRIPP,
Captain S.H.M.R.
(Signed in haste)

The indignation excited by the last paragraph was such that the captain was compelled to exhibit to his company the orders under which he had acted, which were as follows:

Capt. W. O. P. Fripp:
Sir—You are instructed to press into the service of the Confederate States Negroes, boats, and flats, and have them at the most convenient point to bring off our soldiers from Bay Point should it be neces-

sary for them to retreat. This order is to be carried out forthwith.
Mr. Thomas M. Hanckel will carry this.

Jos. Daniel Pope, A.D.C.

It has been suggested that the point off Bay Point opposite Dr. William Jenkins' is the more convenient.

J.D.P.

No further preparation was required at the forts, which calmly awaited the assault. Beaufort was undisturbed, awaiting in calm serenity the sinking of every ship of the attacking fleet by the forts, and Commodore Tatnall's "mosquito fleet," made up of a steam tug towing bomb-boats, was awaiting with banked fires the signal to bring in the vanquished fleet of the enemy.

Early on Monday morning the members of the St. Helena Mounted Volunteer Riflemen assembled at the Jenkins' house, coming on horseback, in buggies and carriages, followed by servants, wagons, and baggage. Felicitations were exchanged in billiard and dining rooms. Wives and sweethearts tearfully buckled on sabers, while mothers warned servants to keep near their masters, to bind their wounds, and to bring back their bodies if——

The dinner at Jenkins' was never eaten. St. Helena, Hilton Head and other islands had passed out of the hands of their long-time owners forever, and, with Beaufort, were abandoned by every white citizen, with a single exception. Nothing was removed from the houses on the islands, not even jewelry from bureaus or money from desks. . . .

PART **X**

The Port Royal Expedition

"Executive Mansion,
September 18, 1861

"To the Secretary of the Navy [Gideon Welles],

"My Dear Sir: To guard against misunderstanding, I think fit to say that the joint expedition of the Army and Navy, agreed upon some time since, and in which General T. W. Sherman was and is to bear a conspicuous part, is in no wise to be abandoned, but must be ready to move by the 1st of, or very early in October. Let all preparations go forward accordingly,

"Yours, truly,
A. LINCOLN."[1]

---

[1] *Official Records of the Union and Confederate Navies* . . . Series I, Vol. XII, p. 208.

Samuel F. DuPont

THREE HARBORS

*After months of investigation, a committee, appointed by Gideon
Welles, Secretary of the U.S. Navy, submitted its report and recommendations regarding a point on the Atlantic coast vital for naval
operation and occupation.*

*Captain DuPont, it will be recalled, was well acquainted with the
objective points under consideration, for he had spent many summers
as a guest at Grahamville in Beaufort County, a favorite resort of the
neighboring planters.*

Washington, D.C., July 13, 1861

Hon. Gideon Welles,

Secretary of the Navy:

Sir: We have the honor to inform you that, in further prosecution
of the duties assigned us, we have made a careful study of three of the
most important of the secondary bays or harbors on the Southern
coast, for the purpose of military occupation. These are Bull's Bay,
Saint Helena Sound and Port Royal Sound, all on the coast of South
Carolina. . . .

Of those three places . . . we have no hesitation in recommending the
immediate military occupation of the first, . . . [because of] its acces-
sibility, direct channel, safe anchorage, . . . which make it a most convenient harbor of refuge, and its being securely held by the possession
of a single point. With regard to Saint Helena Sound and Port Royal
Bay there is more room for doubt. We have compared the two somewhat as follows:

If Port Royal has the greater depth on the bar (twenty-three to
twenty-five feet), yet the bar of the former is eight miles from the
land, while that of the latter is only three miles and a half. Saint Helena
is held by the occupation of a single point. Port Royal requires that
three points should be taken and fortified. The entrance of the former
is six miles wide, and the best channel can only be molested from

Hunting Island; that of the latter is only two miles wide, and the attacking fleet will be subject to fire from both sides. The resources for wood and water are about the same in each. Saint Helena is more central between Charleston and Savannah; Port Royal commands a larger interior communication and trade. The noble bay of Port Royal comprises one large open space, capable of containing any number of vessels anchored in one body. The anchorages of Saint Helena are divided and distinct from each other. It seems to us that Saint Helena ought to be seized before Port Royal, because it will be so much more easily taken and held. The former is a comparatively obscure place, little known and but little resorted to, while the latter is constantly talked of as the first point of attack and is closely looked after.

Stephen Elliott, Jr., of Parry's [Parris] Island, a nephew of George P. Elliott, has been employed in fortifying Port Royal, every foot of which he is familiar with, while not a planter knows Saint Helena.

Finally, believing that the three points we have recommended will suffice for the purposes of coaling stations and harbors of refuge for the blockading squadrons, we are not disposed to recommend any immediate measures for the taking of Port Royal. The putting of 12,000 or 15,000 men thus in the immediate neighborhood of Charleston and Savannah and the presence of a considerable fleet in this noble harbor would doubtless be a sore annoyance to the rebels, and necessitate the constant maintenance of large forces in those cities and on those shores. Yet the same force, naval and military, organized as an expedition and held in hand at New York for a blow anywhere, would threaten not only Savannah and Charleston but the whole Southern coast.

If, in the organization of such a force, its destination should be absolutely undefined, the threat would be equally against every important point of the Southern coast from Hatteras to the Rio Grande. The simple putting to sea of such a force, if it were only to return to its port, would cause general alarm, and the Gulf States could no longer permit their troops to swell the armies of Virginia. The force thus organized, after being, by frequent embarkations and disembarkations, used as a means of threat and thus perfectly drilled to its intended service, might at last be permitted to strike its blow. Whether at New Orleans, or Mobile, or Pensacola, or Savannah, or Port Royal, or that focus of rebellion—the scene of the great indignity offered our flag—Charleston, might be decided at the last moment.

We have the honor to be, very respectfully, your obedient servants.

> S. F. DuPont,
>> Captain, U.S. Navy, President.
>
> A. D. Bache,
>> Superintendent U.S. Coast Survey.
>
> J. G. Barnard,
>> Major, U.S. Engineers.
>
> Chas. H. Davis,
>> Commander, U.S. Navy, Secretary.

Samuel F. DuPont

"WE ARE OFF!"

The ships that sailed from Hampton Roads—described by an on-the-scene reporter as constituting "the greatest war fleet that the United States has ever assembled"—were in the general charge of Flag Officer DuPont. The accompanying expeditionary force was under General Sherman.

Fifty-eight-year-old Samuel F. DuPont, who had a record of distinguished service in the United States Navy, had on September 18, 1861, been assigned to the command of the South Atlantic blockading squadron with control of all naval operations on the Atlantic coast on the boundary between North and South Carolina.

General Thomas West Sherman was born in Rhode Island in 1813. He was graduated from West Point in the class of 1836, had served in the Mexican War and at one time had been stationed at Fort Moultrie.

The following announcement of the departure from Hampton Roads was sent to the Navy Department in Washington.

> U.S.S. *Wabash*,
> Under Steam, Tuesday, October 29, 1861, 9 A.M.

Hon. G. V. Fox,
  Assistant Secretary of the Navy, Washington.

My Dear Sir: Please inform Mr. Welles that we are off, and the pilot will soon leave. . . .

Twenty-eight days ago this expedition, though long meditated by the wisdom of the Department, had in reality no form or substance. In my judgment nothing more could well have been added in that time. I felt at the time of the final decision at Mr. Seward's house, October 1, that the embarkation at Annapolis was an error. The troops have been too long on board, and are too raw, but the generals are able.

The ships of my squadron are in as high condition as I can expect, and I am thankful to the Department for its endeavors to make it as efficient as possible, and to your practical, intelligent, and personal supervision and zeal I shall ever recur, whatever the results in store for us may be.

We have considerable power to carry on an offensive warfare; that of endurance against forts is not commensurate. But in so righteous a cause as ours, and against so wicked a rebellion, we must overcome all difficulties. . . .

S. F. DuPONT,
Flag-Officer, etc.

ON THE *ATLANTIC* WITH THE
THIRD NEW HAMPSHIRE

The anonymous "John" of the Third New Hampshire had reported from Hampton Roads in the following brief letter to his mother. Further happenings aboard the Atlantic *are given by Lieutenant Henry H. Ayer.*

The hurricane which the fleet experienced was one of the most disastrous ever to hit the Atlantic coast.

"John"

On Board Steamer *Atlantic*,
Bound for Somewhere, etc.
18 Oct. 1861

Dear Mother: Though I wrote you yesterday, will add that our regiment embarked on this steamer this forenoon. There are several steamers lying here, taking on board the troops. God and Gen. Sherman only know where we are going; and perhaps Gen. Sherman isn't sure. Some say New Orleans, and some say Charleston. All sorts of rumors float through the air; and [believing them] all is trying indeed to us poor soldiers. We shall soon start—appearances indicate today or tomorrow—so good-bye. We will try to do our duty wherever it may be required; and until you hear from me again believe me to be your loveing and loyal son

John

P.S. (4 P.M.): There is a mail just going ashore and said to be our last chance. Good-bye again.

John

Lieutenant Henry H. Ayer

Off Hatteras, Oct. 30, 1861 (Wednesday)
We are about 40 miles from land . . . accompanied by the whole expedition. The whole number is 48, and 33 are now in sight. . . . The old steamer *Governor*, that used to run from Boston to Kennebec, is with us. . . . The great steamship *Vanderbilt* has one full regiment on board and several companies of another. She is towing the *Great Republic* with 500 horses on board. . . . The sailing ships are towed by the steamers. The principal war ship . . . the *Wabash* . . . is right ahead of us. It is getting rough, and the small gunboats are beginning to pitch and roll badly. One, the *Ottawa*, is rolling fearfully, and the sea breaks over her.

Oct. 31. Great anxiety was felt yesterday for some of the gunboats that could not keep up. About 3 P.M. yesterday our ship turned right about and went back to look them up and found them before dark . . . took one in tow . . . the other refused. The latter, the *Isaac Smith*, is with us this morning. 12 P.M.: We are again on the back track to hunt up five more. . . . 1 P.M.: We have lost sight of the fleet. . . . 4 P.M.: We have found the rest of our fleet . . . found the great steamship *Illinois*, with part of her smoke stack gone and a sailing vessel in tow . . . offered assistance and it was refused. Evening: We have all steam on and will probably overtake the fleet by morning. The *Atlantic* is said to be 288 feet long, 48 feet across, including paddle-boxes, and 50 feet deep in the hold.

Nov. 1. We caught up with the fleet at three this morning. Reporters

on board: *New York Tribune*—Mortimer Thompson, "Doesticks";
New York Herald, also.

Nov. 3, Sunday morning. We have experienced a tremendous gale
... which has blown our fleet God knows where. Only seven vessels of
our fleet in sight. Yesterday morning the little steamer *Mayflower*
was seen with signals of distress, and our ship at once steered in that
direction and found her . . . with upper works badly stove . . . the sea
sweeping clean over her main deck. We took her in tow and she is still
at our stern. One gunboat had broken her rudder chains and lost her
bow gun overboard, staving the bulwarks as it went over. This was
night before last; and she has not been seen since. The sea was so rough
we could not help her. The commotion was terrible; and if our ship
had struck her it would have dashed her to pieces. . . . Am sorry to say
the measles has got among us.

Egbert L. Viele

"UNEXPECTED, ABSOLUTE AND DECISIVE VICTORY IN PORT ROYAL HARBOR"

*Egbert Ludovicus Viele was born in Waterford, New York, in 1825.
After his graduation from West Point in 1847 he took part in the
Mexican War and served on the southwestern frontier. When he re-
signed his army commission he became chief engineer of the proposed
Central Park in New York City, but his design for it was discarded in
favor of one by Frederick Law Olmsted.*

*At the outbreak of war he had been commissioned Captain of En-
gineers in the famous Seventh New York Regiment. On August 17,
1861, he had been made a Brigadier General of Volunteers. Now he
was second in command to General T. W. Sherman of the land forces
on the Port Royal expedition.*

*After leaving Port Royal General Viele played a part in the capture
of Fort Pulaski and Norfolk. He was military governor of Norfolk from
May to October, 1862.*

*In his account of Port Royal General Viele introduces evidence that
the "secret" destination of the armada was known promptly by President Davis and other Confederate officials. The "woman in the case"
may have been Rose Greenhow, the amazingly adept Confederate spy*

in Washington, though she had been under arrest since August 23, 1861.

... A great armada, surpassed by few expeditions of like character in the history of war, passed out into the ocean from Hampton Roads on the 29th day of October [1861] in a grand pageant, to a destination utterly and entirely unknown to the thirty thousand soldiers and sailors who composed its military and naval forces, but followed by the prayers of millions for its success—millions who for long days and weeks and months had lived in doubt and despondency. The consternation and alarm aroused throughout the land by the disaster at Bull Run could only be counterbalanced by some great and overwhelming victory; but where the blow would fall, or through what special channels the much-desired victory could be won, was as yet an unsolved problem.

A gun from the flag-ship *Wabash*, at a few minutes past five o'clock of that lovely October morning, gave the signal for starting. Not a cloud was to be seen in all the broad expanse of the blue sky, and scarcely a breeze ruffled the surface of the water. Both shores of the magnificent harbor were lined with spectators. From one side came blessings, from the other curses—for those serene waters constituted the dividing line between the two sections of the country arrayed in deadly warfare. A scene so remarkable in grandeur and effect has seldom been witnessed. The fleet consisted of seventy-seven vessels, including its men-of-war, transports, steam-tugs, and sailing craft. It was under the command of Commodore Samuel Francis DuPont. It sailed in three parallel lines, the steam frigate *Wabash*, the flag-ship of the expedition, leading the men-of-war and gunboats—the *Baltic, Oriental, Empire City, Atlantic, Ericsson, R. B. Forbes, Ocean Express, Vanderbilt, Illinois, Golden Eagle, Great Republic, Ocean Queen, Philadelphia, Roanoke, Locust Point, Zenas Coffin, Matanzas, Star of the South, Potomac, Ben Deford, Parkersburg, Winfield Scott, Belvidere, Union, Daniel Webster, Alabama, Aeriel, Marion, Cahawba, Mayflower, Mohican, O. M. Pettit, Mercury, Osceola*, the United States coast steamer *Vixen*, the *Augusta, Bienville, Curlew, Florida, Isaac P. Smith, Mohican, Ottawa, Pawnee, Pocahontas, Penguin, Pembina, Seminole, Seneca, Unadilla, Curlew* and many others. The vessels were scattered all through that memorable morning over an area of more than twenty miles.

The night before this another scene, also of a remarkable character, had taken place, known to but few, but which resulted in a change of the whole scheme of the undertaking and brought about events entirely unanticipated by those who had originally planned it.

Months of preparation had been given to this expedition to insure a completeness and a potentiality that would make defeat impossible. A careful review of the situation of the country at that time developed the fact that, so long as the disaffected states could have free access to the sea and the benefits of commerce with foreign nations while the servile labor was devoted to the production of the great staple upon which depended all their financial hopes, it would be next to impossible for any force, however large, to suppress the insurrection. . . . Therefore, it became a matter of the most vital importance to suppress foreign intercourse with the people of the South.

In order to do this a complete system of blockade must be established and maintained, to accomplish which a foot-hold must be secured on the sea-board, then controlled and held along the entire coast south of Hampton Roads by the states that had seceded. Along this coast the Government had, during a long series of former years, expended enormous sums of money in the construction of permanent works of defense. . . . They had been regarded as almost impregnable at the time of their construction against any then known ordnance or projectiles. To attack any of those great forts by sea was deemed a most hazardous undertaking. Nothing but the most consummate strategy and the boldest skill could hope for success against them.

The nature of the undertaking proposed in the organization of an expeditionary force against the Southern coast will, therefore, be comprehended at a glance. If, however, there was one thing more than another that might be deemed positively essential to success, it would appear that absolute secrecy as to its destination was paramount. So important was this element of secrecy regarded by the Government, that from the first it was assumed to be a *cabinet* secret, to be confided only to the ranking military and naval commanders.

The first movement toward the formation of this expedition had been the selection of a large area of ground at Hempstead Plains, Long Island, for the encampment and drill of the military portion of it. Twenty or thirty wells were sunk in the plain at convenient intervals. The accumulation of quartermaster and commission stores began, and two regiments, the Third New Hampshire and Eighth Maine, had arrived, when in obedience to orders from General Scott, commander-in-chief of the army, I assumed command of the camp—General T. W. Sherman being military commander of the expedition.

Twenty thousand soldiers were to constitute the military part of the force. Scarcely had the two regiments pitched their tents when one of those periodical stampedes that were constantly occurring at Washington took place, and a telegram directed the immediate transfer of these regiments to the capital, notwithstanding the expense in preparing the ground at Hempstead, digging wells, and accumulating material—which was all thrown away, merely to add two raw regiments (one of whom had only received their muskets three days before) to the forces at Washington, and this on the strength of some cock-and-bull story by a contraband that the enemy was about to attack Washington in force. . . . Thus the camp of the "First Brigade, E.C." was transferred to the water-soaked clay of Capitol Hill, where the Eighth Maine (nearly all six-footers) caught the mumps and measles to a man. After receiving the addition of the Forty-sixth, Forty-seventh and Forty-eighth New York regiments, the brigade was removed to Annapolis, which was the final rendezvous, and from this place was embarked on transports which, with the naval fleet, ultimately assembled at Hampton Roads. . . .

The expedition was now composed of about 20,000 soldiers and 5,000 sailors, all the largest transport vessels, such as the *Vanderbilt*, *Atlantic* and *Baltic*—in fact, all the available vessels that could be obtained and some of the finest men-of-war in the service—the frigate *Wabash* as the flag-ship and Commodore DuPont, an old and experienced naval officer, to command the naval part of the expedition. He had with him the two Rogers, John and Raymond, and Commodore Davis, as associate commanders. The land forces were under the command of General T. W. Sherman, and were divided into three brigades, the first commanded by Egbert L. Viele, the second by Isaac I. Stevens, the third by Horatio Gates Wright. These eight officers were called together on board the flag-ship the night before the proposed departure of the expedition to listen to the final instruction of the Government and learn the destination of the force. The council assembled in the inner cabin of the *Wabash*. The outer door was securely fastened and a marine placed ten paces from it, with strict orders to allow no listeners to approach. Commodore DuPont then unfolded the carefully prepared instructions and read them in a low tone that could not be heard beyond the immediate circle of those assembled.

To my utter astonishment the destination of this formidable armada was stated to be Bull's Bay, South Carolina, and Fernandina, Florida, two comparatively insignificant places. But more than this, the supposed "secret destination" had been imparted to me more than a month before in the City of Washington, as coming from a woman who was on terms of the closest intimacy with one of the members of Mr. Lincoln's Cabinet. He was a widower, and this woman, who possessed unusual attractiveness of appearances and manners, was a constant *habitué* of the Secretary's house, receiving his guests at receptions, accompanying him on occasional visits to the camps, and evidently a favored friend. She was a Southern woman by birth and sympathies; but when I learned, as coming from her, the destination of this great assailing force—which had been officially withheld from me—I treated the idea with ridicule, not only from the insignificance of the destinations named, but from the natural supposition that it was impossible for such a woman to know anything about it.

What, then, was my amazement, not to say consternation, when DuPont communicated in whispered tones to the council of commanders this same destination. I could hardly believe my own sense of hearing. What hope was there for the Union cause if the great secrets of the Government, the plans of her Army and Navy commanders, could be thus thrown to the winds of heaven or communicated, as these were, directly to Jefferson Davis, as will be seen?

As a matter of course I made known the fact to the officers present that this supposed "secret" was no longer a secret. A long conference ensued, lasting into the hours of the early morning. A close and careful examination of the charts furnished by the coast surveys exhibited the remarkable character of Port Royal as a harbor, and after receiving from Commodore Dupont—in answer to a question if this harbor would suffice as a safe place of rendezvous—the assurance that his fondest anticipations had never contemplated the occupation of so spacious a harbor and that it would be sufficient without any other, it was earnestly urged upon the council to adopt Port Royal as the destination. The council adjourned, however, without coming to a decision; but in reassembling next morning, Port Royal was unanimously chosen. Sealed orders were then prepared for every vessel, not to be opened until each one was out of sight of land. . . .

This destination was *our* secret, and was committed only at the last moment to the President at Washington. Nevertheless, a dispatch from Jefferson Davis was found afterward at Fort Walker, one of the captured forts, informing the commander that Port Royal had been selected for the attack. "The woman in the case" had evidently been on the alert, and a preparation to meet us was made that would have destroyed a less thoroughly organized and equipped force. . . .

The three leading principles that govern a true plan of military operation are secrecy, celerity and audacity. The Port Royal expedition started out handicapped with the absence of the first of these, and the elements combined to deprive it of the second. Scarcely had the great fleet lost sight of the American coast when a storm commenced to gather that threatened for a time to disperse if not destroy it. The weather was unsettled from the first, the wind veering to all points of the compass. On the fifth day, or rather on the night of the fourth day, November 1, the powers of the winds and waves culminated in one of the most fearful storms ever known on the Atlantic coast. The exigencies of the case had caused the drafting into the service of every description of craft—ocean steamers, coasters, sailing vessels, ferry boats, river steamers—many of them of light draft, and all were compelled to breast the fury of the gale. The steamer *Baltic*, of the old Collins line of European steamers, had in tow the large ship *Ocean Express*. The ship *Great Republic* was in tow of the steamer *Vanderbilt*. The steamer *Illinois* had in tow the ship *Golden Eagle*. Nearly all parted their hawsers during the night, the long hours of which will never be forgotten by those who passed through them in wakeful uncertainty.

When the morning dawned, the fleet was scattered in every direction. The *Peerless*, the *Osceola*, the *Governor* and the *Union* were wrecked. Several others were saved only by throwing overboard their guns or cargoes. The *Belvidere* found safety in putting back to Hampton Roads. It was almost a miracle that so many escaped. Nevertheless, on Monday the 4th of November, the seventh day after starting, the fleet was at anchor off Port Royal, ready for active work. First, the channel had to be sounded and buoys placed to mark the entrance. A little more enterprise and daring on the part of Commodore Tattnall, who commanded the insurgent fleet inside the harbor, would have made this operation a very hazardous and difficult one. Once the channel was defined, it was not a difficult matter to enter, but it was fortunate for the fleet that the storm had subsided. On the morning of the 5th the light draft gunboats passed over the bar, followed the next day by all the men-of-war.

And now another dilemma presented itself. The *Ocean Express*, a large sailing ship that was in tow of the *Baltic* and had parted her hawser during the night of the storm, contained all the small ammunition of the force as well as the heavy ordnance. This vessel had failed to put in an appearance off Port Royal, and it was feared that she was lost. At any rate, Sherman refused his assent to the commencement of hostilities until this vessel was heard from or, if lost, until more guns and more ammunition could be procured from the North. As we had stripped the arsenals of all their available ordnance, it looked as if the expedition would have to be abandoned at the moment of success. It having been suggested to Commodore DuPont that when the forts were taken, he, if found necessary, could dismantle some of his war vessels and send the guns on shore, he at once acquiesced. And it being further decided that the bayonet could supply the absence of small ammunition, Sherman reluctantly assented, and the order was given out for commencing the bombardment the next morning. During the night the *Ocean Express* arrived off the harbor, and Sherman's mind was greatly relieved.

The planning of the bombardment, the manning of the ships and the effective work done by the fleet will pass into history as one of the most successful achievements of the kind, as it marked an era in naval warfare. It was the first time that the powerful auxiliary of steam was brought to play such a decided part in war operations. It was grander and more audacious under Farragut at New Orleans, but it was superb under DuPont at Port Royal.

The two works to be encountered, Forts Walker and Beauregard, situated on either side of the harbor, were in themselves models in their construction, admirably designed, well mounted with guns of heavy caliber and manned by as gallant a set of men as ever fought for any cause or country. They were well drilled and disciplined and were all sanguine of victory. A telegram from Jefferson Davis had given them the true destination of the fleet; they knew its power to a ship and its strength to a man. Notwithstanding all this they prepared to meet the odds that were pitted against them with calm determination. The manner in which they served their guns to the last while a hurricane of shot and shell poured in upon them elicited the unqualified admiration of every soldier and sailor.

It was all of no avail. DuPont had planned the attack with the utmost precision. Every vessel had its designated place. The fleet sailed in the form of an ellipse, each ship to deliver its fire at each fort as it passed abreast of it. Three times this circle of death passed in its relentless course. Three times the gallant men at the works received and returned the fire of every vessel. The vessels engaged were the *Wabash, Ingraham, Pawnee, Seminole, Bienville, Pocahontas, Mohican* and *Augusta*; the gunboats *Ottawa, Seneca, Unadilla* and *Pembina*. It was a powerful array. For four hours the terrible duel was maintained, and then after a well-directed broadside from the *Wabash,* all was over! The resistless force of numbers prevailed, and the forts so desperately and courageously defended were abandoned, their occupants making an undisturbed and safe retreat to the mainland. . . .

When Fort Walker was taken possession of, a scene presented itself that beggars description. Such havoc and ruin! Such utter destruction probably never overtook a fortification. Certainly no work was ever more valiantly defended.

One of the sad incidents of this engagement was the fact that while General T. F. Drayton of Charleston, South Carolina, commanded the forces at Fort Walker, his brother, Captain Percival Drayton, also a South Carolinian, was the commander of the *Pocahontas,* one of the Union vessels in the attack. General Drayton's residence at Hilton Head was riddled with shells, some of them in all probability coming from Captain Drayton's vessel. This was truly a fratricidal combat.

Thus was accomplished the most important step taken up to that time in subduing the rebellion. It was a serious blow to the South, effecting as it did the complete blockade of all the Atlantic seaports through which the European enemies of America had so successfully introduced the sinews of war. It gladdened the hearts of the loyal people of the North and sent a thrill of joy throughout the vast camps where the legions were gathered for the defense of the Union. But the question will never be answered how often and by whom was the cause of the Union betrayed to its enemies?

Captain Hazard Stevens

"COMMODORE DUPONT . . . LED THE LONG LINE OF WARSHIPS"

Captain Hazard Stevens of the 79th New York Regiment tells his story of the Port Royal expedition. His father, General Isaac I. Stevens, commanded the Second Brigade under General Thomas W. Sherman.

It was a fine, bracing autumn afternoon, October 29 [1861], when the great fleet sailed out of the Chesapeake in two parallel columns a mile apart. The giant warship *Wabash* led the right column, followed in single file by the war vessels, thirty in number, a black and formidable array. The left column was composed of the transport steamers, crowded with troops, each towing one of the sailing-vessels, and also contained some thirty ships. The *Vanderbilt* towed the *Great Republic*, a four-masted, full-rigged ship of four thousand tons, the largest sailing ship then afloat. Besides a vast cargo of stores, she carried on her main and upper decks a great number of artillery horses. Thus the mighty armada steadily ploughed its way out to sea, with flags waving and bands playing—a glorious and awe-inspiring sight—while the troops, exhilarated by the novel and stirring scene and the excitement of sailing to an unknown destination, their hearts swelling with the hope and determination of soon dealing the rebel lion a mighty and perhaps fatal blow, cheered and cheered again until they could cheer no more.

The third day a furious storm struck the combined fleet and scattered it far and wide. At midnight, in the height of the tempest, the great hawsers by which the *Vanderbilt* was towing her consort threatened to tear off her quarters under the terrific strain of the mountain billows and had to be cut asunder with axes, and the *Great Republic* was abandoned to her fate in the raging storm, furious sea and black night. When day broke, no other sail was visible amid the driving and tossing billows. Later in the day General Stevens opened the sealed orders with which every ship was provided—to be opened in case of separation from the fleet—in presence of Captains Le Favre, [Hazard] Stevens and [William] Lilly and announced that the destination and point of rendezvous was off Port Royal, one of the finest harbors on the Southern coast, situated midway between Charleston and Savannah.

The *Vanderbilt*, the swiftest of the fleet, arrived off the entrance on November 3 among the first. The other ships came straggling in and by the 6th were nearly all assembled and anchored just outside the bar, save four, the *Governor* and *Peerless*, that foundered in the storm, and the *Osceola* and *Union*, that were driven ashore. The loss of life was small under the circumstances, being seven drowned and ninety-three captured. The 50th Pennsylvania, on the *Winfield Scott*, came near going to the bottom and were only saved by incessant pumping and bailing and throwing overboard the entire cargo.

Port Royal was defended by earthworks on each side of the entrance, Fort Walker on Hilton Head, the south side, and Fort Beauregard on Bay Point on the north. These were strong and well-constructed forts . . . and were garrisoned and defended by three thousand troops under General Thomas F. Drayton, whose brother, Captain Percival Drayton, commanded the gunboat *Pocahontas* in DuPont's fleet. The enemy had also three small gunboats in the bay, under Commodore [Josiah] Tatnall, formerly an officer of the United States Navy.

After reconnoissance by his gunboats Commodore DuPont decided to attack the forts with his fleet and arranged with General Sherman [for] the troops . . . to land in small boats on the open beach during the naval bombardment and carry the works by assault, in case the navy failed to shell the enemy out. Accordingly, on the morning of November 7 the surf-boats and all the boats belonging to the vessels were launched and brought up alongside or astern of the transports, and the troops of Stevens's and Wright's brigades were provided with ammunition and one day's cooked rations and held in readiness to land and attack. While they awaited this movement, the following order was written by General Stevens and read to them. . . .

Headquarters, Second Brigade, Expeditionary Corps
S.S. *Vanderbilt*, November 7, 1861

General Orders No. 5.

The brigadier general commanding the second brigade trustfully appeals to each man of his command this day to strike a signal blow for his country. She has been stabbed by traitorous hands and by her most favored sons. Show by your acts that the hero age has not passed away and that patriotism still lives. Better to fall nobly in the forlorn hope in vindication of home and nationality than to live witnesses of the triumph of a sacrilegious cause. The Lord God of battles will direct us; to Him let us humbly appeal this day to vouchsafe to us his crowning mercy; and may those of us who survive, when the evening sun goes down, ascribe to Him, and not to ourselves, the glorious victory. . . .

At nine o'clock on the bright, clear morning, with a smooth sea, the great war fleet crossed the bar and deliberately advanced to attack the forts in a long column of single ships while the transports lay at anchor just outside, with their decks, masts and shrouds covered with the troops. Commodore DuPont in the *Wabash* led the long string of warships slowly up the middle of the bay, receiving and replying to the fire of both forts until two miles beyond them, then turned to the left in a wide circle and led back past Fort Walker at a thousand yards distance, opening upon it broadside after broadside. At the same time a flanking column of five gunboats steamed up the bay nearer to Bay Point and poured its broadsides into Fort Beauregard, and, steering towards the other side, advanced against Tattnall's fleet, driving it into Skull Creek which cuts off Hilton Head on the inside, and then, taking position near the shore and flanking the fort, opened upon it a destructive fire. Meantime the main column, led by the *Wabash*, was slowly passing the work, each succeeding vessel opening its batteries upon it in turn as it came within range and maintaining a rapid fire as it drew past. The naval gunfire was terrific, rising at times to a continuous roar. . . . The enemy replied with a brisk and well-maintained fire. . . .

After passing down the bay as far as the depth of water permitted, DuPont turned and again led the fleet in front of Fort Walker, at much closer range than before, pouring upon the work a still more terrific fire. As the admiral repeated this maneuver for the third time, one of the light-draught gunboats, pushing closely in at six P.M., discovered that the enemy had fled, and sent a boat with a small party ashore, who pulled down the rebel flag and hoisted over it the glorious Stars and Stripes. What cheers then burst forth from ship to ship of the crowded transports, what joy and relief from suspense were felt by the officers who had so anxiously watched the bombardment for hours, momentarily looking for orders to land and assault the works which were so stubbornly resisting the navy. . . .

The flight of the enemy was panic. They left their flags flying, their tents standing and all their supplies. Tatnall's mosquito fleet hastened up Skull Creek and, with the aid of some large flatboats, ferried the fugitives across that stream. The fact that the enemy's retreat might have been cut off and his entire force captured by sending gunboats up the inner channels separating Hilton Head and Bay Point from adjacent islands, lent wings to his flight. . . . Fort Beauregard was abandoned in equal haste, although not subjected to nearly so severe a battering as Fort Walker. The navy lost only thirty-one killed and wounded; that of the enemy was sixty-six.

The morning after the bombardment the Highlanders went ashore on Bay Point and occupied Fort Beauregard and the deserted camp, and the rest of the troops were landed on Hilton Head. . . .

The enemy's camp bore witness to his panic flight; clothing, bedding, half-cooked provisions, even a rebel flag over one tent and a sword inside, and in another an excellent repast, with jelly, cake and wine, were found abandoned. General Drayton's headquarters in a large building near Fort Walker was abandoned in such haste that the horses in the stable were left behind, and General Drayton's own charger, a fine, handsome bay horse of medium size but compactly built and of great spirit and endurance, was captured here and became the favorite horse of General Stevens.

Immediately after landing General Sherman held a conference with his general officers as to undertaking an offensive movement. The enemy was evidently demoralized, and either Charleston or Savannah might fall before a sudden dash and offered a tempting prize. But the general opinion was that a movement upon either involved too great risks and that the first duty was to fortify and render absolutely secure the point already gained. General Stevens alone dissented from this view. He strenuously urged an aggressive movement inland to the mainland, then, turning to right or left, against one of the cities. In answer to objections he declared that the overpowering naval force rendered Hilton Head already secure and it could be fortified at leisure. The navy, too, could support an advance and cover a withdrawal in case of need. . . . But the cautious counsel prevailed. . . .

Samuel F. DuPont

"THE BEARER . . . WILL . . . CARRY WITH HIM THE CAPTURED FLAGS"

On the recommendation of President Lincoln, Congress passed a resolution of thanks to Samuel F. DuPont for his victory at Port Royal, and on July 30, 1861, he was made a Rear Admiral.

All but one of the captured Confederate flags were forwarded to Washington shortly after the victory. That one, on March 6, 1862, was sent by Admiral DuPont to the Mayor of Wilmington, Delaware. "I have retained in my possession until an opportunity offered of forwarding it, the American flag first hoisted on Fort Beauregard after its capture on the 7th of November, 1861. I send with it a rebel flag, likewise captured in South Carolina by one of the vessels of my fleet. . . .

*Will you do me the favor to present them in my name to the loyal city
of Wilmington? They are the emblems of a war forced upon us by the
most wicked conspiracy that a forbearing nation has ever had to con-
tend with, the pretensions and crimes of which Wilmington has de-
nounced from the beginning. . . ."*[2]

*The following letters are from Flag Officer DuPont's correspondence
with Gideon Welles, Secretary of the Navy, and with his wife Sophie
Madeleine DuPont, daughter of the founder of the great powder works
of Wilmington, Delaware.*

*Many refugees from Beaufort and the islands had fled to near-by
Grahamville on the mainland. There Charles E. DuPont and his wife
Julia Kirk DuPont, kinsmen of the admiral who captured Port Royal,
are buried.*

Flagship *Wabash*
Off Hilton Head, Port Royal Harbor, November 8, 1861
Hon. Gideon Welles,
   Secretary of the Navy, Washington
   Sir: I have the honor to inform you that yesterday I attacked the
enemy's batteries on Bay Point and Hilton Head, Forts Beauregard
and Walker, and succeeded in silencing them after an engagement of
four hours' duration, and driving away the squadron of rebel steamers
under Commodore Tattnall. The reconnaissance of yesterday made us
acquainted with the superiority of Fort Walker, and to that I directed
my special efforts, engaging it at a distance of, first, 800 and afterwards
600 yards. But the plan of attack brought the squadron sufficiently
near Fort Beauregard to receive its fire, and the ships were frequently
fighting the batteries on both sides at the same time.
   The action was begun on my part twenty-six minutes after 9, and at
half past 2 the American ensign was hoisted on the flagstaff of Fort
Walker, and this morning at sunrise on that of Fort Beauregard.
   The defeat of the enemy terminated in utter rout and confusion.
Their quarters and encampments were abandoned without an attempt
to carry away either public or private property.
   The ground over which they fled was strewn with the arms of private

---

[2] "S. F. DuPont to His Honor Vincent Gilpin, Mayor of the City of Wilmington, March 6, 1862" in *Official Records of the Union and Confederate Navies* . . .
Series I, Vol. 12, p. 623.

soldiers, and officers retired in too much haste to submit to the encumbrance of their swords.

Landing my marines and a company of seamen, I took possession of the deserted ground and held the forts on Hilton Head till the arrival of General Sherman, to whom I had the honor to transfer its occupation.

We have captured forty-three pieces of cannon, most of them of the heaviest caliber and of the most improved description.

The bearer of these dispatches will have the honor to carry with him the captured flags and two small brass field pieces, lately belonging to the State of South Carolina, which are sent home as suitable trophies of the success of the day. . . .

I have the honor to be, very respectfully, your obedient servant,

S. F. DuPont

Flag-Officer, Commanding South Atlantic Blockading Squadron

P.S. The bearer of dispatches will also carry with him the first American ensign raised upon the soil of South Carolina since this rebellion broke out.

[To Mrs. Samuel F. DuPont]

Wabash, Port Royal, November 9, 1861

. . . During the disheartening events of our passage my faith never gave way, but at some moments it seemed appalling. On the other hand, I permit no elation at our success. Yet I cannot refrain from telling you that it has been more complete and brilliant than I ever could have believed. I have been too fatigued to send a detailed account of the battle; I had to content myself with a succinct account, which I think will be liked as well as a more detailed narrative. I kept under way and made three turns, though I passed five times between the forts. I had a flanking division of five ships to watch, and Old Tatnall too, who had eight small and swift steamers ready to pounce upon any of ours, should they be disabled. I could get none of my big frigates up. I believe my plan was clever. I stood against the tide and had the [better] management . . . in consequence.

The confidence of the enemy was extreme that they could drive us away. They fought bravely, and their rifle guns never missed. They aimed at one bridge, where they knew they could make a hole if they were lucky. A shot in the center let water into the after magazine, but I saved a hundred lives by keeping under way and bearing in close. I never conceived such a fire as that of this ship on her second turn, and I am told that its effect upon the spectators outside of her was intense. I learn that when they saw our flag flying on shore, the troops were powerless to cheer, but wept. . . .

[To Gideon Welles]
                                                        Flagship *Wabash*
                                        Port Royal Harbor, November 9, 1861
     Sir: . . . I have sent gunboats to take possession of Beaufort to protect the inhabitants, but I regret to say they have fled and the town is abandoned to the Negroes, represented to me as in a lawless condition.
     The light vessels, which I hoped to save, were destroyed on the desertion of the forts by the rebels.
     The post-office was visited and a number of documents and letters obtained.
     I have covered Skull Creek, mouth of Broad River, and have cut off the communication between Charleston and Savannah. . . .
                                                        S. F. DuPont
                                                        Flag-Officer

                                                        Flagship *Wabash*,
                                        Port Royal Harbor, S. C., November 17, 1861
     Sir: . . . On Tuesday, the 12th instant, I went to Beaufort myself, inviting General Sherman to accompany me, and taking up the *Seneca* with the armed launches of this ship. The *Unadilla* and *Pembina* held possession of the river and town.
     The latter was deserted. A few blacks were standing at the corners of the streets; their plunder and destruction had been arrested. The impression produced by the sight of a city in perfect preservation, and bearing all the signs of the most recent inhabitation yet wanting the animation of ordinary life, was very striking.
     The people left their property in such a state as to show that their precipitate flight was either the result of real terror or of a design to make it appear such.
     They have so long asserted that we carry on the war without regard to the common humanities and courtesies of modern hostilities that some persons have probably become the dupes of their own misrepresentations. Some are actually deceived. . . .

A fear of the slaves is no doubt one of the chief troubles and lies much deeper than even any apprehension of ourselves.

The deserted city and neighboring plantations exhibit a most melancholy example of weakness and dereliction from duty, the only excuse for which must be the well-founded dread of a servile insurrection.

I have held Beaufort long enough to give the inhabitants an opportunity to return to their homes, but since, in the opinion of General Sherman, it is not a strategic point, and the services of the squadron are, as you know, required elsewhere, I have determined to withdraw the vessels.

A flag of truce was sent to Port Royal Ferry (under my escort as far as Beaufort) by General Sherman on Thursday, the 14th instant. . . .

S. F. DuPont
Flag-Officer, Commanding South Atlantic Blockading Squadron

THE DRAYTON BROTHERS REPORT THE BATTLE OF PORT ROYAL

The Drayton brothers, sons of William and Ann Gadsden Drayton, were born in Charleston, South Carolina, Thomas Fenwick Drayton in 1807 and Percival Drayton in 1812.

Thomas, who commanded the Confederate forces at Port Royal, was graduated from West Point in 1828. He resigned from the service in 1836 and went to Beaufort County, South Carolina, to become a planter. He married Catherine Pope, whose family had long been identified with the islands of Beaufort County. Besides his planting interests Thomas was in charge of building the Charleston & Savannah Railroad and served as its president from 1853 to 1861.

Thomas' oldest son, William Seabrook Drayton, served with the Confederate troops on Hilton Head Island—the site of one of Thomas' favorite plantations—at the battle of Port Royal. A younger son was named for Thomas' brother.

Percival entered the U. S. Navy at the age of fifteen as a midshipman and advanced to the rank of Commander. When his native state seceded, he was on ordnance duty at the navy yard in Philadelphia and elected to remain with the Union. After the battle of Port Royal he was promoted to the rank of Captain. Percival took part in the first

*attack on Fort Sumter under Admiral DuPont, and he commanded
Farragut's flagship, the Hartford, at Mobile Bay. At the end of the
war he was named Chief of the Bureau of Navigation. On August 4,
1865, shortly after this appointment, Captain Drayton, who had never
married, died.*

   *At the time of the Port Royal battle the Drayton brothers' mother,
Ann, was dangerously ill. Her last words and thoughts were of her sons.
"Percy fired at Tom; Tom fired at Percy."*

   The following are from the brothers' reports on the battle.

Commander Percival Drayton

U.S.S. *Pocahontas*
Port Royal Harbor, November 9, 1861

   Sir: In obedience to your order I beg leave to state that on the morning of the 7th instant I found myself a few miles from Tybee lighthouse and at once commenced steaming for Port Royal entrance. Soon
after I stood off in pursuit of a schooner which I thought intended
breaking the blockade, but which proved to be laden with coal for the
squadron. As my stock was reduced to one day's supply and it was
reported to me that the fleet was at anchor outside, I thought it a good
opportunity to replenish while towing the vessel to our mutual destination, and this I was doing when about 10 o'clock I heard the beginning of a cannonade. I immediately cast off the schooner and stood for
the scene of action, which I reached at a little after 12 o'clock. In
passing I engaged the batteries on Bay Point and Hilton Head, but
soon getting out of range of the former, I directed my fire on the latter
until signal was made about 2.30 to cease firing.

   During this time, I expended 24 X-inch and 37 32-pounder shell and
5 32-pounder shot and 4 15-pounder rifle shell. I could have fired much
more frequently, but as there were evident signs toward the last that
the enemy were leaving, I thought it well to spare the ammunition.
The only injuries received were a shot through the mainmast and the
boom topping lift and several small pieces of rigging cut away.

   I am, very respectfully, your obedient servant,

P. DRAYTON
Commander, Commanding *Pocahontas*

Flag Officer S. F. DuPont,
   Commanding South Atlantic Squadron, Port Royal Harbor

General Thomas Fenwick Drayton

Headquarters Provisional Forces
Third Military District, Department of South Carolina
Camp Lee, Hardeeville, November 24, 1861

Sir: I have the honor of presenting my official report of the engagement on the 7th instant between the Federal fleet, numbering fifteen war steamers and gunboats, and Forts Walker and Beauregard, upon Hilton Head and Bay Point, at the entrance of Port Royal Sound. . . .

The enemy's fleet had been collecting in our waters since the morning of the 4th instant and had increased in the afternoon to thirty-two war steamers and transports. On receiving a dispatch to this effect from Colonel William C. Heyward, commanding the troops at Camp Walker, I left my headquarters in Beaufort and repaired by steamer to Bay Point, which I reached at 6 P.M., passing on the way the ever-watchful little fleet of Flag Officer Tattnall, Confederate States Navy.

After remaining until 1.30 A.M. with Colonel R. G. M. Dunovant, commandant of the post, I took my departure. . . . I then visited Commodore Tattnall and after an exchange of views, took leave, crossed over to Hilton Head Island, landed there at daylight on the 5th. . . .

About 9 o'clock A.M. of the 5th, Commodore Tattnall, who had boldly attacked the enemy's gunboats on the previous day, again gallantly steamed out to exchange shots with them, but he was met by too large a force and, therefore, retired slowly behind our forts. The enemy followed and engaged both batteries for about forty-five minutes, with no other injury than three men slightly burned in Fort Beauregard from the explosion of a caisson struck by a rifle shell.

On the 6th instant the fleet and transports, which had increased to about forty-five sail, would probably have attacked us had not the weather been very boisterous. . . .

The 7th dawned upon us bright and serene. Not a ripple upon the broad expanse of water to disturb the accuracy of fire from the broad decks of that magnificent armada . . . advancing in battle array to vomit forth its iron hail with all the spiteful energy of long-suppressed rage and conscious strength. At 9:25 A.M. our IX-inch Dahlgren gun opened fire upon the 48-gun steamship *Wabash*, flagship of Captain S. F. DuPont, which led the van, closely succeeded by fourteen other large steamers and gunboats.

The shell from the Dahlgren exploded near the muzzle and was harmless. Other shot followed from both forts, and soon the fire became general on land and water. In spite of our fire . . . the fleet soon passed both batteries, apparently unharmed, and then, returning, delivered in their charging rounds a terrific shower of shot and shell in flank and front.

Besides this moving battery the fort was enfiladed by two gunboats anchored to the north, off the mouth of Fishhall Creek, and another at a point on the edge of the shoals to the south. This enfilading fire on so still a sea annoyed and damaged us excessively, particularly as we had no gun on either flank of the bastion to reply with, for the 32-pounder on the right flank was shattered very early by a round shot, and on the north flank, for want of a carriage, no gun had been mounted. After the fourth fire the X-inch columbiad bounded over the limber and became useless. The 24-pounder rifled cannon was choked while ramming down a shell and lay idle during nearly the whole engagement. The shells for the IX-inch Dahlgren were also too large. The fourth shell attempted to be rammed home could not be driven below the trunnions, and was then at great risk discharged.

Thus far the fire of the enemy had been endured and replied to with the unruffled courage of veterans. At 10:30 our gunners became so fatigued that I left the fort accompanied by one of my volunteer aids, Capt. H. Rose, and went back to Captain Read's battery (1¾ miles in the rear of the fort) and brought the greater part of his men back to take the places of our exhausted men inside the fort. . . .

The vigorous attack from the fleet continued unabated with still no decided damage to any of their ships. About 12:30 P.M. I again went out of the fort with my assistant adjutant general, Captain Young, for the purpose of mustering together the infantry and reserves and have them in readiness for any eventuality. Before leaving, however, I turned over the command to Colonel Heyward, with directions to hold out as long as any effective fire could be returned.

Having mounted our horses, we rejoined the troops near Hospital No. 2. I received information through one of the vedettes that a steamer and small boats were sounding close to the beach. I detached Captain Berry with three companies of his battalion . . . by a road marked "K," to watch the enemy, beat them back if they attempted to land and give notice if he wanted support. I then, with some of my staff, rode to collect together the other troops, who, through ignorance of our island roads, had lost their way and had not yet come up. . . .

On reaching my reserves at Hospital 2, I learned that the enemy had ceased taking soundings and had gone back to sea. . . .

2 o'clock had not arrived when I noticed our men coming out of the fort which they had bravely defended for four and a half hours against fearful odds, . . . only retiring when all but three of the guns on the water front had been disabled and [with] only 500 pounds of powder in the magazine, [having begun] the action with 220 men inside the fort, afterward increased to 255. . . .

The retreat was commenced about 3 P.M. toward Ferry Point, about 6 miles off, Colonel DeSaussure's regiment and Captain J. Read's company of artillery bringing up the rear. At 1:30 A.M. by the aid of Commodore Tattnall's fleet, the steamers *St. Johns* and *Edisto* and three large flats capable of holding 150 men each, the troops were all safely embarked without provisions [and with] no ammunition but what was contained in the cartridge boxes (the 100,000 cartridges I had made requisition for and been anxiously expecting, not having reached us until after the battle). . . . Fearing that our retreat would be cut off by the enemy's gunboats at Skull Creek, no other alternative was left but to leave the island and concentrate upon the mainland. . . .

The muskets captured by the enemy, with the exception of some ten or fifteen, were those left in the fort, shattered by shot and shell. Others [were] left in camp—belonging to men on sick leave or to those engaged in heating hot-shot furnaces two days before the fight, and some boxes of arms which had been left on the wharf the night before the battle, belonging to the sick men of Colonel DeSaussure's regiment, who had been left behind at Lightwood Knot—and which could have been saved, with a box of swords, if the captains of the steamers *Edisto* and *St. Johns* had not refused to take them on board when directed to do so. . . .

Fort Beauregard. The attack upon the fort, though not so concentrated and heavy as that upon Walker, was, nevertheless, very severe. Its armament was nineteen guns, of which the following, viz: one VIII-inch Rodman, bored to 24-pounder and rifled; two 42-pounders; one X-inch columbiad; two 42-pounders, reamed to 8 inches; and one 32-pounder, in hot-shot battery, were the only guns capable of being used against the fleet.

The force on Bay Point was 640 men, commanded by Colonel R. G. M. Dunovant, Twelfth Regiment South Carolina Volunteers. Of the above, 149 garrisoned Fort Beauregard under the immediate command of Captain Stephen Elliott, Jr., Beaufort Volunteer Artillery Company A, Ninth Regiment, South Carolina Volunteers. The infantry force of Colonel Dunovant's regiment was intrusted with the protection of the eastern part of the island and of the defense of the bastion line at the Island Narrows where an attack was expected from the enemy. . . .

Notwithstanding the prompt measures adopted by Colonel Dunovant to effect his retreat in the direction of the Narrows, it is surprising that, with the knowledge possessed by the enemy (through Mr. Boutelle and others connected with the Coast Survey), his retreat had not been intercepted by gunboats passing toward Beaufort, and mine by other steamers taking the passage through Skull Creek toward the ferry landing. Why they did not adopt this course must be left to time to explain.

Casualties. . . . Total killed and wounded 59; missing 4; taken prisoners, sick in hospital, 3. Total number killed, wounded, missing and taken prisoners, 66. . . .

THOS. F. DRAYTON
Brigadier-General, Commanding

To
Captain L. D. Walker,
Assistant Adjutant-General, Charleston, S. C.

PART XI

Behind the Lines with General Robert E. Lee

On his appointment as commander of the coast defenses of South Carolina, Georgia and East Florida, General Robert E. Lee left for Charleston on November 6, 1861. From Charleston he hastened to Coosawhatchie on the Charleston & Savannah Railroad. Here he established headquarters and remained until March 2, 1862, when he was called back to Richmond by President Davis.

The Federals made a series of unsuccessful attempts to establish a hold on the mainland: at Port Royal Ferry on January 1, June 6, July 4, December 6 and 7, 1862; at Coosawhatchie on October 22, 1862; at Pocotaligo on July 9 and 10 and October 22, 1862. Not until January 14, 1865, when Pocotaligo was abandoned by the Confederates did the Federals gain control of the mainland.

General Lee undertook "first, to prepare the defenses of Fort Pulaski, of Savannah, and of Charleston . . . second, to obstruct the waterways up which the Federals might send their ships . . . third, to assemble the scattered Confederate forces at the most probable point of Federal advance toward the railroad, and, in case of an early attack, to offer such resistance as he could in the field."

At the end of four months, "without the loss of a single soldier from the fire of the enemy, he had held off Sherman from the railroad," wrote Dr. Douglas Southall Freeman, "and had put so many difficulties in the way of his advance that the Federals had nowhere moved beyond the cover of their warships."[1]

---

[1] D. S. Freeman, *Robert E. Lee*. New York: Scribner's, 1933-34, Vol. I, pp. 610, 629.

General Robert E. Lee

FROM COOSAWHATCHIE, SOUTH CAROLINA

General Lee describes, in the following letters to Judah P. Benjamin, a native of Beaufort and now Secretary of War of the Confederate States, the situation on the mainland after the battle of Port Royal. Letters to his son Custis tell of further movements of the enemy.

To his daughter Annie he sent "some violets I plucked in the yard of a deserted house I occupy. . . ."[2]

General Lee had with him in South Carolina "a young gray horse he had purchased in western Virginia."[3] This horse was called Greenbrier and was such a "fine traveller" that he won a new name—Traveller.

From Coosawhatchie, South Carolina

Headquarters
Coosawhatchie, November 9, 1861

Hon. J. P. Benjamin,
    Secretary of War:

Sir: On the evening of the 7th, on my way to the entrance of Port Royal Harbor, I met General [R. S.] Ripley returning from the battery at the north end of Hilton Head, called Fort Walker. He reported that the enemy's fleet had passed the batteries and entered the harbor. Nothing could then be done to make arrangements to withdraw the troops from the batteries to prevent their capture and save the public property. The troops were got over during the night, but their tents, clothing and provisions were mostly lost and all the guns left in the batteries. General Drayton's command was transferred from Fort Walker to Bluffton; Colonel [R. G. M.] Dunovant's from Bay Point to Saint Helena Island and thence to Beaufort.

There are neither batteries nor guns for the defense of Beaufort, and Colonel Dunovant crossed Port Royal Ferry yesterday and was halted at Garden's Corner. General Drayton reports that he has but 955 men with him and no field battery, the troops from Georgia that were on

---

[2] *Recollections and Letters of General Robert E. Lee*, p. 56.
[3] D. S. Freeman, *Robert E. Lee*. Vol. I, p. 615.

the island having returned to Savannah without orders. Colonel Dunovant's regiment is in as destitute a condition as General Drayton's command, as they were obliged to leave everything behind, and number between 600 and 700 men. I wrote to general [A. R.] Lawton to endeavor to withdraw the guns from the battery at the south end of Hilton Head. I have received as yet no report from him nor any official account from the commanders of the batteries. I fear every gun has been lost. At present I am endeavoring to collect troops to defend the line of the railroad and to push forward the defenses of Charleston and Savannah.

Colonel Clingman's regiment of North Carolina volunteers, six companies of Colonel Edward's regiment of South Carolina volunteers, and Colonel Martin's South Carolina cavalry compose the force now here. The enemy, having complete possession of the water and inland navigation, commands all the islands on this coast, . . . threatens both Savannah and Charleston, and can come in his boats within 4 miles of this place. His sloops of war and large steamers can come up Broad River to Mackay's Point, the mouth of the Pocotaligo, and his gunboats can ascend some distance up the Coosawhatchie and Tulifiny. We have no guns that can resist their batteries, and have no recourse but to prepare to meet them in the field. They have landed on Hilton Head. Their fleet is in Port Royal Harbor. Four of their gunboats are reported to be approaching Beaufort. I fear there are but few State troops ready for the field. The garrisons of the forts at Charleston and Savannah and on the coast cannot be removed from the batteries while ignorant of the designs of the enemy. I am endeavoring to bring into the field such light batteries as can be prepared.

I have the honor to be, your obedient servant,

R. E. LEE
General, Commanding

Headquarters
Coosawhatchie, S. C., December 3, 1861

Hon. J. P. Benjamin,
    Secretary of War, Richmond, Va.:
Sir: In a letter received to-day from Col. John S. Preston, whom I had assigned to the duty of mustering into the service of the Confederate States such troops as might offer themselves for the war from the State of South Carolina or be transferred by the governor, it is stated that the

only transfers made up to the time are four companies for twelve-months' service. Even for twelve months the recruiting is very languid; for the war not one company has yet offered, and not one new regiment will be organized in three months. The entire levy will be for terms less than the war, and generally for twelve months, for local defense and special service. I fear that there will be great delay in organizing even such a force as can be armed, unless some measures can be resorted to to procure men. . . .

I yesterday visited Port Royal Sound, with the view of organizing a light force to cut off, if possible, the enemy's marauding parties on the islands. No attempts have yet been made on the mainland, nor could I discover any indication of any movement. The fleet in large force lay extended across the sound from Hilton Head to Bay Point, perfectly quiescent, and no troops were visible except a picket at Hilton Head Ferry. . . .

I have the honor to be, very respectfully, your obedient servant,

R. E. LEE
General, Commanding

General Lee to his son Custis

Dec. 29, 1861

. . . The news from Europe is indeed good, but I think the U.S. Government, notwithstanding their moral and political commitment to Wilkes' act, if it finds that England is earnest and that it will have to fight or retract, will retract. We must make up our minds to fight our battles ourselves, expect to receive aid from no one and make every necessary sacrifice of comfort, money and labor to bring the war to a successful close. The cry is too much for help. I am mortified to hear it. We want no aid. We want to be true to ourselves, to be prudent, just and bold. . . .

The enemy is quiet, and safe in his big boats. He is threatening everywhere around, pillaging, burning, and robbing where he can venture with impunity, and alarming women and children. Every day I have reports of their landing in force, marching upon us, etc., which turns out to be some marauding party. The last was from North Edisto. I yesterday went over the whole line in that region from the Ashepoo to the west and found everything quiet and could only see them by black ships lying down the Edisto, where the water is too broad for anything we have to reach them. They will not venture as yet in the narrow waters. I went yesterday 115 miles but only 35 on horseback. I did not get back until 11 P.M. I took Greenbrier the whole distance. Take good care of Richmond. Draw his forage on my account. Send him to me if opportunity offers, if you do not want him. I have two horses now with me. Good-by, my dear son.

R. E. Lee

Coosawhatchie, S. C. Jan. 4, 1862

... We are all well. No news. Enemy quiet, and retired to his Islands. The Main seemed too insecure for him, and he never went 400 yards from his steamers, not even to the extent of the range of his guns. After burning some houses (three) on the river bank, and feeling our proximity unpleasant, he retreated to Port Royal again. I hope we may always be able to keep him close. But he can move with great facility and rapidity and land anywhere he can bring his steamers, and burn, pillage and destroy, and we cannot prevent him. We lost one 12-pounder. It was drawn by mules with Negro drivers, so hard are we pressed for men, who became frightened at the firing, upset the gun in a ditch, broke the carriage, and it had to be abandoned. Do you hear of any more troops coming to me, or can any be sent? ...

Your affectionate father,

R. E. Lee.

Joseph Wilmer Turner

"WE ARE UNDER THE COMMAND OF GENERAL R. E. LEE"

Among the troops commanded by General Lee during his command of the southeast coast of the Confederacy were several regiments of infantry and field artillery which had been sent from Virginia. Young Joseph Wilmer Turner was a private in one of the artillery units. His letters to his father in Virginia are now in the collections of the Maryland Historical Society. One of them follows. On the back of the original is written:

"A letter from My Dear Son, Joseph Wilmer Turner, written while a member of Leake's Battery stationed at Coosawhatchie, Beaufort

District, South Carolina. Don't let it be destroyed. I wish him to take it and have it copied with pen and ink and preserve it and hand it down to his children as an heirloom with his request blended with mine that they will preserve it. He was 17 years of age when it was written.

"GEO. W. TURNER

"Fortuna favet fortibus."

Coosawhatchie, Beaufort District, South Carolina
Dec 10th, 1861

Dear Father

I am now encamped near Coosawhatchie (pronounced Koo-say-hat-chee) River in the District of Beaufort, South Carolina, 60 miles distant from Charleston, near the Charleston and Savannah Railroad and within 45 [miles] of Savannah. [It is] a low, marshy and level country within a few miles of the seacoast and the yankees are within 5 or 6 miles distance of us. The Coosawhatchie flows into the Broad a few miles below in conjunction with the Pocotaligo, and steamboats can come up the Coosawhatchie as high as our camp. The country is quite healthy in the winter season but very sickly in summer, none but Negroes remaining here in that season. . . . Occasionally their overseers come down in the day but dare not remain at night, it being almost certain death for white persons to do so.

There are a number of small islands around Port Royal which produce very fine Sea Island cotton. The enemy have possession of these islands, which we are unable to drive them off of on account of the superiority their fleet gives them over us. Occasionally they land, but when we prepare to give them fight, they flee to their ships for protection. It is thought that they intend attacking Charleston both by sea and land, but the country is very marshy and it would be difficult for an army to invade it. The enemy number some 30,000. We have now encamped along the seacoast between Charleston and Savannah about 17,000 but expect some 10 regiments from Virginia soon. Our company and Captain Thornton's company of Caroline Artillery are the first companies of Virginians that have come to this state; Captain Thornton's arrived about 2 days before ours. The two companies are encamped together just as they were at Camp Magruder.

The climate near the seacoast is quite warm in the day and cool at night, and I would venture to say there is a greater variation in temperature during 24 hours then in Virginia. Ice is seldom seen and the thickest known for several years was a quarter of an inch. . . . It is a fine cotton region, and fine sweet potatoes are raised here in great abundance. . . . I imagine musquitoes are also numerous in the summer season; bad water is also plentiful. We are immediately under the command of Major General R. E. Lee of Virginia. There are few companies of artillery here.

Formerly there was an old Indian tribe that used to inhabit here; William Gilmore Simms wrote one of his novels about this tribe. "Hatchie" in the Indian language is supposed to mean "river" and there used to be a tribe of Coosaw Indians about here and the river is thought to be named after them. General Lee's headquarters are within a few hundred yards of us. So you see I am away down south in Dixie. . . . Direct your letters to "the care of Capt. Leake Turner, Artillery, Coosawhatchie, South Carolina." My love to all.

Your affectionate son
J. W. TURNER

PART XII

Department of the South, Port Royal, South Carolina

Secretary of War Stanton issued the following announcement from Washington on March 15, 1862: "The States of South Carolina, Georgia, and Florida, with the expedition and forces now under Brig. T. W. Sherman, will constitute a military department, to be called the Department of the South, to be commanded by Major General Hunter."

General David Hunter established his headquarters on Hilton Head Island. This was the base used for military operations against Charleston and as headquarters for the blockade.

"The sea islands, especially near Beaufort, became the scene of missionary, educational, economic and military experiments with the Negroes, in which exalted, impractical idealism, religious devotion and rough military impatience of the various Northerners participating were strangely mingled with the stolidity of some of the most primitive and ignorant slaves in the State.

"Here were mustered in November 1862 the first slave, and except for some almost white 'Negroes' of New Orleans, the first Negro troops in the Federal service."[1]

Plantations were seized as "abandoned lands" and either distributed at low prices to Negroes, soldiers or civilians or retained by the Government. The entire town of Beaufort was sold.

---

[1] David Duncan Wallace, *South Carolina; a Short History, 1520-1948*. Chapel Hill: The University of North Carolina Press, 1951, p. 535.

Concerning the sale of lands, the New England Freedmen's Aid Society, in its Second Annual Report, April 1864, states:

"In March 1863, the United States sold at auction 16,479 acres of land out of 76,775 acres subject to sale for non-payment of taxes. The lands, with the buildings, brought but 93⅓ cents per acre. About 3,500 acres were taken by the blacks. The number of acres now owned by the freedmen is said to be not far from 7,350. More recently, at the sale of the town of Beaufort, from seventy-five to eighty houses and house lots were bought by the blacks, at prices ranging from $40 to $1,800...."

Captain Hazard Stevens

"GENERAL STEVENS WAS ORDERED . . .
TO OCCUPY BEAUFORT"

General Isaac Ingalls Stevens, native of Massachusetts, was a gradu-
ate of West Point in 1839. In the Mexican War he was a tentmate of
Robert E. Lee. In 1853 he became the first governor of Washington
Territory and in 1857 its first representative in Congress. When war
came, he accepted the colonelcy of the 79th Regiment of New York,
known as the "Highlanders." In the Port Royal expedition he com-
manded the Second Brigade under General Thomas W. Sherman and
directed the work of fortifying Hilton Head Island.

General Stevens remained in Beaufort until July 1862 when he was
transferred to the Army of Virginia. He was replaced by General Rufus
Saxton. On September 1, 1862, while leading his men at the battle of
Chantilly, he was killed at the age of forty-four.

Captain Hazard Stevens, his only son, served on his father's staff.
The general wrote his wife on February 16, 1862, "Hazard is making a
very superior officer indeed; is a very efficient adjutant-general." Many
years later the son wrote a biography of the father from which the fol-
lowing extract is taken.

. . . General Stevens was ordered, early in December, to occupy
Beaufort as an advanced post threatening the mainland and affording
protection to the Negroes on the islands. . . . Since the bombardment
raiding parties of the enemy were venturing over with encreasing boldness, burning the cotton and terrorizing the Negroes. These numbered
at least ten thousand, thus abandoned by their masters [the "masters"
were in Confederate service, and their wives and children were refu-
gees], and were scattered over the extensive archipelago, but chiefly
upon Port Royal, Ladies' [*sic*], and St. Helena islands.

The more intelligent house servants having gone with their owners,
nearly all the Negroes left on the islands were in the densest ignorance,
some of them the blackest human beings ever seen and others the most
bestial in appearance, and there were even some native Africans,
brought over by slavers in recent years. . . .

These ignorant and benighted creatures flocked into Beaufort on the hegira of the whites and held high carnival in the deserted mansions, smashing doors, mirrors and furniture, and appropriating all that took their fancy. After this loot, a common sight was a black wench dressed in silks or white lace curtains, or a stalwart black field hand resplendent in a complete suit of gaudy carpeting just torn from the floor. After this sack, they remained at home on the plantations and reveled in unwonted idleness and luxury, feasting upon the corn, cattle and turkeys of their fugitive masters.

General Stevens at once cleared the blacks out of town and established a camp in the suburbs for the temporary reception of refugees and vagrant Negroes. He placed the troops under canvas in the outskirts, . . . prohibited their entering the town without a permit, and strictly forbade all plundering or even entering the empty houses. Guards were posted over a fine public library, the pride of the town, which, however, had been thrown about in utter disorder; patrols were kept scouring the streets, and the strictest order and discipline were enforced.

In order to protect the Negroes and keep the enemy within his own lines, General Stevens strongly picketed the western or exposed side of Port Royal and Ladies' [sic] islands, guarding all the landing places, and watching the Coosaw and Broad rivers for twenty-five miles. Knowing the difficulty of maintaining so long and exposed a line of outposts against an enterprising enemy, he threw him on the defensive by the boldness of his advanced line and by a succession of well-planned and daring raids upon his pickets on the opposite shore. . . .

A fine mansion in the edge of town, in the midst of a luxuriant semi-tropical garden, with the Negro quarters and kitchens in detached buildings, served as headquarters. On the open space on one side, brigade guard-mounting was held every morning to the martial and inspiring music of the Highlanders' band. This was one of the finest bands in the service or, indeed, in the country. . . .

Thus well occupied with drills, dress parades, guard-mountings, picketing and study in that beautiful region and delightful winter climate, profusely supplied with fresh beef, poultry and sweet potatoes in addition to the ample regular ration, the troops greatly enjoyed their sojourn at Beaufort, while they rapidly gained soldierly discipline and efficiency. . . .

Susan Walker

A VOLUNTEER ON ST. HELENA ISLAND

In February 1862, General Thomas W. Sherman, commanding the Port Royal area, issued an order calling for agents to operate the abandoned plantations and for teachers "whose duties will consist in teaching [the Negroes] both young and old, the rudiments of civilization and Christianity. . . ."

In the following month, under the auspices of the Treasury Department and with the additional support of charitable organizations such as the Freedmen's Aid Society of Boston, the National Freedmen's Relief Commission of New York, and the Pennsylvania Freedmen's Relief Association, a call was sent out for men and women to go south to teach the Negroes and manage the plantations.

Edward L. Pierce, a young Harvard law-school graduate, was named superintendent-general of the Port Royal project. His orders were to "prevent the deterioration of the estates, secure their best cultivation and promote the welfare of the laborers."

On March 3, 1862, Mr. Pierce and a group of some fifty-four persons boarded the steamship Atlantic *in New York and set sail for Port Royal, "the first missionary expedition to propagate industry, religion and education among the contrabands."*

One of the volunteers was Susan Walker, a native of Wilmington, Massachusetts, who was assigned to the former plantation of Daniel Pope on St. Helena Island, where Mr. Pierce had established headquarters. She remained until June 6, 1862.

Tuesday 18th March. Last night it was decided that we should go to the plantation. We rejoice in this decision, because we believe we can be far more useful there. . . .

Mr. Pierce urges us to the plantation and so we go—four of us together. A "lighter" takes our luggage, and a 6-oar boat, rowed by as many stalwart Negroes, takes us and Mr. [Edward W.] Hooper [of the Educational Commission], who is our escort. Our rowers sing as they row their own songs—some impromptu and all religious—about the

Savior and the kingdom. Their oars dip in the sparkling water, keeping time to the song. It is a clear bright day. The sun [is] warm, but a fine breeze makes our row of half an hour in crossing Beaufort river most delightful. . . .

Mr. [Frederic A.] Eustis [of Milton, Mass.] has invited us to dine with him and sent his carriage to the ferry for us. The carriage, dilapidated now, was Miss Mary Jenkins' but confiscated and appropriated by Mr. Eustis. This is our way of securing comforts. A nice dinner, roast beef, awaited us, and a pleasant reunion with friends we had not seen since we parted on arrival at Hilton Head. After dinner the gentlemen preceded us to the Pope plantation to see if all was in readiness for us. They returned and escorted us to our future *home*, where tea awaited us, also a crowd of blacks—men, women and children—came to welcome us. Ragged and dirty, they offered hands we could not refuse. The men scraped and bowed, the women curtesied. Little children scraped without bowing, most laughable. . . .

Wednesday 19th March. . . . After arranging my room I went with Mrs. Johnson and Mr. Eustis to his overseer-house, now our store house, to open boxes of clothing and select for plantation. Worked all day and returned for 6 P.M. dinner. . . .

Saturday. Visited cabins and preached industry and cleanliness. I am hopeful.

Sunday. Drove 4 miles to church. Avenue leading up to the church [has] natural hedge of Cherokee rose, climbing sometimes 30 or 40 feet on privet and pine tree. Church stands in a grove of live oak deeply fringed with grey moss. A burial place overhung by a wide-spreading live oak, whose luxuriant branches with their pendants of moss seemed like wings of guardian angels spread out to embrace the loved ones buried there, whose white marble monuments tell us they "lived to be loved and died to be lamented." . . .

I taught a class in our morning Sunday school and never have I seen greater earnestness to learn to read. They oftener ask for books than for clothes. After school the church was filled with some 3[oo] to 400 clean dressed, [in] showy gowns left by Sesesh ladies, and trousers, coats and vests made of carpeting taken from the floors. . . .

After service Mr. Pierce, Nellie and I drove to Jenkins' plantation, about 8 miles from Pope's. The house stands near the river, is 5 miles by boat from Hilton Head. An extensive and beautiful flower garden lies between house and river. I gathered a rich and varied bouquet from the large beds of verbena and sweet violet, retinospora from the large trees in the garden, oleander buds from trees larger than the largest quince tree, coral honeysuckle and geranium and many other varieties. . . .

Tuesday. Again at the Jenkins' plantation to look into cabins, talk with women and see what can be done to improve them. Katy has 7 ragged, dirty children—what shall be done? No husband and *nothing*. Some clothes are given for her children—one naked, and must have it at once. Is Katy lazy? Very likely. Does she tell the truth? Perhaps not. I must have faith, and she must at least cover her children. . . . Visited some twenty or more cabins and talked a great deal. Chaplin's plantation is adjoining. He was old and unmarried. They say he was a kind master. He told them to stay when the Yankees came. Many masters told their slaves the Yankees would take them and send them to Cuba and sell them away from their children and that they must run when the Yankees came. One woman said they told her the Yankees had horns and she must run and hide in the woods before they came. She added, "I knowed massa meant to come and get me away an' I didn't go." . . .

I fear the cotton agent, Salisbury, stationed here is not a good man. The Negroes complain of him, and they all look so neglected it is quite evident he has done no good upon the plantation. He drives the finest horses I have seen in Port Royal or St. Helena, gives good dinners, entertains largely, has appropriated all the furniture and nearly all the teams about the place and refuses to give anything to the superintendents placed there by Mr. Pierce. . . .

Thursday 27th March. Visited cabins and found four or five sick. Yesterday Katy gave birth to a child, the first free-born child here, and we mean to call the boy Edward L. Pierce. . . .

Monday 31st March. . . . We have a dinner party today. General Stevens, wife, son and daughter, Mr. Eustis and son and Mr. Hooper, all invited by Mr. Pierce. . . . Our dinner was pronounced a grand success. General Stevens was too busy with trying the pontoon bridge at Beaufort to come and sent his two aids, Captain Stevens—his son—and Lieutenant Lyons, to escort the ladies. . . . We had a merry dinner, though rebel pickets are within 10 miles of us. . . .

Thursday 10th April. Drove with Mr. Pierce and Mary to the far end of Ladies [Lady's] Island—Brickyard Point where Federal troops are stationed. This is opposite the rebel pickets on the mainland, and shots are often exchanged. Captain Gordon Z. Dimock [50th Pennsylvania Infantry] commands here. Had a charming drive through the woods and cotton fields. . . . Stopped at Chaplin's plantation, where the only white man left on St. Helena still lives very secluded, not liking to see any one but his own servants, who still attend him. His family are all Sesesh. He says nothing and is called crazy—did not see him. . . .

Friday 11th April. Heavy firing all morning yesterday and commenced again at 10 last evening, still continued till about 2 P.M.— probably cannonading Fort Pulaski 30 miles distant—so heavy as to shake our house. If Sesesh gain, we will hang from the highest tree. I look at these tall pines in the grove near my window and wonder which branch will hold me. . . .

Sunday 13th April. Sumter anniversary. Went to church and taught Sunday school. Thorpe made an eloquent appeal to the people. . . . His people are troublsome; many are discontented and our young superintendents are tried in many ways. Soldiers and others equally unwise had told them they were "free men and need not work." . . . With a few exceptions, the laborers have gone about their work as in the master's time. All understand the planting better than we can teach them, but they need encouragement. They have not yet become self-reliant. Many are well-disposed and work willingly when made to understand that the corn, which they so willingly plant, is to furnish them food, but the cotton must also be planted for Government, and for this planting wages will be paid them and with their wages they must buy clothes, sweeting and tobacco or have none. . . .

Some are lazy and others grasping. Let us give them a fair opportunity to try here in their native home. . . . Of course Government will not expect to *make anything out of them* this year. . . .

Monday 28th April. . . . The clothing department has finally devolved upon me. It is a great responsibility. . . . I have tried to do the best I could. At first Mr. Eustis, Mrs. [Walter R.] Johnson, Miss [Mary A.] Donaldson and myself assorted clothing at Eustis' overseer house and left it there for Mr. Eustis to send, as packed, to the different superintendents. Mr. Pierce on April 22 had the boxes brought to Pope's cotton house and now I have sole care of it. . . .

29th April, Tuesday. Drove to Gabriel Caper's. He was a bachelor and everything about the place has an exceedingly neglected look. House old and forlorn; cabins wretched and people hopeless. They gathered and gave me some fine white mulberries. . . . Women gathered around me and I tried to explain to them as simply as I could what *government* is: the power that I and they must obey. One bright, intelligent woman expressed herself very much comforted by what I said. She said they had all been so "confuse"; they did not know what to do; did not know where they belonged or "anything about we." Old Gabriel, her master's father, was the person selected by the chief men of the island (St. Helena) to receive Napoleon Bonaparte when they heard of his banishment to St. Helena. . . . Could there be a St. Helena out of cottondom! "Bleeve ye" the Negro would say. . . .

May 2, Friday. Made out pay-roll for laborers on Pope's plantation, "The Oaks." Thirty-nine laborers to be paid proportionally for planting 52¼ acres cotton at 1 dollar per acre. They promise that if they can have another mule they will plant 20 acres more. They must be kept at work for their own good. . . .

6th May, Tuesday. General Hunter has issued an order and sent Jim Cashman to receive colored volunteers for the army. I have tried in vain to inspire desire to fight but none wish to volunteer. This is a sad truth and full of deep meaning. . . . They might and I think would run fast and far to escape their masters and the old condition of slavery. They prove this by daily escapes from the Main, where they were forced to follow their runaway masters. . . . They could, I am sure, be forced to fight, but they will not volunteer to leave their homes. For weeks after the flight of Secesh, with such of the Negroes as could be taken, they would return by night to the plantation to steal others— took them from their beds—took children—till at last the Negroes for many weeks did not venture to sleep in their houses, but hid in the woods or along the creek under the shelving banks or in branches of trees. The children were hidden among the cotton beds every night, in the fields, for weeks after Government took Port Royal and adjacent Islands. . . .

11th May, Sunday. Great excitement! Captain Stevens brings order from General Hunter that all colored men between 18 and 45 capable of bearing arms shall be taken to Hilton Head—no explanation. What can it mean? Are these men contrary to all American usages—U.S. usages rather—to be impressed *against will* to military service? I am called upon, as superintendent of this plantation, to select the persons coming within General Hunter's requisition. . . . Blinded by tears that will not be kept back, I write the names almost as signing their death warrants. The saddest duty I ever performed. . . .

12 May, Monday. Rose early and sought to be prepared for the trials in waiting. Captain Stevens last night brought a company of armed soldiers and paraded before our door previous to distribution over the island. The Negroes became alarmed. They feared the return of Secesh, and, as some of the house servants knew we were invited by Mr. Forbes to go to Hilton Head in his yacht, they were half afraid of our deserting them as their masters had done; that the Hilton Head excursion was but a pretext for escape. They watched the creek all night for fear of attack. Poor creatures, what could they have done against the attack they feared!

Early after breakfast Captain Stevens came with his soldiers to demand the men. I asked to be permitted to speak to them, when assembled, before he should give them his order. He did not give consent but ordered the soldiers to load their guns in the very face of the assembled men and then told them General Hunter had ordered them to Hilton Head, at the same moment ordering soldiers to fire on any one attempting to disobey the order of General Hunter. . . .

I do not think Captain Stevens meant to be so stern as he seemed. He is but a boy and extremely diffident and in no sympathy with our work here for the Negroes. . . . The men were called from the field and thus hurried off without time for coat or shoes or a good-bye to their families. The women stood near by crying, though half assured by my presence in their midst that nothing wrong would be done. The schoolhouse scene was one of great excitement. Captain Stevens drew up with his men to the Negro quarters. Negroes quite unprepared, had no one to give them confidence. Women wept and children screamed as men were torn from their embrace. This is a sad day throughout these islands. . . . Mr. Pierce has gone to Hilton Head to see General Hunter about it. . . .

THE CAPTURE OF COMPANY H, THIRD
NEW HAMPSHIRE

In the summer of 1862, Company H, Third New Hampshire, was sent from Hilton Head Island to outpost duty on Pinckney Island.

*On August 21, news received at Hilton Head told of their capture;
further details remained a mystery for almost six months. Then fourteen of the missing men reported back to Hilton Head.*

*An anonymous member of Company H tells the story of the capture
by Confederates under Captain Stephen Elliott, of the Beaufort Artillery, with Captain J. H. Mickler, Eleventh South Carolina Infantry.
During their six months' absence Company H experienced prison life
in Columbia, South Carolina, and Richmond, Virginia, before being
paroled and exchanged at Annapolis.*

*We have visited Pinckney Island before in the company of the
Pinckney family.*

On the 4th day of July Company H., having been detailed for that
service, went from Hilton Head to Pinckney Island to do outpost
picket duty. The company consisted of between 50 and 60 men, under
command of Lieut. Joseph C. Wiggin, and were quartered at two
plantation houses, headquarters being established at what was called
"The Point"—a house standing at the junction of Broad River and
Skull Creek, and situated on a bluff overlooking both streams. The
other house was about three quarters of a mile south, and 1st Sergt.
Henry F. Hopkins was in command of the men stationed there. The
territory covered by the company in their long tour of duty was about
three miles in extent, posts being established at the most important
points. Soon after going to Pinckney Island many of the men were
taken ill. Several were sent to the hospital at Hilton Head, others were
put on light duty, and still others were excused from duty altogether
for the time being. Orders were received from regimental headquarters to make the duty of the men as light as possible during the day,
but to keep a strict watch at night, as rumors were prevalent of visits
of rebel officers from the troops stationed at Grahamville; and it was
also stated that some of the colored men in their fishing trips were in
the habit of going over to the mainland.

In the afternoon of the 6th of August three men of the company
were granted permission by Lieut. Wiggin to go up the river fishing.
Not returning at retreat, inquiries were instituted, and it was found
that they went from the beach to the "Middle Plantation," so called,
and before going secured the musket of the guard on duty at that point,
discharged it, and then threw the ramrod into the river. As these would-
be fishermen did not return at dark, word was sent to regimental head-

quarters; and an additional force was sent to Pinckney Island to remain during the night, as it was thought quite likely that the rebels would ascertain our exact condition from the men who had apparently deserted and that an attack was liable at any time. The additional force remained through the night; but no demonstrations were made towards us by the enemy.

Things went on as usual with us on the island till the night of the 20th of August. Soon after dark word came from two picket posts of fires burning brightly on the banks of the Broad River, on the mainland above Corn Island; and sounds of oars in the rowlocks were heard quite frequently. Lieut. Wiggin did not attach much importance to these facts and attributed them to fishing parties. Orders were, however, given to the guard to be vigilant and not allow themselves to be surprised. Up to this time no word had been received from the three men who left us so unceremoniously on the 6th of the month; and they had been reported at headquarters as deserters.

The next morning (Aug. 21), about daybreak, an alarm came from boats at the northwest corner of the island. The men of Company H. not on duty were asleep in their quarters; and before they could get out, a detachment of the enemy, commanded by Capt. Mickler, had landed and deployed across the end of the island, which at that point was very narrow, and were preparing to attack the house where the men were quartered. The writer of this was one of the first out; and on his trip down the path leading to the post at the boat landing, through the bushes, was fired at three times, but fortunately escaped injury. He was at once followed by Lieut. Wiggin, who appeared on the scene without coat or vest and without side arms. He inquired as to the cause of the disturbance, and was told that it was apparently an attack by the enemy. He scouted the idea and said he would ascertain what the matter was. He at once started into the woods and was made a prisoner by Capt. [J. H.] Mickler [of the Eleventh Infantry]. As the men made their appearance from the house they were fired at. One rebel fired through one of the open windows, resting his musket on the sill, and wounded Enoch T. Harvey badly in one shoulder. Several others were wounded, and three were killed. The first squad of rebels, having captured all the men about the house, were forming them in line ready to march to the boats, when the second detachment of the enemy, under Capt. [Stephen] Elliott, came up to the edge of the woods and, seeing men in line near the house, apparently mistook them for our men and fired a volley at them, wounding nine men belonging to Capt. Mickler's command, that officer himself being badly wounded besides.

On the firing of the volley, Lieut. Wiggin started for the bluff on a run and was fired at by the rebels; and he fell, receiving eleven wounds. By this time Capt. Elliott and his men came up, and after caring for the wounded, the prisoners were marched to the landing and loaded into boats; and the procession started up the river to the mainland.

On arriving at the mainland the men were disembarked and marched about two miles, when they came to a plantation house, situated in the midst of beautiful grounds, but which showed signs of neglect. Here they were furnished with something to eat. In the course of an hour the wagons came up from the river, where they had been after the boats used by the expedition, which were unloaded at this plantation.

The men of Company H were ordered to take their places in these rude, lumbering vehicles, and soon started for Grahamville, which place was reached soon after dark. No insults were offered the men; but on the contrary, a person meeting them might think the party had been out for pleasure. There were some fine singers among the rebels, and the air resounded with songs the whole day, and many a laugh went up on the conclusion of stories told by men on both sides. We were prisoners, but it was thought best to make the best of it.

On arrival at Grahamville we were escorted up the main street by the whole population, apparently, and the street was made brilliant with bonfires. We were taken to a large unoccupied house, where a generous supper was provided for us, consisting of boiled rice, fried bacon, boiled fresh beef and soft bread. Husks were prepared in abundance for us to sleep on, and we all had a good night's rest. Early the next morning we were called up, provided with breakfast, and then ordered to "fall in." We were marched to the Grahamville depot on the Charleston & Savannah Railroad, and were soon on the cars. Our guard at this time consisted of Capt. Elliott and his men, a detachment of Beaufort Artillery. They were pleasant and agreeable and treated us more like friends than enemies. The detachment commanded by Capt. Mickler went with the wounded to Hardeeville, where there is a hospital.

Our next stop was at Pocotaligo, where we left the cars and marched about four miles to McPhersonville, a small settlement, and were there turned over to Smith's Sharpshooters, a detachment doing duty there and under command of Lieut. Seabrook. We were very well treated here and had plenty to eat.

After staying here a week we received orders early in the morning to fall in, and were taken in wagons to Pocotaligo, where we boarded the train for Charleston, where we arrived at 2 P.M., and were marched across the city to another depot to take cars for Columbia, S. C., 134 miles away. Rumors of a move by the Federals on Pocotaligo was the cause of our hurried removal. . . .

Charles Nordhoff

"HERE THE TRAITORS PLANNED THE RUIN OF THEIR COUNTRY"

Charles Nordhoff, Harper's New Monthly Magazine correspondent, sailed down from New York to Port Royal on the Fah-Kee, *a ship which had on board three thousand loaded shells and three hundred barrels of powder. He was accompanied on his trip by a gentleman known as the "Major," though he was not a military man. "On the contrary," says our correspondent, "he is a civil man—a very civil man, if you smooth him the right way. He has no particular familiarity with gunpowder either, using an entirely different preparation when he has occasion to blow people up."*

The following account was the result of two weeks' observation at Port Royal where Mr. Nordhoff visited Hilton Head, Beaufort, Parris Island and St. Helena Island.

The bay of Port Royal is wide and deep. It has room and to spare for a thousand ships to swing at their anchors; it is not difficult of entrance; and those who know of the dangers which beset the mariner bound to Charleston or Savannah wonder often why this noble piece of water did not secure a share of the Southern trade and become more famous than either of the rival cities I have named. But when you come to see more nearly the islands which make the harbor, and study on the map the intricate system of creeks and swamps by which alone connection can be had with the main land, it is not difficult to believe that neither Charleston nor Savannah is likely to be ruined by Port Royal.

Above: Old Slave Quarters

Below: Abandoned Rice Fields on Combahee River

Old-Fashioned Hand Organ in Old Brick Church, Frogmore, St. Helena Island

Sea Pines Corp.

Old Road to Baynard Ruins, Hilton Head

Courtesy of Frank H. Ramsey

A Magnolia Tree Blossom Which Converts into a Mass of
Seeds Looking Like a Small Pineapple

The famous Sea Islands, in the midst of which you here find yourself, are low, sandy and flat. Apparently Old Ocean, who has been robbed to form them, has not yet given up his claim upon their site, for along the outer beach of Hilton Head Island I noticed, within the sweep of the tide, large stumps of live oak sticking out above the sand, as though there had been, at some time not very remote, firm land where now the tide surged and tried to eat away still more of the loose sand.

The soil on which the famous long-staple cotton was—and is—grown, instead of the rich black mould which I expected to find it, is a pale yellow sand, which seems to you useless for agricultural purposes till you notice that it glistens with white particles, which are the pulverized shells the lime of which gives the soil its strength and substance.

On every hand you see the marks of long settlement, in avenues of fine live oaks, cedars and pines, leading up to the plantation houses and bounding the roads. Among these, as well as in the unreclaimed ground, of which there is a far greater area than I had supposed, you find the palmetto—a tree worthless for timber, unfit for fuel and valuable, I believe, only to use in the shape of piles for wharves, because the marine worm refuses to touch it. One use the planters made of it: in the broad flat cottonfields you see large palmettos standing at regular and wide distances like sentinels. Beneath these the slave-mothers left their infants while they labored near by among the cotton; and hither they came, at appointed hours, to suckle their little ones. . . .

Coming from the blustering and bleak March winds of New York the climate here was enchanting. The breezes are soft, the skies have a tropical radiance; the yellow jessamine was in full bloom on the 15th of March [1863] and filled the air with its strong perfume. The jessamine grows rankly in this loose sand and overruns the trees by the roadside, covering them with its profuse canary-colored bloom. In the gardens roses were already in full flower; the orange trees were white with their odoriferous blossoms, and the splendid magnolia was preparing to flower. . . .

Why could not these wretches be content? I often asked myself, as I rode among the plantations from which the planters fled in such terror—according to the accounts of the Negroes—when, to their dismay, the magnificent *Wabash* drove their panic-struck soldiers out of the forts.

The village of Hilton Head is a place which has grown up since the capture of the forts. . . . The most prominent and ambitious building was originally a plantation house, to which has been added a curious superstructure—a tower—which is used as a signal station. The quarters of General Hunter and his staff front upon the water, and are simple enough to satisfy the demands of the most exacting democrat. . . . If you are an early riser, and chance to take a stroll on the beach, you may see the General practicing with his pistols, and satisfy yourself that he is not a safe man to invite to a duel. I have heard that he is counted among the best shots in the army, and that Mrs. Hunter has as correct an eye and as steady a hand as he. I know that the General is a magnificent horseman—as indeed he ought to be, for he is an old cavalry officer who has spent perhaps the greater half of his life in the saddle. . . .

To visit the rebel lines under a flag of truce was so novel an experience that, when it was hinted to us that we might make it, we were but too delighted to accept. The little steamer *Mattano* set out from the fort about nine o'clock, bearing at her stern the American flag, and at her bow a broad square of milk-white bunting. She steamed rapidly up the tortuous river, till, on rounding a sharp turn, we came in sight of the obstructions by which the rebels have attempted to bar our way to Savannah. Above them, and apparently close to them, lay a nondescript marine monster, which is the iron-clad battery *Georgia*. She lies there, moored with her broadsides down the river, prepared to defend the narrow passage which is left in the barrier for the ingress and egress of rebel crafts.

We steamed up steadily nearer and nearer, up to the mouth of Augustine Creek, past its upper bank, beyond it for some distance, and ever nearer and nearer to the enemy, till at last an angry flash from the broadside of the *Georgia*, and presently after a sharp report from her gun, warned us that we were far enough.

"Down anchor!" said the captain. "Stop her!" and we swung round and lay still, waiting for a rebel boat to come off to us.

It was, I think, the strangest scene I have ever beheld. On the right bank of the river a squad of rebel picket-guards stood near a smouldering fire, in the tall reeds, on the flat and evidently marshy shore, eyeing us, staring at us, in grim silence. I wonder what was in the minds of these grim and somewhat shabby soldiers? Ahead of us, but a short mile away, were the two rows of piles sticking out of the water; and between them, through the opening I have spoken of, a little rusty-looking rebel steamer passed on her way up from Augustine Creek.

Beyond lay the *Georgia*—to a sailor's eye a monstrous creature, something like, in appearance, to the pictures we have of the *Merrimac*; with sides and ends sloping to the water at an angle of, I should think, 45 degrees, and covered with long slabs or strips of railroad iron; with a long box on top of the deck, which also appeared to be armoured; and, with her ports open. It is said that she proved unable to stem the tide in the river, and is therefore useless, except as a kind of floating fort, to bar our way to Savannah.

How strange and incomprehensible it seemed that these men we saw standing on the shore were enemies, ready to take our lives; that, had we attempted to pass a hundred yards further up, yonder gloomy *Georgia* would have belched forth shot at us to blow us out of water; that the fellows pulling down in that trim barge to communicate with us would have been glad to cut our throats; that the gallant young captain who was our "flag-of-truce officer" had a price set on his head by the commander of the men who now pull alongside and address him, and would be hanged if Beauregard could catch him and dared fulfill his threats!

There was one of our company—a very civil man I have called him—who knew right well that the rebels would have been but too glad to have him in their possession; and, curiously enough, picking up the Savannah paper which was given to us, the first paragraph which struck his eye was personal abuse of himself as a "venomous viper." Nor was it a less curious coincidence that the paper which was given the rebel officer in return should be a number of *Harper's Weekly*, opening which, eagerly, as their boat shoved off, "our friends the enemy" saw a broadside picture of the loyal Negro troops of Louisiana. It was a double hit.

The young captain, who was our "flag-of-truce officer," organized the first battalion of colored soldiers in South Carolina. General Beauregard threatened him and all others engaged in that work with death if caught. "I thought they might as well get accustomed to the sight of him," said General Hunter, "so I send him up whenever we dispatch a flag of truce." It must be a charming thing thus to act the part of red rag to this raging rebel bull. I fear General Hunter does not understand the noble art of "conciliating" the enemy, of which our Copperheads talk so much.

They would not communicate. "Our friends the enemy are surly today," said the Captain, as we hove up anchor and steamed down the river again. Not even whisky would tempt them. Sometimes, we hear, they come on board and have a jolly time; but returning in a tipsy state, it is probable that the poor wretches get hauled over the coals for their imprudence.

Fourteen miles above Hilton Head lies Beaufort, a pretty village, made up of what in the South are called "mansions," square, comfortable-looking wooden houses, with verandas and large gardens. This was the summer and winter pleasure resort of many of the South Carolina conspirators and traitors. Here, in cool quiet, they hatched their treasonable plot—and I must say the nest seems a pleasant one, and doubtless the labors of incubation were lightened and cheered with many a fragrant "cobbler." Beaufort—pronounced *Bufort*—stands on the bank of a broad river, where it gets a cool breeze in the hottest summer day. It is a retired nook of the world, where contemplative traitors might cozily chat and fear no sudden arrival of prying strangers. Negroes now live in many of the mansions and seem quite at home there. . . .

As I walked under the generous shade of magnificent live oaks, which abound hereabouts, and drank in the quiet spirit of the scene, I caught with it a sense of the base use to which this piece of earth had been put. Here, beneath these live oaks, in this grove of tall and spreading pines, by these budding orange trees, in the portico of the rural church, the Rhetts, the Barnwells, the Prescotts, the hundred other leading traitors conferred together; here they deliberated; here they planned, in sober councils, the ruin of their country; here was nurtured that gigantic and inexcusable crime which has made so many children fatherless, so many homes desolate, that a few ambitious and unscrupulous aristocrats might have their fling against free government.

It is a pleasant spot, this Beaufort; but I hope whenever our soldiers leave it they will raze it to the ground, nor leave one stone standing on another of its foundations. The whole place is accursed.

One day came in the *Arago*, and in her certain pleasant-voiced ladies on a tour of pleasure. Now the sweet smile of woman is a rarity in the Department of the South. The Secretary of War has forbidden her presence here, except as teacher to the colored children. Only a very few of the officers have their families here. . . .

A more charming spot than even Beaufort, and the coziest nook I found among these islands, is Paris [Parris] Island. Here stands a low-roofed, somewhat rude, broad-verandaed house but a few steps from where the surf beats against the shore; it stands in a garden filled with a wilderness of roses and oranges and tall oleanders; the Negro quarters at a little distance, and not in view; and every thing about it is so quiet, so cool, so shady, the constant murmur of the sea fills the air with so pleasant a dreaminess, that I thought, Hither one might come, weary of the busy world, and live contented forever—nor ever long for a New York paper. . . .

One day we sailed over to St. Helena to witness a review of part of the forces. To see several thousand men drawn up under arms, to see them moving at the word of command like one great machine, one vast body of which the general is the head, to watch the thousands of bayonets glistening in the sun, and to feel, in the tremor of the air, the steady tramp of their feet, is surely a stirring sight. . . .

As the regiments filed past the General and his staff, once in a while would come along an old worn, battle-stained, shot-riddled flag, and then you would hear a murmur of admiration ripple along the line of spectators, and the eyes of the soldiers would gleam, and their swarthy faces fill with the healthy blood stirred by the fine sight; and those regiments which bore such flags walked more proudly and filed by in more solid phalanx, it seemed to me, looking at no one but soberly following that flag.

But it was when I saw the Sixty-seventh Ohio march up, their brave young Colonel Voorhees riding at their head, that I was most deeply touched. They were the only Ohio boys there, and though I know probably not a man of them except their colonel, suddenly the water came into my eyes, and I felt like shouting out, "Hurrah for the old Buckeye State!"

Some people tell you that all state pride is wrong in these days, but they might as well assert that you should not love your mother better than any other elderly lady of your acquaintance.

Walking over the field after the review, I came upon the fragments of an unlucky snake which had got under the hoofs of the prancing staff horses and now lay crushed into at least a dozen lifeless pieces; a type, I hope, of the fate of that serpent, Rebellion, which has reared its head among us.

Such as I have described is the round we made in a short visit to Port Royal. You may, if you are active, go farther—and very likely fare worse. Army officers are very kind; one gallant colonel placed me under lasting obligations by an offer to take me out to see the line of rebel pickets. "It's first-rate fun, and a splendid ride! They *do* take a shot at us, as we dash by, sometimes; but then their powder is poor, and they don't *often* hit anyone." Such were the words with which he sought to charm me. . . .

Thomas Wentworth Higginson

THE ARMING OF THE BLACKS

The first slave regiment of freed slaves mustered into the service of the United States in the Civil War was the First Regiment of South Carolina Volunteers, organized at Port Royal on November 7, 1862. Recruiting had begun in May under Major General David Hunter, who was then in command at Port Royal, and the undertaking was further sponsored by Brigadier General Rufus Saxton, Military Governor of the Department of the South. General Saxton gave the command of the regiment to Thomas Wentworth Higginson.

The Confederate Congress passed on May 1, 1863, the following Act: "That every white person being a commissioned officer, or acting as such, who, during the present war, shall command Negroes or mulattoes in arms against the Confederate States, or who shall arm, train, organize, or prepare Negroes or mulattoes for military service against the Confederate States, or who shall voluntarily aid Negroes or mulattoes in any military enterprise, attack, or conflict in such service, shall be deemed as inciting servile insurrection, and shall, if captured, be put to death, or be otherwise punished at the discretion of the court."

Thomas Wentworth Higginson, who wrote the history of his regiment from which extracts here are taken, was born in 1823, in Cambridge, Massachusetts. He was graduated from Harvard College at seventeen and from the divinity school in 1847. Following in the footsteps of his ancestor, Francis Higginson, first minister in the Massachusetts Bay Colony, he entered the ministry as pastor of First Religious Society of Newburyport, Massachusetts. He served also at the "Free Church" in Worcester. At both churches it was said he "preached himself out of his pulpit." He became a leader of the extreme abolition

movement, *"pledged to use whatever means were in his power to promote the dissolution of the Union." He was in sympathy and close
touch with John Brown.*

*Higginson was no stranger to the South, when he reported for duty
at Port Royal for he had often paid visits to Virginia during his college
days and he had many near kinsmen in that state who were all seces-
sionists. He held his command of the First South Carolina Volunteers
from November 1862 to May 1864, when he returned home after being
wounded. He resigned from the service in October 1864.*

*On May 12, 1881, now a literary man of distinction, Colonel Hig-
ginson went to South Carolina from his home in Cambridge to represent the New England states at the anniversary of the battle of the
Cowpens. General Wade Hampton represented the Southern states.
The governor of South Carolina was then Johnson Hagood, who had
been the general commanding the Confederate land forces in the Port
Royal neighborhood during Higginson's service there.*

*Before returning to Massachusetts, Colonel Higginson visited Beau-
fort and the site of his old camp. "The large white houses still look
peacefully down the placid river," he wrote. "The fortifications on the
old shell-road have almost disappeared . . . there are changes enough,
and yet the general effect of the town is unaltered . . . it is the same
pleasant old sleepy Beaufort. . . ."*

One day in November 1862, I was sitting at dinner with my lieutenants, John Goodell and Luther Bigelow, in the barracks of the
Fifty-First Massachusetts, Colonel Sprague, at Worcester, Mass., when
the following letter was put into my hands:

Beaufort, S.C., November 5, 1862
My dear Sir,—I am organizing the First Regiment of South Carolina
Volunteers, with every prospect of success. Your name has been spoken
of, in connection with the command of this regiment, by some friends
in whose judgment I have confidence. I take great pleasure in offering
you the position of Colonel in it, and hope that you may be induced
to accept. I shall not fill the place until I hear from you, or sufficient
time shall have passed for me to receive your reply. Should you accept,
I inclose a pass for Port Royal, of which I trust you will feel disposed to
avail yourself at once.
I am, with sincere regard, yours truly,
R. SAXTON, Brig.-Genl., Mil. Gov.

Had an invitation reached me to take command of a regiment of Kalmuck Tartars, it could hardly have been more unexpected. I had always looked for the arming of the blacks, and had always felt a wish to be associated with them; had read the scanty accounts of General Hunter's seemingly abortive undertaking, and had heard rumors of General Saxton's renewed efforts. But the prevalent tone of public sentiment was still opposed to any such attempts; the government kept very shy of the experiment....

For myself, I was at the head of a fine company of my own raising, and in a regiment to which I was already much attached. It did not seem desirable to exchange a certainty for an uncertainty; for who knew but General Saxton might yet be thwarted in his efforts by the pro-slavery influence that had still so much weight at headquarters? It would be intolerable to go out to South Carolina, and find myself, after all, at the head of a mere plantation-guard or a day-school in uniform.

I therefore obtained from the War Department permission to go and report to General Saxton, without at once resigning my captaincy. Fortunately it took but a few days in South Carolina to make it clear that all was right, and the return steamer took back the resignation of a Massachusetts commission. Thenceforth my lot was cast altogether with the black troops, except when regiments or detachments of white soldiers were also under my command....

Camp Saxton, near Beaufort, S.C.
November 24, 1862

Yesterday afternoon we were steaming over a summer sea, the deck level as a parlor-floor, no land in sight, no sail, until at last appeared one lighthouse and then a line of trees and two distant vessels and nothing more. The sun set; ... it grew dark; after tea all were on deck, the people sang hyms; then the moon set, a moon two days old ... Toward morning the boat stopped....

Hilton Head lay on one side, the gunboats on the other; all that was raw and bare in the low buildings of the new settlement was softened into picturesqueness by the early light. Stars were still overhead, gulls wheeled and shrieked, and the broad river rippled duskily towards Beaufort.

The shores were low and wooded; ... there were a few gunboats, twenty schooners, and some steamers. The river-banks were soft and graceful, though low, and as we steamed up to Beaufort on the flood-tide this morning, it seemed almost as fair as the smooth and lovely canals which Stedman traversed to meet his Negro soldiers in Surinam. . . . Then we saw on a picturesque point an old plantation, with stately magnolia avenue, decaying house and tiny church amid the woods; behind it stood a neat encampment of white tents—"and there," said my companion, "is your future regiment."

Three miles farther brought us to the pretty town of Beaufort, with stately houses amid Southern foliage. Reporting to General Saxton, I had the luck to encounter a company of my destined command, marched in to be mustered into the United States service. They were unarmed, and all looked as thoroughly black as the most faithful philanthropist could desire; there did not seem to be so much as a mulatto among them. Their coloring suited me, all but the legs, which were clad in a lively scarlet, as intolerable to my eyes as if I had seen a turkey. I saw them mustered; General Saxton talked to them a little; they gave close attention, though their faces looked impenetrable. Then I conversed with some of them. The first to whom I spoke had been wounded in a small expedition after lumber, from which a party had just returned, and in which they had been under fire and had done very well.

I said, pointing to his lame arm, "Did you think that was more than you bargained for, my man?"

His answer came promptly and stoutly: "I been a-tinkin', Mas'r, *dat's jess what I went for.*"

I thought this did well enough for my very first interchange of dialogue with my recruits.

November 27, 1862

Thanksgiving Day: it is the first moment I have had for writing during these three days, which have installed me into a new mode of life so thoroughly that they seem three years. . . .

It is a holiday wherever General Saxton's proclamation reaches. The air is full of noisy drumming and of gunshots; for the prize shooting is our great celebration of the day, and the drumming is chronic. My young barbarians are all at play. I look out from the broken windows of this forlorn plantation house, through avenues of great live oaks, with their hard, shining leaves, and their branches hung with a universal drapery of soft, long moss, like fringe-trees struck with grayness. Below, the sandy soil, scantly covered with coarse grass, bristles with sharp palmettoes and aloes; all the vegetation is stiff, shining, semitropical, with nothing soft or delicate in its texture. Numerous plantation buildings totter around, all slovenly and unattractive, while the interspaces are filled with all manner of wreck and refuse, pigs, fowls, dogs, and omnipresent Ethiopian infancy. All this is the universal Southern panorama; but five minutes' walk beyond the hovels and the live oaks will bring one to something so un-Southern that the whole Southern coast at this moment appears to tremble at the suggestion of such a thing—the camp of a regiment of freed slaves. . . .

Already I am growing used to the experience, at first so novel, of living among five hundred men, and scarce a white face to be seen—of seeing them go through all their daily duties, drilling, eating, frolicking, talking, just as if they were white. Each day at dress parade I stand with the customary folding of the arms before a regimental line of countenances so black that I can hardly tell whether the men stand steadily or not; black is every hand which moves in ready cadence as I vociferate, "Battalion! Shoulder arms!" nor is it till the line of white officers moves forward, as parade is dismissed, that I am reminded that my own face is not the color of coal.

The first few days on duty with a new regiment must be devoted almost wholly to tightening reins; in this process one deals chiefly with the officers, and I have as yet had but little personal intercourse with the men. But as the machine comes into shape, I am beginning to decipher the individual parts. At first, of course, they all looked just alike. . . . Most of them are wholly raw, but there are many who have already been for months in camp in the abortive "Hunter Regiment," yet in that loose kind of way which, like average militia training, is of doubtful advantage. I notice that some companies, too, look darker than others, though all are purer African than I expected. . . .

It needs but a few days to show the absurdity of distrusting the military availability of these people. They have quite as much average comprehension as whites of the need of the thing, as much previous knowledge of the gun, and, above all, a readiness of ear and imitation, which, for purposes of drill, counterbalances any defect of mental training. To learn the drill, one does not want a set of college professors; one wants a squad of eager, active, pliant schoolboys; and the more childlike these pupils are, the better. . . . They are simple, docile, and affectionate almost to the point of absurdity. The same men who stood fire in open field with perfect coolness, on the late expedition, have come to me blubbering in the most irresistibly ludicrous manner on being transferred from one company in the regiment to another.

The men seem to have enjoyed the novel event of Thanksgiving Day; they have had company and regimental prize-shootings, a minimum of speeches and a maximum of dinner. Bill of fare: two beef-cattle and a thousand oranges. The oranges cost a cent apiece, and the cattle were Secesh, bestowed by General Saxby, as they all call him.

December 3, 1862—7 P.M.

What a life is this I lead! It is a dark, mild, drizzling evening, and as the foggy air breeds sand-flies, so it calls out melodies and strange antics from this mysterious race of grown-up children with whom my lot is cast. All over the camp the lights glimmer in the tents, and as I sit at my desk in the open doorway, there come mingled sounds of stir and glee. Boys laugh and shout; a feeble flute stirs somewhere in some tent, not an officer's; a drum throbs far away in another; wild kildeer-plover flit and wail above us, like the haunting souls of dead slave-masters; and from a neighboring cook-fire comes the monotonous sound of that strange festival, half powwow, half prayer-meeting, which they know only as a "shout." These fires are usually enclosed in a little booth, made neatly of palm leaves and covered in at top—a regular native African hut, in short, such as is pictured in books. . . .

This hut is now crammed with men, singing at the top of their voices, in one of their quaint, monotonous, endless, Negro-Methodist chants, with obscure syllables recurring constantly, and slight variations interwoven, all accompanied with a regular drumming of the feet and clapping of the hands, like castanets. Then the excitement spreads; inside and outside the enclosure men begin to quiver and dance, others join, a circle forms winding monotonously round some one in the centre; some "heel and toe" tumultuously, others merely tremble and stagger on, others stoop and rise, others whirl, others caper sideways, all keep steadily circling like dervishes; spectators applaud special strokes of skill; my approach only enlivens the scene; the circle enlarges, louder grows the singing, rousing shouts of encouragement come in, half bacchanalian, half devout, "Wake 'em, brudder!" "Stan' up to 'em, brudder!" and still the ceaseless drumming and clapping, in perfect cadence, goes steadily on. Suddenly there comes a sort of snap, and the spell breaks, amid general sighing and laughter.

And this not rarely and occasionally, but night after night, while in other parts of the camp the soberest prayers and exhortations are proceeding sedately. . . .

December 5, 1862

Give these people their tongues, their feet, and their leisure, and they are happy. At every twilight the air is full of singing, talking, and clapping of hands in unison. One of their favorite "sings" is full of plaintive cadences. . . . I wonder where they obtained a chant of such beauty.

> "I can't stay behind, my Lord, I can't stay behind!
> O, my fader is gone, my fader is gone,
> My fader is gone into heaven, my Lord!
>   I can't stay behind!
> Dere's room enough, room enough,
> Room enough in de heaven for de sojer;
>   Can't stay behind!"

This evening, after working themselves up to the highest pitch, a party suddenly rushed off, got a barrel, and mounted some man upon it, who said, "Gib anoder song, boys, and I've gib you a speech." After some hesitation and sundry shouts of "Rise de sing, somebody," and "Stan' up for Jesus, brudder," irreverently put in by the juveniles, they got upon the John Brown song, always a favorite, adding a jubilant verse which I had never before heard—"We'll beat Beauregard on de clare battlefield." Then came the promised speech, and then no less than seven other speeches, each orator being affectionately tugged to the pedestal and set on end by his special constituency. . . . "Our mas'rs dey hab lib under de flag, dey got dere wealth under it, and ebryting beautiful for dere children. Under it dey hab grind us up, and put us in dere pocket for money. . . ."

December 20

Philoprogenitiveness is an important organ for an officer of colored troops; and I happen to be well provided with it. It seems to be the theory of all military usages, in fact, that soldiers are to be treated like children; and these singular persons, who never know their own age till they are past middle life, and then choose a birthday with such precision—"Fifty year old, sah, de fus' last April"—prolong the privilege of childhood.

I am perplexed for countersigns—their range of proper names is so distressingly limited, and they make such amazing work of every new one. At first, to be sure, they did not quite recognize the need of any variation; one night some officer asked a sentinel whether he had the countersign yet, and was indignantly answered, "Should tink I hab 'em, hab 'em for a fortnight"; which seems a long epoch for that magic word to hold out. To-night I thought I would have "Fredericksburg," in honor of Burnside's reported victory, using the rumor quickly for fear of a contradiction. Later, in comes a captain, gets the countersign for his own use, but presently returns, the sentinel having pronounced it incorrect. On inquiry, it appears that the sergeant of the guard, being weak in geography, thought best to substitute the more familiar word, "Crockery-ware"; which was, with perfect gravity, confided to all the sentinels and accepted without question. . . .

January 12 [1863]
. . . It was very dark the other night—an unusual thing here—and the rain fell in torrents; so I put on my India-rubber suit and went the rounds of the sentinels, incognito, to test them. . . . Sometimes I tempted them by refusing to give any countersign, but offering them a piece of tobacco, which they could not accept without allowing me nearer than the prescribed bayonet's distance. Tobacco is more than gold to them, and it was touching to watch the struggle in their minds; but they always did their duty at last, and I never could persuade them. . . .

It rained harder and harder, and when I had nearly made the rounds I had had enough of it and, simply giving the countersign to the challenging sentinel, undertook to pass within the lines.

"Halt!" exclaimed this dusky man and brother, bringing down his bayonet, "de countersign not correck."

Now the magic word, in this case, was "Vicksburg," in honor of a rumored victory. But as I knew that these hard names became quite transformed upon their lips, "Carthage" being familiarized into Cartridge, and "Concord" into Corncob, how could I possibly tell what shade of pronunciation my friend might prefer for this particular proper name?

"Vicksburg," I repeated blandly but authoritatively. . . .

"Halt dar! Countersign not correck," was the only answer.

The bayonet still maintained a position which, in a military point of view, was impressive.

I tried persuasion, orthography, threats, tobacco, all in vain. I could not pass in. Of course my pride was up; for was I to defer to an untutored African on a point of pronunciation? Classic shades of Harvard, forbid! Affecting scornful indifference, I tried to edge away, proposing to myself to enter the camp at some other point where my elocution would be better appreciated. Not a step could I stir.

"Halt!" shouted my gentleman again, still holding me at his bayonet's point, and I wincing and halting. . . .

"Call the corporal of the guard," said I, at last, with dignity, unwilling either to make a night of it or to yield my incognito.

"Corporal ob de guard!" he shouted lustily. "Post Number Two!" while I could hear another sentinel chuckling with laughter. This last was a special guard, placed over a tent, with a prisoner in charge.

Presently he broke silence. "Who am dat?" he asked in a stage whisper. "Am he a buckra [white man]?"

"Dunno whether he been a buckra or not," responded doggedly my Cerberus in uniform, "but I's bound to keep him here till de corporal ob de guard come."

Yet when that dignitary arrived, and I revealed myself, poor Number Two appeared utterly transfixed with terror and seemed to look for nothing less than immediate execution. Of course I praised his fidelity, and the next day complimented him before the guard and mentioned him to his captain; and the whole affair was very good for them all. Hereafter, if Satan himself should approach them in darkness and storm, they will take him for "de Cunnel" and treat him with special severity.

January 13

. . . It is time for rest; and I have just looked out into the night, where the eternal stars shut down, in concave protection, over the yet glimmering camp, and Orion hangs above my tent door, giving to me the sense of strength and assurance which these simple children obtain from their Moses and the Prophets. Yet external Nature does its share in their training; witness that most poetic of all their songs. . . .

"I know moonrise, I know star-rise;
    Lay dis body down.
I walk in de moonlight, I walk in de starlight,
    To lay dis body down.

I'll walk in de graveyard, I'll walk through de graveyard,
　　To lay dis body down.
I'll lie in de grave and stretch out my arms;
　　Lay dis body down.
I go to de Judgment in de evening ob de day
　　When I lay dis body down;
And my soul and your soul will meet in de day
　　When I lay dis body down."

May, 1863

. . . The only thoroughfare by land between Beaufort and Charleston is the "Shell Road," a beautiful avenue, which, about nine miles from Beaufort, strikes a ferry across the Coosaw River. War abolished the ferry and made the river the permanent barrier between the opposite picket lines. For ten miles, right and left, these lines extended, marked by well-worn footpaths, following the endless windings of the stream. Upon their maintenance depended our whole foothold on the Sea Islands; and upon that again finally depended the whole campaign of [W.T.] Sherman. . . .

There was thus a region ten or twelve miles square of which I had exclusive military command. It was level, but otherwise broken and bewildering to the last degree. No road traversed it, properly speaking, but the Shell Road. All the rest was a wild medley of cypress swamp, pine barren, muddy creek and cultivated plantation, intersected by interminable lanes and bridle paths, through which we must ride day and night and which our horses soon knew better than ourselves. The regiment was distributed at different stations, the main force being under my immediate command, at a plantation close by the Shell Road, two miles from the ferry, and seven miles from Beaufort.

Our first picket duty was just at the time of the first attack on Charleston, under DuPont and Hunter; and it was generally supposed that the Confederates would make an effort to recapture the Sea Islands. My orders were to watch the enemy closely, keep informed as to his position and movements, attempt no advance, and, in case any were attempted from the other side, to delay it as long as possible, sending instant notice to headquarters.

As to the delay, that could be easily guaranteed. There were causeways on the Shell Road which a single battery could hold against a large force; and the plantations were everywhere so intersected by hedges and dikes that they seemed expressly planned for defense. Although creeks wound in and out everywhere, yet these were only navigable at high tide, and at all other times were impassable marshes.

There were but few posts where the enemy were within rifle range, and their occasional attacks at those points were soon stopped by our enforcement of a pithy order from General Hunter, "Give them as good as they send." So that, with every opportunity for being kept on the alert, there was small prospect of serious danger. . . . The picket station was therefore always a coveted post among the regiments, combining some undeniable importance with a kind of relaxation. . . . The whole region always reminded me of the descriptions of La Vendée, and I always expected to meet Henri de la Rochejaquelein riding in the woods. . . .

Our house possessed four spacious rooms and a piazza; around it were grouped sheds and tents; the camp was a little way off on one side, the Negro quarters of the plantation on the other; and all was immersed in a dense mass of waving and murmuring locust blossoms. Indoors, the main headquarters seemed like the camp of some party of young engineers in time of peace. A large, low, dilapidated room with an immense fireplace and with windowpanes chiefly broken, so that the sashes were still open even when closed—such was our home. The walls were scrawled with capital charcoal sketches by R. of the Fourth New Hampshire, and with a good map of the island and its woodpaths by C. of the First Massachusetts Cavalry. . . .

It was pleasant all day, with the different visitors who were always streaming in and out, officers and soldiers on various business; turbaned women from the plantations, coming with complaints or questionings; fugitives from the mainland to be interrogated; visitors riding up on horseback, their hands full of jasmine and wild roses; and the sweet sunny air all perfumed with magnolias and the Southern pine. . . .

Till about the time when we went on picket, it had been the occasional habit of the smaller gunboats to make the circuit of Port Royal Island—a practice which was deemed very essential to the safety of our position, but which the Confederates effectually stopped a few days after our arrival by destroying the army gunboat *George Washington* with a single shot from a light battery. I was roused soon after daybreak by the firing, and a courier soon came dashing in with the particulars. Forwarding these hastily to Beaufort, I was soon at the scene of action five miles away. Approaching, I met on the picket paths man after man who had escaped from the wreck across a half mile of almost impassable marsh. Never did I see such objects—some stripped to their shirts, some fully clothed, but all having every garment literally pasted to their bodies with mud. Across the river, the Confederates were retiring, having done their work, but were still shelling, from greater and greater distances, the wood through which I rode. Arrived at the spot nearest the wreck—a point opposite to what we called the Brickyard Station—I saw the burning vessel aground beyond a long stretch of marsh, out of which the forlorn creatures were still floundering. Here and there in the mud and reeds we could see the laboring heads, slowly advancing, and could hear excruciating cries from wounded men in the more distant depths. . . . During that morning we got them all out, our last achievement being the rescue of the pilot, an immense Negro with a wooden leg. . . .

A naval gunboat, too, which had originally accompanied this vessel and should never have left it, now came back and took off the survivors, though there had been several deaths from scalding and shell. It proved that the wreck was not aground after all, but at anchor, having foolishly lingered till after daybreak, and having thus given time for the enemy to bring down their guns. The first shot had struck the boiler and set the vessel on fire; after which the officer in command had raised a white flag, and then escaped with his men to our shore. . . .

February 23, 1864

There was the sound of revelry by night at a ball in Beaufort last night, in a new large building beautifully decorated. All the collected flags of the garrison hung round and over us, as if the stars and stripes were devised for an ornament alone. The array of uniforms was such that a civilian became a distinguished object, much more a lady. All would have gone according to the proverbial marriage bell, I suppose, had there not been a slight palpable shadow over all of us from hearing vague stories of a lost battle in Florida,[1] and from the thought that perhaps the very ambulances in which we rode to the ball were ours only until the wounded or the dead might tenant them.

General Gillmore only came, I supposed, to put a good face upon

---

[1] Battle of Olustee.

the matter. He went away soon, and General Saxton went; then came a rumor that the *Cosmopolitan* had actually arrived with wounded, but still the dance went on. There was nothing unfeeling about it—one gets used to things—when suddenly in the midst of the "Lancers" there came a perfect hush. The music ceasing, a few surgeons went hastily to and fro as if conscience-stricken; then there "waved a mighty shadow in," as in Uhland's "Black Knight," and, as we all stood wondering, we were 'ware of General Saxton, who strode hastily down the hall, his pale face very resolute and looking almost sick with anxiety. He had just been on board the steamer; there were two hundred and fifty wounded men just arrived, and the ball must end. Not that there was anything for us to do, but the revel was mistimed and must be ended; it was wicked to be dancing with such a scene of suffering near by.

Of course the ball was instantly broken up, though with some murmurings and some longings of appetite, on the part of some, toward the wasted supper.

Later, I went on board the boat. Among the long lines of wounded, black and white intermingled, there was the wonderful quiet which usually prevails on such occasions. Not a sob nor a groan except from those undergoing removal. It is not self-control, but chiefly the shock to the system produced by severe wounds, especially gunshot wounds, which usually keeps the patient stiller at first than at any later time.

A company from my regiment waited on the wharf, in their accustomed dusky silence. . . .

I found our kindhearted ladies, Mrs. Chamberlin and Mrs. Dewhurst, on board the steamer, but there was nothing for them to do, and we walked back to camp in the radiant moonlight. . . .

Elizabeth Hyde Botume

TEACHER TO THE FREEDMEN

On October 25, 1864, Elizabeth Hyde Botume received the following message: "You are hereby appointed by the New England Freedmen's Aid Society a teacher of freed people at Beaufort, S. C." Shortly afterward she sailed from New York to Hilton Head Island. There she

took the oath of allegiance, "swearing I would give no aid nor information, etc., to the enemy."

While waiting for her assignment, she was the guest of General Rufus Saxton in Beaufort. There she found "Negroes, Negroes, Negroes.
They hovered around like bees in a swarm. . . . There were soldiers
everywhere. . . . Not a white woman to be seen, excepting some officers' wives and a few teachers expecting friends, and who only appeared
in public under escort."

In a short while Miss Botume was sent to Old Fort Plantation,
formerly the home of Captain John Joiner Smith, where she began
her school for contrabands. This school, which was later to be known as
the Whitney School, was destroyed by the hurricane of June 1866.
Old Fort Plantation had experienced many changes since 1861; it had
been the site of a number of military encampments and used also as a
hospital.

I found my location was to be at Old Fort Plantation, a place of
historic renown and great beauty. A large number of colored refugees
had been brought here. These were part of the eight hundred brought
off by General Montgomery on his raid to Combahee, as poor and destitute a class of human beings as could possibly be found. Dr. Marsh
had warned me against these people, assuring me "the slaves on the rice
plantation were the most degraded of the race." And he considered
them "the connecting link" between human beings and the brute
creation. . . . My subsequent experiences in teaching the freed people
proved that the good doctor was wrong in his estimate of their character and condition. I found those from the mainland more intelligent
and better bred than the mass of those from the islands.

Sunday afternoon I drove in an ambulance down to the old plantation. My road lay along the riverbank, which was thickly bordered by
large oaks and tall pine trees. We passed through one or two plantations abandoned to the Negroes, and past the contraband village, a
collection of low buildings called by the people themselves "Mon-
'gomery Hill." Why a "hill" I could never learn, as there was not the
slightest perceptible elevation. All the people—men, women, and
children—came out to greet us, with bows, scraping of the feet, courtesies and a general shouting of "How d'ye, missis?" . . . "How de'ye?"
. . . "Us glad to see you'n'a!" . . . "How's all de folks when you lef' 'em?"

This last inquiry they consider a special mark of respect and one they never forget.

The plantation house at which we stopped, and which was to be my future home, was one of the oldest on the island. It was a low, two-storied mansion, built in a wonderful grove of live oaks and water oaks which covered an area of sixty acres. All these trees are heavily draped with the long gray moss, which is never found in greater luxuriance than on and around the sea islands.

It hung dank and heavy from the recent rains; and as we entered the grove, this bright afternoon, the place seemed like a solemn, grand old cathedral.

The house contained nine small rooms. The outside door opened into a medium-sized apartment, which was called "the hall," but had always been used as parlor and dining room. Out of this opened a butler's pantry and buttery, which enclosed one end of the open piazza. At the other was an office or waiting room. There was adjoining this a small room which the servants designated as the "drawing room." A door opened from this room directly upon a narrow front piazza, from which there was a pleasant view of the broad river and of the islands beyond.

A narrow flight of winding stairs led up outside from the back piazza to a small square entry, from which four doors opened into the bedrooms. The kitchen and laundry and servants' rooms were in separate buildings. A row of these houses faced the back entrance. Not far away and in plain sight were the "Negro quarters," a row of small houses placed diagonally, where the "field hands" lived.

In front of the house was an avenue of magnolias leading to the river, which was bordered with a thick hedge of "Spanish daggers" or "bayonets"—the *Yucca filamentosa*.

When the war broke out this place was mentioned as "Smith's Plantation," taking its name from the old owner. On one of the posts of the front piazza was found some writing, supposed to be by the former owner. It said that for more than fifty years he had moved from this place to his house in town and back again, making the change over eighty times, and he devoutly thanked God for all the blessings he had received.

It seemed indescribably pathetic to me, thus to walk into a stranger's house and take quiet possession. There was nothing within to remind one of the original owner. It was only when I walked around and saw the carefully arranged grounds, with fine shrubs and vines and graveled walks bordered with flowers, that I realized what the place had been. In spite of years of neglect—for it was first left to the care of the Negroes and then taken by the Union troops and used for soldiers' barracks and hospitals—in spite of all this, there was much beauty left. As I walked around, I was more and more overwhelmed by a realization of the cruel necessities of a civil war. . . .

From the banks of the river, which is a broad arm of the sea, I could distinctly see the Union gunboats lying peacefully at anchor at Bay Point and Port Royal Harbor.

My first night spent in this old deserted plantation was full of troubled dreams. The novel and isolated position, with remembrances of the stories I had been listening to of its past and recent history, with the sighing of the wind and the dashing of the waves against the shore as the tide came in, all combined to weave around me strange and fantastic visions. But the early morning brought a healthy reaction, for there was work enough to do. Like soldiers, we had come with knapsacks in our hands. We were to live on "soldier's rations" and draw our supplies from the *commissariat*. In army fashion we "formed a mess." To each member of this was delegated some special duties, and each one in turn took charge and looked after supplies. By the *we* I mean a young man from Massachusetts who was superintendent of that part of the island, and a young woman sent out by the New York society, and who had charge of the plantation school.

The house was stripped of all furniture. The windows were without curtains and had only board shutters to protect us from the sun by day and unwelcome intrusion at night. When these shutters were closed we were in absolute darkness. When they were open the windows were so shattered there was nothing to protect us from the wind and the weather. There were no domestic utensils. A few articles of household furniture had been gathered together for our immediate use. This place was first deserted by its owners, then stripped of every movable thing by the Negroes, and then entirely devastated by the soldiers. . . .

Our house was a cheerless place at first. It took time and patience to bring around us anything like homely comforts. Three times a day our "rations" were spread on a solid-mahogany table, a relic of "secesh times," too big and heavy to be carried away. We drew up our camp-stools to this festive board and enjoyed our repast as only tired, busy and hungry people can.

One bright November morning I started to take possession of my contraband school. The air was soft as June; birds were singing; the cotton fields were gay with blossoms which contrasted charmingly with the white matured bolls. My path lay through a grand old live-oak grove. It was wonderfully attractive, with its great trees covered with long gray moss, through which the broad sunshine cast fantastic lights and shadows. From this I emerged into an open field. There was no regular path, and the walk over the old cotton hills was exceedingly rough and uncomfortable.

The schoolhouse to which I was appointed was a rough, wooden building standing on palmetto posts two or three feet from the ground, with an open piazza on one side. When I first came in sight of this building, the piazza was crowded with children, all screaming and chattering like a flock of jays and blackbirds in a quarrel. But as soon as they saw me they all gave a whoop and a bound and disappeared. When I reached the door there was no living thing to be seen; . . . so I inspected my new quarters while waiting for my forces.

There was one good-sized room without partitions; it was not ceiled, but besides the usual heavy board shutters its six windows were glazed. . . .

The furniture consisted of a few wooden benches, a tall pine desk with a high office stool, one narrow blackboard leaning against a post, and a huge box stove large enough to warm a Puritan meetinghouse in the olden times. The pipe of the stove was put through one window. . . .

I believe this was the first building ever erected exclusively for a colored school. It was built for the colored refugees with a fund sent to General Saxton for this purpose by a ladies' freeman's aid society in New England. All the "contraband schools" were at that time kept in churches, or cotton barns, or old kitchens. Some teachers had their classes in tents.

Inspection over, I vigorously rang a little cracked hand bell which I found on the desk. Then I saw several pairs of bright eyes peering in at the open door. But going towards them, there was a general scampering, and I could only see a head or a foot disappearing under the house. Again I rang the bell, with the same result, until I began to despair of getting my scholars together. When I turned my back they all came out. When I faced about they darted off. In time, however, I succeeded in capturing one small urchin, who howled vociferously, "O Lord! O Lord!" This brought out the others, who seemed a little scared and much amused. I soon reassured my captive, so the rest came in. Then I tried to "seat" them, which was about as easy as keeping so many marbles in place on a smooth floor. Going towards half a dozen little fellows huddled together on one bench, they simultaneously darted down under the seat, and scampered off on their hands and feet to a corner of the room. Hearing a noise and suppressed titters back of me, I looked around and saw four or five larger boys rolling over and over under the benches towards the door—whether for fun or freedom I could not tell; but as the first boy sprang to his feet and out of the door, I concluded they all planned escape. But I "halted" the rest and got them on to their feet and into their seats. They saw I was not angry but in earnest, so they quieted down. The runaway peeped in at the door, then crept along and sat down by his companions.

All these children were black as ink and as shy as wild animals. . . . They all looked alike to me now. I tried in vain to fix upon some distinguishing mark by which I might know one from another. Some of these children had been in a school before, but they were afraid of white people, and especially of strangers. As they said of a teacher on a subsequent occasion, "Us ain't know she." . . .

These children had been born and bred in troublous times. They had always been surrounded by conflict and confusion. They were in a constant state of effervescence. In time, after some more skirmishing, the little gang before me was brought into a degree of order. They listened, apparently, with open mouths and staring eyes to what I had to say. But I soon discovered my words were like an unknown tongue to them. I must first know something of their dialect in order that we might understand each other.

Now I wished to take down the names of these children; so I turned to the girl nearest me and said, "What is your name?"

"It is Phyllis, ma'am."

"But what is your other name?"

"Only Phyllis, ma'am."

I then explained that we all have two names; but she replied, "Nothing but Phyllis, ma'am."

Upon this an older girl started up and exclaimed, "Pshaw, gal! What's you'm title?" whereupon she gave the name of her old master.

After this each child gave two names, most of them funny combinations. Sometimes they would tell me one thing, and when asked to repeat it, would say something quite different. One boy gave his name as Middleton Heywood, shouting it out as if it were something he had caught and might lose. Whereupon another boy started up, saying angrily, "Not so, boy. You ain't Massa Middie's boy. I is."

All were now busily studying up their cognomens, and two or three would try to speak together before being called on. One boy was "Pumpkin," another "Squash," and another "Cornhouse." The girls were "Honey," and "Baby," and "Missy," and "Tay," with an indiscriminate adoption of Rhetts, Barnwells, Elliotts, Stuarts and Middletons for titles. . . .

The next morning I called roll, but no one answered, so I was obliged to go around again and make out a new list. They looked like so many peas in a pod. The woolly heads of the girls and boys looked just alike. All wore indiscriminately any cast-off garments given them, so it was not easy to tell which was which. Were there twenty-five new scholars, or only ten?

The third morning it was the same work over again. There were forty children present, many of them large boys and girls. I had already a list of over forty names. Amongst these were most of the months of the year and days of the week, besides a number of Pompeys, Cudjos, Sambos, and Rhinas and Rosas and Floras. I now wrote down forty new names, and I began to despair of ever getting regulated. . . .

In time I began to get acquainted with some of their faces. I could remember that "Cornhouse" yesterday was "Primus" today. That "Quash" was "Bryan." . . .

One boy gave the name of Middleton, but afterwards came to me, wishing to have it changed, saying, "That's my ole rebel master's title. Him's nothing to me now. I don't belong to he no longer, an' I don't see no use in being called for him." But when I asked what other name he would choose, the poor fellow was much puzzled. In time he decided on Drayton, as "that was a good name in secesh times, and General Drayton was a friend to we, an' no mistake. He fight on our side 'gainst his own brother when the first gun shoot." . . .

Rear Admiral John A. Dahlgren

A MOVEMENT TO ASSIST SHERMAN

Rear Admiral John A. Dahlgren had replaced Admiral DuPont on July 6, 1863, as commander of the South Atlantic Blockading Squadron.

Orders from Gideon Welles, Secretary of the Navy, on November 22, 1864, gave this information and instruction: "Major General Sherman, with about 50,000 men, left Atlanta, Georgia, on the 16th instant, with the intention of reaching the Atlantic coast somewhere in the vicinity of Savannah. He may be expected about the middle of December, and the Department directs that you will be prepared to give him any needed co-operation that may be in your power."[4]

In answer Admiral Dahlgren promised: "General [John G.] Foster and myself will do what our forces allow to assist in establishing a connection with Gen. Sherman. General Foster proposes to move on the night of the 28th for this purpose. I am to cover his landing and furnish a battery of six howitzers to march with his troops. . . ."

After the capture of Savannah, the admiral kept up demonstrations to draw attention from General Sherman, who was on his way to Columbia. When Charleston was taken, he attended the celebrations held at Fort Sumter. He sailed from Charleston on June 17—"and so ends," he noted in his diary, "a command of two years of one of the largest fleets ever assembled under American colors—as many as 96 ships at one time."

The following is from this same diary.

November 24 [1864]. About 3 arrives a note, confidential, asking if I will aid in a movement to assist Sherman. Certainly I will, and before I sleep the orders are issued to collect the light artillery, sailors, and marines—the vessels, too, are assigned.

November 25. *Harvest Moon* went up at 3 A.M. for marines and *Pontiac*, Captain [George Henry] Preble, etc. About 10 A.M. another letter from General Foster asks two to six gunboats to cover and six

---

[4] *Official Records of the Navy*, Series I, Vol. 16, p. 57.

naval howitzers to assist, to be ready Monday evening. Start the *Bibb* off for *Mingoe* and men; send south for *Winona* and men; very busy with the detail.

November 27. Very foggy. *Mingoe* got in last night. No Sabbath to-day for us. The naval detachment must move to-morrow night with the troops, and they are very raw, so we must drill on Sunday. The officers are clever, and with zealous men, so we get off. The battery will have six 12-pounders, two of them rifled. The sailor skirmishers, about 160, in four companies, and the marines, 180, in —— companies. Very difficult to get the officers into the idea of light drill and open order; they will mass the men. *Wissahickon* and *Winona* came in. I was ashore morning and afternoon looking on. Broad River is to be the scene of action.

November 28. Port Royal. Ashore in the morning; got all parts together and had a grand drill. Gave them some notion of my idea. They scampered through bushes and over sand hills with howitzers. In the afternoon all getting ready to embark. At sundown the gunboats *Pontiac* and *Mingoe* were brought to the wharf and took in sailors, marines, and howitzers.

November 29. At 4 o'clock A.M. I looked out; there was a low fog hanging over the water, through which vessels might be glimpsed for two or three hundred yards; the stars clear above. As signals were uncertain and inexpedient, the *Harvest Moon* had to steam round and order each of six steamers to get underway, so that daylight was relieving the horizon as the party was steering for Broad River, I ahead, for Bradford is a good natural pilot. It was a bitter reflection that the army must be far ahead and the gunboats not ahead to cover. The fog had thickened, so that the shores were just seen dimly and only the vessel ahead and astern. I ordered the *Pontiac* to lead.

At last, about 8:30, the pilot announced that we were at the landing. Not ten minutes before I had heard one or two loud hallos, and supposed they came from some of our soldiers; but there was not a soldier nor a steamer but my own, nor a sign of life, but there was a little hut under a tree for a picket, and the fire was still burning, and the said picket had been suddenly astonished by the sight of many large steamers, seen like ghosts in the fog; so close, too. He was at his breakfast, for the sweet potatoes were found on the fire; gave a yell for some one and was off.

And here I was, not a sign of the troops; they had left at 2 o'clock, three hours before me, and were somewhere in the river. The pilot was sure of the name of the place, and the fleet captain was sure of the spot on the sketch. Perhaps the army had gone elsewhere. I lingered for a moment in doubt, and was turning downstream to make sure of the place when a solitary transport was descried moving up. It was all right, so in a twinkling the howitzers were put ashore, and the men. I landed on the relics of a wharf. A beautiful spot, truly, woodland and uncultivated fields, but silent as the grave. The sailors moved quickly, and the lesson of yesterday was put in practice, howitzers and men advancing to the front in skirmishing order. I walked up the farm road with the foremost men, and it was hot as summer.

Leaving the boys at a halt about a mile from the river, I went back. It was about 11 o'clock. A few companies of colored troops were near the shore, some formed in companies and others about loose—not a sign of a move, but rather like a colony about to settle. Some were building fires, as if for a meal. Many transports were arriving, some with black troops, some with white.

About 2 P.M. Major General Foster appeared, denoted by a square blue flag with two stars. This is the new arrangement, to correspond with the navy flags. About 3 a master's mate came from Captain Preble, saying he had advanced about 4 miles, but the army as yet had only a company between him and the shore. So I sent the master's mate to General Foster, who replied that General Hatch was hurrying the troops ashore. Got to Port Royal about 8, and returned to the *Philadelphia*, a wiser man than when I left.

November 30. The mail steamer leaves at noon and I must send a word to the Secretary. So I was occupied till noon, when I left for Broad River, for the sound of cannon had been heard during the morning. General Foster went up about 10 o'clock. Took the *Philadelphia* this time. It was 4 o'clock when I got into the creek. Did not get up to the landing; got ashore. General Foster a little higher up, and left soon after I arrived. Captain Balch came on board, said all was going well; the troops near Grahamville had some fighting with the rebels,[5] but drove them. Navy howitzers doing well. I started to return about 6 P.M.

December 1. I started at 11 A.M. for Broad River; got to Boyd's Landing and was grieved to hear that the fighting had been going on

---

[5] Battle of Honey Hill, near Grahamville, November 30, 1864.

yesterday very unfavorably to us. The rebels had retired to a strong position on our road to Grahamville. General Hatch assaulted the work and was repulsed with heavy loss; he then fell back to a crossroads some 3 miles from the landing.

During the day General Foster was absent reconnoitering and got back in the evening. I went to see him; unfortunate that he is crippled by an old wound and moves only with a crutch. His course of remark amounted to the men not fighting hard, which also seemed evident to me through all my experience here. He wanted to look around to see if he could get in at any other place.

December 2. Thick and foggy. Sound of field guns from 7:30 for an hour. General Foster sent a telegram from Hatch saying the rebels were gathering in our front and firing from two fieldpieces, but it was not serious enough to answer. The general was going to reconnoiter Whale Branch to Port Royal Ferry; wanted Balch and the tugs to go along. Last night I found that we had not a single picket boat out, nor a single feeler on our right and left. I had both done. Started at 3 P.M. to reconnoiter the Coosawhatchie; tug grounded in the Broad River a mile and a half above Boyd's Creek; could not get off and I went back in a boat. At 7 P.M. returned to Port Royal in the *Philadelphia*.

December 3. The same fine weather, but too warm to be seasonable. Gave directions about affairs and at 10:30 went up Broad River. Foster ahead. Sent the fleet captain to the general to say that if he wished the batteries in the Coosawhatchie attacked I would send vessels, but it would be to no purpose if there were no troops to hold them. The general wished to have them attacked and I might have my brigade—and then he would not ask it officially. I told Balch to be ready.

The *Harvest Moon* came up about 9 P.M. with 4 deserters from Beaulieu, real native Georgians, who had been conscripted and would not stand it. They report Beaulieu very strong and that Sherman was coming on.

In the afternoon Colonel Mulford, the agent for exchange, came to see me. He said that the exchange at Savannah was interrupted by present operations and he desired to go on at Charleston. General Foster had given leave; would I? Certainly.

December 4. Sent the *Pawnee* and *Sonoma* to Coosawhatchie with the launches. The general started off with some small steamers and a

regiment for Whale Branch. About noon I started after them only to
look on. Found the *Pawnee* and *Sonoma* very busy pounding a small
battery not far up the Coosawhatchie; it fired a few shots and was soon
shut up. General Hatch was reconnoitering in force on the left, and
the boats of the *Pontiac* which I had ordered up Boyd's Creek peeped
out of the marsh on the left.

December 5. Started with General Foster up Broad River. Stopped
off at the confluence of the Coosawhatchie and Tulifinny rivers; the
latter was reconnoitered, and I sent up for a few Negroes that appeared
on the shore. Meanwhile the steamers were pelting the little battery
on the Coosawhatchie as a feint. Got three very decrepit old cuffeys,
but their information was valuable for the operation which the general
and I had agreed on up the Tulifinny to-morrow. We go in force and
hope to reach the railroad.

December 6. Soon after light the troops and steamers began to move
from Boyd's Creek. We got to Tulifinny about 8, dead low water, and
it looked as if we were not to get in. General Potter, who was to command, came on board and said General Foster doubted if it were not
best to wait for the tide. What did I say? Go ahead offhand. General
Potter concurred in my reasons, and soon was the water covered with
the boats filled with the soldiers and sailors and guns. No opposition,
not a rebel visible. Our men got ashore and were soon lost in the
woods. In the afternoon word came in that we [had] met the rebels
and were driving them. In the evening learned that several of my men
had been wounded. The *Pontiac* sent me half a dozen prisoners, just
nabbed, all Georgians. One said he was at the battery we fired at on
the Coosawhatchie, and they had 600 men in ambush waiting for us;
so I was right; if the boats had landed I should have lost heavily.

After dark some heavy and continued firing was heard in a direction
north of Savannah and some rockets seen. Hoping it might be Sherman I had guns fired and rockets thrown up.

December 7. Firing ashore. The brigade of the fleet has lost about
20 men here and at Boyd's Creek. I went ashore to the upper landing
to look at the wounded sailors. Firing steadily, heard it was only skirmishing, rebels trying to force our position. We have cut the county-
road bridge on the right and can see and hear the cars.

December 8. Little or no firing, the rebels quiet and our lines certainly near the railroad. Our casualties swell to 23 in all.

December 9. As I understood yesterday from the general, to-day the effort was made to open the view to the railroad through the dense wood in front of our position. Accordingly 500 axmen started on the right, covered by the fire of strong columns of skirmishers. The firing was sharp but not serious while the axes were advancing, but as soon as we began to retire (the work being done) the rebels came down like a house on fire. All I learned by night [was] they had been repulsed and we suffered considerably, and among them our marines. A deserter stated that Sherman was within 15 miles of Savannah, so I started down after dark to Port Royal, where I arrived about 11 P.M., and found to my surprise that the *Harvest Moon*, which I sent down yesterday afternoon, was here; had been kept back by the heavy gale that blew all day.

December 10. Tulifinny. Disposed of all the business by 4 P.M., and once more turned up the river to know how we finally stood after the action of yesterday. Reached the mouth of the Tulifinny about 8 o'clock. Balch came on board and, though senior officer, absolutely knew no more than I knew last night; said he had not heard from the front to-day; so I dispatched an aid and he got back by 11 P.M. Things were substantially as represented last evening, except the disaster to the marines, though our total casualties amounted to 20 at least. We were in position, well intrenched, and a lane cut to the railroad through the trees ready for the rifle cannon.

December 11. At 9:30, finding matters all secure, turned down the river, got to Port Royal by noon. About 10 at night an army tug brought a dispatch from *Wissahickon*, at Tybee, saying that heavy firing was heard up the river about Savannah; sent word over to Foster.

December 12. General Foster came in his steamer astern of me and secured. General lame, so I went on board. He thought news of last night good. I told him a steamer I sent (*Dandelion*) was coming in from Ossabaw and would bring letters, as that alone could bring her. In a few minutes an officer was announced with a dispatch from General Howard, the advance of Sherman's army.

It was Captain William Duncan, of the Illinois cavalry, with a sergeant and private. They had found their way down the Ogeechee to Ossabaw and U.S.S. *Flag*. Had left the army just outside of Savannah and a fight going on. The dispatch from General Howard was short, in pencil, on a scrap of paper.

Captain Duncan left General Howard at 9 P.M. of the 9th with two men; went down the Ogeechee in a boat. At daylight of the 10th started; passed McAllister, and at daylight was 6 miles below it; reached the *Flag* at noon; left in the *Dandelion* at 2 P.M. (11th), but was detained by a gale.

After a brief chat with General Foster about dispositions, I left and gave orders for collecting my steamers about the rivers near Savannah. Sent the monitor *Sangamon* to Savannah River and about noon was able to leave myself and reach there about 4. After giving directions about buoying the channel of the river I left after dark for Ossabaw; reached there about 11 P.M.

December 13. Reached Savannah River about daylight. Found things moving as indifferently as if nothing of interest was proceeding. General Foster arrived in the morning from Ossabaw and Wassaw; not communicated yet with Sherman.

December 14. At 8 A.M. an officer came in a boat from the *Passaic* with dispatches from Ossabaw; had communicated by signal last night with Sherman. So I determined to go to Ossabaw by way of Wassaw, where I wished to have things right for stopping the rebel ironclads in case they made a dash. So I started by the inland passage, Lazaretto Creek and Tybee River. On getting into Wassaw Sound saw General Foster's steamer outside, which changed course and stood in on seeing me. I stood on to speak to the *Pawnee* and *Passaic*; was near the former when the signal officer reported signals from General Foster that General Sherman was with him. Anchored immediately, and in a few minutes the steamer came alongside, and I jumped aboard, walked into the cabin, and met General Sherman. He had left his army to see me. Sherman told me a division had just walked into McAllister (December 13, at 5 P.M.), but that no ships could have taken it, so powerfully was it fortified toward the water. Well, finally it was agreed that Sherman should go back with me, and General Foster would go to Hilton Head.

December 15. After breakfast I went ashore with General Sherman to look over Fort McAllister; a truly formidable work; so crammed with bombproofs and traverses as to look as if the spaces were carved out of solid earth, a very strong and complete work. The rebel garrison were still there cooking, etc., as if nothing had happened. Then we went up the river, and I landed with General Sherman at the rice mills. Here we looked around, and we parted; he took horse for his army, and I returned to my vessel. . . .

Brigadier General George P. Harrison

PRISONER OF WAR ON HILTON HEAD

Brigadier General George P. Harrison who commanded the Con-
federate forts at Savannah was captured on December 9, 1864, by
Sherman's Twentieth Army Corps. His home was at Monteith near
Savannah. More than six hundred Confederate prisoners were sent to
Hilton Head Island. General Harrison sent the following letter to
Richmond.

Prisoners' Barracks,
Hilton Head, S.C., January 9, 1865

Hon. Julian Hartridge; Richmond, Va.

My Dear Sir: You will see from where this is written that I am a
prisoner of war, captured about a month since at my home by General
Sherman's forces on their advance to Savannah. I reached this place
about two weeks since with about 600 prisoners. With the officers I
was sent to the prison on this island, where 200 officers are confined
and upon retaliatory treatment. Having shared their privations, hardships and sufferings for two months, I propose to give you, and through
you to the authorities of the Government, somewhat in detail what
we have been called to endure and what these 200 officers are still
enduring. (Sherman's prisoners are now drawing better rations, in
other respects the same treatment.)

The prison bounds embrace about fifty square yards. Upon this
stand two buildings, lightly weatherboarded, about seventy-five by
twenty-four feet in size, one small kitchen, and fifteen tents. The remainder of the ground is used for cooking place and exercise for about
260 men; about 100 of these are lodged on one floor of each of these
buildings; remainder (privates) occupy the tents. Cells are arranged
on both sides of these buildings, about seven by six feet, and are occupied by from four to nine officers. But one door opens to the buildings
and no windows, consequently the larger portion of the building is
too dark even at midday for either reading or writing. No fire is allowed
in these buildings. At about 5 P.M. is roll-call, when the inmates are
locked in until 7 A.M. next morning. The cold here is severe. Once
since my arrival water would be ice in a moment after it touched the
floor.

Many of these officers are in rags, scarce enough clothing to cover their nakedness. Many, well-nigh shoeless, lay at nights upon a rough, naked board, and in some instances two cover with one blanket, with their hips covered with a rough, horny scab from their nightly contact with their bedless bunks. To avoid freezing to death when the weather is cold much of the night is spent running up and down the building to keep up the circulation. This is done by almost the entire prison.

The daily allowance to each man is one pint of stale meal, about two spoonsful of which is husk and weevils, four ounces of bread, and one-fourth pint of pickles. Three camp kettles are allowed to each prison as cooking utensils. One stick of green wood about eight feet long and eight inches in diameter for fuel. The cooking is done in the open yard by the prisoners. Old coffee pots, tin kettles, frying pans—in a word, everything upon which a hoecake can be baked or in which water can be boiled—is brought into requisition and used thus. Two or three of a mess pick up their bunch of chips, cup of meal, etc., select a place, open a hole in the sand, pile it around the edge to keep off the wind. Into this the chips are deposited, the fire applied, down drops an officer, his mouth near the coals, and blows until sufficient fire is kindled to prepare his mush or hoecake. From the scanty supply of provisions and wood only two meals are taken per day. It is not uncommon for officers to cut the wood for the hospital for the privilege of picking up and using the chips. I have seen a little piece of dirty grease carefully picked out of the sand, carefully cleaned and put away for use. So perfectly ravenous are the cravings of nature for meat by men thus circumstanced that every cat about the prison has been eaten, and rats are eaten as readily as a chicken would be at home.

The officers and privates garrisoning the prison are kind and courteous, and although a portion of the troops are Negroes, still we have no cause of complaint, as they confine themselves strictly to a performance of their duties. I write this letter by the consent of the provost-marshal of the department, who, whilst he enforces with fidelity the orders of his government, is deeply anxious that Federal prisoners in Confederate prisons might be better treated, so as to bring about an amelioration of the Confederate prisoners both here and elsewhere. May I hear from you? Write via Charleston.

While I remain, as ever, your friend,

GEO. P. HARRISON

Elizabeth Hyde Botume

SHERMAN'S ARMY COMES TO BEAUFORT

A *letter from Beaufort on January 15, 1865, reported that "some twenty steamers arrive daily at Beaufort direct from Savannah, bringing the troops and wagons, artillery and animals. . . . The greater part of the whole army seems to be coming around this way and marching over the ferry towards Pocotaligo."*

Along with the army from Savannah came Secretary Stanton and other officials from Washington.

On that day, January 15, General W. T. Sherman issued his Field Order No. 15, reserving for Negroes the sea islands from Charleston "to and including the lands bordering the St. John's River, and the abandoned rice fields for thirty miles from the sea."

Miss Botume, from her school at Old Fort Plantation, gives her account of the passing of Sherman's army.

It was an exciting time when Sherman's army marched through Georgia. The left wing, or "Tenth Army Corps," marched to Beaufort. A long procession of gunboats sailed up the river past our place. No one knew at first whether these were friends or foes. So there was a regular stampede amongst the colored people, who hid away or locked themselves into their houses. The children stood on the riverbank and shouted, ready to fly to the schoolhouse should danger threaten them. They soon made out the Union colors, and then there were the wildest shouts and manifestations of delight.

The first soldiers who landed in Beaufort supposed they were still in hostile territory, and they immediately took possession of the town, helping themselves to whatever they could lay their hands on. They were intoxicated with success, and for a few hours ran riot. General Saxton placed a strong guard around the town, with strict orders that no colored people should enter the lines. As soon as the superior officers arrived, order was restored. But with the army came a great gang of contrabands to be housed and rationed and taken care of.

For forty-eight hours we were barricaded from the town; then General Saxton sent an orderly with a permit for us to enter the lines, "good for thirty days." . . .

We soon learned that life in a military department, especially near the camping ground, had many tribulations.

For the month that Sherman's army was stationed in and around Beaufort all supplies were used for the military. The weather became exceedingly cold. Ice formed and did not melt all day. For three weeks we could get no rations from Beaufort, and we were very nearly reduced to our own supply of sweet potatoes and hominy and milk. . . .

I find in my notebook, dated January 14, 1865, this entry:

"We hear that Sherman's army is crossing to the mainland today. Are glad that the soldiers are leaving our neighborhood. For a month we have been demoralized. It has been almost impossible to keep the contrabands under our care in order, and it has been difficult to ration the newcomers and make them comfortable. All our supplies have been stopped. It was not possible to get our letters, the mails have been so crowded with military documents. We hear there is a mass of boxes at Hilton Head waiting to be moved, but no room for them yet on the overloaded boats. Truly, our lives have been like a seething caldron."

PART XIII

Reconstruction

1865-1877

The Nation, March 1870, stated: "The Legislature which has just adjourned in South Carolina was one of the most corrupt assemblages of men ever legislated for a state, and one of the most contemptible in point of ability. . . ." South Carolina was "completely at the mercy of the white and black corruptionists."

A Negro represented Beaufort County in the Senate of the General Assembly of 1868; two whites and five Negroes were members of the state House of Representatives.

The last session of the South Carolina General Assembly under Negro rule met in November 1875. Shortly afterward, Mr. B. C. Pressley, a lawyer, voiced the opinion of the native whites: "I tell you that we have drunk the last drop of the bitter cup that we intend to drink, unless the United States Army says so. . . . The time has come for action. . . ."[1]

---

[1] John S. Reynolds, *Reconstruction in South Carolina, 1865-1877*. Columbia, S. C., The State Co., 1905, p. 324.

"MASSA RICHARD" RETURNS

When Secretary Chase visited Port Royal shortly after the close of the war on a tour of inspection, among those he invited to accompany him was Dr. Richard Fuller, who had owned a plantation on St. Helena, including some 200 or 300 slaves.

Richard Fuller, a descendant of our old friend Dr. Henry Woodward, was born in Beaufort, April 22, 1804. His father was Dr. Thomas Fuller, a minister and also one of the wealthiest cotton planters in South Carolina. His mother was Elizabeth Middleton, whose ancestors included a signer of the Declaration of Independence. After being graduated from Harvard in 1824, Richard Fuller practiced law in Beaufort. He gave up the law in 1832 to serve as minister to the Beaufort Baptist Church. From Beaufort he was called to the Seventh Baptist Church in Baltimore, Maryland. When war came, he opposed secession and stayed in Baltimore. His father died a refugee in Greenville, South Carolina.

On March 13, 1862, Dr. Fuller had conferred in Washington with Secretary Salmon P. Chase about his plantation and slaves at Port Royal and his rights in the matter. Chase's diary of that date noted the meeting. Dr. Fuller was "willing to acquiesce in the experiments of the Government, but expressed grave doubts of the success of the undertaking at Port Royal."

He died in Baltimore on October 20, 1876.

"Agate" of the Cincinnati Gazette, was in Secretary Chase's party and duly reported what happened at Port Royal.

[Port Royal, July 1865]
While our party stood looking about this scene of the past, a white-woolled deacon came, with the politeness, if not the grace, of an old-world master of ceremonies, to summon us: "De people is gathering, sah, and was ready for the suvvices to begin." It was a natural sensation when the major generals, the chief justice and the ladies of the party were led through the crowd to the little platform under the live oaks; but it was when Rev. Dr. Fuller—"Massa Richard"—made his appearance that the wondering stare brightened, and eyes grew moist, and ancient Negresses could be heard vehemently whispering,

"Bress de Lod, bress de Lod!" . . . "Hebenly Marster!" . . . "Gra-a-ate
King!" No word had been sent of our coming, and it was but within
the last half hour that the old slaves of Dr. Fuller heard that he was
to address them. There was no way of estimating the number of those
in attendance (he had owned between two and three hundred); but
probably half of them were now at Beaufort. Every adult Negro in
the assemblage, however, seemed to know him.

The scene was a striking one. In front of us was the old church;
behind, the new schoolhouse. Half a dozen superb live oaks spread
their gnarled branches over us, the silvery, pendulous streamers of
Spanish moss floating down and flecking with the sunlight the up-
turned faces of the great congregation of Negroes; while the breezes
made mournful music among the leaves, and the mockingbirds sent
back a livelier refrain. The little valley between the platform and the
church was finally packed with Negroes, all standing, and, as the deacon told us, "eagah fur de Wud." They clustered, too, about the platform, leaned over the railing behind and at the sides, and spread away
in all directions among the carts and wagons that formed a sort of
outer line of defenses.

A quaint old African, clad in cotton checks and bowed with many
years of cotton-hoeing, stepped out on the platform where all this
party had been seated. Leaning like a patriarch on his cane and gently
swaying his body to and fro over it as if to keep time, he struck up, in
a shrill, cracked voice, a curiously monotonous melody, in which, in a
moment, the whole congregation were energetically joining. For the
first time I observed what had often been told me, that the languages
of these sea-islanders (and I am told that, to some extent, the same
is true of the majority of plantation hands in South Carolina) is an
almost unintelligible *patois*. Listening carefully to the swaying old
leader, I found it almost impossible for a time to make out his meaning; and the vocal contortions to which the simplest words seemed
to subject him was a study that would have amazed a phonetic lec-
turer. The words were those of an old song which our soldiers found
them singing shortly after the fall of Bay Point:

> "Ma-a-a-assa Fullah a-sittin' on de tree ob life,
> Ma-a-a-assa Fullah a-sittin' on de tree ob life.
> Roll, Jordan, roll!
> Ma-a-a-assa Fullah a-sittin' on de tree ob life.
> Roll, Jordan, roll!"

And so on, with repetitions that promised to be endless. The grateful Negroes had cherished the memory of Dr. Fuller, who had abandoned his large legal practice to preach to them, and, long after his departure to the North, had still kept his name green among them by thus associating it with their ideas of heaven. But as freedom came, and no Dr. Fuller with it, they gradually forgot the old benefactor and substituted the name of the new one. To them, Gen. Saxton was law and order and right. He secured their plantations; he got them rations till they were able to support themselves; he decided disputes, defended privileges, maintained quiet, and was the embodiment of justice; and so it gradually came to pass that "Gen-e-ul Sa-a-axby" . . . took the place of "Ma-a-a-assa Fullah" in the song. The presence of the good doctor recalled their old love and they gave him the first place: but they could not depose their later favorite and greater benefactor; and so, after interminable repetitions, we came to the second stanza:

> "Gen-e-ul Sa-a-axby a-sittin' on de tree ob life,
> Gen-e-ul Sa-a-axby a-sittin' on de tree ob life.
> Roll, Jordan, roll!
> Gen-e-ul Sa-a-axby a-sittin' on de tree ob life.
> Roll, Jordan roll!"

The patriarchal old African, swaying on his cane before the congregation, threw the whole power of his lungs into the harsh tones with which the concluding "ro-o-o-oll" was given. And then came the great feat of the African reception to the visitors. Wherever we had been, the Negroes seemed to know something of Mr. Chase. Their ideas were very vague; but they thought that, in some way, he was a great large friend of theirs, who had done something or another for them (what they scarcely knew), and was to be held beside "Linkum" in their esteem. So now, with a droll look of intelligence toward the crowd . . . the antique leader struck out in harsher tones and more indescribably bewildering difficulties of pronunciation than ever:

> "Me-is-ta-ah Che-a-ase a-sittin' on de tree ob life,
> Me-is-ta-ah Che-a-ase a-sittin' on de tree ob life.
> Roll, Jordan, roll!
> Me-is-ta-ah Che-a-ase a-sittin' on de tree ob life.
> Roll, Jordan, roll!"

The chorus was sung with vehemence that pierced the ears and swayed the leaflets of the live oaks above our heads, while pickaninnies crowed, and their mothers smiled, and there was a general bustle in the crowd, and all fixed beaming eyes . . . on the embarrassed Chief Justice, whom they were establishing in all his avoirdupois on the identical limb where Dr. Fuller and Gen. "Saxby" were already perched.

When Dr. Fuller came to speak to them, they evidently understood him and undoubtedly meant to obey his instructions. When, for example, he told them that, at the North, their enemies were declaring that they would be idle and dissolute, and asked if they were going thus to bring shame upon those who had befriended them, there was an emphasis of response, and an earnestness in the looks men and women gave each other, that spoke both for their understanding and their intentions.

"I know that new machinery will work a little rough," said the doctor. "I am not surprised that at first there were some blunders and faults; but it is time you had got over that. If a man who has been shut up for a long time in a dark room is suddenly brought to light, it dazzles his eyes, and he is apt to stumble. Well, then, what will you do? Put him back in the dark again?"

"No, no!" energetically exclaimed the crowd, with many an earnest shake of the head.

"What then?"

"Tell him what to do," suggested some. "Lead him a little while," whispered others.

"*Give him more light!*" at last exclaimed the doctor, and it was curious to watch the pleased noddings of the woolly heads, the shakings of the turbans, the sensation, exchange of smiles and other indications that the doctor's solution of the difficulty was thoroughly understood in its application to their own condition.

Mr. Chase followed in a few words of calm advice as to the necessity of industry, economy, study and the like. When he added that, for his own part, he believed, too, that the best way to teach them to swim in the ocean of suffrage was to throw them in and let them take care of themselves, the emphatic nods and smiles, and cries of "Yes, yes!" showed that the figure was not thrown away upon them.

But there remained a scene that showed how, if not anxious to return to their old masters, they were still glad to have their old masters return to them. Dr. Fuller rose to pronounce the benediction, and all reverently bowed their heads . . . bowed altogether before God—the freedmen and the major generals, the turbaned young women from the plantations and the flower of Northern schools and society, the woolly-headed urchins who could just remember that they once "belonged to" somebody, and the Chief Justice of the United States.

The few words of blessing were soon said; and then came a rush to the stand "to speak to Massa Richard." Men and women pressed forward indiscriminately. The good doctor in a moment found both his hands busy and stood like a patriarchal shepherd amid his flock. They pushed up against him, kissed his hands, passed their fingers over his hair, crowded about, eager to get a word of recognition. "Sure you 'member me, Massa Rich'd: I'm Tom." . . . "Laws, Massa Rich'd, I mind ye when's ye's a little un." . . . "Don't ye mind, Massa Rich'd, when I used to gwine out gunnin' wid ye?" . . . "How's ye been dis long time?" . . . " 'Pears like we's never gwine to see 'ou any more; bu, bress de Lord! you'm cum." . . . "Oh, we's gitting on cum'table like; but ain't ou gwine to cum back and preach to us sometimes?" So the string of interrogations and salutations stretched out.

"I haven't liked him much," said an officer of our cutter standing near, whose rough and ready oaths had sometimes provoked the rebuke of the doctor, "but I take back every harsh thought. I'd give all I'm worth, or ever hope to be worth in the world, to be loved by as many people as love him." . . .

Mary S. Hamilton

"SALE OF THE LAND"

Mary S. Hamilton was a descendant of Paul Hamilton, Secretary of the Navy (1808-1812), whom we have met. Refugees from "The Oaks" in Beaufort since November 1861, Mary and other members of the family came back in November 1866 to witness the sale of homes "for the taxes due." "Some few females have returned since the war," she wrote, "but the greater part have found homes elsewhere, many 'where the wicked cease from troubling and the weary are at rest.'"

In a large four-horse wagon we came back, packed, as we said, "like sardines," and in spite of all happy to see once more the salt water and our dear old home, which the authorities would not allow my father to hire for fear he might show them that "possession was nine tenths of the law." We succeeded in hiring it, however, in the name of our uncle, who lived with us.

And now comes one of the strangest facts in modern history, which I believe is unknown at the North, and only half understood in our native state. I refer to the sale of the land on our sea islands for taxes during the war, a sale which was continued even eighteen months after peace—the so-called peace—had been declared, when we were promised our rights of life and property.

On our return home we found nearly all the houses occupied by Negroes or Northern families who had come here "in the wake of the army," as one of them expressed it. The churches were dismantled of pulpits, pews, carpets and organs, and the former Sunday school was the only place of worship in the town for the whites, as both the large churches had been used as hospitals, as well as the houses which had been bought in by the Government for that purpose when the tax sales took place.

In November 1866 they offered these houses for sale, as the Government commissioners said, "for the taxes due." Ours was included among the number, and long will that day be remembered in the Southern part of the community when their homes were bid up by different parties, in spite of the assertion of the real owners that they were homeless and wished to try to purchase or redeem these homes by paying the amount claimed by the Government.

Our father succeeded in outbidding a "Northern philanthropist" who "wanted our home for a charitable institution," and the commissioners promised to give him three days to visit the city of Charleston and try to make arrangements for the payment of the sum, which was six times more than the amount of taxes due.

I am glad, among so many acts of unkindness, to be able to record the following. The day before my father could possibly return, two Northerners heard that the commissioner intended to sell the house at private sale, after sunset, unless the money was paid before. They collected the required amount, at their own risk, and one of them went to the commissioner and paid it down just before the time was up.

As he was leaving the office, the sun set, and the man who expected to purchase entered, so that he heard the commissioner say: "You are too late, the money has been paid." We shook hands with the Northerner that night, though up to that time we had said we would never give a handshake to any Yankee.

The house of one of our friends was bought in for him by a Frenchman who was here on a visit, and who sympathised very much with the Southerners and would not even leave his address on going away, so that the money advanced could never be paid.

I must say in justice to them, however, that many of our Northern friends would not buy property here unless they could purchase from the true, original owners or, at least, buy their titles. Strange to say, the plantations are still known by the names of the Southern owners.

These lands and homes thus forfeited here have never been returned, and the surplus tax money has never been refunded to the owners. . . .

The papers, even in Washington, have had lately a full account of the desolate condition of the grave of ex-Secretary Paul Hamilton on one of the plantations on this island. This grave, with all the rest of his family enclosure, was sold at tax sale by the Government in 1863. The iron fence surrounding the enclosure was destroyed or carried off during the war, and the stones leveled by the troops or other persons. This property was bought by a Northern colored man, who, from feelings of common humanity, has never planted over the spot. A naval officer while out hunting came across the sacred grave and, being attracted by the stones, dismounted and found out whose resting place it was. He applied to Congress for money to put the grave in order. One hundred dollars was generously appropriated for this object, and the grave has been enclosed with galvanized wire. Would it not have been more suitable for the Government to purchase the grave and enclosure from the present owner, who holds their titles, so that future owners of the soil may not encroach on the spot where rests one of the country's heroes?

Our country is lost, our hopes are dead, yet we must "be still" and know that He who doeth all things well will show us the why and wherefore in His own good time. If not now, at least then the verdict shall be: "Thy works, O Lord, pass understanding. Thy mercies are very great."

Committee on Finance of the United States Senate

"PETITION . . . FOR THE RESTORATION OF PINCKNEY ISLAND"

Pinckney Island has experienced many changes of fortune since General Pinckney sent his boats "a-drum-fishing" in 1818.

The following petition from members of the Pinckney family, heirs to the island, was presented in the United States Senate on April 7, 1868.

The Committee on Finance to whom the petition was addressed fails to note the great and distinguished part "General Charles Cotesworth Pinckney, an officer of the revolutionary army," afterward played in the service of his country.

In the Senate of the United States
April 7, 1868.—Ordered to be printed.

Mr. Morgan, from the Committee on Finance, submitted the following

REPORT

The Committee on Finance, to whom was referred the petition of the heirs and representatives of Miss Harriott Pinckney, of South Carolina, praying the restoration to them of Pinckney island, in South Carolina, the same having been confiscated for the non-payment of taxes, submit the following report:

The facts set forth in the petition of the heirs of General Pinckney for the restoration of Pinckney island, and in the other papers, herewith submitted, are as follows:

Pinckney island is situated in St. Luke's parish, Beaufort district, South Carolina, and contains about 2,000 acres of land, together with about 500 acres of marsh, called respectively "the Cresent" and "Espatanque." In 1863 it was valued on the tax-roll at $8,000. Major Everston, inspector, etc. values it at $10,000 to $15,000, and says that the present rate of rent represents a valuation of $17,000. Mr. Wording, United States direct tax commissioner, says a fair intrinsic valuation of the island would, in his opinion, be about $10 per acre.

Major General Charles Cotesworth Pinckney, an officer of the revolutionary army, died on the 25th of August, 1825, possessed of the island in question, leaving three daughters to represent him:

I. Maria Henrietta, who inherited one-third, and who died unmarried, prior to the rebellion, her one-third interest at her death passing to the surviving sisters.

II. Eliza Lucas married Mr. Izard, and died without issue before the rebellion. She made a will in November, 1849, which, with the codicil, was proven in June, 1851. Under this the title to one-half of Pinckney island, subject to the life interest of her sister Harriett, became vested in the father of the petitioner, who was also the cousin of Eliza.

III. Leaving only surviving Harriett, maiden. The latter, it appears, never married. She died in 1865, aged 91 years. By her death the family of her father became extinct. She made a will, which with the codicil, was admitted to probate in March, 1866. By this she gave her one-half interest to the petitioner, Rev. C. C. Pinckney.

The present petitioners are the Rev. Charles Cotesworth Pinckney, and his sisters, Caroline Seabrook (born Pinckney) and Mary E. Pinckney, who are first cousins, once removed, of Harriott, and grandchildren of Thomas, the brother of General Pinckney. They claim to be the sole representatives, and, with a single exception, sole heirs of the said Harriott, the exception being Thomas, brother of the petitioner, who in March, 1867, released his eighth interest to his brother, the petitioner. . . .

The island was not occupied by the owners when the national forces took possession of it. Being situated in that portion of South Carolina in which the provisions of the direct tax operated, the government sold it, on the 1st of December, 1863, for non-payment of taxes, and, as it had been selected for military, naval, police, and other purposes, it was bid in for the United States, at the sum of $2,100. It was found unsuitable for these objects, and was leased, at public auction, for the term of four years from the 1st of January, 1865, at an annual rent of $3,475. The lessee being unable to pay this amount, the rent, after the first year, was reduced to $1,500 for the remainder of the term.

The number of persons entitled to land under the law in force in January, 1867, did not exceed 600, and it is shown that there would be enough to supply all claimants thereunder without this island.

There are three or four families, consisting of about 20 persons in all, who were formerly the servants of the Pinckneys, now living on the island; and about 200 freed people are employed thereon, the greater number of whom live on Hilton Head island, and go daily to Pinckney island to labor.

The government have expended in improvements on the island about $2,000; taxes and interest due when the government took possession of it in 1863, $160: Penalty 80: Costs 36: 10 per cent 34.

The government had received up to the 29th of January, 1867, through the United States direct tax commissioners, as rent for the island, the sum of $6,475. . . .

The papers show that little or no part was taken by the family in the rebellion, although what share, if any, Thomas, the brother who claimed an eighth interest, had, does not appear. Archibald H. Seabrook, the husband of Caroline E., the latter one of the heirs and petitioners, it would appear, has, for a long time past, been a cripple, and therefore could take no active part in the war. The assistant commissioner of the Freedmen's Bureau says the Rev. Mr. Pinckney took no part in the rebellion, and adds that, from his general character and his interest in the education of the colored race, he would be a valuable man in their midst. Harriott was 85 years of age at the opening of the rebellion, quite too old, it may be presumed, to render any efficient aid, and the two female petitioners, it is claimed, gave no assistance to the insurgents. But, while it is asserted that the petitioners took no part in the war, Major Everston, inspector, etc., to whose statements we are indebted for several important facts in this report, says that "the proclivities of the whole family favored strongly the rebel cause." . . .

As the tax commissioners and the assistant commissioner of the Freedmen's Bureau, who, "being on the ground and cognizant of all the facts in this case, have recommended the restoration of the property," General Howard, Commissioner, unites in asking the favorable consideration of Congress to the petition. General Grant concurs with General Howard in this, and the Secretary of the Treasury expresses the opinion that the property should be released.

The inquiry into the title of the petitioners has been made more particularly for the purpose of ascertaining whether or not the petition of the heirs should be rejected on the ground of disloyalty of the parties in interest. . . .

While we do not recommend that the prayers of the petitioners in this case be granted, nor, indeed, be considered with a view to releasing property taken in the manner and under the circumstances in which that under consideration was, nor until the policy of the government upon so grave a question shall be settled, yet the committee beg leave to say that this case affords a proper one for favorable attention, should Congress determine to restore property in the insurgent States.

Elizabeth Hyde Botume

"WE SEEMED TO BE LIVING OVER A VOLCANO"

Miss Botume, whom we have met twice before, gives a last account of her experiences as a teacher to the Negroes of Beaufort County. The Freedmen's Bureau's educational effort in South Carolina ended in 1870. Its funds were exhausted and Northern interest had waned. Miss Botume seems to have become discouraged in her mission.

As we were returning south in the fall of 1868, we heard disheartening stories about the freedmen. We were told in Washington they were becoming usurpers. They realized their power and began to feel they could do without white influence. It was said they had taken the entire direction of their schools, putting into office colored trustees and a colored superintendent, and they had removed several white teachers and put inefficient colored teachers in their places.

Miss Amy Bradley, who was giving her life to help the "poor whites" in Wilmington, N.C., spoke to us of the arrogant assumption of the Negroes around her as a serious evil.

In Charleston we heard of riots in different parts of the state. . . . We feared there was a growing hostility between the two races, *as races*.

We took a small steamer from Charleston for Beaufort. Here we found a decided change since we went north. Then no colored person was allowed on the upper deck, now there were no restrictions—there could be none, for a law had been passed in favor of the Negroes. They were everywhere, choosing the best staterooms and best seats at the table. Two prominent colored members of the State Legislature were on board with their families. There were also several well-known Southerners, still uncompromising rebels. It was a curious scene and full of significance. An interesting study to watch the exultant faces of the Negroes, and the scowling faces of the rebels—rebels still against manifest destiny and the new dispensation. Until now we had but little understood these portentous changes, the meaning of which we must study out for ourselves.

We were summoned to dinner. When we reached the table we found there only colored people occupying more than half the seats on each side. They were doing the honors with something of an air that said, "Receive this from me or go without." In all respects, however, they were courteous and attentive. There was no loud talking or laughing.

The stewardess came behind us and, leaning over, whispered we had better wait a little, as they were obliged to give the colored passengers the first table. The white passengers would come to the second. We thanked her, but preferred to keep our seats. A few Northerners joined us. One, who we knew had been a first-class Democrat and "down on the Negroes," was obliged to leave us and sit next to a man as black as ink. He swallowed his prejudices and took his seat, and fraternized with his neighbor to the best of his ability; besides, it was no longer a question of inclination, it was business. This was the point in which our fears were most aroused. The freedmen, no longer slaves, were fast becoming tools.

The Negro who sat not far from me was an immense fellow, seemingly an iron man, with powerful physique and indomitable will. He had made an incendiary speech in July, telling his people this was their government, and they no longer needed or had any use for white people. All the morning he had walked around scanning and apparently marking the passengers. His looks seemed to say, "If you are with us, well and good; if not, stand back," whilst the scowling faces and muttered words of the Southerners implied, "If you stand back, well and good; if you fraternize with the Negroes, be——"

The little group of Northerners noted and translated what they saw. Each one watched his neighbor. I now understood why we were so frequently asked in Charleston if we were not afraid to return to Beaufort just now. Some friends had earnestly urged us to wait until after election on Tuesday, but that was the time we wanted to be with the people in our own district. We had no fears for ourselves, but grave apprehensions for our friends. These were exciting times. We seemed to be living over a volcano.

On arriving in Beaufort we found no excitement amongst the freed people, and no apparent antagonism. All was quiet in our own district. Rumors of disaffection had reached our colored neighbors. They came to us to know what it all meant. . . .

But election day came and went without conflict or confusion. Fortunately for all concerned, the barrooms were closed, and no riotous or disorderly people were allowed on the streets. . . .

In the fall of 1869 we found grave causes for anxiety cropping out in our district. The old people were fast breaking down; the younger people had not the patience and endurance of their parents. The children ran more at large and acquired bad habits. . . .

Speculators had succeeded in getting hold of much of the land near us. From the friends of the freed people in town, who tried to shield them against sharpers and carpetbaggers, the women had learned that they too had independent rights in their ten-acre lots. . . .

Most of the field work was done by the women and girls; their lords and masters were much interrupted in agricultural pursuits by their political and religious duties. When the days of *"conwentions"* came, the men were rarely at home, but the women kept steadily at work in the fields. As we drove around, we saw them patiently cleaning up their ground, listing, chopping down the old cotton stalks and hoeing them under, gathering sedge and "trash" from the riverside, which they carried in baskets on their heads and spread over the land. And later, hoeing the crops and gathering them in. . . .

Many of these same workingwomen were in school at odd times, eager to learn, but they thought they could go through a book as they hoed a task. "Please read me quick, and let me go!" was usually their first exclamation. It took time to make them understand that learning was not given by weight or measure. As soon as they saw that school, too, required steady work, many of them dropped out.

These men and women no longer left everything to come "to catch a lesson," as in the first days of freedom. Many things conspired to check their zeal, the chief of which was the little importance placed on education throughout the country. The men were eager to hold office, and positions of trust were frequently given to those who could neither read nor write, while those who were studying were set aside. In time they decided that for all practical purposes the ignorant got along as well as "those that have book learning." . . .

Ambrose Elliott Gonzales

"THERE WAS NOTHING, SAVE FLOWERS, LEFT TO GIVE"

Ambrose Elliott Gonzales, who tells the story of an exiled family's return to Oak Lawn in 1870, was the son of a Cuban patriot, General Ambrose José Gonzales, and Harriet Rutledge Elliott, daughter of William Elliott of Beaufort. His father had served as colonel and chief of artillery on the staff of General Beauregard; after the evacuation of Charleston, Colonel Gonzales joined Johnston's army in North Carolina. His family meantime refugeed in Flat Rock, North Carolina.

Oak Lawn, on the mainland in Beaufort County, was burned by W. T. Sherman's corps in January 1865.

The Gonzales family returned to Cuba in 1869. After the death of Mrs. Gonzales, the young children were brought back to Oak Lawn, home of their maternal grandparents, and here the following story begins. The narrator is thirteen years of age at this time.

In 1891 the State, the daily paper of Columbia, S. C., was founded by Ambrose Gonzales and his brothers, Narciso Gener Gonzales and William Elliott Gonzales. Ambrose wrote a long list of stories about the Gullah Negroes and life at Oak Lawn. Among his published books were The Black Border, The Captain *and* With Aesop Along the Black Border. *He died in 1926.*

When it was all over we returned to the ruined low-country and to Reconstruction! Far worse than the poverty and privation was the constant realization in the minds of the boys of the physical and mental strain upon the grownups they loved. And the hopelessness of it all! We felt, young and old, like rats caught in a trap. We couldn't think our way out and could see no light ahead. . . .

Back at the old plantation, the boys took up the new life under changed conditions. The sturdy English brick walls of the old house still stood, but they were now green with ivy and wreathed with climbing roses. The only stick left standing on the place was the "washkitchen," a servants' house, which the pleadings of an old caretaker induced the Federal colonel to leave for the Negroes' occupancy. Before the family returned, the weather-boarding had been stripped away and stolen, but the framework and the chimneys remained, and about these a crude habitation was constructed that sheltered the family for years.

Servants, there were none. The two or three fine old men, who served their master's family with such loyalty and devotion during and after the war, were now dead, and the other house servants were far-scattered, living in homes of their own or serving in the cities those who had money to pay for service. So the boys undertook such tasks— each according to his strength—as came to hand, and as each of us was doing something for the common good, all of us were happy.

We were seldom idle, for there was always something to do—water to be brought from the "Big Spring" three hundred yards away, wood to be cut, and the vegetable and flower gardens to be worked. And the flower gardens were at once a great delight and a heavy responsibility. In the old days they had been cared for by a French gardener and his half-dozen trained Negro assistants, all of them under the constant supervision of one of our aunts; but now the task was upon the former taskmistress, an occasional hireling and such labor of love as the boys would contribute. And chivalry or affection often prompted them to forego an afternoon's fishing at "the Cypress" or a tramp in the woods, in order to relieve one of the ladies of the family, so often engaged in raking up the fallen leaves in the avenue or in the holly walks that threaded the shrubbery, now but a tangle of sweet myrtles, spice plants and other fragrant things.

Some of the dwarf box hedges and "standards" were still intact, but the cedar and wild-orange hedges, once so trim, so beautifully clipped, were now young trees, still in alignment, but rearing their tousled and uneven heads like the awkward squad of a village militia company. Climbing roses—La Marque, multiflora and seven sisters—clambered boldly to the tops of tall magnolias and flung wide their variegated banners forty or fifty feet aloft. And there were beautiful Lady Banksias —white and yellow—some on trellises, while others followed their sturdier sisters and ran riotously up the magnolias, scattering the mintage of their gold and silver blooms far up among the dark, glossy leaves.

And all about this lovely war-made *chaparral* were blooming, singly and in clumps, the delicious old-time sweet roses, whose French names the boys mastered only after a fashion, but whose fragrance they understood and reveled in. In a sequestered corner of the garden, among the "tea" and the "musk" roses, was an old bush, watched over and tended reverently, for 'twas our "great-grandmother's tea rose" and had been in the family for more than a hundred years! Blooming in Charleston ten years before the Revolution, it was first transplanted to Cheeha [a plantation on Cheeha River] and brought, fifty years later, to Oak Lawn. Though gnarled and scraggy now, the boys approached the old bush as though it were a shrine, for its delicate loose-petaled blossoms had blessed with exquisite fragrance four generations of our people. So we dug around the old rosebush and put fresh clay about its roots; but only the ladies gathered the sparse blooms, whose poignant sweetness gripped the heart of even a boy—of sensibilities.

Of all the gracious hospitality of the old times there was nothing, save flowers, left to give, but flowers we had, and flowers we gave to all in the neighborhood that cared for them, while on Memorial Day cartloads of beautifully made crosses and wreaths were sent to Charleston for the Confederate graves at Magnolia Cemetery.

There were no schools, of course, but the boys were obliged to study such antiquated textbooks as we could command, and were encouraged to dip into Plutarch's *Lives*. . . . Our grandfather's splendid library had gone up in smoke with the old house, but we had taken to the up-country, when we refugeed, fine editions of Shakespeare and other English poets, Burns, and Scott's Waverley novels, and these were now a priceless blessing, for one of the ladies would read Shakespeare aloud on winter evenings while the boys listened with rapt attention. . . .

All through this period of our lives there was the constant hope in the hearts of the grownups that out of the French spoliation claims, or out of the refund of the direct tax on confiscated lands, would come the means of giving the boys an education, but the ships of our hopes never came to port. After the two older boys had spent a few months at school in Beaufort, the former home of our maternal grandfather [William Elliott], the elder was sent to a private school in the valley of Virginia. . . .

A year passed, and upon my return, N[arciso] G[ener], too, had his turn, and went for a year to a private school in Fairfax County, Virginia, while the elder, now sixteen, went to Grahamville, a station on the Charleston and Savannah Railway, to learn telegraphy. . . .

Grahamville, in Beaufort County, was far within the black belt, and the preponderance of Negro population was tremendous. . . .

In those days, under the constant strain of a man's responsibilities, boys soon developed into men, and long before we were out of our teens, we took an active part in the work of the Democratic Clubs into which the handful of white men in the vicinity had organized themselves in the fight for the redemption of the state from the horde of blacks and the vicious whites who controlled them.

The telegraph office at Grahamville was, at that time, the only one between Yemassee and Savannah, and, serving twenty-five hundred square miles of territory, was, at election time, a gathering point for those in search of news from the outside world. In 1876, during the momentous Hampton campaign and the equally exciting contest for the Presidency between Tilden and Hayes, parties of men rode on horseback twenty-five miles or more from points in Barnwell County along the Savannah River, and from Lawtonville and Brighton far up in old Beaufort district, in quest of news, and, picketing their horses in the pineland, accepted such primitive hospitality as we were able to extend, while, by day and by night, we tapped the through wires for such news as might be gleaned.

In 1876, too, the brothers took the Grahamville Democratic Club to Beaufort, to the Hampton rally, where we sported the first two "red shirts" ever seen in that historic town.

About this time the "Combahee Riots" occurred. The Negroes in that section went on strike and, abandoning their work in the rice fields, became riotous and turbulent. The Combahee Mounted Rifles, a crack "red shirt" company organized for the protection of that district, was beleaguered at Ballouville by thousands of half-crazed Negro men and women, armed with hoes, rice hooks and axes, besides firearms of every description. For several days the situation was tense, and only the courage and coolness of Captain D. Elliott, commanding the Rifle Company, averted disaster. Captain Elliot, however, restrained his men, gradually got the situation in hand and restored quiet. . . .

Alfred B. Williams

GENERAL WADE HAMPTON CAMPAIGNS IN
THE "BLACK BELT"

*In 1876, on the one-hundredth anniversary of the signing of the
Declaration of Independence, white South Carolina Democrats nomi-
nated General Wade Hampton as candidate for governor to oppose
the incumbent Republican, Daniel H. Chamberlain. Hampton in
accepting the nomination said: "You are struggling for the highest
stake for which a people ever contended, for you are striving to bring
back to your prostrate state the inestimable blessings which can only
follow orderly and regulated liberty under free and good government...."*

*Followers of Wade Hampton wore red shirts, symbol of the cam-
paign of 'Seventy-six. During the campaign Hampton spoke at all but
one of the thirty-two counties of the state. "Their whole tour was a
vast triumphal procession," readers of the* Atlantic Monthly *for February 1877 were informed; "at every depot they were received by a tremendous concourse of citizens and escorts of cavalry. ... They were
preceded by processions of the rifle clubs, mounted and on foot, miles
in length, marching against the strains of music. ... At night there
were torchlight processions equally imposing. ... The enthusiasm, as
Confederate veterans pressed forward to wring their old general's hand,
was indescribable...."*

*On October 26, 1876, Hampton spoke in Beaufort, and for the first
time met a hostile audience. Beaufort had sent a Negro senator and
several Negro representatives to the General Assembly in Columbia,
and the county had sent a Negro to the United States Congress.*

*Alfred B. Williams, a young reporter who became a distinguished
journalist, accompanied the campaign party. Hampton did not carry
Beaufort County in the coming election in which he was chosen governor. He was re-elected in 1887, and afterward served in the United
States Senate until 1891.*

The morning of [October] 25th, 1876, a special train from Augusta,
already well filled with people and the Irish Volunteer band, picked

up the Hampton party at Allendale and bore it toward the center of the black belt. When the train reached Brunson it was necessary to stop to take on more cars. People from that section had gathered in the hope of seeing Hampton and, when they learned he would be there a short while, stopped cheering long enough to call on him for a speech. He responded briefly and departed, followed by cheers which could be heard a mile above the noise of the train for one of the most remarkable meetings of the campaign—that at Early Branch, a mite of a town, hardly more than a mere railway station.

Hampton arrived there at noon and found a lane of mounted Red Shirts 400 yards long, the men formed on both sides of the street, and a tempest of cheers began as soon as the train was in sight. This small community had constructed and decorated a stand which would have been creditable to any city, using flowers, Spanish moss and evergreens. The place was the new depot. A tall pole carried the Stars and Stripes and at the top of a pine tree growing alongside was a mammoth picture of Mr. Tilden. A strong club of colored Red Shirts was given place of honor and followed directly after the campaign party as the ranks wheeled in to form the procession. The Gardner's Corners Campaign Club, Negro, had a place on the stand and sang at intervals songs composed by F. M. Turner, each having as its theme the good time coming when the thieves and disturbers would be sent away, honest folk would conduct the government and the races would be at peace.

Prayer was offered by the Rev. Mr. Peeples. The speakers were: Hampton, Youmans, Tillman, Judge Cooke. Three or four hundred Negro men present wore no red shirts and were not with Democratic clubs and, presumably, were Republicans. At the end of his speech Judge Cooke called on all those who were convinced that it would be better for them and the state to have Hampton elected to hold up their hands. Whether really convinced or carried by the enthusiasm of the moment, all but about a dozen lifted their hands quickly and held them high; whereat there was a tremendous demonstration and something like a general love feast. A Democratic Negro, veteran or recruit, could get anything for which he chose to ask in that wonderful patriotic bit of a town that day. Judge Cooke was in extra high feather, not foreseeing the calamity the next day was to bring. . . .

Hampton could have had an escort of from 500 to 1,000 armed men, but he preferred to go with nobody but the speakers and reporters. Possibly the spice of danger appealed to his spirit of adventure. Per-

haps he thought best to avoid the possibility of serious collision between his followers and the intensely antagonistic Beaufort population. He went unguarded and unattended, except by his regular party,
and stepped directly from a warm atmosphere of love and adulation to
chilling surroundings of hostility. When he arrived at Beaufort at 10
o'clock at night nobody met him but a few friendly, faithful white
men, silent, dubious of what the next day would bring. A stand had
been built at the clubhouse and the white women had decorated it
handsomely and tastefully, but the night of the 25th, Negro roughs
showered stand and decorations with brickbats and seemed to be preparing to destroy both when the local police—nearly, if not quite, all
Negroes—were induced by the earnest remonstrances of leading white
citizens to interfere.

There was no attempt at a procession before the meeting, which
consisted of 400 to 500 Negroes and perhaps 100 white men, with a
number of ladies on the veranda of the clubhouse. The Rev. Mr. Johns
offered prayer, and Hampton began his first speech before an un-
friendly audience. What kind of devil, or angel, or giant, the Beaufort
Negroes expected to see is beyond white imagination. As the general
arose one old fellow in the crowd shouted, in tones of amazement and
relief, "Why, he ain' nuttin' buttah man, attaah all!"

It is something in Negro psychology beyond Caucasian comprehension, perhaps, or maybe it was the power of personality. Whatever
the cause, the crowd picked and sent, as appeared from later develop-
ments, to disturb and interrupt and start a riot, listened to Hampton
silently and as attentively as it was allowed to do. The intendant of the
town and the police, on pretence of keeping the road clear, did all they
could to prevent the speaker from being heard and to make trouble by
pushing back everybody, of either color, who tried to approach the
stand. Hampton spoke along steadily, taking no heed of the noisy
efforts of the officials. He challenged Lieutenant Governor Gleaves,
Negro, who was circulating busily about the town almost within ear-
shot, to come on the stand and speak and defend his party and chief,
if he could. He warned the Republicans that even if they could elect
Chamberlain he never could be governor because there was evidence
to convict him of felony and flatly accused the governor of cowardice
in failing to come out and face the people. Even this was heard without
show of resentment. . . .

When Hampton concluded his speech, the meeting took a new turn.

LeRoy F. Youmans of Columbia spoke next. He, too, was heard in silence until he began attacks on the Republican government and officials. Then shrieks and howls arose from front and rear and center and both flanks, from men, women and boys. The crowd was permitted to approach and from it came a tangle and mixture of epithet and insulting and derisive cries. Mr. Youmans shouted and pleaded until perspiration streamed down his face, but he could not make three consecutive words heard, despite his orator's voice. He yielded at last and Judge Cooke tried it. The storm became wider and louder and more furious, and epithet began to give way to definite threat. The judge had become accustomed through nearly two months to enthusiastic applause from his opening to his closing sentence. This steady, unrelenting bombardment of evil names and denunciation, taunt and fierce declaration of purpose to destroy him forthwith, was too much for him. He lost his temper, became so hoarse with shouting defiance that he could not hear himself and at the end of his strength had the mortification of retiring amid a roar of African laughter, caused by some gesture of disgust that appealed to the risibles of his volatile foes.

Then came another marvel. Hampton advanced again, and again there was silence. He spoke quietly and without show of resentment, like a man rebuking a crowd of disorderly children. He said those before him might be interested to know that a large party of naval officers from the fleet at Port Royal was in the clubhouse, had seen all that had happened and would be able to tell their friends at the North what the conduct of the Negroes and Republicans and the officials had been.

This concluded the one failure of the campaign, if it really was a failure in the long run. Three or four United States deputy marshals were in the crowd and did nothing toward suppressing disorder. . . .

After the Beaufort meeting we campaigners dined at the hotel and emerged baggage in hand, bound for the depot, a mile or so away, at the other end of a beautiful stretch of shell road—perhaps the one beautiful stretch of road in South Carolina at the time. There were 15 or 20 of us, and the Negro hackmen clustered about the entrance looking for a harvest. Judge Cooke addressed us briefly. Now was the time, he said, for us to be true to our declared principles and refuse to hire any hack unless driven by a Democrat. So off we trudged. Greedy as they were for fares, no Negro hackman in Beaufort dared declare himself a Democrat that day.

About halfway to the depot we met a Negro driving two miles to a wagon loaded with lumber. The judge was in the middle of the road and took his stand there. He proclaimed that he had been run over by these people all day and was tired of it and did not intend to submit further. Therefore, he ordered the driver to drive around him. The wrathful judge, tall and portly, holding the middle of the road and the perplexed and enraged darky slowly guiding his mules in a semi-circle, made one of the most ludicrous scenes of the campaign.

Probably General Hampton was being driven to the depot by friends. I cannot recall that he was along with us. If he had been he would have enjoyed it intensely. Those of us in the party laughed until the judge became infected, relaxed and laughed with us; and so we ended a disastrous day hilariously. And Walterboro, next day, and Charleston, on the 30th, more than compensated for the troubles at Beaufort.

What a contrast it was! Leaving Beaufort in the afternoon unattended, as we arrived, with hardly a cheer heard, surrounded by black people with black looks, made to feel hatred every minute and at every step, we reached Green Pond amid a swirl of light and cheering and welcome, red-shirted horsemen of both colors waving their hats joyously, friendly hands reaching out from every side, vehicles waiting to take us over the 14 miles of road—very bumpy road it was then—to Walterboro.

PART XIV

The Big Storm of 1893

On August 27, 1893, a great hurricane swept the coast of South Carolina. A tremendous wave submerged the sea islands, spreading along the coast from the Savannah River to the North Edisto inlet. When the "sea invaded the land" it swept all before it and, although esimated at 1,000, the number of fatalities was never known. Property damage was estimated at $10,000,000.

Outside help came from all quarters of the state and nation. The President of the United States dispatched a cutter equipped with officers and men well supplied with medicines, disinfectants, and turnip seed. Clara Barton of the National Red Cross came down to offer assistance.

The Negroes of St. Helena Island remember the "big storm" in a song which they sing each year.

Rachel Crane Mather

"FEARFUL NIGHT OF TERRORS"

Mrs. Rachel Crane Mather of Boston established in 1868 a school for Negro girls near Beaufort. Her pupils were witness to the storm of August 27, 1893, and from their accounts Mrs. Mather assembled the following story of the "Big Storm."

On that sad Sabbath, never to be forgotten, when a thousand men, women and children looked out on sea and shore for the last time, the pitying heavens put on a pall of sackcloth and early in the morning brooded in silence over the doomed islands. Ere noon the wind wailed piteously and the bay moaned ominously as if aware of the death and destruction they were bringing in, as if conscious of the pain and woe they were about to inflict on man and beast. The wind rose higher and shrieked hoarsely, driven on with relentless fury, till it attained the fearful velocity of one hundred and twenty miles an hour; and thus the hurricane raged without a lull for nearly fourteen hours—nothing movable could stand before its sweeping power.

Strong arms had secured everything afloat firmly as possible, boats and steamers were made fast as chains and cables could hold them, but the fury of the storm ruthlessly snapped them asunder and beat wildly against the tottering wharves, till vessel and wharf went down in a common wreckage. Boats dashed madly against the shore and were broken in pieces, or washed far in upon the land. Wind and wave clasped hands and quickly reduced to ruins the pretty city of Beaufort, prostrated its majestic trees and demolished nearly every warehouse and wharf. Stores and offices were inundated and borne swiftly over the frantic waves down the angry sea, where they quickly went to pieces exposed to the fury of the cyclone. Their contents were found washed ashore miles distant. The iron safes remained a black spot standing in the water. Immense guano factories were blown down, and the yawning sea swallowed their phosphate dredges with the heroic crews on board vainly struggling to save them. Men and boys driving their animals from the shore to higher ground were overtaken by the furious waves, swiftly borne back by the receding plunge, and both man and beast were drowned. Whole villages with their panic-struck inhabitants were swept into the raging sea. A score of brave men buffeted the waves and reached the substantial Government wharf on Paris Island where a noble army surgeon had stationed himself to rescue and save, but a mad wave, pursuing, suddenly overleaped the wharf and engulfed them all, including good Surgeon Hazel in his vain efforts to save them.

Heavy crops of rice and cotton ready for harvest were utterly destroyed by the encroaching, all-devouring sea. When the waters retreated, many a fertile field had become a sandy desert on the lower land, while on the higher the corn was imbedded in the earth. Over a thousand men, women and children perished, over twenty thousand it is estimated escaped with their lives only, and seventy thousand, it is said, on the islands and low shores of the mainland, lost their crops. These are destitute of food and many of them have no shelter. And the distress is wide spread, extending over eighty populous islands and the mainland from Georgetown to Savannah. The vast extent of this devastated district is a broad network of islands and tortuous peninsulas with sinuous creeks, and many of them very inaccessible. . . .

As night drew on and darkness obscured their vision of the appalling scenes, the horror of the poor islanders increased. The encroaching tidal wave, driven in by the fierce hurricane, continued more and more to submerge the islands. Men, women and children, knowing that the sea surrounded them on all sides, groped vainly for higher ground, and many perished in the attempt. Others climbed to the top of their houses, but this was sure death, as their roofs were soon broken up by the angry waves and carried out to sea.

Wiser men and women seized their little ones and hastened to the woods fast as possible, through the deep water; those who could climb the trees were comparatively safe, but the raging waves tore many little ones from their mothers' grasp and carried them beyond their reach. Children climbing the trees fell in the presence of their parents and were drowned. Some, perched among the boughs, fell with the falling trees and perished in the billowy sea below. Fathers and mothers stood all night on stumps on the highest ground they could find, with their little ones on their shoulders, fearing to step in any direction lest the flood should overwhelm their precious charge.

Happy they who were washed out to sea in their sleep and knew nothing of the terrors of that awful night; still happier they who resigning themselves to the raging billows, could sing as they went down into the sea,

> "Jesus, lover of my soul,
>   Let me to Thy bosom fly,
> While the nearer waters roll,
>   While the tempest still is high."

A young woman from Eustis plantation on Ladies [Lady's] Island, where over fifty were drowned on that fearful night, came to me leading a little girl. "Dis chile I done save from perishing in de storm. I seizes her Missis and rush out one door ob de house while Ma snatches up de two little ones an' runs for tother door, but Missis we neber meets again."

A man in Seabrook took his sick wife in his arms and groped his way among fallen trees to a neighbor's house, leaving his little children asleep in the loft of the cabin. He was starting back, as the tidal waves came up and he had to abandon the task. When with morning light the tide had receded, he went home and found his cabin washed up on higher ground, and his children still sleeping in their little loft.

One woman took her infant and climbed up into a tree, holding onto the baby's garment with her teeth. In the morning she was found dead, still holding onto the baby's dress.

Another, in her fright and haste, gathered a little bundle of clothes and, taking up her baby, fled for high land. When she became exhausted, to lighten her burden she threw away the bundle, as she thought, but to her horror found she had thrown away her little one! As a consequence the mother became insane.

On Port Royal Island, a little cabin and two lives were saved almost by a miracle. A strong vine had grown near the cabin and wound itself firmly into the framework of the house and roof. The high wind only twisted the cabin on the blocks for the vine held it fast, and so the house and the inmates were saved....

Maggie Waring's Story of the Storm

In the morning I went to a friend's house, where I spent the day. When I got home in the evening, I found my people bracing doors and windows, and we could not think of cooking any supper that night, as it was all we could do to keep out the storm. After a while, we found it was no use: we could not keep the doors and windows shut, and my mother had lain down with a feeling of despair, not being very well. My brother called out, "The tide is rising. Get up, mother, or you will be drowned. The house is going to fall, I fear. We must all get out."

So we all started for the door, and, sure enough, the tide met us, roaring and filling the house instantly. My mother could only grab a quilt to put around my little sister Blossom, and call to us to follow. We plunged into the water, for we looked for the house to fall, and if we stayed inside those who might escape being drowned would certainly be crushed by the timbers. After we left the house it floated off, and we had to wade about a task and a half up to our waists in water. We went to a neighbor's house, but it was so crowded with people we could hardly get in, and finally the roof came off, and we had to get out at the windows. We sat down under the housetop, which had floated onto the ground, but after the tide reached us there we went to another neighbor's.

About the middle of the night my brother went to let our dogs loose, but the tide was too high and he could not get there. The next morning we found them dead and the crops gone.

In the morning when we went to see if we could find the house and get some dry clothes, there was no house. It had floated off, with all that was in it. So we had to make a fire on the marsh sedge and dry the clothes we had on. . . .

Clara Chaplain's Story

On the day of August 27th I was at Mrs. Von Harten's on Bay Street, Beaufort. The storm being so severe I could not go, and the lady kindly invited me to pass the night there. On awakening in the night, I was terribly frightened to find the room full of water, up even with my bed. The house shook violently, and there was great commotion all around. Then Mr. Von Harten took his wife on his back and his brother took me in the same way, and they rushed out of the house, that seemed tumbling into the bay, until they crossed three streets and reached the house of Colonel White, in the highest part of the city, where we found many of our neighbors had already gathered, and there we all had to go upstairs and remain till morning. An old man and his wife, while attempting to go there, fell down in the street exhausted and were drowned. In the morning we found the outbuilding and kitchen on Bay street, where we fled from, all gone, swept away by the tide, and the houses and wharves all along Bay Street in ruins, and so many trees blown down we found it very difficult to go about at all. Boxes of provisions and barrels and bales of dry goods were floating along the shores. We saw also dead horses, cows, pigs and poultry drowned through the town.

Margaret Weary's Experiences on St. Helena

I was so busy that evening cooking supper I never minded the wind and rain, nor the great roaring of the waves, till I looked out through the shutter and saw the sea all around the house. Then we were all frightened, as we saw the waves rushing up to the door. Ma seized my little sister Grace, wrapped her in a blanket and ran to a neighbor's house on the hill. Brother and I jumped out into the water and ran as fast as we could, but I fell down into the water. My brother picked me up, and we pressed on through the waves till we reached the house where Ma was. The water had come up all around that house too, and so we had to run to another, up on higher land, and there stayed all night.

Next morning we went home, but there was no house there, nor anything left. All had been washed away into the marsh, and the sedge and seaweed were piled up all around higher than my head. We saw dead cats and dogs, dead horses and hogs all along the shore, and some dead men and women and children. We saw one dead woman holding onto a timber of her house by her teeth. Pretty soon we built up a fire on a heap of sedge and we dried ourselves by the fire.

Charlotte Edwards' Experience on Parris Island

That evening the tide came up high on Parris Island. It covered the piazza and was three feet deep in the house. About midnight the house shook violently till it was blown off the blocks, and the boards fell off. Many people gathered near us, coming through water up to their waists. The stairs fell on a neighbor's neck and killed her. In the morning we could find no pigs nor poultry. At our back door lay good Dr. [W. Gowan] Hazel who perished trying to save two colored boys. Nineteen men lay in one boat, all drowned. Nearly half the people on Parris Island perished that awful night, among whom were nearly all my relatives.

Arthur Tolliday's Story

Six o'clock came and with it worse weather. I looked up and down the road but not a living thing could be seen. The wind increased in violence. Three tall pines fell near my door. Another tremendous crash. The rain was beating through every crevice, pouring down the chimney and running over the floor. Another violent gust of wind gave the old house a shake-up that made me quake with fear. I prayed the Lord that I might not perish there alone, but among friends. Then extinguishing my lamp and locking the door, I ran as best I could, over fallen trees, till I reached my neighbors' house. As I drew near, I heard them singing to the top of their voices,

> "Hide me, O my Savior, hide,
> Till the storm of life be past."

I entered the cabin breathless and dripping. I told them I could remain alone no longer—was compelled to seek companionship in this hour of peril. It was ten o'clock; the storm was raging fearfully and roared like a heavy mail train, while every few seconds a terrific crash was heard above the hurricane as a giant tree was laid low. . . . Never, never, have I passed such a fearful night of terrors. By and by . . . day had come at last. How can I describe the scenes outside? The road between my place and the ferry, which yesterday was a perfect one, was now passable only by good jumpers. Huge trees lay all along across the road, and marsh sedge covered it in drifts six feet deep. Trunks, household furniture and farmers' utensils were strewn everywhere; numerous carcasses of hogs, dogs, cows and poultry lay scattered over the land.

On Stuart's Point was the greatest loss, almost every house being demolished. I saw the body of a farmer's daughter, whose neck was broken by falling timber. She looked peaceful as if asleep.

Everywhere around reigned desolation and destruction, where two days before the outlook was so bright and promising—fields smiling with a bountiful harvest of corn, cotton, rice, peas and sweet potatoes. Where was it all gone now? Where those glorious green patches of sugar cane? All gone for a twelve months, swallowed by the all-devouring sea, and no money in the hand of the poor husbandman. . . .

Joel Chandler Harris

"THE SEA ISLANDS WERE DUMB"

Shortly after news of the devastating hurricane of August 27 reached the outside world, Joel Chandler Harris, beloved author of the Uncle

Remus stories, was sent to Port Royal by Scribner's Magazine. He came from Savannah by steam launch and tugboat and spent several weeks in Beaufort and among the islands questioning those who had experienced the disaster.

The following is from his articles in Scribner's, which appeared under the title "The Sea Island Hurricanes" in the issues for February and March 1894.

At the ancient town of Beaufort, one is nearer to the group of islands devastated by the storm than at any other point. The autumn days pass pleasantly at this old place. The midday sun throws the shadows far northward, but there is no sign of winter. The summer foliage is still fresh and green, and June seems to have taken the place of November. But the lonely and far-reaching marshes, with their rank and waving sedge, yellow as if waiting for the sickle, give a sombre touch to the scene that does not belong to spring, nor yet to summer. And the long gray moss, streaming from the trees like ghostly signals long hung out for succor unavailing, is another element that subdues the mind and imparts a sense of solemnity. The birds may sing never so gaily, and the sun shine never so brightly, but they are all overshadowed by the brown marshes, and by the gray beards of these immemorial oaks.

All day long, the Negroes go by in their queer little two-wheeled carts, each drawn by a diminutive steer, or a more diminutive donkey. All day long the Negro pedestrians tramp back and forth. All day long the Negro boatmen shoot out from, or disappear in, the tall marsh grass. There is not much noise of vehicles; the sand prevents that. There is not much noise from the passers-by or from the boats that flit in and out the marsh grass. There is no loud laughter in the streets; there are no melodious songs wafted back from the water.

The streets swarm with Negroes, on the sidewalks, in the middle way, and on the corners. At the headquarters of the Red Cross Society, which has in hand the work of relief, they are huddled together until they block the way. And yet there is no loud talking, no loud laughter, no singing. The mind resents this as unnatural. Where there are Negroes there ought to be noise, surely there ought to be laughter and song. What is the trouble? You look into those black faces and see it is not sullenness. You note these quick smiles and discover that it is not depression. If the puzzle brings a frown to your face, as it did to mine, an old Auntie will look at you steadily until she catches your eye, and then, dropping a courtesy, will exclaim:

"You look worry, suh!" And then when you turn to her for an explanation, "I bin worry myse'f, suh—many time."

Whereupon you will be no longer puzzled, for here is a type of Negro different from that of the upland regions—a type that knows how to be good-humored without being boisterous, and that has the rare gift of patience. Coming or going, men, women and children will pause to salute you, and their courtesy is neither familiar nor affected. Their pensiveness fits in with the sombre marshes and the gray moss that swings solemnly from the trees.

"It is a great pity," says the oldest inhabitant, waving his shining cane in the air, "that you could not have come here before the storm struck this grove. You see how the trees are stripped and twisted."

At last your companion has hit upon the matter that is uppermost in your mind, and so, gently—very gently and cautiously, for fear of a relapse—you lead the genial old gentleman to forget about the antiquity of the old fort and the practical utility of Port Royal harbor, and tell you some of the experiences of the August tornado; to give you some idea of the horror and confusion of that vast elemental disturbance; and to present to your mind a clear outline of results.

But this seems to be out of the question. The memory of the oldest inhabitant is more to be depended on in the recital of events that have become matters of tradition. He gives you details that bear no definite relation to the large results. The storm blasted hundreds of landmarks that were a part of his daily associations. Curious incidents occur to his mind. A lad clinging to an overturned dredge for thirty-six hours, finally gave up all hope and sank back into the water. The tide brought him twenty miles to Beaufort and landed him in a pile of driftwood near his mother's door, where he was found and, strange to say, restored to life. Immense lighters employed in the phosphate business were lifted out of the water and driven far on shore. The barometer on the tug *Weymouth* dropped to 27.60 and stood there quivering like the hammer of an alarm clock. Yes! and a great many Negroes were drowned—hundreds of them, poor things!

The impression left seems to be as vague and as shapeless as the tempest was. . . . There are those who know what was and who know what is; but between what was and what is lies the awful cataclysm of the storm. The curtains of the cavernous clouds enveloped it; the raging tempest drowned it; the thundering tide covered it. The leaf from the tree, the ship from the sea and man that was set to rule over all, became companion atoms, and all were caught by the storm and hurled into chaos. And when the morning dawned, and the tide fell, and the sun shone serenely over the scene of wreck and devastation, there was none left to tell the definite story of the hurricane on the Sea Islands. There is none left to tell it today.

The oldest inhabitant is able to remember some very severe storms, but not such another year of storms. He is able to measure the intervals that have elapsed between these disturbances, and from this measurement he has constructed the comfortable theory that after every severe storm there must be a peaceful interlude of ten or fifteen years. But today as he stands in the bright sunshine, the solemn mystery of the marshes stretching away before him as far as the eye can reach, he shakes his head sadly and digs his cane feebly into the sand. His theory has been blown northeastward into the sea, and it is no wonder he sighs as he walks by your side and points to signs of the storm's devastation that might otherwise escape the eye of a stranger. A house was here or a cabin. Near by a shoal of dead bodies had been seen drifting along or were washed ashore. Here was where a magnificent dock or warehouse stood, but there is nothing now to mark its site except a few scattered piles which, at low tide, are important only as showing the architectural ability of the teredo, the insect that eats them away. . . .

All around, and for miles and miles, farther than the eye can reach, as far as a shore bird can fly, the results of the storm lie scattered. Here a house has staggered upon its end, there a boat has been flung into the arms of a live oak, and yonder a phosphate dredge, weighing hundreds of tons, has been lifted from the water and turned completely over; here a magnificent grove of live oaks has been uprooted; there a broad-beamed lighter has been lifted across the marshes; and yonder hundreds of tons of marsh sedge have been spread over arable land.

The old man casts his eyes seaward across the long stretch of marshes that lead to the inland shore of St. Helena. A small column of smoke stands out against the sky and seems to be fixed there. "The poor things!" he sighs. "They are trying to burn the marsh sedge off their potato patches."

Then he grows reminiscent. He has heard his father tell of the great storm of 1804, which began on the morning of the eighth of September and raged until ten o'clock at night. . . . In 1830 a storm curved in from the sea. . . . On September 10, 1854, a storm of great violence passed over Savannah and the Sea Islands, devastating the whole coast region. . . . In 1873 a violent storm passed between Cape Hatteras and the Bermudas. . . . In 1881 a storm passed over the Sea Island region. . . .

On these dates, the oldest inhabitant had formulated his storm-period theory. Every tenth year he expected a storm. If it failed then it was sure to come on the twentieth year. . . .

The August hurricane was not unexpected. In fact it had been heralded, and for at least three days before it made its appearance, warnings had been given. The Weather Bureau . . . had found it in West Indian waters, and so the announcement went forth that a storm was forming in the neighborhood of St. Thomas. Next day the bulletins stated that the disturbance near St. Thomas had moved slowly westward. The day after came the announcement that the West Indian storm, after moving to the west and then to the south, had turned and was heading directly for the South Atlantic coast. . . . Savannah was more directly in the path of the storm, and the Sea Islands, that lie between that city and Charleston, were exposed to the full fury of the tempest. And the winds fell upon them as if trying to tear the earth asunder, and the rains beat upon them as if to wash them away, and the tide rose and swept over them twelve feet above high-water mark. Pitiable as the story is, it may be condensed into a few words: near three thousand people drowned, between twenty and thirty thousand human beings without means of subsistence, their homes destroyed, their little crops ruined, and their boats blown away. . . .

No just and reasonable estimate of the loss of life on these islands has been made. The adjacent coast was prompt to tell of its losses over the long tongue of the telegraph. Its dead were known and identified. Its searching parties found them out. Its tugs and launches brought them ashore.

But the Sea Islands were dumb, and they are dumb to this day. When the tide was friendly, it carried their dead ashore, or lodged them in the rank marsh sedge, but when the tide was careless it drifted the bodies seaward. In one little corner of St. Helena, the coroner inspected eighty bodies that had been thrown ashore. Some were known, but a great many were not identified and never will be. All about the channels and through the boat ways in the waving marsh grass, the bodies of the unknown drifted, and some floated miles away. Some had their clothes torn from them, mute witnesses of the fury of the tornado. All this is to be heard away from the islands. The islands themselves have not spoken, and they will not speak. Gentle, patient, smiling and good-humored, the Negroes have no complaint to make. They discuss the storm among themselves, but not in a way to impart much information to a white listener. They speak in monosyllables. . . .

"Were many lives lost around here?" an old man was asked. He stood with his hands folded in front of him and his eyes seeking the ground. . . . He stood stock-still, his bare feet placed close together.

"He gone deaf, suh," said a woman standing near.

She touched him gently on the arm, and instantly he was alert. The question was repeated: "Were many lives lost around here?"

"Oh, yes, suh; 'bunnunce!" His voice sounded as if it came from far away.

"How many?"

"One, two, t'ree—" he held up the fingers of one thin hand— "mebby se'm. Mebby l'em. Enty?" He turned to the woman to confirm his figures, but she merely smiled. "We no count dem," he went on, shaking his head and shutting his eyes. "Dee gone!"

Then the old man relapsed into his former attitude. His eyes sought the ground, his hands clasped in front of him, his bare feet close together.

The woman who had spoken for him formed part of a little group standing near by. She was rubbing the head of a four-year-old pickaninny.

"How many children have you?" she was asked.

"T'ree, suh. Two boy; one lil' gal."

"Were any of them drowned?"

"How dee gwan drown, suh?" she answered, laughing. "I up'd de tree," she said, after a pause, with a gesture that explained how she saved them. "Dee choke—dee strankle—I up'd de tree!" The woman turned and pointed to another woman who was standing apart by the water's edge, looking out over the lonely marshes. "She los' dem chillun, suh. She have trouble. . . ."

Station Creek divides St. Phillips' Island from St. Helena. On this creek, on the St. Helena side, our exploring party found a fine old two-story house. It had evidently been the home of one of the old-time planters, who had chosen to build here, miles away from all the lines

of communication. . . . As our little launch steamed toward the landing the Negroes swarmed out of the house—there must have been
fifty of them, big and little—and stood on the shore silent and watchful. . . .

There was not much to see there—not much to learn. All their
cabins had been destroyed, their crops ruined, and they were far from
Beaufort, the centre from which relief was distributed. They had taken
refuge in the big house, which had weathered the storm. There was no
other shelter for them. . . .

Though the Negroes here were far from the relief fund, they had
been visited by a Red Cross Committee, and their immediate wants
supplied. . . .

The Negroes at this place had a mystery to deal with, and they were
very much perplexed by it. The mystery was in the shape of a little old
man, who had come into the settlement in the very middle and height
of the storm. The Negroes were not afraid of the little old man, but it
was plain they regarded him with something more than a shade of
superstition. One of the Negro men, trying to reach the big house, was
tossed by the rising tide against a live oak, into which he clambered
with all possible haste. He sat there all night, and at dawn found at his
side the little old man. . . . He was an entire stranger. The Negro asked
him who he was and where he came from, but all the reply he could
get was "John Omcum." None of the Negroes had ever seen him before, and none had ever heard of him. Where did he come from? Was
he blown from Hilton Head Island across the long sweep of Port
Royal Sound, or did he drift from one of the little islands in the Chech-
essee River?

The little old man was pointed out to me. He stood apart, for he
was too much of a mystery to invite familiarity on the part of the
other Negroes. He smiled shrewdly, blinked his little eyes, and seemed
to feel some sort of pride in his peculiar position. He was old, and
wrinkled, and dried up, and yet wonderfully alert. . . .

We sailed away from the old place, the screw of the little launch
making a mighty stir and splutter in the quiet waters of Station Creek.
The Negroes stood watching us. One of them waved a handkerchief
listlessly, and the little steamer responded with its whistle, sending
a ringing farewell over the water. Apart from the rest stood John
Omcum, as still as a statue, with one hand raised and his head craned

forward a little. He stood thus, until a turn in the creek hid him from view. . . .

What is it about these islands that attracts the Negroes and holds them here? What subtle influence brings them back again when they venture to go away? There is a saying that those who once drink water on one of these islands will never rest contented until they return. But this fancy, or superstition, has its origin with the white race, and is common to all sections and communities.

I overheard a conversation between two Negro women and a Negro preacher on the little steamer that plies occasionally between Savannah and the islands. One of the women had some property in Beaufort and was going there to look after it. The other woman lived on St. Helena. The preacher lived in Savannah, and was going to the islands to see if he could be of any service.

The three were talking about the storm. The preacher said he couldn't understand why any human being would want to live on the islands, exposed to the "relements" (as he put it), and cut off from the world.

"You smell de ma'sh when you'n young—you mus' smell 'im when you ol'—enty?" remarked the woman who was going back to Hilton Head.

"T'ank God!" exclaimed the Hilton Head woman. "I been deer, I stay deer, I gwan die deer!"

She had been in the worst of the storm, and had been rescued more dead than alive. Afterward she had gone to visit some of her old master's family in Savannah, and now she was returning, happy to get home again, although there was no home there—"nuttin' 'tall but chimley stack," as she said. She was leaving food and shelter behind her and going back to the devastated island where squalor and destitution had taken up their abode. . . .

And, somehow, as I draw near the limit that has been set for this record, one frail and shrunken figure seems to typify it all. The loneliness and the helplessness seem concentrated in the pathetic figure of John Omcum—poor old John Omcum, who was blown out of the very body of the storm! Standing on that desolate shore, his thin hand lifted, his ragged coat waving in the wind, he seems to be the essence of everything that is to be seen and heard and known in this remote region.

Evelyn L. Beardslee

"DEEPEST SYMPATHY"

*Dr. W. Gowan Hazel, whose plantation on St. Helena had been
sold to Negroes by the United States Government during the war and
never recovered by him, started life anew with a small stock of drugs
on credit, as a doctor to the island people.*

*When the hurricane swept down, Dr. Hazel was at the Port Royal
Navy Yard. He was drowned while trying to save two young colored
boys. "When found next day," said his friend J. Mikell Jenkins, "he
was lying beside his two little friends. In death, as in life, he was ever
at their call."*

*Writing from the Naval Station at Port Royal, Mrs. Evelyn L.
Beardslee, wife of the Station commander, offers her sympathy to Dr.
Hazel's sister.*

> Naval Station
> Port Royal, S.C.

My dear Mrs. Rice,

All the Station and indeed the whole island are in the deepest sympathy with you in the sad, sad loss of your dear brother. As for myself I
am in deep affliction, for I have lost my good friend whom I loved and
admired for his gentle kindness to everybody and everything. There
are many Negroes drowned and many have lost their houses.

The Station is almost a wreck—both launches are at the bottom of
the river and every boat but one small bateau destroyed, but these
things are all lost in our grief over our good friend. God bless you and
help you to bear it! I will come to see you as soon as I can get to Beaufort and tell you all I can learn in regard to the accident. His house is
entirely demolished and all his belongings washed away. Eleven members of Baches Green's family perished with him. . . .

> Sincerely yours,
> EVELYN L. BEARDSLEE

August 28, 1893

PART XV

Twentieth-Century Beaufort and the Sea Islands

"It is always Sunday on sea islands."

—DuBose Heyward

More than four hundred years have passed since the Spanish discovered the Sea Islands. Greatest have been the changes in the last sixty, but they leave the immemorial charm quite unimpaired.

Some of these changes are noted in the concluding pages of our book. Here are a few others, to illustrate the spirit of the new day.

"Come for a visit—and you'll want to come back for life," invites the Beaufort Chamber of Commerce. A spectacular Water Festival is held there each year, over which reigns a Queen of the Sea Islands.

Hunting Island is now a state park, a "dreamer's paradise," as a recent visitor called it, with its magnificent beach and its wild-life sanctuary.

The James F. Byrnes Bridge, linking Hilton Head Island with the mainland, was opened in May 1956. All signals are flying to attract vacationers and sportsmen.

On the banks of the Okatie River near Bluffton, the National Foundation for Infantile Paralysis own and operate a monkey farm. It is a "March of Dimes" project, and the work done is making a valuable contribution to scientific research.

On Lady's Island and St. Helena are great private hunting preserves, small farms and many new houses.

Each year fresh thousands of sleek yachts and boats of every description pass through the islands along the intracoastal waterways.

The resorters love them and decide to stay on or to return next year, the more attracted because the islands, for all their offshore sport, never assume the usual resort aspect but remain history-haunted in their serene beauty, with endless expanses of sea and sky.

> "I, a latecomer, hear the waves break still,
> High tide, by the sea oats, on this quiet shore,
> And hold an arrowhead picked off the land."[1]

---

[1] From "Fort Frémont, 1562; 1958," by Edith Bannister Dowling, in Charleston *News and Courier*, February 8, 1959.

THE MARINE CORPS RECRUIT DEPOT ON
PARRIS ISLAND

The man who gave his name to the island which is known the world over for the men trained there, was [Colonel] Alexander Parris.

The Lords Proprietors of South Carolina, on August 12, 1698, created Major Robert Daniell, a landgrave of Carolina. This title carried with it the right to grants of land to the extent of 48,000 acres. Among the lands selected by Landgrave Daniell was the island now known as Parris. On April 17, 1701, he conveyed the island to Edward Archer, of Barbados, mariner, in consideration of £100, current money of the province.[2]

On July 1, 1715, Edward Archer transferred it to Alexander Parris, a prominent colonist and for many years Public Treasurer. After his death in 1736, the island came to be called by his name.[2]

In the intervening years until it was acquired by the United States Government, the island was the site of plantation houses; the money crop was sea-island cotton.

Forty-one thousand recruits trained on Parris Island during World War I. During World War II, between 1941 and 1945, the number trained reached 204,509. The value of the island is estimated at $29,668,763.72; quite an increase in value since it was purchased by Edward Archer in 1701.

Approximately two thirds of all our Marines are sent through the recruit training on Parris Island. The only other "boot" camp is located at San Diego, California, where men west of the Mississippi River are trained.

The Woman Marine Recruit Training Battalion, the Marine Corps' only organization for training women recruits, is on Parris Island.

"When a recruit leaves Parris Island, he wears a new uniform that has been individually tailored to fit him. Every sleeve, including shirt sleeves, and every trouser leg has been measured to his exact length. He has successfully completed one of the most important phases of his Marine training. He talks like a sailor, walks like a soldier, but boasts that he is a Marine."

[2] Quoted from *Parris Island*, by A. S. Salley. Bulletins of the Historical Commission of South Carolina, No. 5, Columbia, 1919, pp. 8, 9.

The land comprising the Marine Corps Recruit Depot at Parris Island was acquired by the United States Government between 1878 and 1941. . . .

The first Marine Corps post was established on Parris Island on June 26, 1891, when a small detachment, with First Sergeant Richard Donavan, USMC, in charge, was posted for duty in connection with the Naval Station. It was highly commended for its service in preserving life and property during the hurricane and tidal wave which swept over the island in 1893, and again commended for like action during the several storms which rendered havoc on the island in 1898.

In 1909, a school for Marine officers was established on the island, and in 1911 a small recruit depot was started. It, however, was transferred during the latter part of 1911 to Norfolk, Virginia, and the building used by the Marines was turned over to the Navy for use in connection with the Naval Disciplinary Barracks.

By General Order 122, August 28, 1911, the designation "U.S. Naval Station, Port Royal" was changed to "U.S. Naval Disciplinary Barracks, Port Royal, S.C." . . .

By order dated October 28, 1915, the naval station, Port Royal, South Carolina, was transferred to the United States Marine Corps to be used as a recruiting depot or for such purposes as the Commandant of the Marine Corps might, with the approval of the Navy Department, direct. On November 1, 1915, the Recruit Depot, then located at Norfolk, Virginia, was moved back to Parris Island. From that date on, the island has flourished under Marine Corps activities and has become famous as a training place for Marines.

In 1917, the entire island was taken over by the government and utilized to train Marines for World War I.

From the time the first Marine Corps Post was established on the island in 1891, until 1929 when the Horse Island bridge was built, practically all transportation on the island was carried on by a "kicker" which operated between the docks near the present Port Lyceum and Port Royal.

In addition to the regular supply and liberty boats which used to run between the island and Port Royal, two or three trips would be made for the purpose of obtaining household supplies at Port Royal and Beaufort.

Marines going on liberty to Savannah could make the trip by boat

from Beaufort. There was a regular passenger service maintained between these two important seacoast cities at one time.

The water transporation era went out in 1929, however, and the
Horse Island bridge and causeway were completed, connecting the
island with the mainland.

The bridge across Battery Creek, near the present Main Gate, was
not built until the late 1930s, and until that time the road to Beaufort
was the roundabout route along the Burton road.

In the late 1930s, the state highway system was extended from Beaufort direct to Jerico Point, and the bridge built across Battery Creek.
This brought both Beaufort and Port Royal closer to Parris Island, and
made transportation onto the island during the period of increased
activity in World War II a great deal simpler.

In 1941, the eastern, or outgoing side of the Horse Island bridge was
added to allow for the increased load of traffic, and later the Main Gate
was moved to its present location. . . .

The First Recruit Training Battalion was organized on the sixth
of August, 1940, followed by the Second, Third and Fourth Battalions.

In August of 1940, a tropical hurricane struck Parris Island, and
caused severe damage to the electrical and water-supply systems. From
August 4 through 7, no lights could be furnished. Because the causeways leading to the island were torn up, men scheduled for training at
the Recruit Depot were re-routed to Quantico for approximately two
weeks, where an improvised recruit-training program was inaugurated
as a temporary expedient.

All military and civilian personnel on Parris Island had been moved
to the most secure buildings the moment the alarm sounded. Although
many structures were heavily damaged, personnel came through safely
and training returned to normal after a week of repairs and policing. . . .

During the period 1941 through 1945, a total of 204,509 recruits were
trained on Parris Island. . . .

Effective December 1, 1946, the organization of the post was re-
vised, the designation was changed to Marine Corps Recruit Depot,
Parris Island. . . .

On June 24, 1948, Public Law 759, known as the Selective Service
Act of 1948, was approved and went into effect. With it came the
authorization to accept one-year enlistees.

According to information received at Parris Island from Headquarters Marine Corps, approximately 333 one-year enlistees would arrive each month, in addition to normal recruit loads, the first of which were to arrive July 22, 1948. . . .

On February 15, 1949, the Third Recruit Training Battalion, Marine Corps Recruit Depot, Parris Island, was activated specifically for the training of Women Marines. . . .

The War Memorial Building, plans for which were discussed in 1946, was erected by October of 1951. . . . The building stands as a monument to Marines of the past as well as a source of inspiration for Marines of the future. Its motif is simple—memorial. It stresses the importance of sportsmanship, teamwork and physical conditioning which emphasize Marine Corps traditions and, most specifically, the recruit-training program at Parris Island. . . .

The memorial chimes, located in the New Post Chapel, were dedicated on October 28, 1951, at a service in front of the Chapel. The chimes . . . were dedicated to the memory of all Parris Island personnel who lost their lives in Korea. . . .

On March 24, 1952, a new record for recruits aboard the Recruit Depot reached an all time high. For the first time in Marine Corps history, as many as 24,424 recruits were mustered. This figure included 128 women recruits of the Women Marine Recruit Training Battalion. The male recruits totaled 24,296. Eight battalions were in operation at the time. . . .

On the morning of September 5, 1952, Colonel John R. Lanigan, then Depot Chief of Staff, unveiled the statue on the main parade field which stands to commemorate the heroic flag-raising on Mount Suribachi by the 28th Marines during the siege of Iwo Jima.

Colonel Lanigan and Major Harold G. Schrier, both present at the ceremony, were instrumental in the successful attack on the Pacific island and the famous flag-raising there.

In his dedicatory address, Major General Merwin H. Silverthorn said: "Let every American viewing this monument be proud of his country, inspired by the deeds of his fellow Americans, be humble in the presence of sacrifice, and be dedicated to the principles of true citizenship." . . .

Throughout his entire indoctrination into the Marine Corps the recruit is taught the need for a close relationship between a man and his rifle.

This relationship is best expressed in the following:

"MY RIFLE"
The creed of a United States Marine
by
Major Genearl W. H. Rupertus, USMC

This is my rifle. There are many like it, but this one is mine. My rifle is my best friend. It is my life. I must master it as I must master my life.

My rifle, without me, is useless. Without my rifle, I am useless. I must fire my rifle true. I must shoot straighter than my enemy who is trying to kill me. I must shoot him before he shoots me. I will. My rifle is human, even as I, because it is my life. Thus I will learn it as my brother. I will guard it against the ravages of weather and damage. I will keep my rifle clean and ready, even as I am clean and ready. We will become part of each other. Before God I swear this creed. My rifle and myself are the defenders of our country. We are the masters of our enemy. We are the saviors of my life. So be it, until victory is America's and there is no enemy, but Peace!

Don Lewis and "Billy"

"THE LAND IS THE SAME!"

The letters that follow were written by Don Lewis, of Greenville, South Carolina, and by "Billy," who prefers to be otherwise anonymous. They were Marine recruits in 1956, two boys out of the many thousands who have received their training on Parris Island and have all reported their experiences to the home folks.

Like the soldiers of Jean Ribaut nearly four hundred years ago, Don and Billy could gaze out on the broad expanses of Port Royal Sound, and their feet could travel the same tangled paths. The land—and the sea—are the same.

[Parris Island, South Carolina,
April 1956]

Dear Mother,

You've asked so often about Parris Island, and here is a letter answering your questions.

Although I've been here almost four months, it wasn't until the last few weeks that I've really seen the place. In boot camp we were busy all the time, and then I thought that Parris Island was just a big pile of sand. Now that I'm through with that training I've had time to look around, and I can see that there's a lot more to it than that.

The marshes begin right behind our barracks and stretch for about a hundred yards out into the water. They tell us that no one has ever made it across them alive, but they look quite harmless—like wild strong grass growing in soft sand. Actually the earth in the marshes is all bog, treacherous and deep.

Also from the barracks we can see Beaufort and the bridge that is the only way off the island. It gives me a feeling of isolation, knowing that such a small span of water separates us from the rest of the world.

The Marines have transformed the body of the island into an efficient city of barracks and men and parades, but the place still looks as if it had just been discovered by a fifteenth-century Spaniard. The land is the same, not cultivated or altered.

I can't help but think that Parris Island would be a lonely place even if there were a million people packed on it. There is no animal life here (except for a few snakes and a lot of sand fleas) and there are no natural sounds. We can't even hear the water lapping because of the break the marshes provide.

It seems to me that the land is now as it has been for hundreds of years, oblivious of what goes on upon it, giving none of its own soil to yield to its inhabitants. It's not at all like the red earth at home that changes with the crops or is excavated and altered.

Needless to say, I'll be glad to get off. But if it was not a Marine base, I think Parris Island might fulfill a romantic soul's longing for an island paradise.

Your son,
DON

Parris Island, S.C.
August 3, 1956

Dear Mom,

This is the first time that we could write a letter since we have been here. We have been pretty busy so far. We have already had a few shots. . . .

They told us to tell our parents not to come down here for a while. So, if you can, wait and come the day before graduation. I may can go home the next day. I am doing just fine so far, so don't worry about me. Let me do the worrying until I get out of boot camp.

Boy, it is sure hot down here running around like a monkey! We go to bed at 9:30 at night and get up at 5:00. There are a lot of homesick boys. . . . I wouldn't mind being home myself, but I will make the best out of it.

We sleep in Quonset Huts. There are 24 people in each hut. . . .

We have to say "Sir" to everybody with a stripe.

Well, guess I had better hush for now.

Love,

BILLY

Sunday, August 6, 1956

Dear Mom,

A line or two to let you know that I am still kicking. I am doing just fine. . . . We have to wash our own clothes. . . .

We have to take a strength [test] tomorrow, which I can pass . . . ; then we have to take a written test.

They have changed down here now. All we do is march, and that's not hard. We got our rifles yesterday. I got a brand-new one. These Quonset Huts are cool. But the black gnats and mosquitoes eat me up every morning. . . . The Drill Instructors are pretty good ones. I had to do 10 push-ups yesterday but I didn't mind it. We have to shave every morning. We have 7 minutes to do it. There are guys in here who don't even shave, but they have to shave anyway.

I went to church this morning. Boy, it was big! I bet there were 1500 people there. . . . I bet I will gain 30 lbs. We were divided up into squads today. We have to know 11 General Orders, 8 Attention Rules word for word. . . . They let us write letters every night. . . .

Love,

BILLY

August 26, Saturday

Dear Mom,

Thought I would write you to let you know that I am still kicking. I am just sitting here doing nothing for we get Saturday evenings off after 12.

Haven't got much news for you except I am doing just fine.

Boy, it sure is hot today! . . . I just got through washing my clothes—

it took me about a hour and a half. Got to clean my rifle after I come back from chow. We eat at 4:30 every evening. . . .

This place is just like a prison, but I hate to leave in a way. You meet a lot of people from all over the country of all nationalities and races. Well, this is all the news for now so tell every one hello for me and write when you get a chance.

Love,
BILLY

Ruth Batchelder

"ISLES OF THE BLEST"

Ruth Batchelder, a frequent visitor to the sea islands, contributes an account of a voyage from Savannah to Beaufort on an old steamer in 1917. The Beaufort-Savannah steamers have long since made their last trips along the winding inland waterway.

Perhaps the longest to retain the romantic atmosphere of ante bellum days are the picturesque Sea Islands of the lower Carolina, which lie midway between Charleston and Savannah. This group is composed of over 150 low, sandy islands, in the heart of which lies the beautiful old colonial town of Beaufort. There has always hung over these charming islands of the sea a veil of delicate mystery which the commercialist of the present age has not been able to penetrate.

The casual traveler may embark from Savannah in a roomy, old-fashioned boat which, after plying down the sluggish, yellow Savannah River, passes the home of the "Waving Girl," who lost her lover at sea twenty years ago and for twenty years has waved at every incoming and outgoing vessel with a kerchief by day and a lantern by night. She is known to the sailors of nations all over the world, and none fails to salute her as he passes. She lives on a marshy peninsula extending out into the river, and her brother earns her living and his by tending one of the Savannah River lights.

A few miles farther down the river the boat turns suddenly off into Rams' Horn Creek, well named, for its waterways are so narrow and twisting that the captain has to exert all his strength and skill to keep the boat on her course between the low-lying islands, fringed with palmettos and quaint, century-old water oaks, hung with Spanish moss.

These islands make ideal hunting preserves. . . . The climate is ideal, as the islands are warmed by the Gulf Stream in the winter and made comfortable in summer by the breeze from the Atlantic.

As the boat swings in and out among the islands, points of historical interest begin to appear. On the right we pass Fort Frémont, an army post, while a little farther up the bay on the left is the Port Royal Naval Station, well known as having the best natural deep-water harbor of the southern Atlantic.

A pause is made at the Naval Station while supplies are being un-loaded by the "hands." Powerful Negro boys are stationed at intervals from the hold of the vessel up the wharf, and boxes and barrels, as the case may be, are thrown from one to the other with unerring accuracy as their bodies sway in rhythm to a song which runs something like this:

> Marster's nigger is fat and slick,
>   *Oh-oh-ho*
> Case dey gets enough to eat,
>   *Oh-oh-ho.*
> I love marster and mistis too,
>   *Oh-oh-ho.*
> Case dey's rich an' kin' an' true,
>   *Oh-oh-ho.*

Soldiers and sailors in the blue of the Navy or the khaki of the Marines are either on duty receiving the supplies or loll around the deck, basking in the mellow sunshine and exchanging idle remarks with the crew of the boat.

Again the *Pilot Boy* pushes her blunt nose out, on past the ruins of the old Spanish Fort. . . .

Another turn in the harbor and in front of us, . . . like a perfect jewel in a perfect setting, lies Beaufort, with her row of galleried houses, relics of an old regime. This queen city of the Sea Islands is, indeed, ideally located on a peninsula of Port Royal Island. . . . Her whole water front is taken up with beautiful, old ante bellum residences whose rose gardens, masses of luxuriant bloom, mingle their perfume with the sweet odors of the orange and the magnolia.

Many of the beautiful old homes in Beaufort are built of tabby, a mixture of oyster shells and cement, a very substantial composition on which time has little effect and which is in color a beautiful, grayish pink. The oldest house[3] in the town was built in 1690 and is so constructed, with long piercings in the foundations, that muskets can be aimed in either direction. It has a ledge running along underneath on which munitions may be stored. This house was built when the Yemassee Indians used to make war on the whites. In those days warning was sent from island to island of an uprising by the waving of a red flag.

During the War of 1812 the British fired upon Beaufort and it was said that one of the cannon balls had penetrated a house on the water front. The hole had been sealed up and the exact location was not known until a fire occurred in 1906 which burned the house down, and the ball was found in the ruins wedged in among the masonry....

The Beaufort Volunteer Artillery has the honor of being one of the oldest military organizations in the country. It was organized by Colonel William Harden, of Marion's staff, and is housed in a picturesque old arsenal constructed of tabby with "B.V.A., 1776" mounted on its gates.

On the walls of the old Episcopal Church ... is placed a great tablet of bronze on which is inscribed the names of those who went out from Beaufort to die for the Lost Cause, and above them is written this inscription:

"The triumphs of might are transient, they pass and are forgotten. The memories of right are graven deepest in the chronicles of nations."

And under this tablet, on the tenth of every May, the rapidly thinning ranks of gray-haired veterans gather with the Stars and Bars floating sadly over them while they pay their tribute to the comrades who have gone before....

The Negroes of the Sea Islands are a source of never-failing surprise and delight to the tourist. ... Many of them speak "Gullah," a perversion of the English language hardly intelligible to anyone except a resident of that section....

---

[3] The house located at the southwest corner of New and Port Republic streets. The exact date when it was built is unknown, but it is indeed believed to have stood since the days of the Yemassees. It was later used as a Masonic Hall, and here the Order of the Eastern Star is rumored to have originated. The story goes that young Peggy Johnson hid in a closet to overhear a session of the Masons. When the outraged Masons realized their secrets were in the possession of a woman, they then and there organized the Order of the Eastern Star with the eavesdropper as charter member.

They are a kindly people, and on St. Helena Island 40 white people and over 8,000 Negroes live together without the slightest friction between the races. On St. Helena is established Penn Normal and Industrial School, which is doing a great deal for the Negro in teaching him how to learn his living by skilled labor. . . .

Vendors of vegetables, shrimp, fish and other edibles invade the streets in the early morning hours with their hardly articulate but wholly melodious cries. One ancient "Mauma" drives a still more ancient ox, and her voice can be heard for blocks around as she chants in a singsong tone: "My mistis, my marster, come an' git yo' nice fresh vegetables, yo' clean little sweet potato! Come, buyers, fo' dey is five cents a measure an' ah can' go no highrer nor no lowrer." And she passes down the street with a rich, oily chuckle of pure happiness on account of the day, the time and the place. . . .

One of the quaint superstitions of these Sea Island Negroes is a fear of being married while the minute hand of the clock is going down or the tide is going out. They think it bodes bad luck and, strange as it may seem, it is recorded that every death that occurs among them takes place when the tide is at its ebb.

The trip back to Savannah shows the islands as night draws on and the moon rises and bathes them in a silvery light, which transforms the old plantation houses into semblance of their former grandeur. On the farther shore lies Beaufort like a city of dreams, and one is reminded of the ancient legend still whispered among the natives that these were originally the Isles of the Blest, since Christ's crucifixion the abode of human beings.

Talbot and Jessica Hamlin

"BEAUFORT . . . A BLESSED HAVEN"

From Boston to Beaufort is 1241 statute miles. On one of the many boats to travel along the inland waterway by Beaufort were two re-tired Columbia University professors, Talbot and Jessica Hamlin. On board the Aquarelle I, *they arrived in Beaufort around Thanksgiving, en route to Florida.*

The following is from the book We Took to Cruising: from Maine to Florida Afloat, *which they wrote about their experiences.*

Some people complain that the trip across the Carolinas is monotonous. We did not find it so except in a couple of seemingly endless swamps—such, for instance, as the one in South Carolina across what is euphemistically called Bull Bay on the charts. Here the waterway is a straight marsh cut for miles, and at low tide (there is a rise and fall of nine feet in that part of the world) one is hedged in on both sides by walls of black mud, with a cornice of bright green salt grass at the top. Here only the birds give variety. But elsewhere one twists and turns, goes up rivers, across cuts, down estuaries into a sound or toward an inlet where suddenly, by the change of color in the water from coffee-brown to blue and perhaps by feeling the distant reflection of the ocean swell, one is conscious of the purity and might of the sea off to the eastward. Those subtle variations, to us at least, were endlessly fascinating. . . .

We stayed three days in Charleston, drinking in the elegance of its fine old buildings, savoring the charm of its streets, delighting in the compelling rhythm, almost universal, of garden, colonnade and gable. . . .

But we had to get on; regretfully we left behind the gardens and the white houses . . . and on a blustery cold gray day set out for Beaufort. It was a long run for *Aquarelle I*, nearly 70 miles, and we wrapped warmly against the chill northeaster. . . . "We're going to catch it," the skipper said. As the clouds passed, the wind whipped around into the northwest and increased to a gale; the temperature dropped violently from chilly to downright cold. And just then we came out of protected marsh passages into the full sweep of the Coosaw River, up which we had to struggle in the teeth of the wind for eleven long miles. The chop was extraordinary; every wave was white-ridged and spray slashed madly across *Aquarelle*, deluging her windscreen. The skipper leaned out one side, the mate the other, to identify the course markers, our faces stung with driven spray and our muscles aching from efforts to balance against the ship's leaping. The river's length seemed greater and greater, and we were a relieved pair when the mouth of Brickyard Creek was reached and we turned in again into narrower and more sheltered passages.

Perhaps it was the dramatic suddenness of the change, but now the rolling meadows and fields and the luxuriant enframing woods, brilliant in the cold sunshine, seemed to have even more than the customary air of pastoral loveliness and peace, and Beaufort when we reached it after circling through the creek and tied up alongside a fisherman seemed a blessed haven indeed.

And the town is a wonderful place. It was in the old days a great seasonal social center for the rice-raising families of the great swamp and inland plantations; each family tried to outdo his neighbors in the size and monumentality of the columned mansions built there. The city is on a peninsula, with cross streets from water to water, and each city block contains two or three of these gorgeous homes standing as memorials to a vanished culture and wealth lost. In some of them there are mantels and cornices and paneling to rival the best of Salem or even of Annapolis, and it is all on a scale of size and grandeur seldom found elsewhere. There are charming churches too, and churchyards solemn with moss-hung live oaks, an old arsenal quaint with its miniature parade of Gothic windows and battlements, and an excellent library with a librarian who has the history of the place and its houses at her finger tips.

Fortunately Beaufort is far from dead today; it is a living, prosperous town of charming people who have the good sense to appreciate and to preserve the beauty they have fallen heir to. We spent delightful days there both going south and on our return....

We ran from Beaufort into the broad clean stretches of Port Royal Sound, by Parris Island, past the elaborate piers and ordered buildings of the Marine Corps station. *Aquarelle* rose and fell and threw rhythmic fans of spray to either side as she felt the ocean swell making up the Sound; despite the continuing cold our hearts rose, and a sense of accomplishment stayed with us all the day—through Calibogue Sound—Ramshorn Creek—across the Savannah River....

Herb Bryant

THE "PORT" OF PORT ROYAL

Until the beginning of the twentieth century, Port Royal was a prosperous port, well known to ships from all over the world. In one year, 1886, 92,022 tons of cargo worth $1,058,791.60 were shipped from Port Royal; and during 1880-1881, 65,000 bales of cotton. Here also was one of the largest cotton presses in the world.

It was from the Port Royal Naval Station that the Maine *began her fateful voyage to Cuba.*

On October 4, 1958, old Port Royal, renovated by the State Ports Authority, was reopened to commerce. Along with the South Carolina state flag, the South Carolina State Ports Authority flag, the United States flag, flew the flags of Spain, France and England.

The festivities connected with the official opening of the port are described by Herb Bryant of the Charleston News and Courier.

Port Royal [October 2, 1958]—Port Royal's ship came in Wednesday. It was the first commercial craft to tie up at the $1.5 million S.C. State Ports Authority Pier 21.

Pier 21 will be dedicated in a ceremony Saturday, October 4, by the authority. The rites originally were scheduled for September 27, but, because of Hurricane Helene, were postponed.

Bright-eyed children and grownups who had never seen a large commercial ship enter Port Royal Sound came in droves to witness the 7:35 A.M. arrival. And they continued to come afterward.

The *Georg Russ,* a German ship, is the vessel that is making history in this developing port. It came in drawing fifteen feet, six inches of water and bringing a cargo of native lumber from South America.

It is the first time a commercial ship has brought a cargo into the port since 1922, according to Mayor J. L. Ritter. Ritter said the 1922 ship was the *Silver Leaf,* which came here to pick up a load of lumber.

Pilot William Santos brought the 2,606.6-gross-ton ship into port. Santos, of Charleston and Port Royal, said he was "tickled to death to see shipping start at Port Royal again, especially so since it's my home."

After the ship docked Mayor Ritter went aboard to welcome the captain, Harns Boge, to Beaufort. Captain Boge described the pier and channel as "very nice."

Port Royal [October 4, 1958]—This historic port was officially opened for commerce Saturday morning when South Carolina State Ports Authority Pier 21 was dedicated. . . . The U.S. Navy sent four ships, the Marine Corps sent the Parris Island drum and bugle corps, and the Beaufort High School band turned out. . . .

A crowd of approximately 1,000 persons was present for the ceremony, although they came in a light rain which lasted all morning. Isla Atkinson, "Miss Port Royal," raised the South Carolina State Ports

Bobbs-Merrill COMPANY, INC.

AN ASSOCIATE OF HOWARD W. SAMS & CO., INC.

1720 EAST 38th STREET • INDIANAPOLIS 6, INDIANA

PORT ROYAL UNDER SIX FLAGS
by Katharine M. Jones

Price $5.00

Publication date ~~April 25th~~ MAY 24

Authority flag after Senator Olin D. Johnson's speech. The flag-raising ceremony was conducted by U.S. Marines from this area. . . .

A number of local, county, state, national and military figures were present at the dedication, which was conducted by G. G. Dowling, chairman of the Beaufort County Ports Authority.

State Senator E. Burton Rodgers told the crowd that "this is a great day in my life. . . ." Port Royal Mayor J. L. Ritter also addressed the crowd. "The dream that I have had has reached its culmination," he said. He presented [to the visiting dignitaries] ten gavels, made from wood recovered from the original site of Charlesfort. . . .

Dinners for the visitors and town folks were served at Port Royal and the Lady's Island Country Club. The Port Royal Masonic Lodge was opened to visitors.

The four ships, minesweepers, the *King Bird, Blue Bird, Meadowlark* and *Parrot,* which arrived at Port Royal for the occasion, are holding open house Sunday. . . .

John Pennington

THE "DEMON STORM" OF 1959

Hurricane Gracie struck the South Carolina coast on September 29, 1959, leaving Beaufort and her sea islands battered but unbowed. "We are proud to be a part of a community whose residents, for the most part, were able to take the suffering and financial loss inflicted by this disastrous hurricane with a becoming grace," wrote the editor of the Beaufort Gazette.

Parris Island Marines dropped their rifles and shouldered axes to clear streets and aid homeowners who were surrounded by masses of fallen limbs and trees. Evacués from other islands found food and shelter on the Marine base.

"We won't be the same in a hundred years," Mayor Angus Fordham of Beaufort commented. "But," said the Charleston News and Courier, *"his very words are in the tradition of Beaufort, site of the white man's settlement on the soil of North America before the* Mayflower *sailed or Captain John Smith landed at Jamestown. Not for an instant does Mayor Fordham, or anyone else in his right mind, countenance the*

idea that Beaufort could fail to survive this and any number of other buffetings from nature or mankind.

"Though it takes time to grow great oaks, Beaufort will grow them as long as there are acorns. . . ."

John Pennington of the Atlanta Journal was in Beaufort when Hurricane Gracie struck.

I was condemned by Hurricane Gracie to watch part of her devilish blow from South Carolina's Beaufort County Jail.

With three other newsmen, deputy sheriffs, assorted prisoners and six evacués, I stood in the jail and watched the demon storm unexpectedly break up a town.

The wind moaned like the low tones of a great organ. It whined like a hillbilly fiddle. It rumbled, as they say in the disaster stories, like a freight train, or a flight of jets. And it broke up the town.

Nobody here expected what happened. The hurricane advisories warned that Gracie was dangerous. They said she would strike inland near Charleston, with winds of 120 miles an hour. Beaufort (a quaint seaport town, they call it) expected to get by with fringe damage.

But at 11 o'clock on Tuesday morning, Gracie "got ripe," Chief Deputy Sheriff C. O. Michael said.

She "got ripe" and trapped four Atlanta newsmen at the county jail, along with the other assortment of people, most of whom belonged there, because to travel through her fury would have been folly.

She "got ripe," and the big locust tree in front of the jail entrance began to creak and groan. Slowly but surely, the great tree broke up before our eyes. Great limbs were snapped like so much dry macaroni, popping loudly as they went. The big aerial atop the jail came tumbling down. "Hot wire," somebody yelled.

Just before it fell, the radio dispatcher in the sheriff's office announced loudly: "We've had our first fatality. A tree fell on a car out on the edge of town."

It later developed this was the hurricane's only known fatality in South Carolina. A trip later to the scene revealed a new red convertible twisted into a grotesque shape by the impact.

Two houses away from the jail, a chimney crumbled. Trees came out of the ground and skidded along with the wind, which whistled through the trees and set power lines to humming as it broke them in two.

Suddenly there was an ominous, rumbling sound. The floor of the iron-and-concrete jail shook like a bridge with a car crossing it, and across the front of the jail, coming with the angry wind, sailed a big sheet of corrugated tin off somebody's roof. The roof was not in sight, so it had come a distance, and fast. It stopped at the door.

"Grab that thing and bring it inside," Deputy Michael gruffly yelled, "before it cuts somebody's head off." He was not kidding. The tin was hurtling along fast enough to do just that.

All the while the scene in front of the jail gradually turned to one of destruction. The local citizenry, blasé at first about the storm, eyed one another quizzically. The deputy sheriffs wondered about their own homes, their families.

Somebody ventured that Beaufort (the residents pronounce it Bufort, as in beautiful) seemed to be getting more of Hurricane Gracie than she had bargained for. And soon that was confirmed. Sheriff J. E. McTeer[4] radioed in from his home on Coffin Point, fourteen miles east and near the ocean's brink, that things had suddenly shifted from fury to deathly silence. The air was still "so quiet you could go fishing." He was, Sheriff McTeer related, in the eye of the hurricane, the dead center of it.

Before long he radioed back that the winds had resumed. The eye had passed. And all the while, Gracie lambasted Beaufort without let-up, angrily ripping the town to shreds, it seemed.

Chief Deputy Michael ventured forth into the storm in his car. He dodged wires and trees and flying debris and came back shaking his head sadly.

"This town is a wreck," he said, "a total wreck."

Next time out he took along the Atlanta newsmen, all stranded here in pursuit of the hurricane by her very fickleness.

They found that Chief Deputy Michael was not exaggerating. The town was a total wreck. Victim of hundreds of thousands of dollars worth of damage.

He drove through water that was knee-deep, over broken limbs that bumped the bottom of the car roughly, through hanging wires, around fallen trees.

---

[4] Sheriff J. E. McTeer's home was on St. Helena and was "completely wrecked," he reported. "The island is in desolation." The sheriff was cut off from Beaufort when the high winds and water blocked roads leading to St. Helena Island.

Every street—every one—was littered with fallen trees and limbs. Some houses and cars had trees across them. Nearly every store on Bay Street, the town's main thoroughfare, had its plate-glass window blown out, displays littered and soggy. The roof was rolled off the Methodist Church.

Deputy Michael's own home had two trees across it—they fell with his wife and children inside the house while he worked. Every tree in Beaufort, it seemed—and this is a town of many trees—was uprooted or broken.

The town was, putting it mildly, a scene of devastation.

And no one outside knew what had happened to Beaufort. Newsmen on the scene tried repeatedly, but could not communicate. Every telephone was out. Long-range radio was knocked out when the antenna fell. And deadlines, like the hurricane's eye, went on by.

National Guardsmen were called into duty through the local radio station. They quickly went on guard to prevent looting.

Two hours after the winds "got ripe," they began to mellow. Still the rain came, but the winds subsided to gale force. The attempted exodus began. And again Gracie thwarted those whom she had trapped.

Across the only two highway exits from the town numerous big trees and wires had fallen. It took this reporter over two hours, battling blockades like a rat in a maze, to get out of battered Beaufort. When finally the last fallen tree was behind, it had been six hours since Gracie "got ripe"—six tempestuous hours. Gracie really went on a rampage in this "quaint little seaport town."

Thomas R. Waring

THE AWAKENING OF THE ISLE OF HILTON HEAD

Thomas R. Waring, native Charlestonian, now editor of the Charleston News *and* Courier, *contributes the following account of "The Awakening of the Isle of Hilton Head."*

Hilton Head, S.C.—

This island, which was almost inaccessible until 1956, when a toll bridge linked it with the mainland, is now awakening from a centuries-old slumber which was most violently disturbed by the Civil War.

That was when a Union fleet captured the island and established the base for blockading Southern ports, thus strangling the Confederacy's lifeline.

From its known beginnings, the area has been ranged successively by Indians, Spaniards, French and English, and until recently, although rich in history and composing one of the most unspoiled seaside regions in the United States, it was in truth a backwater. But in 1950 Georgia interests bought 20,000 of Hilton Head Island's 30,000 acres and began rearranging the place as a vacation and retirement resort.

The toll bridge was put up from the mainland in 1956 and has proved so successful that all tolls were lifted December 1, 1959. For the ensuing year traffic on the bridge, and hence to the island, is expected to jump to 200,000 cars.

A new motel, the William Hilton Inn, was opened last July [1959] for year-round occupancy. Its eighty rooms were built on a sand dune within sight and sound of the Atlantic surf.

Thirteen miles of magnificent hard-sand beach rim the island, one of the largest on the Atlantic Coast. For swimming, surf fishing, strolling, cycling and, until it becomes too congested, motoring, this beach is among the finest on the seaboard. Miles of trails and wooded roads, some paved and some as the planters built them a century or so ago, cross the island. Indian mounds, plantation ruins and remains of military fortifications supply sight-seeing objectives.

Naturalists will find both wildlife and plants of great variety. Among the trees are pine, bay, magnolia, laurel, sassafras, live oak, palmetto, cassina and holly. Deer, turkey, wild pigs, alligators, possums, raccoons, squirrels, rabbits and marsh tackies—descendants of horses brought here by the Spaniards—roam the fields and forest. Fish include channel bass, drum, pompano, whiting, mullet, trout, flounder and bluefish, as well as oysters, clams and crabs. Shrimp trawlers ply their vocation outside one's picture window.

The island is on the intracoastal waterway, and a marina services transient yachts. More facilities for boating are being built.

When the Indians first came here is not known, but tests by the radioactive carbon 14 method on oyster shells and other remains in the mounds indicate a period of about 4,000 years ago. Soon after Columbus discovered the New World, Spanish explorers touched here. The name Spanish Wells labels the place where they filled their casks with fresh water.

Across Port Royal Sound one can see Parris Island, where a great Marine Corps base now stands. French Huguenots in 1562 founded a settlement there, called Charlesfort, as a bastion against Spain. . . .

The first English tourists arrived in 1663 when William Hilton, captain of the *Adventure*, dropped anchor in Port Royal Sound. They found friendly Indians. The Spanish had been coming to these shores already for more than a century and called the locality Santa Elena. The English named a high sand dune that supplied a landmark for their charts Hilton Head in honor of their captain.

A couple of years later another English vessel brought Henry Woodward, a surgeon at the age of 19, to the same spot to begin a fabulous adventure with the Indians. As described in a novel by the late Josephine Pinckney called *Hilton Head*, Woodward lived with the Indians, learned their language and paved the way for treaties that helped the first permanent settlers of Carolina to survive when they built Charles Town in 1670.

Many years passed before there was permanent settlement of Hilton Head Island. Indigo was grown for a time, but sea-island cotton was the money crop that flourished in the burgeoning era after the Revolutionary War. About a thousand Negro slaves worked the plantations when the Civil War started with the firing on Fort Sumter at Charleston.

Inadequately fortified by the Confederates, although it dominates the magnificent harbor of Port Royal, Hilton Head soon became the target of a Federal fleet. The same strategic reasons that prompted Spain, France and England to seek control of Port Royal Sound caused the North to move heavily into this Southern theatre. A fleet of fifty United States Naval vessels besieged Fort Walker, and on November 7, 1861, 13,000 blue-clad troops made a beach landing. They captured the island in one of the largest of amphibious operations until World War II.

The Union fortified Hilton Head and built up the garrison to as many as 50,000 troops, including liberated slaves who flocked here from mainland plantations.

Scores of supply vessels and warships plied these waters. The Federal blockade strove to shut down commerce through Savannah, Charleston, Wilmington and other Atlantic cotton ports. Great earthworks, a couple of miles of which still can be seen in the thickets back of the beach, surrounded the coastal forts. . . . Buttons from Yankee uniforms, bullets and other souvenirs from the great force stationed here throughout most of the war still are being found after a high tide disturbs the sand.

Another military memento remains from a later war. The emplacement of a huge steam cannon, one of the two developed for the Spanish-American War, forlornly stands on the beach among the ruins of a brick furnace. Near the Civil War fort and the spot where Hilton landed, this coast artillery weapon of 1898 was designed to repel a Spanish armada. It is said to have been fired only once in practice. The result was a woods fire on Bay Point on the other side of Port Royal Sound.

Woods have played an important part in the recent history of Hil-ton Head. After the cotton plantations were ruined by war and boll weevils, Hilton Head Island was all but abandoned to descendants of plantation slaves. Many Negroes still own small holdings on the island. Acreage passed through hands of carpetbaggers and others.

From 1870 to about 1900, shipping interests owned large tracts of island land. In that year, Roy Rainey, a New York yachtsman, acquired control, which he held until 1940. Then the land was bought by Landon K. Thorne and Alfred L. Loomis, New York public-utilities men. They developed Honey Horn Plantation. Aside from sportsmen in search of game, scarcely any visitors bothered to hire a boat to come to this somnolent island over which men had fought in the past.

In 1950, a syndicate of Georgians bought out Messrs. Loomis and Thorne for more than $1,000,000 cash. The transaction reversed the usual flow of Northern capital to exploit Southern properties. It represented a substantial beginning of an even larger enterprise. They brought in bulldozers to carve out roads and homesites in a modern style of settlement very different from the pioneering of 300 years earlier.

Two companies—Hilton Head Company and Sea Pines—are engaged in developing the island. South Carolina interests have joined with Georgians in Sea Pines, constructors of the inn and the golf course. Chairman of the board of directors is Lieutenant General Joseph B. Fraser, U.S.A. (Retired) a Hinesville, Ga., lumberman. He is a veteran of both World Wars and the Korean War. His son, Charles Fraser, is president.

About 200 cottages, some of the summer variety and some designed for year-round living, have been constructed so far and many more are planned. The William Hilton Inn alone represents an investment of $900,000, of which $600,000 went for construction, $100,000 for furnishings, and the rest for a heated swimming pool, land and other expenses. . . .

Developers are striving not to spoil the island, however, by over-crowding. Five years of careful planning have gone into the Sea Pines project on the southern end of the island.

For each acre this company sells, it reserves an acre to preserve the atmosphere of wilderness. The company quotes Julian Huxley's remark that "wilderness-lovers constitute a sizable minority—and also a siz-able proportion of interesting characters and original thinkers. Wilder-ness is, in the long run, one of the major functions humanity demands from the surface of the earth."

To reach Hilton Head, which lies about 110 miles south of Charles-ton, a south-bound motorist should turn left off U.S. Route 46, which leads directly to the resort. North-bound from Savannah, a right turn from U.S. 17 on State Route 170 leads to State Route 46.

Samuel Hopkins Adams

MY FAVORITE TOWN—BEAUFORT—AND THE
SEA ISLANDS

Samuel Hopkins Adams, native of Dunkirk, New York, and his sec-ond wife, Jane Peyton Van Norman, came to Beaufort in 1935 and for more than twenty years made it their winter home. He died in Beaufort on November 16, 1958, at the age of 87. Funeral services were held at St. Helena's Protestant Episcopal Church.

Mr. Adams was the author of more than fifty books and numer-ous short stories and articles. Seventeen of his novels have been made into movies. Much of his best writing is about the South Carolina sea islands, which he loved.*

We were just a pair of tourists, seeking a winter spot. The familiar and lavish blandishments so insistently capitalized on the wayside bill-boards of the South left us cold. "Historic Interest," "Typical Dixie

---

* From "My Favorite Town" by Samuel Hopkins Adams. First published in the *Lincoln-Mercury Times*. Copyright 1950 by Ford Motor Company.

Homeland," "Old-Time Atmosphere," "Aristocratic Associations," "Playground of Millionaires" and similar large-print tourist-bait, were just so many blemishes on the landscape to our eyes. Town after town might well be all that it claimed as a Shrine of Southern Culture in the midst of a Sportsmen's Paradise and Anglers' El Dorado; we simply did not care. We were looking for a place to settle.

With a tourist and a town, it is either love at first sight or pass on and look elsewhere.

The spell was cast as we turned off the main route, pursuing the vague report of an old and quiet city out among the sea islands. Too many American communities welcome the stranger via the city dump or between rows of grimy hovels. The approach to Beaufort threads through broad marshlands and across shining rivers. There are far vistas of wooded islets, unpeopled and unapproachable across the high-waving reeds of the morasses. The effect is strangely other-worldly.

One's initial response to a locality is likely to be made up of trivialities. There was a feeling of unreality in the spectacle of five dollars' worth of terrapin on the hoof, leisurely crossing the highway and vanishing in the tawny depths of the marsh where two snowy egrets posed in philosophic reverie. It set a keynote. We entered the town proper between a long double row of royal palmettos and rounded a curve to blink amazedly at a floral riot in a privet yard. There were camellias enough in that one clump to choke the biggest display window on Fifth Avenue. Overhead a pair of chinaberry trees were festooned with the soft gray of the Spanish moss and spangled with the golden traceries of the wild jasmine. For background there spread the broad expanse of reed and river with a lordly white yacht on its way to Florida, poised in mid-stream while two sweating bridge-tenders toiled at the hand-lever of the turntable, aided by a pair of sails which they had rigged on the ironwork.

Before us on the asphalt an authentic oxcart labored and creaked, with a white-bearded Gullah drowsing on the high seat. It stopped in front of the post office. So did we. Across the street a mockingbird improvised elaborately in the branches of a live oak which might have been two centuries old but was more probably three.

We turned to one another. "This is it," we said.

That was fifteen years ago. To the one of us who is left, Beaufort is still it.

Other towns may equal or even surpass my favorite in conventional **advantages**: its lovely, belvedered mansions, the picturesqueness of the old arsenal and the older slave quarters, the ancient "tabby" buildings, constructed from a unique amalgam of oyster-shell mortar, the noble architecture of St. Helena's set in the bowered luxuriance of its church-yard, its spreading live oaks and the bewildering profusion and variety of its flowers, both wild and cultivated. Yet, with all these attractions for the tourist, it is—and this is its distinction—the least tourist-ish of resorts. For that matter, I doubt whether the term, "resort," would not be locally resented. The town has not even any night life!

This does not mean that the stranger within Beaufort's gates is not welcome enough. There are several excellent inns wherein he can find comfort. But Beaufort is not going to put itself out to impress or even to retain him. He is never made to feel, as in so many wintering places, that he is a commodity. Here nobody seizes upon your undefended elbow and drags you forth, prescribing, "You MUST see the beauties of Beaufort." Assuming that you would like to wander about and enjoy your surroundings, you will be blessedly uninterfered with in doing so. If you wish to go fishing, you can go, but no maritime huckster with a boat to rent will pester you with his solicitations. It is the same way with crabbing or shrimping or shooting or sightseeing. I doubt whether a guide could exist in Beaufort; I hope not. You could live there ten years and never be importuned to hire a rig or go on an excursion. In fact, there is complete and refreshing immunity from the uncomfortable feeling that somebody is after your dollar. This may go far to explain why people who have once discovered Beaufort return to it year after year until they cease to be regarded as tourists.

Beaufort lies two islands out from the mainland toward the open sea. It is one of a group of sixty-four, ranging in size from forty square miles to a few rods-length of sand and marshweed. Through and around them wind the convoluted branches of the great Inland Waterway which joins north and south by sheltered passage. These tributaries form one of the most intricate waterscapes in the world, and one of the most fascinating to explore.

The very names have a touch of magic; Coosaw, Dahtah, Ashepoo, Dahfuskie, Huspah, Albergottie, Pope Gall, Old Woman's Folly, Cuckold's Creek, Calibogue, and—echoes of Africa?—Tuckassa King and Little Pon Pon. Here, enfolded in the coils of the rivers, lived and prospered the early settlers, grown rich on indigo, then rice, and finally cotton—all abandoned industries now. In their place spread the vast truck gardens, shipping from their own railroad spurs direct to the northern markets. The great Trask fields have twenty-nine varieties of crops, ranging from collards to gladioli.

Hither were brought from a forgotten coast of West Africa the Gullah slaves whose descendants are perhaps the purest-blooded strain of all American Negroes. They are now the overwhelmingly predominant populace of the islands. They are largely property owners, law-abiding, self-respecting, and pious, their Christianity, however, still bearing the indelible impress of ancient and mysterious tribal rites. From their small, sometimes windowless, and remote praise-houses in the pine woods, as well as from the more public Penn School Community House, issue spirituals such as are unknown to New York stages or Hollywood night spots, the true, rich-voiced music of an ancient tradition. How many pay audiences have ever heard "I Got a Home in the Rock," or the swinging refrain of "Ain' Gonna Study War No More"? . . .

Throughout the adjacent islands there is a profusion of wild life. The lazily-waving marsh growth secretes seldom-seen creatures which thrive, hidden and secure in the sanctuary of their depths. Here live thousands of marsh hens, fewer thousands of terrapin, not infrequently their huge cousins, the green sea turtles, and a few surviving alligators. Along the side-waters are found rare waterfowl: godwits, willets, skimmers, water turkey, that grotesque caricature of a bird, the oyster-cracker, and, rarely in the depths of the forest, the pigeon-size pileated woodpecker.

A plantation-owning friend on Lady's Island just across the river from town can stand in his doorway of an evening and watch two or three hundred herons settling down for the night upon their chosen rookery in his swamp. Within gunshot of the city there is an uninhabited island, guarded by the hostile bayonets of the barrier cacti, where the huge, black buzzards nest and breed, undisturbed, year after year. For the visiting hunter, there are quail, dove, and at least ten varieties of duck. On any strip of beach in the season, myriads of snipe scamper and flit. The wild turkey still gobbles on Hilton Head which harbors, also, less desirable inhabitants, the black widow spider, the diamondback rattlesnake, some moccasins, and a few of that most deadly of Western Hemisphere creatures, the coral snake.

A dozen varieties of fish, edible and sporting, succeed one another in the main waterways and adjoining creeks: sea trout, cobia, blackfish, drum, bass, rockfish, sheepshead, and (for my taste, the most toothsome of all) flounder. The delicious blue crab is everywhere. I can walk fifty yards from where I sit and catch a mess in an hour. If there is anywhere a better oyster than the local variety, I have not met with it. Clams are also plentiful, and of prime flavor, but the local markets do not carry them and nobody eats them raw. Why? The best answer I can get from my friends is that "People always have dug their own" and for chowder use only. They always have, hence they always will. That, also, is Beaufort.

One of the best fishing spots in the locality is a deep, tidal-swirl pool crossed by the tracks of the Seaboard Airline Railroad. Sportsmen with a taste for extra excitement make up parties for what is known as trestle-fishing. The excitement is furnished by unscheduled freight trains. Members of the party take turns acting as sentinel. When a locomotive looms around the not-so-distant curve, the outpost raises a lusty cry. The game then is to reach the nearest shore ahead of the train. The unblemished score of the anglers was nearly ruined when 220 pounds of tourist hooked onto six pounds of trout, with an oncoming freight just around the corner. The sentinel yelled, the party broke for safety, but the tourist hung on. So did the fish. Hooting madly, the locomotive bore down upon the trestle. At the last moment the persistent angler rolled off the end of the ties and disappeared in a vast waterspout thirty feet below. Doggedly clinging to his rod he came up and swam to shore, with the trout still on the other end. Use of the trestle for fishing is now suspended.

The local islands have seen no less than six flags raised above them by a long and varied succession of tourists. First to arrive were the Spaniards in 1520. They did not commend themselves to the aboriginal inhabitants, the Yamassee Indians, who departed hastily for the interior. Except for an unfavorable impression, these early invaders seem to have left nothing permanent. The French came next, in 1562, and settled Parris Island, subsequently taken over by the United States Marines who still hold it. Then the British arrived in force and had some lively skirmishes with the Indians who had begun to seep back. After the Revolution, the culture of the locality remained predominantly English with some slight admixture of Huguenot.

A patriotic and enthusiastic Carolina historian expressed his conviction that Beaufort was "the wealthiest, most aristocratic and cultivated town of its size in America."

BIBLIOGRAPHY

Part II—*The French at Port Royal*

"You Shall Be Registered for Ever as the First That Inhabited This Strange Country"
Richard Hakluyt, *The Principal Navigations Voyages Traffiques & Discoveries of the English Nation* . . . , VIII. Glasgow, 1904.

"No Fayrer or Fytter Place Then Porte Royall"
Jean Ribaut, *The Whole & True Discouerye of Terra Florida*. A Facsimile Reprint of the London Edition of 1563, Together with a Transcript of an English Version in the British Museum, with Notes by H. M. Biggar and a Biography by Jeannette Thurber Connor. Deland, Fla.: The Florida State Historical Society, 1927. By permission of the Florida State Historical Society.

The Fate of the Charlesfort Colony
Richard Hakluyt, *The Principal Navigations* . . . , VIII. Glasgow, 1904.

Part III—*The Spanish at Santa Elena*

"A Fort Was Built . . . and the Adelantado Called It San Felipe"
Jeannette Thurber Connor, ed., *Pedro Menéndez de Avilés, Adelantado, Governor and Captain-General of Florida*. Memorial by Gonzalo Solís de Merás. Deland, Fla.: The Florida State Historical Society, 1923. By permission of the Florida State Historical Society.

"In the City of Santa Elena"
Jeannette Thurber Connor, ed., *Colonial Records of Spanish Florida*, I. Deland, Fla.: The Florida State Historical Society, 1925. By permission of the Florida State Historical Society.

"From the Ships They Saw the Houses Burning"
Jeannette Thurber Connor, ed., *Colonial Records of Spanish Florida*, I. Deland, Fla.: The Florida State Historical Society, 1925. By permission of the Florida State Historical Society.

"Give Me Some Grant of Land There, Where I Might Live for Always"
Jeannette Thurber Connor, ed., *Colonial Records of Spanish Florida*, I. Deland, Fla.: The Florida State Historical Society, 1925. By permission of the Florida State Historical Society.

Santa Elena Rebuilt
Jeannette Thurber Connor, ed., *Colonial Records of Spanish Florida*, II.

Deland, Fla.: The Florida State Historical Society, 1930. By permission of
the Florida State Historical Society.

Part IV—*The English*

"All They That Want a Happy Settlement of Our English Nation"
South Carolina Historical Society Collections, V (1897).

"That Never-Enough-to-Be-Valued Country"
South Carolina Historical Society Collections, VIII.

"The Land Was Good Land"
South Carolina Historical Society Collections, V (1897).

Part V—*The Scotch at Port Royal*

"It Shall Be a Port Toun for Ever"
George Pratt Insh, "Arrival of the Cardross Settlers," *The South Carolina
Historical and Genealogical Magazine*, XXX (April 1929).

"Stewarts Town at Port Royal Is the Frontier of the Whole Settlement"
South Carolina Records, 1685-1690, II. British Public Record Office.

"The Spaniards Burnt the Towne Downe to the Ground"
J. G. Dunlop, contributor, "Spanish Depredations, 1686," *The South Carolina Historical and Genealogical Magazine*, XXX (April 1929).

Part VI—*An English Frontier Colony*

"The Yammosees . . . Fell upon Port-Royal"
B. R. Carroll, comp., *Historical Collections of South Carolina . . .* , II. New
York, 1836.

"We Being a Frontier Parish"
Copy of letter in St. Helena's Episcopal Church, Beaufort.

The Swiss Settle Purrysburg
Henry A. M. Smith, "Purrysburg," *South Carolina Historical and Genealogical Magazine*, X.

Visits to Port Royal
Percy Livingstone Parker, ed., *The Heart of John Wesley's Journal.* . . .
New York: Fleming H. Revell, n.d.

Fort Frederick
J. H. Easterby, ed., *The Journal of the Commons House of Assembly, September 12, 1793-March 26, 1741.* Columbia, S. C.: The Historical Commission of South Carolina, 1952. By permission of Dr. J. H. Easterby, Director of the South Carolina Archives.

J. H. Easterby, ed., *The Journal of the Commons House of Assembly, November 10, 1736-June 7, 1739*. Columbia, S. C.: The Historical Commission of South Carolina, 1951. By permission of Dr. J. H. Easterby, Director of the South Carolina Archives.

Part VII—*War for Independence*

"Proceed with the Sloop *Beaufort*"
A. S. Salley, ed., *Journal of the Commissioners of the Navy of South Carolina, October 9, 1776-March 1, 1779*. Columbia, S. C.: The Historical Commission of South Carolina, 1912.

"My Dear Harriott"
Jack L. Cross, ed., "Letters of Thomas Pinckney, 1775-1780," *South Carolina Historical Magazine*, LVIII (October 1957).

Battle for Beaufort
William Moultrie, *Memoirs of the American Revolution . . .*, I. New York, 1802.

"I Expected Nothing but Death"
South Carolina Historical and Genealogical Magazine, X.

"The Enemy Have Landed at Beaufort"
William Moultrie, *Memoirs of the American Revolution . . .* , II. New York, 1802.

"I Had Some Hair Breadth Escapes"
"Extracts from a Private Manuscript Written by Governor Paul Hamilton, Sr., During the Period of the Revolutionary War, from 1776-1800," *Charleston Year Book*, 1898.

"Ravages of War"
George Howe, *History of the Presbyterian Church in South Carolina*. Columbia, S. C., 1870.

Part VIII—*Periclean Age of the Sea Islands*

President Washington Passed This Way
John C. Fitzpatrick, ed., *The Diaries of George Washington: 1748-1799*, IV. Boston: Houghton Mifflin Company, 1925. Copyright by the Mount Vernon Ladies' Association of the Union and used with their permission.

Recollections of an Island Boyhood
Samuel Gaillard Stoney, ed., "The Autobiography of William John Grayson," *The South Carolina Historical and Genealogical Magazine*, XLVIII (July 1947), XLIX (January 1948).

"Sent the Boat a Drum Fishing"
J. H. Easterby, ed., "Charles Cotesworth Pinckney's Plantation Diary, April 6-December 15, 1818," *The South Carolina Historical and Genealogical Magazine*, XLI (October 1940).

President Monroe Visits Beaufort
Carolina Gazette (Charleston, S. C.), May 15, 1819.

Beaufort Celebrates the Anniversary of American Independence
Carolina Gazette (Charleston, S. C.), July 17, 1819.

Lafayette Comes to the Sea Islands
A. Levasseur, *Lafayette in America in 1824 and 1825*, II. Philadelphia, 1829.

Southern Patriot and Commercial Advertiser (Charleston, S. C.), March 23, 1825.

Plantation Missions
W. P. Harrison, ed., *The Gospel Among the Slaves*. . . . Nashville, 1893.

Devil Fishing at Hilton Head
William Elliott, *Carolina Sports by Land and Water*. . . . New York, 1859.

"We Passed Between Low Sandy Islands"
Sir Charles Lyell, *A Second Visit to the United States of North America*, I. New York, 1849.

Part IX—*The Confederate Flag Waves over Port Royal*

"Pledging Allegiance to the Confederate States of America"
A. W. Dimock, "A Story of the Sea Islands," *The Outlook*, February 4, 1905.

Aspects of a Sea Island Plantation
William Howard Russell, *My Diary North and South*. New York: Harper and Brothers, 1863.

"Our Coast Will Be Attacked"
Manuscript letter by permission of Mrs. Nellie Fripp, Beaufort, South Carolina.

The Last Trip from Edisto
I. Jenkins Mikell, *Rumbling of the Chariot Wheels*. Columbia, S. C.: The State Company, 1923. By permission of the State Company.

"The Fleet Is upon Us"
A. W. Dimock, "A Story of the Sea Islands," *The Outlook*, February 4, 1905.

Part X—*The Port Royal Expedition*

Three Harbors
The War of the Rebellion: A Compilation of the Official Records, Ser. 1, LIII.

"We Are Off!"
Official Records of the Union and Confederate Navies . . . , Ser. 1, XII.

On the *Atlantic* with the Third New Hampshire
Daniel Eldredge, *The Third New Hampshire* . . . Boston, 1893.

"Unexpected, Absolute and Decisive Victory in Port Royal Harbor"
Egbert L. Viele, "The Port Royal Expedition, 1861: The First Union Victory of the Civil War," *Magazine of American History*, XIV (October 1885).

"Commodore DuPont . . . Led the Long Line of Warships"
Hazard Stevens, *The Life of Isaac Ingalls Stevens*, II. Boston: Houghton Mifflin Company, 1900.

"The Bearer . . . Will . . . Carry with Him the Captured Flags"
Official Records of the Union and Confederate Navies . . . , Ser. 1, XII.
Magazine of American History, XIV (October 1885).
Official Records of the Union and Confederate Navies . . . , Ser. 1, XII.

The Drayton Brothers Report the Battle of Port Royal
Official Records of the Union and Confederate Navies . . . , Ser. 1, XII.

Part XI—*Behind the Lines with General Robert E. Lee*

From Coosawhatchie, South Carolina
Official Records . . . Army, Ser. 1, VI.
J. William Jones, *Life and Letters of Robert E. Lee*. . . . New York: Neale Publishing Company, 1906.

"We Are Under the Command of General R. E. Lee"
William D. Hoyt, Jr., ed., "To Coosawhatchie in December 1861," *The South Carolina Historical and Genealogical Magazine*, LIII (1952).

Part XII—*Department of the South, Port Royal, South Carolina*

"General Stevens Was Ordered . . . To Occupy Beaufort"
Hazard Stevens, *The Life of Isaac Ingalls Stevens* . . . , II. Boston: Houghton Mifflin Company, 1900.

A Volunteer on St. Helena Island
Henry Noble Sherwood, ed., "Journal of Miss Susan Walker, March 3d to June 6th, 1862, "*Historical and Philosophical Society of Ohio's Quarterly Publication*, VII (January-March 1912). By permission of the Historical and Philosophical Society of Ohio.

The Capture of Company H, Third New Hampshire
Daniel Eldredge, *The Third New Hampshire* . . . Boston, 1893.

"Here the Traitors Planned the Ruin of Their Country"
Charles Nordhoff, "Two Weeks at Port Royal," *Harper's New Monthly Magazine*, June 1863.

The Arming of the Blacks
Thomas Wentworth Higginson, *Army Life in a Black Regiment*. Boston: Houghton Mifflin Company, 1900.

Teacher to the Freedmen
Elizabeth Hyde Botume, *First Days Amongst the Contrabands*. Boston, 1893.

A Movement to Assist Sherman
The diary of Rear-Admiral John A. Dahlgren in *Official Records of the Union and Confederate Navies* . . . , Ser. 1, XVI.

Prisoner of War on Hilton Head
Official Records . . . *Army*, Ser. 2, VIII.

Sherman's Army Comes to Beaufort
Elizabeth Hyde Botume, *First Days Amongst the Contrabands*. Boston, 1893.

Part XIII—*Reconstruction*

"Massa Richard" Returns
"Agate," *Cincinnati Gazette*, n.d., reprinted in J. H. Cuthbert, *Life of Richard Fuller, D.D.* New York, 1878.

"Sale of the Land"
Our Women in the War, The Lives They Lived; The Deaths They Died. Charleston, S. C.: The News and Courier Company, 1885.

"Petition . . . for the Restoration of Pinckney Island"
U. S. Congress, Senate Finance Committee (40th Cong., 2d sess.)

"We Seemed to Be Living over a Volcano"
Elizabeth Hyde Botume, *First Days Amongst the Contrabands*. Boston, 1893.

"There Was Nothing, Save Flowers, Left to Give"
Narciso Gener Gonzales, *In Darkest Cuba*. Foreword by Ambrose Elliott Gonzales. Columbia, S. C.: The State Company, 1922. By permission of The State Company.

General Wade Hampton Campaigns in the "Black Belt"
Alfred B. Williams, "Hampton Faces Both Friends and Foes," *The State* (Columbia, S. C.), January 23, 1927. By permission of *The State*.

Part XIV—*The Big Storm of 1893*

"Fearful Night of Terrors"
Mrs. R. C. Mather, *The Storm Swept Coast of South Carolina*. Woonsocket, R. I., 1894.

"The Sea Islands Were Dumb"
Joel Chandler Harris, "The Sea Island Hurricane," *Scribner's Magazine*, XV (February and March 1894).

"Deepest Sympathy"
Manuscript letter by permission of Mrs. Nellie Fripp, Beaufort, South Carolina.

Part XV—*Twentieth-Century Beaufort and the Sea Islands*

The Marine Corps Recruit Depot on Parris Island
"Four Centuries of Progress: A Short History of Parris Island, S. C." Information Section, Marine Corps Recruit Depot, Parris Island, South Carolina. January 1958. Courtesy of Joseph C. Bridgers, Captain, U. S. Marine Corps, Informational Services Office, Marine Corps Recruit Depot, Parris Island, S. C.

"The Land Is the Same!"
Manuscript letter by permission of Don Lewis, Greenville, South Carolina.
Manuscript letter by permission of an anonymous mother.

"Isles of the Blest"
Ruth Batchelder, "Beaufort, of the Real South," *Travel* Magazine, XXVIII (February 1917). By permission of *Travel*.

"Beaufort . . . a Blessed Haven"
Talbot and Jessica Hamlin, *We Took to Cruising: From Maine to Florida Afloat*. New York: Sheridan, 1951. Copyright 1951 by the authors. Used by permission of Sheridan House, Inc.

The "Port" of Port Royal
Herb Bryant, "First Ship Is Off Loaded at Port Royal Terminals," *News and Courier* (Charleston, S. C.), October 2, 1958.
Herb Bryant, "Historic Port Royal Assumes New Role," *News and Courier* (Charleston, S. C.), October 5, 1958.

The "Demon Storm" of 1959
John Pennington, "Wind 'Got Ripe,' " *Atlanta Journal*, September 30, 1959. By permission of the author.

The Awakening of the Isle of Hilton Head
Thomas R. Waring, "The Awakening of the Isle of Hilton Head," *New York Times*, December 6, 1959. Reprinted by permission.

My Favorite Town—Beaufort—and the Sea Islands
Samuel Hopkins Adams, "My Favorite Town." First published in the *Lincoln-Mercury Times*. Copyright 1950 by Ford Motor Company. By permission of Brandt & Brandt.

ACKNOWLEDGMENTS

It is a pleasure to express my appreciation to the many kind and wise persons who helped in the making of this book.

Mrs. Nellie Fripp of Beaufort shared with me family letters and a journal; also her own vast store of island lore and history.

The late Miss Mabel Runnette and the staff of the Beaufort Library gave me invaluable help.

Frank Ramsey of Beaufort shared his photographs of the islands and helped in many other ways.

James W. Busch of Beaufort allowed me use of his excellent collection of military histories of the 1861-65 period and supplied many beautiful photographs of the islands.

I thank Mr. and Mrs. A. E. Samuel for the hospitality of the Gold Eagle in Beaufort.

Special thanks go also to Mrs. Mary B. Prior, editor of the *South Carolina Historical Society Magazine*, to Dr. R. W. Patrick of the University of Florida, and to Samuel Gaillard Stoney.

Captain Joseph C. Bridgers of the Marine Corps Recruit Depot of Parris Island was generous in his help and co-operation.

Charles E. Fraser of Hilton Head Island furnished many beautiful photographs and other valuable assistance.

For their co-operation and help I am grateful to Mary Simms Oliphant, Greenville, S. C.; S. L. Latimer, editor and publisher of *The State*, Columbia, S. C.; David C. Mearns of the Library of Congress; John Pennington of the Atlanta *Journal*; Thomas R. Waring of the Charleston *News and Courier*; Mr. and Mrs. Don Lewis of Greenville, S. C.; John McKay of Greenville, S. C.; Cornelia Huggins Hensley and Alfred Rawlinson of the University of S.C. library; Mrs. Edith Bannister Dowling of Beaufort; and Herb Bryant of the Charleston *News and Courier*.

My thanks go also to Dr. J. H. Easterby, Director of the South Carolina Archives, for permission to reprint from *The Journal of the Common House of Assembly*.

The late Mrs. Helen Morgan Wallace of Greenville, whose kinsmen, the De Saussures, were early landowners of Beaufort County, gave me much help and encouragement.

I thank the many persons of the Bobbs-Merrill Company who had a part in the making of this book. To my editor, Harrison Platt, I owe a debt of gratitude. My special thanks go also to Andrée Fé Coers.

KATHARINE M. JONES

Greenville, South Carolina